PERSPECTIVES IN STATE SCHOOL SUPPORT PROGRAMS

Edited by

K. FORBIS JORDAN
Congressional Research Service
Library of Congress

and

NELDA H. CAMBRON-McCABE
Miami University, Oxford, Ohio

**Second Annual Yearbook of the
American Education Finance Association**

BALLINGER PUBLISHING COMPANY
Cambridge, Massachusetts
A Subsidiary of Harper & Row, Publishers, Inc.

International Standard Book Number: 0-88410-197-5

Library of Congress Catalog Card Number: 81-8074

Printed in the United States of America

Library of Congress Cataloging in Publication Data

Main entry under title:

Perspectives in state school support programs.

  (Annual yearbook of the American Education Finance
Association ; 2nd)
  Bibliography: p.
  Includes index.
  1. State aid to education—United States—Addresses, essays, lectures.
I. Jordan, K. Forbis (Kenneth Forbis), 1930- . II. Cambron, Nelda H.
III. Series.
LB2828.P47   379.1'22'0973   81-8074
ISBN 0-88410-197-5   AACR2

CONTENTS

LIST OF TABLES

PREFACE

Following the tradition established by the first yearbook of the American Education Finance Association (AEFA), this second yearbook addresses significant issues related to the financing of education. As an extension of AEFA's role as a facilitator for public policy debate and communication between policymakers, researchers, practitioners, fiscal planners, and students of school finance, the yearbook has been designed not only to serve as a basic source but also to stimulate debate and additional research.

As education fiscal policymakers contemplate the decade of the '80s, they find themselves confronted with increasing challenges in design and implementation of state school support programs. In designing this second AEFA yearbook, the editors have identified emerging problems and considerations concerning components of state school support programs. The book is organized into three parts: educational need and fiscal capacity, current state school support programs, and accountability and adequacy.

The task of developing a sound state school support program is much more complex than merely counting the students, totalling the assessments on real property, determining an amount to be paid per pupil or per teacher, and devising a simple formula that can be used in allocating funds to local school districts. Pressures are mounting for more precise measures to be used in quantifying the level of educational need in local districts, for inclusion of various support activities in state aid programs, and for procedures to ensure that local school districts give ample consideration to fiscal planning and reporting, student educational attainment, and adequate educational opportunities for all students.

In the aftermath of school finance reform efforts of the '70s, the focus of attention appears to be shifting toward refinements in state school support programs that recognize differences among students and school districts. Issues include the importance of recognizing educational needs of special populations, adjusting the state payment to consider differences in education costs and prices among local school districts for equivalent educational programs and services, and developing better measures of local school district fiscal capacity. State funds are comprising an increasing percentage of the average educational dollar, and fiscal and economic pressures are mounting for all governmental services. In this context, state legislatures have become increasingly interested in enacting legislation that will ensure adequate fiscal and educational planning in local school districts. Policymakers are also seeking to impose reporting requirements related to fiscal expenditures and educational results.

Rather than assuming an advocacy position for a particular point of view, the goal of each author has been to present a balanced discussion that includes a review of the relevant research and literature, an overview of current practices among the states, and a discussion of problems and issues from a policy perspective.

PREVIEW

The yearbook Introduction is written by R.L. Johns, an emeritus professor at the University of Florida and first president of the American Education Finance Association. Johns has had an illustrious and productive career as a major consultant and researcher in the field of state school support programs for over forty years. While a professor of educational administration at the University of Florida, Johns was involved in school finance research and design activities that contributed to the reformulation of state school support programs in over half the states of the nation. His advocacy for equalization and adequacy in educational funding has significantly influenced the course of state school support programs. As director of the National Educational Finance Project, Johns provided the leadership for development of a research base that was invaluable to state fiscal planners during the school finance reform movement of the '70s. In the Introduction to this second yearbook, Johns has traced the historical development of state school support programs and has placed current concepts within the context of this historical evolution.

Part I contains five chapters that focus on educational need and fiscal capacity. Chapter 1 addresses the educational needs of special populations, reviews existing state programs for these students, and identifies a series of issues related to recognition of special populations in state school support programs. The author is Michael Hodge, research associate for the School Finance Project in the U.S. Department of Education.

In Chapter 2, Jay Chambers of Stanford University has provided a comprehensive discussion of both the theoretical and empirical aspects of education cost and price level adjustments to state aid for local school districts. As state school support programs have become more refined and as disparities in per pupil expenditures have been reduced, increasing attention has been given to the need for factors through which education cost or price adjustments may be made or used in the allocation of funds to local school districts.

Chapter 3 focuses on the potential relationships between municipal overburden and state aid for education. Interest in this concept has been increasing because of the multiple pressures for governmental services in urban areas and the declining fiscal condition of many older cities. The author of Chapter 3 is Jane Sjogren, currently on the faculty at Wellesley College and formerly with Abt Associates.

The focus of Chapter 4 is school finance reform and the cities. Drawing upon recent research in the state of New York as well as upon other efforts throughout the nation, Margaret Goertz of the Education Policy Research Institute, Educational Testing Service, has examined the manner in which school finance reform has affected the inner cities and has identified a series of problems or issues that merit the attention of state school finance fiscal planners.

In Chapter 5, E. Kathleen Adams and Allan Odden of the Education Commission of the States discuss the use of alternative wealth measures in calculating local school district fiscal capacity and allocating state school support. They also discuss specific techniques that might be used by fiscal planners and policymakers who desire to include other measures of fiscal capacity besides real property in determining the relative wealth of local school districts.

Part II is devoted to three chapters that provide an overview and analysis of current state school support programs for the basic instructional program, school facilities, and pupil transportation. Chapter 6 includes criteria for the review of state school support programs and an analysis of current programs. In this chapter, Orlando Furno and Dexter Magers of the U.S. Department of Education draw upon various federally funded research activities conducted by several states as well as previous research efforts. Attention is given to a series of issues that should be of interest to fiscal planners as they design state school support programs.

Chapter 7 contains a discussion of the various ways in which states participate in the financing of school facilities in local school districts. Written by William R. Wilkerson of Indiana University, the chapter reviews current programs among the states, discusses the relative merits of current options, and identifies issues for consideration by state level policymakers in the formulation of state programs for financing school facilities.

In Chapter 8, Thomas Melcher of the Minnesota Department of Education has reviewed the evolution of research efforts related to state support for local school district pupil transportation programs. Discussion also includes a series of factors that should be considered in the development of programs, state program options, and issues for consideration by fiscal planners.

Part III includes three chapters that provide the background for interesting scenarios about funding education in the '80s. A variety of indicators suggest that policymakers and interest groups will become increasingly concerned with accountability from both an educational and student performance perspective and with adequacy in educational programs for students. One of the concerns about the school finance reform movements of the '70s has been the impact that the quest for fiscal neutrality has had on efforts to address educational needs of students.

The focus of Chapter 9 is fiscal accountability and the challenges of formulating responsive policies for both state and local educational agencies. Walter Hack and Carla Edlefson of the Ohio State University and Rodney Ogawa of the University of Utah use a research and literature background to analyze case studies, review developments in Ohio, and identify a series of problems or issues.

Chapter 10 addresses educational needs and the accounting of them in school finance programs. Arthur Wise and Linda Darling-Hammond of the RAND Corporation have reviewed various approaches that are currently being used to assess the relative success of educational programs or identify pupil needs. Discussion includes the implications of minimum competency programs, individualized plans, and mastery programs.

In Chapter 11, Martha McCarthy of Indiana University discusses adequacy in educational programs from a legal perspective. Although attention is given to the various approaches used by states and voluntary agencies to assure minimal levels of quality in educational institutions and offerings, the major focus of the chapter is litigation trends. Recent developments suggest an interest in ensuring that adequate levels of funding or educational programs are provided for all students.

The editors wish to express their appreciation to those persons who gave support and encouragement during the preparation of this second AEFA yearbook. Richard Rossmiller, immediate past president, and Edwin Steinbrecher, current president, were most supportive in the venture. Various members of the AEFA board of directors also provided valuable advice and constructive criticism. Recognition is due as well to the members of the publications committee—Bob Brischetto of Trinity University, Terry Geske of the University of Illinois at Urbana–Champaign, Jim Guthrie of the University of California at Berkeley, and L. Dean Webb of Arizona State University.

Special appreciation is extended to Monique Austin, Jan Fulton, and Helen McKoy for their assistance in preparation of the manuscript and for their tolerance of the editors during various stages of transforming a rather vague concept into a cohesive publication. Finally, the editors wish to express their sincere thanks to Professor R.L. Johns not only for his contribution to the yearbook but also for the professional role model and encouragement that he has provided for the editors and many others for the past several decades.

Annapolis, Md.   **K. Forbis Jordan**
April 1981   **Nelda H. Cambron–McCabe**

INTRODUCTION

*Roe L. Johns**

Financing the public schools has been one of the most important political issues during the 1970s, and it appears that it will continue to be a keenly contested issue in the 1980s. More than half of the states made significant changes in their school finance programs between 1970 and 1980. These changes have been good, bad, or ineffective as judged by persons with differing philosophical beliefs. It is appropriate at this time to consider the political theory and the philosophical beliefs that affect policies of public school financing.

Hickrod, Layman, and Hubbard (1974) argue that "there is an identifiable *democratic theory of school finance* and the roots of this political theory can be found in the works of such classical authors as Aristotle, Thucydides, Thomas Jefferson, Alexis de Tocqueville, Caleb Mills, and others." These writers point out that Jefferson was a rigorous student of Hellenic civilization, and his familiarity with Aristotle's famous work *Politics* was revealed in his "Bill for the More General Diffusion of Knowledge" which he introduced in the Virginia general assembly.

Jefferson's philosophy was best expressed in these often quoted words from the Declaration of Independence which he wrote: "We hold these truths to be self-evident, that all men are created equal,

---

*Roe L. Johns, Professor Emeritus, University of Florida, and first President of the American Education Finance Association.

that they are endowed by their Creator with certain unalienable rights, that among these are Life, Liberty and the pursuit of Happiness." This statement of philosophy in the Declaration of Independence was followed by the Bill of Rights of the Constitution and supplemented by the thirteenth, fourteenth, fifteenth, and sixteenth amendments. These legal provisions in the federal Constitution have been implemented by numerous federal statutes. Furthermore, the constitutions and the statutes of the states cannot deny a citizen his rights and privileges guaranteed by the federal Constitution.

The literature of public school finance is filled with statements of philosophy based on our cultural heritage. Every well-known writer on school finance has advocated a program of financing which provides equity for pupils and equity for taxpayers. It would be difficult to find a legislator, state or federal, who would not support this philosophical concept. However, what is equity for pupils and what is equity for taxpayers? Legislators and educators have not reached agreement on these definitions. The general consensus is that society should provide for "equalization of educational opportunity." But there is far from agreement on either the arrangements that should be made to equalize educational opportunity or the kind and level of educational opportunity that should be equalized.

The words "public education" are not included in the federal Constitution and its amendments. However, in view of the philosophical commitments of the founding fathers as expressed in the Declaration of Independence and the federal Constitution, it is strange that public education developed so slowly in the United States. According to the Seventh Census of the United States, in 1850, free education was provided to only about half the children in New England, one-sixth in the West, and one-seventh in the middle states (Edwards and Richey 1963). With few exceptions, the southern states provided free education only for the paupers in 1850. In fact, free public elementary and secondary education did not become generally available in all states until the first quarter of the twentieth century. It should not be implied from these statements that educational opportunities were equal either interstate or intrastate. During the early twentieth century, however, certain educational leaders began to protest against the inequalities in educational opportunity and advanced proposals for remedying the situation. In yearbooks such as this, it is appropriate to review briefly some proposals from these pioneer theorists of school financing and to trace the roots of contemporary theorists of school financing.

The original theorist of school financing was Ellwood P. Cubberley. He stated his theory of school financing in the following words:

> Theoretically, all the children of the state are equally important and are entitled to have the same advantages; practically this can never be quite true. The duty of the state is to secure for all as high a minimum of good instruction as is possible, but not to reduce all to this minimum; to equalize the advantages to all as nearly as can be done with the resources at hand; to place a premium on those local efforts which will enable communities to rise above the legal minimum as far as possible; and to encourage communities to extend their educational energies to new and desirable undertakings
>
> (Cubberley 1905: 16).

Cubberley advocated that a minimum program funded as high as possible should be available to all, but he also recommended state reward for local effort. Contemporary theorists on school finance differ on whether state reward for local effort should be included in a state's school finance program.

Harlan Updegraff (1921) proposed a plan of school financing under which state funds would be allocated in inverse relationship to the valuation of property per unit of need in the district but in direct relationship to the local tax effort made by a district in proportion to its taxpaying ability. Therefore, he proposed that the plan of state support be "fiscally neutral"—that is, that the quality of a child's education should not depend upon the wealth per unit of need of the district but upon the local tax effort made by the district. Contemporary theorists of school financing commonly refer to this plan of financing as "district power-equalizing." Present-day experts on school financing differ widely on the desirability of this plan.

Strayer and Haig in 1923 proposed the following theory of school financing:

> The state should insure equal educational facilities to every child within its borders at a uniform effort throughout the state in terms of the burden of taxation; the tax burden of education should throughout the state be uniform in relation to taxpaying ability, and the provision for schools should be uniform in relation to the educable population desiring education. Most of the supporters of this proposition, however, would not preclude any particular community from offering at its own expense a particularly rich and costly educational program. They would insist that there be an adequate minimum

offered everywhere, the expense of which should be considered a prior claim
on the state's economic resources (1923:179).

Contemporary experts on school financing generally call this model
the "foundation program" plan of school financing. Strayer strongly
opposed reward for local tax effort as advocated by Cubberley and
Updegraff. He contended that "any formula which attempts to
accomplish the double purpose of equalizing resources and rewarding effort must contain elements which are mutually inconsistent"
(1923:175).

The plans of state support advocated by Cubberley, Updegraff,
and Strayer all required some measure of the taxpaying ability or
taxpaying capability of local school districts. School finance experts
differ widely on what is being measured or how it should be measured. Is local taxpaying ability or local accessibility to taxes being
measured? Should local tax effort be based exclusively on the equalized valuation of property, or should it include such factors as income and municipal overburden?

Henry C. Morrison (1930) advocated complete state support for
the public schools. He noted that great inequalities in wealth among
school districts had created great inequalities in educational opportunity. He argued that education was a state function and that attempts to equalize educational opportunity by enlarging school
districts or by providing state equalization funds had failed. Morrison
even advocated the abolishment of local school districts and state
assumption of both the administration and financing of the public
schools. In 1930, 0.3 percent of school revenue was provided by the
federal government, 17 percent from state sources, and 82.7 percent
from local resources.

A number of contemporary experts on school finance advocate
complete or nearly complete state and federal support of the public
schools, and it appears that states are moving slowly in that direction. The National Education Association (NEA) estimated in 1979–
80 that 9.3 percent of public school revenue was provided by the
federal government, 48.1 percent by the states, and 42.5 percent by
local sources (Sheridan 1980:34). The President's Commission on
School Finance in 1972 recommended the following:

Our investigation of present school financing and our deliberation on the
issues confronting us lead us to an inescapable conclusion: the most practical
system for fulfilling the requirements of reform would be one in which reve-

nue raising and the distribution of educational resources were centered at the state level. We recommend such a system, in contrast to the traditional separation of revenue sources by state and local government, as the means of coming to terms with and correcting the unequal tax burdens and the inequitable distribution of the state's educational resources" (McElroy 1972:30).

Contemporary authorities differ on whether it is desirable to have complete state and federal funding of the public schools, but there seems to be general support of a fiscal policy of providing 75 percent or more of public school revenue from state and federal sources.

Milton Friedman (1955) recommended a system of vouchers for financing elementary and secondary schools. The purpose of these vouchers was not to equalize educational opportunity but to break up the alleged monopoly of the public schools and to increase competition among institutions. The vouchers would be issued to parents and children under this plan and could be redeemed at either public or private schools. This theory of school financing is not new. It was recommended in the eighteenth century by Thomas Paine in his "Rights of Man" primarily to aid the poor in the education of their children, although he did not propose restricting it exclusively to the poor. Many leaders of private schools support this plan, but it is vigorously opposed by leaders of the public schools (Levin 1980).

What progress has been made in the equalization of educational opportunity in the United States since 1900? Cubberley (1905), Updegraff (1921), Strayer (1923), Morrison (1930), Mort (1933), the Committee for the White House Conference on Education (McElroy 1956), the National Educational Finance Project (Johns, Alexander, and Stollar 1971), the President's Commission on School Finance (McElroy 1972), and the Education Commission of the States (Odden, Berne, and Stiefel 1979) all pointed out that educational opportunity had not been equalized at the times their studies were made. The Education Finance Center of the Education Commission of the States noted that considerable improvement had been made in equity in school financing between 1970 and 1979, but that many inequities still exist (Odden, Berne, and Stiefel 1979: 34–36).

Much progress was made from 1930 to 1980 in reducing the differences in educational expenditures per pupil among the states. Mort (1933) reported that in 1930–31 the median expenditure per weighted pupil in the district of average wealth ranged from $23.66 in Arkansas to $115.74 in New York. This was a ratio of almost five to one. The NEA estimated that the current expenditure per pupil in average daily attendance (excluding Alaska) ranged from $1,414 in Georgia to $3,041 in New York (Sheridan 1980). This ratio is a little over 2 to 1. The reduction in the range in educational expenditure per pupil among the states has been largely due to a major reduction in the differences in per capita income among the states. In 1930 the range in per capita income among the states was 5.1 to 1, and in 1980 the range was 1.6 to 1.

Despite the progress that has been made in equalizing the financial resources of the districts of a state, it is not unusual today, especially in states with numerous small districts, to find ranges of 3 or 4 to 1 in expenditures per pupil among the districts of the state.

Even though acceptable equity has not been attained for pupils or taxpayers, the long-range trends for the financial support of the public schools have been quite favorable. Table I-1 presents some interesting trends in expenditures for the public schools from 1929-30 to 1979-80. To make the data comparable from year to year, amounts are expressed in terms of the purchasing power of 1979-80 dollars. Expenditures per pupil increased 389.7 percent in constant dollars between 1929-30 and 1979-80, whereas the per capita gross national product (GNP) increased only 214.1 percent over this fifty-year period. This suggests that taxpayers placed a higher value on education in 1979-80 than they did in 1929-30. Further evidence of this increased preference for education is shown in the 2.4 percent of the GNP allocated to expenditures for the public schools in 1929-30 and the 3.7 percent in 1979-80.

Data in Table I-1 indicate that expenditures for the public schools increased the most during the decades when the per capita GNP increased the most. The decade of 1930-40 was a depression decade with a slow growth in the GNP, and the 1970-80 decade was an inflationary decade with a relatively slow growth in the GNP. The percent of the GNP allocated to public school expenditures also declined during the 1970s. Part of that decline was probably due to the decline in school attendance in the latter part of that decade, but part was no doubt due to frustrations of taxpayers concerning inflation which increased their resistance to taxes.

What are the prospects for improving the financial support of the public schools in the decade ahead? As the nation enters the 1980s, inflation has not yet been brought under control, and the per capita GNP is growing very slowly. These are unfavorable indicators. Another unfavorable factor is the aging population. Estimates from the

Table I-1. Trends in Per Pupil Expenditures for the Public Schools and the Per Capita GNP Expressed in Terms of 1979–80 Dollars

Year	Total Expenditures Per Pupil in ADA Expressed in 1979–80 Dollars[a]		Per Capita GNP Expressed in 1979–80 Dollars[b]		
	Amount	Percent Increase Over Previous Decade	Amount	Percent Increase Over Previous Decade	Percent of GNP Expended for the Public Schools
1929–30	$ 494	—	$ 3,582	—	2.4
1939–40	567	14.8	4,000	11.7	2.4
1949–50	844	48.9	5,767	44.2	2.1
1959–60	1,268	50.2	7,233	25.4	3.2
1969–70	1,992	57.1	9,661	33.6	4.2
1979–80	2,419	21.4	11,250	16.5	3.7
Percent increase 1920–30 to 1979–80	389.7	—	214.1	—	

a. U.S. Office of Education except for the year 1979–80 which was estimated by the National Education Association.
b. Survey of Current Business, U.S. Department of Commerce.

U.S. Bureau of Census indicate that the total population will increase about 8 percent between 1980 and 1990 but that the number of persons 65 years of age and over will increase approximately 19 percent.

Persons sixty-five years of age and over are less supportive of taxes for education than younger persons with children in school. The National Retired Teachers Association–American Association of Retired Persons (NRTA–AARP), an organization with more than 11 million members, released a publication in 1980 entitled "State Laws Enacted Pertaining to the Interest of the Elderly" and reported the following legislation passed by state legislatures which took effect in 1979 and 1980 (NRTA–AARP 1980):

1. Reduction in local property taxes
    a. Property tax limitation   — 5 Acts
    b. Circuit breaker   — 3 Acts
    c. Homestead exemption   —19 Acts
    d. Credits and rebates   —10 Acts
    e. Total of 37 Acts in twenty-five states

2. Reduction of state income taxes—22 Acts in fifteen states

3. Reduction in state sales taxes—13 Acts in twelve states

4. Reduction of inheritance and gift taxes—8 Acts in six states

5. Total number of Acts reducing state or local taxes taking effect in 1979 or 1980—80 Acts in thirty-two different states.

This bulletin indicates that the various NRTA–AARP state legislative committees supported all of these laws. Retired people on fixed incomes have felt the impact of doublt-digit inflation. Also, the wages and salaries of many workers did not keep pace with the inflation of the 1970s.

These conditions provide some explanation for the public interest in reducing taxes. Despite these unfavorable indicators for the immediate future, the historical commitment of the American people to equality, justice, fairness, and a better life is strong and not likely to waiver. The reductions of the rate of economic growth and inflation have no doubt been the two principal factors causing present difficulty in obtaining adequate financing of public education. Will this decline in the rate of economic growth continue until there is no economic growth in the United States? The economist Rohatyn was asked the following question in 1980: "Can we get by on limited or no growth in times ahead?" His reply was: "No, the idea of a zero-sum society is baloney. One cannot function as a zero-sum society, because we are not equipped to handle the taking away from some to give to others that a zero-sum society involves. We need sustained, relatively non-inflationary private-sector growth" (Rohatyn 1980: 31). Zero-sum is a term used by economists in game theory in which the amount one player wins in an economic game is exactly equal to the amount the other player loses (Mansfield 1979: 342).

The zero-sum concept is somewhat similar to the Pareto–Optimal Concept under which no one can be made better off without making someone worse off (Mansfield 1979: 444). A fixed quantity of goods and services is implied by both concepts. As pointed out by Rohatyn, the people of the United States have never been satisfied by a no-growth society. They have always sought the better life. In order to have economic growth, a society cannot consume all it produces. Some current production must be saved and invested in both physical and human capital. As pointed out by many, including Schultz (1961) and Denison (1962), one of the surest ways to provide for economic growth is an adequate investment in education. Adequate investment in the private sector of the economy also is essential for economic growth, but sophisticated machines produced by investment in the private sector would not contribute to productivity in a society of illiterates.

A number of court decisions have affected school financing during the 1970s. Starting with the *Serrano* v. *Priest* decision of the California Supreme Court in 1971, the method of financing education has faced court challenges in a number of states. In the *Serrano* case, it was held that the quality of a child's education could not be a function of the wealth of his parents and neighbors. This decision denied the legality of making the level of school expenditures in a district a function of the wealth of the district. The *Serrano* decision was soon followed by the *San Antonio Independent School District* v. *Rodriguez* decision in a federal court in Texas which held that the Texas school finance plan violated the fourteenth amendment to the federal Constitution. The Supreme Court of the United States reversed that opinion in 1973 holding that education was not a fundamental constitutional right under the Equal protection Clause of the fourteenth amendment. Since that time the constitutionality of the school finance plans of a number of states has been successfully challenged because of violations of one or more provisions of state constitutions.

These court decisions have no doubt influenced school finance reform in a great many states in addition to the states in which the school finance plan was being litigated. The school finance reforms in the 1970s in general have increased state funding for education and improved the equity of school financing for both pupils and taxpayers.

The problems of school financing will never be solved for all time. Each year, each biennium, each quadriennium, and each decade new problems will require that decisions be made by local boards of education, by state legislatures, and by the Congress of the United States. This second yearbook of the American Education Finance Association presents a review of current problems of school financing and alternative solutions. Experts in school finance are not likely to solve the problems of school financing by developing a perfect model of federal, state, and local financing of the public schools. Decisionmakers in different generations vary in their concept of the marginal utility of public education as they allocate scarce resources. Leaders in school finance will continue to face many decisionmakers in the school finance arena who have the zero-sum or Pareto–Optimal Concept of the economy. History indicates that the future will consist of periods of depression, low productivity, and inflation, and also periods of prosperity, high productivity, and low inflation. All of these factors will continue to affect school financing. The American Education Finance Association will never complete its mission because the need for educational and fiscal leadership will be as great in the future as in the past.

REFERENCES

Cubberley, Ellwood P. 1905. *School Funds and Their Apportionment.* New York: Teachers College, Columbia University.

Denison, Edward J. 1962. *The Sources of Economic Growth in the United States and the Alternative Before Us.* New York: Committee for Economic Development.

Edwards, Newton, and Herma C. Richey. 1963. *The School in the American Social Order.* Boston: Houghton Mifflin Company.

Friedman, Milton. 1955. "The Role of Government in Education." In *Economics and the Public Interest,* edited by Robert A. Solo. New Brunswick, N.J.: Rutgers University Press.

Hickrod, Alan G.; Ronald L. Layman; and Ben C. Hubbard. 1974. "Toward a Political Theory of School Finance Reform in the United States." *The Journal of Education Administration* 12, no. 2 (October).

Johns, Roe L.; Kern Alexander; and Dewey Stollar. 1971. *Status and Impact of Educational Finance Programs.* Gainesville, Fla.: The National Educational Finance Project.

Levin, Henry C. 1980. "Educational Vouchers and Social Policy." In *Care and Education of Young Children in America*, edited by J. Gallagher and R. Haskens. Norwood, N.J.: Ablex.

Mansfield, Edwin. 1979. *Micro-Economics—Theory and Practice.* New York: W.W. Norton and Company.

McElroy, Neil H. 1956. *A Report to the President.* Washington, D.C.: The Committee for the White House Conference on Education, U.S. Government Printing Office.

_____. 1972. *Schools, People and Money—The Need for Educational Reform.* Washington, D.C.: The President's Commission on School Finance.

Morrison, Henry C. 1930. *School Revenue.* Chicago: University of Chicago Press.

Mort, Paul R. 1933. *State Support for Public Education.* Washington, D.C.: The American Council on Education.

National Retired Teachers Association-American Association of Retired Persons. 1980. *State Law Enacted Pertaining to the Interests of the Elderly.* Washington, D.C.: NRTA–AARP, National Headquarters.

Odden, Allan; Robert Berne; and Leanna Stiefel. 1979. *Equity in School Finance.* Denver: Education Finance Center, Education Commission of the States.

Rohatyn, Felix G. 1980. "Bitter Medicine for Ailing U.S. Economy." *U.S. News and World Report*, (September 1), p. 31–32.

Schultz, Theodore W. 1961. "Education and Economic Growth." In *Social Forces Influencing American Education*, 60th Yearbook National Society for the Study of Education, Ch. 3. Chicago: University of Chicago Press.

Sheridan, Alton B. 1980. *Estimates of School Statistics 1979–80.* Washington, D.C.: National Education Association.

Strayer, George D., and Robert Murray Haig. 1923. *The Financing of Education in the State of New York*, Report of the Educational Finance Commission 1. New York: MacMillan Company.

Updegraff, Harlan. 1922. *Rural School Survey in New York State: Financial Support.* Uthica, N.Y. (Published by author).

EDUCATIONAL NEED AND FISCAL CAPACITY

As school finance theorists, fiscal policymakers, and spokespersons for educational interest groups contemplate the future direction of state school support programs, increasing attention is being devoted to the degree to which differences in educational needs among students are recognized in the calculations and the process used to ensure that all students in similar circumstances are treated equally. The chapter on educational programs for special populations focuses on the rationale for supplementary support for three groups of students and discusses alternative approaches through which these students will be provided equality of educational opportunity.

Another area of intense interest is cost or price differences among local school districts for equivalent levels of educational programs and services. Even though there may be differences of opinion as to the best solution, authorities are in general agreement that the differences do exist and that they affect the quantity and quality of educational programs and services that local school districts make available to their students. The chapter on this issue provides some interesting insights into the theoretical and empirical considerations related to adjusting state school support programs for cost and price differences.

Problems of the cities are addressed from two somewhat different but complementary perspectives by the chapters on municipal overburden and the effect of school finance reform on the cities. The first discussion explores the concept of municipal overburden and its implications for state school finance programs. The second chapter addresses the problems of financing education in the central cities and the relative fiscal need of these school districts.

For three-quarters of a century, the principal measure of local wealth has been the value of real property. A variety of observers have raised questions about the relative merits of the use of assessed value of real property as an indicator of local school district ability to support education. This issue and the rationale for utilizing multiple measures of local district wealth will be discussed in the chapter on alternative measures of wealth. Attention will also be given to the experiences of states that use measures other than the value of real property and the potential impact of using a broader based wealth measure.

1 IMPROVING FINANCE AND GOVERNANCE OF EDUCATION FOR SPECIAL POPULATIONS

*Michael V. Hodge**

School finance reform was the most significant undertaking of state and local governments in the field of education during the 1970s. However, the presumed goal of reform differs even among those intimately involved in the quest. Two perspectives on the goal and impact of reform demonstrate this diversity of viewpoint. For the observer of post–*Serrano*[1] activity, school finance reform and the achievement of fiscal neutrality among school districts may appear to have been collateral goals. From that vantage point, education finance reform may be seen as but one vehicle to achieve greater taxpayer equity in state–local financing systems. There is convincing evidence to show that this effort has been relatively successful. New state laws have held property tax rates in check and have resulted in new infusions of state school aid that have narrowed disparities in school tax burdens (Brown and Ginsburg 1977; Callahan and Wilken 1976; Odden, Berne, and Stiefel 1980).

On the other hand, those witnessing the rapid shift in legislative and litigation strategies that accompanied the failure of *McInnis*[2] and the triumph of the *Serrano* model may hold a somewhat different view. These observers may suggest that reform activity was initially prompted by the release of evidence documenting systematic

*Michael V. Hodge, Research Associate, School Finance Project, U.S. Department of Education.

underinvestment in the education of low-income and minority children (Coleman et al. 1966; Guthrie 1976; Hansen and Weisbrod 1969; Wise 1967). Finance reform was to compensate for this long-standing imbalance by bringing about a fairer distribution of school resources to these children. For such observers, the pursuit of fiscal neutrality may therefore be viewed as a second strategy which presented fewer analytical and ultimately fewer judicial and political limitations than the strategies based on pupil need which appear to have sparked the initial flurry of reform activity. However, it has been difficult to assess the effects of reform from this vantage point. The absence of reliable data on the level and direction of resource flows below the school district level has prevented observers from obtaining an accurate picture of the impact of reform activity on children with special educational needs. The purpose of this chapter is to take a closer look at some of those analytical problems and, more generally, to explore issues in the finance and governance of education for pupil populations with special needs.

INTRODUCTION AND OVERVIEW

Present concepts of equity in school finance systems are by-products of the 150-year-old effort to develop an operational definition of equality of educational opportunity. It is not at all surprising, therefore, that today the concept of equity attracts a diverse following which seeks varied and often conflicting goals. Although it is generally recognized that a concept of equity should entail some quantitative or qualitative notion of distributional fairness, there has been considerably less agreement regarding how the good is to be fairly distributed, what would constitute fair treatment, and who should be the primary beneficiary. Odden, Berne, and Stiefel (1979: 7-16) have noted several theoretical equity concerns and related equity principles in school finance. For purposes of this introductory discussion, only two aspects of equity are briefly explored.

The notion of *horizontal equity* —equal treatment of equals—is the enduring principle in the field of public school finance that guided much of the earlier effort to establish state systems of free public schools. In the 1970s, this aspect of equity also gave shape to the fiscal neutrality standard which spurred more recent efforts to reduce tax rate, revenue, and expenditure disparities among school districts. In general, fiscal neutrality refers to equalization of the fiscal ability of governmental subdivisions to support local public services. *The achievement of fiscal neutrality among school districts rests on breaking the link between district property wealth and the level of education expenditures.*

The concept of *vertical equity*—different treatment of dissimilarly circumstanced groups—is of more recent vintage and has not been the major focus of recent state school finance reform efforts. Only during recent years have efforts been undertaken to operationally define equality of educational opportunity in such terms. This aspect of equity gave rise to the principle of student educational equity that emphasizes equalization of resources and services among children. *Vertical student educational equity, or, more simply, educational equity, may be said to be attained when the quantity and mix of school resources and services vary in direct relation to discernible differences in the educational needs of students.*

The application of the educational equity principle need not conflict with the use of the fiscal neutrality standard. For example, where there are uncontrollable differences in the distribution of special needs pupils among districts, the state aid system may legitimately provide additional resources for these children without jeopardizing its fiscally neutral standing. During the 1970s, however, many observers thought that competition for funds between general aid and support for special needs pupils was inevitable. Strained public coffers and increasing overall tax burdens had produced a reform constituency preoccupied with attaining essentially two objectives: (1) securing sufficient tax rate revenue and expendiure equalization to satisfy the courts or to ward off judicial intervention, and (2) reducing the growth in or the absolute level of local property taxes. Such tendencies would in turn curtail, if not reduce, further support for special needs students.

Funding programs for special needs students have increased, and, as shown in the following discussion, there has been a net increase in the number of state programs for such children. Yet, this can be misleading. The mere existence of supplemental aid programs reveals very little information about how new state laws have affected the flow of resources to children identified as having special educational needs. Thus, one of the more crucial issues that will be addressed here concerns the extent to which state aid supplements are likely to have been used to purchase additional resources and services for the children generating the funds.

This chapter offers a brief account of the development and implementation of federal and state reforms that have sought to allocate supplemental education resources and services to children with special educational needs. Because an inordinate number of these children attend central city schools, the chapter necessarily documents some of the more obvious demographic trends affecting those systems. However, the concern is primarily with addressing some of the issues and problems associated with efforts to target resource supplements to needy children regardless of their geographic location. While compensatory and bilingual education programs are the principal focus, special education programs are also included in the discussion. Data limitations continue to withhold a definitive answer to the question of whether new state initiatives have appreciably increased the flow of resources and services to high-need pupils. However, by reviewing relevant state school finance programs and by discussing the policy instruments (formulas and regulations) governing the flow and use of funds, it will be possible to gain some indication of how these children have fared.

Because it is important that these efforts be viewed in their social and historical contexts, a rationale for uneven distribution of public resources is developed in the first section. For similar reasons, the second section includes a discussion of federal influences on the development and use of pupil-need-based resource supplements. The third part of the chapter presents a panoramic view of state initiatives of the past decade, notes some of the specific issues and problems associated with pupil-need-based allocations, and discusses some of the strategies that can be used to overcome these problems. In the last section, conclusions are presented for policy consideration.

EDUCATIONAL NEED AND SOCIAL JUSTICE

The contention that supplemental education resources should be directed to specific categories of pupils rests on several assumptions concerning the distribution of opportunity within the social system. In an egalitarian society, the rationale for distributing public resources unequally must be based on some notion of social justice or public benefit, designed to compensate for imbalances in social arrangements, and tied to the achievement of a legitimate social end. The suggestion that some children should receive extra school resources implies the existence of some objective notion of resource equality. Supplemental allocations, then, must represent a defensible deviation from this standard. Although variation in per pupil expenditures in a given year has been the most widely used measure of educational inequality, it is, at best, a highly restrictive and crude estimate of educational resource inequity.

Educational Need

Neither children nor school systems operate in isolation from society but function within the larger social system which, absent government subventions, tends to produce resource flows that correlate with factors such as social status and wealth. When viewed from this perspective, education is seen not as a simple commodity but as a process that can be represented as the interaction of the cumulative public and private investments that accrue to children in the form of experiences, services, and tangible resources.

From this vantage point, the use of per pupil expenditures as the sole criterion of resource equality has several failings, namely:

- it disregards the influence of public and private "out-of-school" resources on preparedness for the mainstream (middle-class) orientation of school systems;

- it ignores the existence of intradistrict resource disparities associated with variations in economic and political power;[3]

- it assumes the existence of expenditure equality in years not covered by the analysis;[4]

- it assumes that such differences as may exist in educational needs, associated costs, and resource prices are randomly distributed among the units of comparison, generally school districts; and,

- it ultimately overlooks the fact that children from affluent families are likely to remain in school for a greater number of years and are therefore more likely to consume the progressively more expensive educational resources associated with secondary and higher education than their less-advantaged counterparts.[5]

Thus, current educational expenditures per pupil are, at best, a useful starting point from which to assess the distribution of educational opportunity.

Of course, more comprehensive measures of resource inequality might be identified that have a bearing on the education consumption patterns of children. (While the education system is unable to compensate fully for social and economic imbalances, it is generally recognized to be one of the prime vehicles of upward mobility. The attempt to overcome systematic disadvantages has therefore been viewed as an important role of education.) To gain a better assessment of the distribution of educational opportunity, it might be appropriate, for example, to include a broader complex of investment estimates such as the level of resources available to families for the purchase of health care services, cultural or recreational activities, home reading materials, and other factors associated with middle-class socialization and considered important for the healthy growth and development of children (Kirst et al. 1980). Such estimates could be tallied for five-, ten-, or fifteen-year periods, since it is the cumulative effect of disparities that is of greatest import. Contemporary societies, however, have found it unnecessary to undertake repeatedly this kind of massive data collection and analysis.

In the interest of social justice and social stability, most Western societies attempt to neutralize the negative effects of rigidities in their social systems. These cultures tend to demand that individuals internalize the predominant value system and behavioral patterns of their society (Parson 1967: 7-8). This inevitably places at a disadvantage those who differ because of social, economic, cultural, or even physical attributes. Societies, in effect, attempt to diminish such individual and group differences by applying sanctions that withhold or constrain access to social institutions and resources, and by limiting opportunities for effective political expression. The perpetuation of structural inequities of this sort is considered to be against the interests of advanced democratic societies in particular. Class-based disparities in educational investment and attainment, for example, also perpetuate social disadvantages and solidify economic stratification to the extent that unrestricted access to certain academic and social resources is a prerequisite to a more advanced education that, in turn, is associated with greater and more rewarding employment opportunities.

In education, Western societies generally recognize at least two categories of children who are affected by the legacy of such systemic discrimination: children who by virtue of their historic cultural or economic situation are less socialized to the mainstream culture that forms the basis for present patterns of school organization, educational instruction, and behavioral expectations; and children who because of mental or physical exceptionality have been excluded from full participation in school or otherwise have not benefitted from traditional schooling (Organization for Economic Cooperation and Development 1980). In the United States, these categories correspond to at least four overlapping groups of children who have been targeted for supplemental school resources and services, namely, Native American children, children whose household language is not English, children who are from low-income families, and children who possess mental or physical exceptionalities.

Unlike the equal per pupil expenditure doctrine, the application of the social justice principle to education funding implicitly recognizes that, in a society committed to the maximization of human potential, it is essential that attempts be made to neutralize the impact of social and economic disadvantages resulting from faults in the social system. In addition, it implicitly acknowledges that efforts to compensate for differential levels of preschool and out-of-school resources potentially increase the benefits of education and strengthen society (Hansen 1980: 22).

The first concerted effort to implement programs of pupil-need-based resource supplements in the United States began with passage of the Public Law 89-10, the Elementary and Secondary Education Act of 1965 (ESEA). Title I and Title VII of ESEA, Public Law 94-142, and the related education programs that emerged at the federal and state levels owe their genesis to raised levels of social consciousness caused by the black political reawakening of the 1950s and 1960s.[6] The evolution of this effort is briefly discussed in the next section of this chapter.

Social Justice

During the formative years of public education in America, black children were included in the school census to maximize the federal land grant allocation to territories; however, these children did not receive immediate benefit from public education. Until the second half of the present century, black Americans either had been either refused access to schooling or were legally bound to attend separate facilities that were scarce and underfunded. "By refusing to build sufficient schools for black children . . . [states] ensured that a disproportionate part of state aid would accrue to white schools" (Weinberg 1977). Because state school aid was also based on a census of all school-age children, the lower expenditure of funds for black children "created a surplus of unspent state aid that was then used for the benefit of white schools . . ." (Weinberg 1977: 2–7). Blacks were required to pay school taxes in Illinois, Ohio, Rhode Island, Maryland, and Virginia, for example, but were excluded from schools in those states. By 1860, only about 2 percent of the 1.4 million black children under the age of ten were in school compared to 55 percent for white children.

Despite the fact that freedmen had built and operated a number of schools—contributing between one-half and one-third of total support—by 1860, nine out of ten black children were still not in school. During Reconstruction and under black political influence, public education was expanded, and race-based per pupil expenditure disparities began to close in many states. But the end of the Reconstruction period and the dawn of the Jim Crow era brought a reversal of this brief trend. Compulsory segregation laws resulted in inferior facilities and programs for blacks. Thus, state aid systems again produced surplus funds that accrued to the exclusive benefit of white pupils. Between 1900 and 1930, the school year for blacks grew at a less rapid pace than for whites; class size in black schools was in some cases found to be one and one-half times that for whites; and the average salary of black teachers dropped from 86 to 52 percent of whites from 1900 to 1920, reflecting decreasing expenditures for black students. It was not until the 1950s that this pattern of discrimination was successfully challenged.

The 1954 decision of the U.S. Supreme Court in *Brown* v. *Board of Education* and the subsequent passage of Title I of the ESEA in 1965 offered implicit recognition of the long history of systematic underinvestment in the education of black children. Shortly thereafter, the relationship between socioeconomic status (and race) and per pupil expenditure as well as lifetime educational investment was unveiled by Coleman and others in their 1966 national survey of the distribution of educational opportunity in the United States (Coleman et al. 1966).

OVERVIEW OF FEDERAL INFLUENCES

By 1978–79, the federal government had enacted supplemental aid programs for the handicapped, disadvantaged, and bilingual students. Each program is funded separately.

The *Education for All Handicapped Children Act, Public Law 94–142, of 1975* provides federal financial assistance to states for the education of children having one or more of nine physical or mental disabilities. The level of federal assistance is based on a state biannual census of handicapped children between the ages of three and twenty-one years and is intended to pay a percentage of the excess cost associated with educating handicapped children. Payments to states are affected by the authorized federal reimbursement ceilings and the annual congressional appropriation. The 1979–80 estimated federal contribution was $804 million or about $204 per student, approximately 40 percent of the authorized level.

Title I of ESEA was funded at $3.3 billion under the FY 1981 Continuing Resolution. Federal funds are allocated to counties on the basis of poverty criteria. The State Education Agency (SEA) makes subcounty allocations to school districts that, in turn, allocate funds to schools using either poverty or achievement criteria. Schools use achievement criteria to identify needy children. Payments to states are based on a ratio of the state average per pupil expenditure to the national average per pupil expenditure. In 1975–76, the federal government provided a national average of $347 per client served. These funds accounted for 3 percent of total elementary and secondary education expenditures.

The *Bilingual Education Act — Title VII* authorizes the distribution of federal funds to school districts for programs to serve students with limited-English-speaking (LES) and non-English-speaking (NES) ability who have sufficient difficulty speaking, reading, writing, or understanding English to deny them the opportunity to learn successfully in classrooms where English is the language of instruction. Title VII of the 1978 Education Amendments authorized the expenditure of $200 million in 1979 and an additional $50 million for each year thereafter until 1983. In addition, a $20 million annual appropriation is made to the National Institute of Education(NIE) for administration of research and demonstration projects first funded under the 1968 Amendments to ESEA 1965. Unlike compensatory and special education programs that allocate funds according to formulas, Title VII funds are distributed through a grant application process.

The principal policy instrument used by the federal government in these targeted aid programs has been the categorical grant directed to either the state or local school districts. These intergovernmental grants generally carry certain sanctions against the use of federal funds for "nonfederal purposes": for example, substitution of federal funds for state or local general support. In addition, states are generally required to maintain separate accounts for federal funds that must be spent in a manner consistent with federal law and regulation. For example, the 1972 Education Amendments required that Title I funds be used to "supplement and not supplant" local funds. The "maintenance of effort" and "non-commingling of funds" requirements were designed to increase the likelihood that federal supplementary funds aided the intended beneficiaries. Public Law 94–142 and Title VII contain similar requirements.

In summary, the specific federal purpose in funding for each of the target groups just discussed has been threefold: (1) to insure the provision of services to children currently unserved or underserved by state programs; (2) to supplement instructional services provided to these children; and (3) to stimulate state–local adoption and support of similar programs.

STATE PROGRAMS OF THE 1970s

Current state programs for special populations provide supplementary funding of special education programs for the handicapped, compensatory education programs for the underprivileged, and various programs for NES or LES children. Following a brief discussion of the current state programs, some of the issues and problems related to these efforts are addressed.

State support of programs for special needs pupils appears to be a function of the interaction of several factors. Among these are the wealth of the state, the degree to which school districts (and states) are heavily impacted by large numbers of pupils with particular disadvantages, and the extent to which representatives of these children have successfully exerted pressures through the legislative or judicial systems.

During the 1970s, many school finance reform advocates, principally those representing older central cities of the North–East and North–Central regions and low-wealth rural districts, argued for the enactment of pupil-need-based supplemental aid programs on grounds that these districts needed financial help to offset the costs of additional resources and education tasks required to provide adequate service for large numbers of educationally needy, low-income, and language-minority children.[7] Recognizing the possibility of also redressing their grievances, parents of handicapped children successfully challenged the practice of denying their children full and equal access to the education programs of school districts (*Mills* 1972; *PARC* 1971).

The combination of federal action and legal opinion had already lent credence to claims on behalf of both handicapped and LES or NES students. By 1978–79, three years after passage of P.L. 94–142, most of the fifty states had substantially increased formula-based allocations for special education. The federal government first began supporting bilingual education through a 1967 amendment to ESEA (Title VII). Only three states funded bilingual programs in 1971, but one year after the Supreme Court's decision in *Lau* v. *Nichols* (1973), eleven states funded bilingual education programs. By 1978–79, at least fourteen states supported such programs.

The enactment of ESEA Title I and the political pressures of the 1960s were the most significant factors influencing the early expansion of state compensatory education support. In 1965, five states funded such programs, but five years later, in 1970–71, sixteen states funded the programs on the basis of the number of disadvantaged pupils or supported compensatory education programs. School finance reform activities of the 1970s had a positive but somewhat less dramatic effect on the number of such state school support programs. The number of states funding compensatory education has increased by seven since 1970–71,[8] but two states eliminated their programs while two others reduced support in that period. During 1978–79, twenty-three states provided additional funds to districts on the basis of the number of low-income or educationally disadvantaged children.

Special Education

During 1978-79, ten states and the District of Columbia accounted for one-half of all the children served under P.L. 94-142 (*Progress* 1979: 161), but these jurisdictions also enroll approximately the same percentage of the nation's public school enrollment. Table 1-1 shows that between FY 1972 and FY 1978 aggregate state special education revenue grew by an estimated 226 percent or $2 billion above the FY 1972 allocation of $900 million. Reported growth in special education support was highest in the East-South-Central and West-South-Central census regions. This uneven growth reflects a reduction in interstate spending disparities. During this period, Mississippi, for example, increased support from only $240 thousand to over $29 million—an increase of over 12,000 percent. *The state share of total federal-state allocations for special education is 90 percent* (Table 1-2). The federal share was highest in New Hampshire (60 percent) and lowest in Delaware and Alaska where an estimated 98 percent of total special education revenue came from state sources.

Compensatory Education

Table 1-1 also shows that the growth in state allocations for compensatory education was over $360 million between 1971-72 and 1978-79. During this period there was a net increase in the number of states supporting compensatory education. While programs were eliminated in Delaware and Arizona, new support programs emerged in nine states—Florida, Georgia, Indiana, Maryland, Minnesota, Missouri, Nebraska, New Jersey, and Utah.

States in the industrial North with large numbers of low-income children have generally been most inclined to provide compensatory education. The number of Title I poverty eligibles is highest in the North-East and North-Central regions of the United States and in California and Texas. Eight states—California, Illinois, Michigan, New Jersey, Ohio, Pennsylvania, Texas, and New York—contained nearly one-half of the nation's Title I poverty eligible population in 1975 (NIE 1977b: 32-33). Of these, only Texas did not report making compensatory education allocations in 1978-79 (see Table 1-1).

Compensatory education support is most prevalent in the North-Central region where ten of the twelve states supported such programs in 1978-79. All East-North-Central states currently fund compensatory education. These states contained nearly 17 percent of the nation's 1975 poverty eligibles. Three West-North-Central states—Minnesota, Missouri, and Nebraska—provide compensatory education resource supplements. Utah is the only Mountain state to provide such support. About 42 percent of the 1975 poverty eligibles are reported to reside in seventeen Southern states, but this high count of poverty eligibles may be something of an aberration since regional differences in the cost of living are not taken into account when defining poverty. Only three Southern states funded special programs for economically or educationally disadvantaged children. Total state allocations for compensatory education grew by about 226 percent between 1970-71 and 1978-79. *State governments provided an estimated twenty-nine cents of every combined federal-state dollar allocated for compensatory education.*

Bilingual Education

Aggregate growth in state allocations for bilingual-bicultural programs amounted to about $55 million between 1971-72 and 1978-79. Nine states added new programs in the post-*Lau* period—principally between 1973 and 1978—and no states eliminated programs. The states of Connecticut, Wisconsin, and Utah are the only states to have enacted programs since 1975-76. The largest number of programs is found in the Western states—Alaska, Arizona, California, Colorado, New Mexico, and Utah. California and Illinois reported the highest level of bilingual education revenue in 1978-79—$14.6 million and $12 million, respectively (see Table 1-1).

Ten states contain nearly 95 percent of the nation's Hispanic children identified as being of LES or NES ability (National Center for Education Statistics 1980: 56). Total allocations from eight of the states with the greatest number of these children account for 83 percent of total state allocations for bilingual education. Three of these states (California, New York, and Texas) have almost three-quarters of the nation's identified potential Hispanic clients. California and Texas account for 21 and 36 percent, respectively, of the eligible

Table 1-1. Revenue from State Sources for Selected Programs

State (Grouped by Census Region)	Special Education		1978-79 Increase over FY 1972 (%)
	Special Education Revenue from State Sources		
	FY 1971-72[a] (000)	1978-79[b]	
Northeast			
New England			
Connecticut	15,706	51,400	227
Maine	1,353	6,600	388
Massachusetts	18,120	e	—
New Hampshire	336	500	49
Rhode Island	13,500	4,000	-70
Vermont	2,070	11,100	436
Middle Atlantic			
New Jersey	32,656	88,100	170
New York	0	146,600	—
Pennsylvania	81,403	149,300	83
North-Central			
East-North-Central			
Illinois	59,575	154,200	159
Indiana	3,757	34,000	805
Michigan	55,000	114,700	109
Ohio	66,246	142,800	116
Wisconsin	22,282	93,600	320
West-North-Central			
Iowa	3,700	50,000	1,251
Kansas	3,841	22,400	483
Minnesota	18,633	78,100	319
Missouri	14,005	46,300	231
Nebraska	3,472	13,900	300
North Dakota	671	6,100	809
South Dakota	350	1,500	329

Table 1-1. continued

Compensatory Education			Bilingual–Bicultural Education		
State Compensatory Education Allocation		1978–79 Increase over 1970–71 (%)	State Bilingual Education Allocation		1978–79 Increase over 1971–72 (%)
1970–71[c]	1978–79[b]		1971–72[d]	1978–79[b]	
(000)			(000)		
8,375	7,300	−13	—	1,400	—
—	—	—	—	—	—
—	—	—	1,500	—	—
—	f	—	—	—	—
2,000	2,000	0	—	100	—
—	—	—	—	—	—
g	69,000	—	—	7,900	—
52,000	140,000	169	—	—	—
1,000	1,000	0	—	—	—
200	h	—	805	14,600	1,714
—	12,200	—	—	—	—
21,500	32,700	52	—	4,000	—
22,254	40,100	80	—	—	—
1,975	1,200	−39	—	1,400	—
—	—	—	—	—	—
—	—	—	—	—	—
—	i	—	—	—	—
—	j	—	—	—	—
—	700	—	—	—	—
—	—	—	—	—	—
—	—	—	—	—	—

Table 1-1. continued

State (Grouped by Census Region)	Special Education		
	Special Education Revenue from State Sources		1978-79 Increase over FY 1972 (%)
	FY 1971-72[a]	1978-79[b]	
	(000)		
South			
South Atlantic			
Delaware	8,800	33,800	284
District of Columbia	e	—	—
Florida	42,842	202,200	372
Georgia	18,178	60,900	235
Maryland	27,066	61,900	129
North Carolina	22,556	65,700	191
South Carolina	10,074	52,600	422
Virginia	11,107	38,800	249
West Virginia	2,004	7,000	249
East-South-Central			
Alabama	9,844	25,600	160
Kentucky	11,666	63,800	447
Mississippi	240	29,200	12,067
Tennessee	13,459	57,800	329
West-South-Central			
Arkansas	485	14,000	2,787
Louisiana	1,675	75,000	4,378
Oklahoma	1,250	21,500	1,620
Texas	74,186	250,800	238

Table 1-1. continued

Compensatory Education			Bilingual-Bicultural Education		
State Compensatory Education Allocation		1978-79 Increase	State Bilingual Education Allocation		1978-79 Increase
1970-71[c]	1978-79[b]	over 1970-	1971-72[d]	1978-79[b]	over 1971-
(000)		71 (%)	(000)		72 (%)
500	—	—	—	—	—
—	—	—	—	—	—
—	26,500	—	—	—	—
—	19,800	—	—	—	—
—	9,800[k]	—	—	—	—
—	—	—	—	—	—
—	—	—	—	—	—
—	—	—	—	—	—
—	—	—	—	—	—
—	—	—	—	—	—
—	—	—	—	—	—
—	—	—	—	—	—
—	—	—	—	—	—
—	—	—	—	—	—
—	—	—	—	—	—
—	—	—	—	5,200	—

Table 1-1. continued

State (Grouped by Census Region)	Special Education		1978-79 Increase over FY 1972 (%)
	Special Education Revenue from State Sources		
	FY 1971-72[a]	1978-79[b]	
	(000)		
West			
Mountain			
Arizona	3,209	28,300	782
Colorado	6,750	34,300	408
Idaho	1,901	11,400	500
Montana	5,676	26,700	370
Nevada	3,566	11,100	211
New Mexico	4,500	30,200	571
Utah	10,057	23,300	132
Wyoming	744	14,700	1,876
Pacific			
Alaska	4,095	20,000	388
California	154,010	373,800	143
Hawaii	6,637	14,200	114
Oregon	3,963	24,500	518
Washington	24,384	49,000	101
Totals	$901,600	$2,937,300	

a. Figures for 1972 taken from Wilken (1977:8).

b. All 1978-79 self-reported by states in Tron (1980).

c. Compensatory and bilingual education support from states sources for 1970-71 and 1971-72, respectively, taken from Bothwell (1976).

d. FY 1978 federal allocation under Part B taken from *Progress Toward a Free Appropriate Public Education* (1977:214).

e. Data not available for Massachusetts and District of Columbia.

f. Massachusetts has weightings for special, bilingual, and Aid to Families with Dependent Children (AFDC) pupils. Data not reported.

Table 1-1. continued

Compensatory Education			Bilingual–Bicultural Education		
State Compensatory Education Allocation		1978–79 Increase over 1970– 71 (%)	State Bilingual Education Allocation		1978–79 Increase over 1971– 72 (%)
1970–71[c]	1978–79[b]		1971–72[d]	1978–79[b]	
(000)			(000)		
200	—	—	100	1,100	1,000
1,547	6,400	313	—	2,400	—
—	—	—	—	—	—
—	—	—	—	—	—
—	—	—	—	—	—
—	—	—	100	2,700	2,600
—	1,000	—	—	300	—
—	—	—	—	—	—
—	—	—	—	5,200	—
42,021	130,100	210	—	12,000	—
1,175	13,400	1,040	—	—	—
1,385	1,000	-28	—	—	—
4,000	7,300	83	—	—	—
160,132	521,500		2,505	58,300	

g. New Jersey offered AFDC weightings under the pre-reform Bateman–Tanzman Act. Not reported in Bothwell.

h. The Illinois equalization formula provides additional funds for Title I eligibles; 1978–79 data not reported.

i. Minnesota's basic support program offers additional weights for the number and concentration of AFDC pupils; not separately reported.

j. Missouri's program offers a .25 add-on weight for each AFDC and orphan child; not separately reported.

k. Maryland's density program allocation of $13,982,460 requires that two-thirds of the district allocations be used for compensatory education programs.

Table 1-2. Comparison of State Support and Federal Allocation for Selected Programs

State (Grouped by Census Region)	Special Education — 1978-79 State Spec. Rev. as % of Total 1978-79 State and Federal Allocation—Part B[a]	Compensatory Education — 1978-79 State Allocation as % of Total 1978-79 State Allocation and FY 1977 Title I Allocation[b]	Bilingual-Bicultural Education — 1978-79 State Allocation as % of Total 1978-79 State and 1978 Title VII Allocation[c]
Northeast			
New England			
Connecticut	93	27	59
Maine	82	—	—
Massachusetts	d	d	—
New Hampshire	40	—	—
Rhode Island	79	21	55
Vermont	95	—	—
Middle Atlantic			
New Jersey	90	54	—
New York	90	41	75
Pennsylvania	92	1	—

North–Central

East–North–Central

Illinois	91	e	97
Indiana	85	31	—
Michigan	92	27	75
Ohio	93	40	—
Wisconsin	96	4	78

West–North–Central

Iowa	94	—	—
Kansas	90	—	—
Minnesota	94	f	—
Missouri	88	g	—
Nebraska	89	7	—
North Dakota	90	—	—
South Dakota	68	—	—

South Atlantic

Delaware	98	—	—
District of Columbia	d	d	—
Florida	96	25	—
Georgia	91	28	—
Maryland	92	22	—
North Carolina	91	—	—
South Carolina	91	—	—
Virginia	88	—	—
West Virginia	77	—	—

(Table 1–2. continued overleaf)

Table 1-2. continued

State (Grouped by Census Region)	Special Education 1978–79 State Spec. Rev. as % of Total 1978–79 State and Federal Allocation—Part B [a]	Compensatory Education 1978–79 State Allocation as % of Total 1978–79 State Allocation and FY 1977 Title I Allocation [b]	Bilingual–Bicultural Education 1978–79 State Allocation as % of Total 1978–79 State and 1978 Title VII Allocation [c]
East–South–Central			
Alabama	87	—	—
Kentucky	94	—	—
Mississippi	93	—	—
Tennessee	91	—	—
West–South–Central			
Arkansas	88	—	—
Louisiana	93	—	—
Oklahoma	88	—	—
Texas	94	—	30
West			
<u>*Mountain*</u>			
Arizona	92	—	34
Colorado	92	—	58
Idaho	93	—	—

Montana	97	—	—
Nevada	95	—	—
New Mexico	96	—	—
Utah	92	13	62
Wyoming	97	—	44
Pacific			
Alaska	98	—	NA
California	94	43	41
Hawaii	94	69	—
Oregon	91	5	—
Washington	91	21	—
Totals	90	29	59

a. FY 1978 federal allocation under Part B taken from *Progress Toward a Free Appropriate Public Education* (1977:214).

b. FY 1977 Title I information found in Title I Funds Allocation: The Current Formula (NIE 1977a).

c. Title VII data for 1978 reported by National Center for Education Statistics.

d. Data not available for Massachusetts and District of Columbia.

e. The Illinois equalization formula provides additional funds for Title I eligibles; 1978–79 data not reported.

f. Minnesota's basic support program offers additional weights for the number and concentration of Aid to Families with Dependent Children (AFDC) pupils; not separately reported.

g. Missouri's program offers a .25 add-on weight for each AFDC and orphan child; not separately reported.

NA = Data not available.

population. Their allocations for bilingual–bicultural education pro-grams equal 21 and 8 percent, respectively, of the total state program contributions. Florida and New York, which together contain over 20 percent of this group of potential clients, report no current ex-penditures under this category. *ESEA Title VII revenue accounts for about 40 percent of combined federal–state revenue for bilingual education students.*

Issues and Problems

Intergovernmental aid programs designed to benefit specific sub-populations are subject to misinterpretation and potential abuse at all levels of the intergovernmental system. In turn, these problems may influence the behavior of service providers and affect the flow of funds as well as their efficient and effective use. Rules and regu-lations may either reduce or exacerbate these problems. Some of the potential programmatic effects of the various state funding programs are discussed below.

Current Formulas.   States employ a variety of approaches for fund-ing programs for the handicapped, disadvantaged, and bilingual stu-dents.[9] During 1978–79, full or partial excess cost reimbursement was the principal mechanism used for funding special education. Twenty-two states used this method, while sixteen used the unit approach, and at least eleven employed some form of weighting tech-nique. Most of the twenty-three states reporting expenditures for compensatory education were using a flat- or formula-based grant method, while another eight used a weighting approach. Only Ore-gon funded the total cost of approved programs or services. Of the fourteen states reportedly funding bilingual–bicultural education programs, two made payments based on excess cost; four used a weighting approach; and eight made flat- or formula-based grant payments.[10]

Although states use several types and combinations of formulas, the distinctions between them are more nominal than substantive. Support for this notion is suggested by the fact that state special education formulas in Utah and Oregon, for example, yield approxi-mately the same amount per pupil in spite of the fact that Utah em-ploys a comprehensive weighting system and Oregon uses the cost reimbursement approach. Hartman has noted that with "comparable regulations, guidelines, and constraints, each of the formulas can be made to yield the same amount of money" (Hartman 1980: 7-8). Regulatory features and procedural guidelines may also cause the formulas to wield influence outside as well as within the funding programs. For example, formulas may be made part of the state's general aid program, in which case the special program fund is distributed in inverse proportion to school district wealth. These facts suggest that the potential fiscal and programmatic effects of the various formulas are influenced by rules and regulations governing eligibility criteria and the use of funds as much as by the level of state support.

For reform advocates, the issue of the types of state aid formula adjustments that should be adopted was one of the principal problems associated with the finance and governance of education for special needs populations during the 1970s. A related issue that received much less attention, but goes to the heart of the effort to improve education for these children, is related to the question of whether supplemental funds are actually translated into effective resources and services for the children generating the funds. This concern has two aspects. One aspect is whether resource supplements, in fact, accrue to needy children through the use of targeting and spending provisions and whether funds are used effectively. A second aspect is the extent to which special funding programs encourage misclassification of pupils.

Disadvantaged Pupils. Once the impetus of reform was redirected from pupils to school districts and taxpayers, it became clear that needy children were not likely to benefit even indirectly from new state general aid programs unless they attended schools in property-poor districts (Berke and Callahan 1972: 21). While a substantial number of needy low-income, language-minority, and handicapped children attend low-wealth rural and affluent suburban districts, it was suspected that these children tended to be concentrated in large city systems. Many analysts felt that special attention should be devoted to detecting educationally significant fiscal and demographic trends within these systems and to projecting the differential impact that reform might have on large city systems (Callahan, Wilken, and Silberman 1973; Levin, Muller, and Sandoval 1973).

One of the assumptions of some fiscal neutrality advocates of the early 1970s—that the highest incidence of special needs children was to be found in low-wealth districts—came into question when evidence was produced showing a disproportionate concentration of these children in central city districts of average to above-average wealth. Analysts sensitive to the plight of fiscally declining central cities in North–East and North–Central states argued that central city wealth was overstated by outmoded and inappropriate measures of their financial condition and resource needs. They further maintained that strict application of the fiscal neutrality standard would reduce rather than increase state assistance to many of the school districts with the highest concentrations of needy children. Today, few people would argue with the suggestion that large central cities are faced with higher than average educational tasks. (The capacity of the fiscally declining central cities of the North–East and North–Central states to meet the educational needs of their client population is discussed by Goertz in Chapter 4.)

Blacks and Hispanics are disproportionately represented among low-income families in the United States. The 1978 poverty rate was 31 percent for blacks and 22 percent for Hispanics. This compares with a 9 percent rate for whites. Increasing proportions of Hispanics and blacks are concentrated in the nation's central cities. Fifty-six percent of all blacks and 50 percent of all Hispanics live in central cities. Indeed, more than half of all low-income (Title I poverty eligible) children reside in eight urbanized states. Between 1970 and 1979, white population in central cities declined by 4.1 million, while blacks increased by 1.2 million and Hispanics by 1.4 million. In eighty-nine large city systems, between 1970–75, white public school enrollments dropped by 19 percent, while black and Hispanic school populations grew by 5 and 37 percent, respectively. In thirty-seven of these systems, minorities made up over half of the school enrollments in 1976 (Callahan and Wilken 1976). A detailed study of the distribution of minority-group children found, for example, that over 65 percent of Colorado's black students attended schools in Denver, and 70 percent of Florida's Hispanic pupils were enrolled in the Dade County (Miami) school district.

While the urban concentration of low-income black children has taken place over the past fifty years, the rapid shift in the attendance patterns of Hispanic children only has occurred during the past ten years. In 1970, 65.4 percent of all Hispanic students were enrolled in schools with more than 50 percent minority enrollment. Significant numbers of Chicanos and Spanish-speaking immigrants continue to concentrate in low-wealth rural districts of the Southwest. Nevertheless, by 1976 more than seven of ten Hispanic children could be found in schools with enrollments which consist of between 90 and 100 percent black, Hispanic, or other minority children.

Additionally, because of the general availability of more comprehensive health care and social services in central cities, programs for handicapped children often have disproportionate enrollments in large city systems. For example, the findings of Wilken (1977: 60–63) suggest that districts with higher average daily attendance tend to serve larger concentrations of special education pupils.

Formula Components.   One option available to policymakers wishing to direct assistance to needy children in low-wealth rural and some central city districts is the inclusion of pupil categorical support programs in the states' wealth-equalized general aid formula. The resulting wealth-equalized payments direct state aid to districts on the basis of both local wealth and the level of educational need. This is accomplished by making payments in an inverse relationship to local district wealth and distributing state aid on the basis of the number of enrolled pupils, then adding a cost adjustment (weights) for the number of children in the more expensive supplemental programs. Adjustments may also be made for variations in the concentration of high-need children. Twenty-four states use some form of wealth-equalized weighting techniques for special education. Three states provide compensatory or bilingual education support in this manner. However, no single funding approach seems to be uniformly effective in simultaneously compensating for differences in measured fiscal capacity and for educational need. This is not only because the internal distribution of educationally needy children and wealth varies among local school districts within a state but also because other factors will affect the distribution of aid within different states.

Generally, states have not modified their wealth measures or otherwise made adjustments for the impact of competing public service demands on the capacity of fiscally declining urban school systems to support education. Thus, needy children in those central cities that are not poor in terms of the wealth measure in the state aid formula may not benefit greatly from equalized categorical weightings. Similarly, equalized categorical weightings will provide little benefit to special needs pupils in states that have low-level foundation programs or that otherwise support a relatively small fraction of total school costs through the equalization for these children. Wealth-equalized weightings could provide these districts with only marginal increases in aid, and the districts themselves would have to carry the brunt of any additional expenditures. Under these circumstances, unequalized categorical grant programs may provide more support for these children.

In summary, the relative effectiveness of the equalized weighting approach or the unequalized grant method in a given state is a function of at least three factors that should be carefully considered: (1) the distribution of the target population among types of districts; (2) specific features of the state general aid program; and (3) the fiscal capacity of districts heavily impacted by high-need pupils. Both fiscal and educational equity can be most easily and directly achieved if states adopt a comprehensive weighting program and underwrite the full cost of education. Expenditure caps and limitations on the number of pupil or categorical weightings would control for unbridled growth in state aid and could help to limit pupil classification abuses.

Expenditure of Categorical State Aid. A further concern is how to increase the likelihood that supplemental funds accrue to the educational benefit of the target population. Although states may allocate additional resources on the basis of the number and concentration of needy pupils, they often do not stipulate that these funds should be used to purchase supplemental resources and services for these children. This is frequently the case with compensatory and bilingual education. In addition, present school-budgeting and accounting procedures make it virtually impossible to determine the level of resources devoted to children within and among schools. With the exception of Florida, which has school-by-school accounting, spending, and reporting requirements, all other states aggregate relevant information to the school district level. In attempting to assess the distribution of school resources to special needs children, for example, analysts encounter problems that are the direct result of data limitations.

In the absence of intradistrict data, analysts simply cannot accurately estimate resource flows to these children who typically represent only a small percentage of the district's total population. On the other hand, even where special needs students represent a high percentage of the total population, or where there is a high degree of segregation within the district, analysts may obtain only rough estimates of resource flows by weighting schools according to the concentrations of needy pupils. In either case, the distribution patterns between and among the district's pupils remain unknown. Under such circumstances and in the absence of expenditure requirements, the funding cannot be verified as being pupil-targeted. In an era of budget constraints and social and fiscal conservatism, the increased assistance may be diverted to other uses: for example, regular instructional programs, central office administration, or even property tax relief. While some indication of the flow of resources can be discerned by examining relevant policy instruments, a precise answer to the question of whether increased state aid actually accrues to the intended beneficiaries is still largely open to question.

Policymakers wishing to maximize the efficiency and effectiveness of pupil-need-based supplemental aid programs should consider the adoption of targeted aid spending requirements, and school-by-school budgeting and accounting procedures. Although the problem of local system adaptability is, by definition, best handled at the local level, it is the state policymaker who is empowered to offer districts the needed flexibility to adapt instructional programs and services to meet specific needs.

One approach to achieving this end appears to be the formation of school site advisory councils, chaired by the school principal and consisting of elected or selected teachers, parents, community representatives, business leaders, and, in the case of high schools, students (Guthrie 1976; *Improving Education* 1976). Under such a decentralized management and budgeting system, the council could make decisions on the selection of the appropriate mix of resources and services based on annual resource projections, individual education plans of all pupils, and the achievement profile of the school site. The enactment of this type of reform, which offers a mid-range option to the status quo and a voucher program, is likely to result in different levels and combinations of resources, activities, and pupil-teacher class ratios among schools and districts. Such differences are, however, more likely to reflect local needs and preferences than the present central office mandate (Longstreth 1978).

Misclassification. In public education, as in other publicly financed social service programs, the attempt to provide supplemental resources and services to specific target groups carries with it the potential for misclassifying clients. Critics have argued that need-based allocations may provide incentives for districts to "overclassify" and "misplace" children in order to maximize state aid. While it is not likely that this problem is the principal source of legislative reluctance to provide pupil-need-based supplements, the issue must be addressed if policymakers and representatives of school clients are to consider seriously the adoption of pupil-targeted programs.

Partial resolution of the misclassification issue appears to rest on the choice of the funding formula. In seeking to examine their policy effects, Hartman (1980) grouped the formulas according to the main factor that drives the funding formula and the criteria that determine the amount and use of funds. From this he isolated three types of approaches which simply supplement payments on the basis of either: (1) the units of service or number and type of personnel, with regulations on the cost of allowable resources and on resource use per student (resource-based); (2) the number and type of eligible clients, with regulations on the cost and use of resources (child-based); and (3) partial or full reimbursement of the costs of approved resources and services, with regulations on the children served and use of resources (cost-based).

Conceivably, the resource- and cost-based approaches are equivalent. The apparent difference between them rests on the decision of whether or not to emphasize the *cost* if services or the *type* (and by implication, the cost) of the units of service. In practice, however, the *reimbursement* feature of the cost-based approach produces the more significant differences. In general, any reimbursement approach has disadvantages for low-wealth districts or districts under tax and revenue constraints. These districts may be unable to fund levels of support out of local funds, even though they later would be reimbursed in the same manner as other districts. On the other hand, since records of costs are required, the approach appears to offer greater assurances that funds are, in fact, used for the specific target group. Because nearly half of the states fund special education in this manner and because there exists a large body of accountability rules, these program funds can be more easily tracked to the handicapped population than for other special student populations. Again, accountability features can be incorporated into any formula to improve the targeting of resources.

Hartman (1980) contended that *child-based formulas* tend to encourage misclassification since the actual amount of aid is directly tied to the number and type of eligible pupils. Further evidence of misclassification was found in a recent study of the impact of reforms on poor and minority children. In conducting a school-by-school analysis of the impact of Florida's pupil weighting system, Brischetto and Vaughan (1979: 38–39) found that black students were disproportionately represented in classes for the educable mentally retarded. This "overrepresentation" was as high as 563 percent. White students were classified as gifted in 33 percent greater number than would be expected from random assignment. The significant point here is that the associated pupil weightings yielded an average of two times as much revenue as would a classification for the regular school program.

Resource-based formulas, such as payments for classroom units or personnel, provide fewer incentives to misclassify because an increase in state support for teacher or classroom units, for example, will only occur with a sizable and noticeable increase in the eligible population. Under such formulas, target pupils are counted in order to determine the number of fundable units.

Cost-based formulas, such as partial excess cost reimbursement programs, require that districts put up local matching funds for each additional increment of state support. This approach would offer the least incentive for overclassification; however, if the program is not equalized, it will create problems for low-wealth districts that cannot afford the "front end" costs or the matching funds.

From the foregoing, it is clear that the misclassification issue does not have a simple resolution, since some type of procedure is required to identify and serve the target children. Nevertheless, the funding approach, accountability measures, and caps on the number of eligible clients or limitation on approved costs can help to reduce both the extent of financial abuse and the potential for misclassification.

SUMMARY

State school finance systems that base resource allocations on the happenstance of local property wealth often have been found to be irrational, discriminatory, and unconstitutional. Yet, the earlier notion that a rational system of education finance should provide for the distribution of school resources in relation to discernible differences in the educational needs of children lay dormant for nearly a decade. Analysts and policymakers have focused attention primarily on equalizing revenues and expenditures among school districts. However, the use of current per pupil expenditures as the criterion of educational equality has been found wanting since it disregards the powerful influence of economic and political power on the distribution of resources and services within school districts and also ignores the reality of systematic underinvestment in the education of low-income and minority children.

The evidence appears to suggest that during the past decade, some states have, nevertheless, made important strides toward increasing support for special populations. In this sense, some states seem to have reconciled the demands of the apparently conflicting objectives of fiscal equity and educational equity. Still, federal initiatives and the court decisions of the 1960s and 1970s appear to have had a more significant impact on state support for compensatory, bilingual, and special education programs than the *Serrano*-inspired reforms of the 1970s. State efforts to achieve fiscal equity among school districts have benefitted taxpayers and improved the financial standing of property-poor districts; but, in general, the resulting laws cannot be said to have increased directly the flow of resources and services to needy children, particularly those from low-income and language-minority backgrounds. Even more important, because Title I aid is targeted to low-income and lower achieving pupils and because Title VII funds are used specifically to establish and maintain programs for language minorities, both programs tend to compensate for the historically lower level of resources devoted to poor and minority children. Similarly, while targeting and reporting requirements increase the likelihood that supplemental federal resources will benefit the target population, few states would offer such assurances regarding their compensatory (NIE 1978: 7–29) or bilingual education programs. Even where state programs are in place, it is not necessarily the case that supplemental resources and services actually benefit the children generating the funds.

In the preceding discussion, an attempt was made to demonstrate that it is possible to devise pupil-need-based allocation systems at the state level that minimize many of the problems often associated with such programs. While the choice of the type of funding program was found to affect the distribution of funds for special needs pupils, the accompanying rules and regulations regarding spending requirements were also shown to be of critical importance.

While it is important to ensure that the combination of state and local funds is sufficient to support an adequate educational program for special populations, to increase the effectiveness of such efforts, the specific funding programs should include accountability features that ensure that the intended beneficiaries actually receive the resource supplements. Various approaches may be used to help ensure that the funding is adequate: for example, equalized unit weightings or unequalized categorical programs. However, fiscal and educational accountability dictate that more direct efforts be made to assure that funds are expended on those who generated the increased support.

NOTES TO CHAPTER 1

1. *Serrano v. Priest*, 5 Cal. 3d 584, 96 Cal. Rptr. 601, 487 P.2d 1241 (1971), subsequent opinion, 135 Cal. Rptr. 345, 557 P.2d 929 (Dec. 30, 1976), *rehearing denied*, Jan. 27, 1977; *as modified* Feb. 1, 1977. In this class action suit, plaintiffs contended that the California school financing system discriminated against children and taxpayers in low-wealth districts because local taxable property wealth determined the level of district revenue and expenditures. The court accepted the plaintiff's argument in support of "fiscal neutrality," ruling that the quality of public education should not be "a function of local wealth" but should be related to the wealth of the state as a whole. The successful litigation strategy became the model for most other state school finance suits. The fiscal neutrality doctrine is developed by John Coons and others (1970).

2. *McInnis v. Ogilvie*, 394 U.S. 322 (1969). Originally *McInnis v. Shapiro*, 293 F. Supp. 327, 331 (N.D., Ill., 1968). In this case, plaintiffs claimed that the Illinois school finance system did not offer equal protection to children who were in low-wealth school districts and who also had greater educational needs. In rejecting plaintiff's argument that school funds should be distributed in direct relation to educational need, the court held that this remedy offered no judicially manageable standard since the court could not develop an objective measure of educational need. The failure of this litigation strategy and the success of the *Serrano* approach effectively shifted the emphasis of reform activity from individual children to school districts (and thus from a focus on student educational equity to an effort designed to achieve fiscal equity among school districts).

3. For evidence of this tendency in the District of Columbia schools see Baratz (1975). See also *Hobsen v. Hansen*, 269 F. Supp. 401 (1967).

4. During the 1960s research findings indicated that the "Richest fifth of all families have their children in schools that spend 20 percent more than the schools serving the poorest fifth" (Jencks 1972: 27).

5. It has been estimated that twice as much is spent on the education of children of the rich as on the children of the poor (Jencks 1972).

6. For information on earlier efforts to secure equal access to quality public education see Chapter XXVIII, "Social and Cultural Strivings," Franklin (1969).

7. See, for example, Levin, Muller, and Sandoval (1973) and Guthrie (1976). At least three of the court cases of the 1970s broached the adequacy issue: *Robinson* v. *Cahill*, 62 NJ 473, 303 A.2d 273 (1973) wherein the court held that . . . "the (state) constitutional guarantee must be understood to embrace that educational opportunity which is needed in a contemporary setting to equip a child for his role as citizen and as a competitor in the labor market" (303 A.2d 273); and *Board of Education, Levittown* v. *Nyquist*, 94 MISC 2d 466, 408 NYS 2d 606 (Nassau County Supreme Court 1978), wherein the trial court found the New York system unconstitutional in part because of its failure to compensate for "educational overburden." This issue is currently under litigation in *Somerset County Board of Education* v. *Hornbeck*, File No. A–58438, Docket 119A, Folio 159 (Circuit Court of Baltimore City).

8. Figures for 1970–71 taken from Bothwell (1976: 32).

9. Seven funding approaches are identified by Chambers and Hartman (1980).

10. For a description of need-based funding approaches, see Alexander and Jordan (1976), Chambers and Hartman (1980), and Leppert and Routh (1979).

REFERENCES

Alexander, S. Kern, and K. Forbis Jordan, eds. 1976. *Educational Need in the Public Economy*. Gainesville: University Press of Florida.

Baratz, Joan. 1975. "A Quest for Equal Education Opportunity in a Major Urban School District: The Case of Washington, D.C." Report prepared by the Educational Policy Research Institute. Washington: Educational Testing Service.

Berke, Joel S., and John J. Callahan. 1972. "*Serrano v. Priest*: Milestone or Millstone for School Finance." *Journal of Public Law* 21: 23–71.

Bothwell, Robert O. 1976. "Geographic Adjustments in School Aid Formulae." In *School Finance Reform in the 1970's: A Legislator's Handbook*, edited by John J. Callahan and William H. Wilken. Washington, D.C.: National Conference of State Legislatures.

Brischetto, Robert, and David Vaughan. 1979. *Minorities, The Poor and School Finance Reform.* (9 vols.) San Antonio, Tex.: Intercultural Development Research Association.

Brown, Lawrence, and Alan Ginsburg. 1977. "School Finance Reforms in the Seventies." Washington, D.C.: U.S. Office of Education. Mimeo.

Callahan, John J., and William H. Wilken, eds. 1976. *State School Finance Reform in the 1970's: A Legislator's Handbook.* Washington, D.C.: National Conference of State Legislatures.

Callahan, John J.; William H. Wilken; and Seymour Sachs. 1976. *Big City Schools: A Profile of Changing Fiscal Pressures.* Washington, D.C.: National Conference of State Legislatures.

Callahan, John J.; William H. Wilken; and M. Tracy Silberman. 1973. *Urban Schools and School Finance Reform: Promise and Reality.* Washington, D.C.: National Urban Coalition.

Chambers, Jay G., and William Hartman. 1980. "A Cost-Based Approach to the Funding of Education Programs: An Application to Special Education." Stanford, Calif.: Stanford University, Institute for Research on Education Finance and Governance.

Coleman, James S., et al. 1966. *Equality of Educational Opportunity.* U.S. Department of Health, Education, and Welfare. Washington, D.C.: U.S. Government Printing Office.

Coons, John et al. 1970. *Private Wealth and Public Education.* Cambridge, Mass.: Harvard University Press.

Franklin, John Hope. 1969. *From Slavery to Freedom: A History of Negro Americans.* Vintage Book ed. New York: Alfred Knopf.

Guthrie, James W. 1976, "Social Science Accountability and The Political Economy of School Productivity." In *Determinancy in Education,* edited by John E. McDermott. Berkeley, Calif.: McCutheon Publishing Corporation.

Hansen, Erik Jorgen. 1980. "Analysis of Principles and Issues: Rationale for Distributing Resources Unequally." In *Financing, Organization and Governance of Education for Special Populations.* CERI/SF/80. Paris: Organization for Economic and Cooperation and Development.

Hansen, Lee W., and Burton A. Weisbrod. 1969. *Benefits, Costs and Finance of Public Higher Education.* Chicago: Markham Publishing Company.

Hartman, William T. 1980. "Policy Effects of Special Education Funding Formulas." *Journal of Education Finance* 6, no. 2 (Fall): 135–159.

Improving Education in Florida: A Reassessment. 1976. Tallahassee, Fla.: Select Joint Committee on Public Schools for the Florida Legislature.

Jencks, Christopher. 1972. *Inequality: A Reassessment of the Effect of Family and Schooling in America.* New York: Basic Books.

Kirst, Michael, et al. 1980. "State Services for Children: An Exploration of Who Governs." *Public Policy* 28, no. 2 (Spring): 185–206.

Lau v. Nichols. 472 F.2d 909 (9th Cir. 1973). Upheld by U.S. Supreme Court 414 U.S. 563 (1974).

Leppert, Jack, and Dorothy Routh. 1980. *Policy Guide to Weighted Pupil Education Finance Systems: Some Emerging Practical Advice.* Washington, D.C.: National Institute of Education.

Levin, Betsy; Thomas Muller; and Corazon Sandoval. 1973. *The High Cost of Education in Cities.* Washington, D.C.: The Urban Institute.

Longstreth, James. 1978. "School Site Management and Budgeting: A Guide for Effective Implementation." Unpublished paper, National Institute of Education.

Mills v. Board of Education. 348 F. Supp. 866. (D.D.C. 1972).

National Center for Education Statistics. 1980. *The Condition of Education for Hispanic Americans.* Washington, D.C.: U.S. Department of Education.

National Institute of Education. 1977a. *Compensatory Education Services.* Washington, D.C.: U.S. Department of Health, Education, and Welfare.

_____. 1977b. *Using Achievement Scores to Allocate Title I Funds.* Washington, D.C.: U.S. Department of Health, Education, and Welfare.

_____. 1978. *State Compensatory Education Programs*, A Supplemental Report from the National Institute. Washington, D.C.: NIE.

Odden, Allan; Robert Berne; and Leanna Stiefel. 1979. *Equity in School Finance.* Denver: Education Commission of the States.

Odden, Allan; John Augenblick; and Kent McGuire. 1980. *School Finance Reform in the States: 1980.* Denver: Education Commission of the States.

Organization for Economic Cooperation and Development (OECD). 1980. *Financing, Organization, and Governance of Education for Special Populations.* Paris: Center for Educational Research and Innovation.

Parsons, Talcott. 1967. *Sociological Theory and Modern Society.* New York: The Free Press.

Pennsylvania Association of Retarded Children (PARC) v. Commonwealth of Pennsylvania. 334 F. Supp. 1257 (E.D.Pa. 1971).

Progress Toward a Free Appropriate Public Education, A Report to Congress on the Implementation of P. L. 94–142: The Education For All Handicapped Children Act. 1979. Washington, D.C.: U.S. Department of Health, Education, and Welfare.

Weinberg, Meyer. 1977. *Minority Students: A Research Appraisal.* Washington, D.C.: U.S. Department of Health, Education, and Welfare.

Wilken, William H. 1977. *State Aid for Special Education: Who Benefits?* Washington, D.C.: U.S. Department of Health, Education and Welfare.

Wise, Arthur E. 1967. *Rich Schools, Poor Schools: The Promise of Equal Educational Opportunity.* Chicago: University of Chicago Press.

2 COST AND PRICE LEVEL ADJUSTMENTS TO STATE AID FOR EDUCATION
A Theoretical and Empirical Review

Jay G. Chambers *

As the responsibility for school funding has become increasingly centralized at the state and federal level and pressures mount for improving the equity of school finance, policymakers have come to realize that efforts to equalize should not be limited to improving the distribution of nominal differences in school spending, but rather should be directed toward improving the distribution of "real" educational services. It has become increasingly accepted that some nominal variations in school spending are justified on the basis of differing needs of student populations as well as a whole host of other factors such as differences in school size, sparsity of student populations, and declining enrollments. All of these factors create differences in resource requirements and, hence, costs of providing educational services. More recently, a number of states have been considering the possibility of adjusting state aid distributions for education to account for the differences in the prices and costs of particular school resources and services. The purpose of such an adjustment would be to provide local school districts with the same purchasing power and thus enable districts in similar fiscal circumstances to have access to the same real educational services.

Adjustments to intergovernmental aid for differences in resource prices across regions or local agencies (for instance, school districts)

* Jay G. Chambers, Associate Director and Senior Research Economist, Institute for Research on Educational Finance and Governance (IFG), Stanford University.

have not been widely used at either the state or federal level. The state of Florida has taken the lead in this arena by using an estimate of the variation in the local price of living to adjust state aid to schools. Only Alaska has begun to employ similar procedures in adjusting state aid (see Scott 1977).

Previous research in a number of states has demonstrated the existence of significant variations in the cost of services across local school districts (for example, Augenblick and Adams 1979; Chambers 1978a, 1978b, 1980b; Kenny, Denslow, and Goffman 1975; and Wendling 1979). Moreover, there has been a reasonable basis established, both in theory and in practice, for incorporating an adjustment for variations in the price of educational resources into the formulas for the distribution of state aid to local school districts.

The purpose of this chapter is to present a review of the current state-of-the-art in the assessment and measurement of resource price adjustments in education and to show how such adjustments might be implemented within school finance systems. Although a more general conceptualization of educational cost differentials would include both resource price differences and differences in educational technology arising out of varying pupil needs and scale of school or district operations, this discussion is focused primarily on resource price variations with some attention to technological cost factors as they relate to energy and transportation costs. In the first section of the chapter, price level adjustments are reviewed as they are currently implemented in state school finance systems. A cost-of-education index is defined in the second section, while some of the methodological issues in the construction of an education cost index are presented in the third section. How a cost-of-education index might be constructed is described in the fourth section, and a review of empirical results of education cost studies is offered in the fifth section. Finally, in the last two sections, some issues about the application and implementation of a cost-of-education index are raised, followed by some concluding remarks on equity and efficiency in school finance.

ADJUSTING FOR PRICE LEVEL DIFFERENCES

There are currently two basic approaches being used by states to adjust state aid to local school districts for differences in resource costs. As of 1979, two states, Florida and Alaska, adjusted state aid distributions to local school districts for differences in the levels of consumer prices. Eight states made adjustments for the costs of teacher training or experience in state aid appropriations. Each of these approaches is reviewed and evaluated below.

Cost of Living Adjustments

As indicated above, both Florida and Alaska use cost-of-living-type adjustments in their school finance formulas. Although the Florida Price Level Index (FPLI) involves a good deal more elaborate data collection and analysis than the Alaskan version, both are essentially directed at adjusting school funding for differences in the purchasing power of the consumer dollar in different regions of the state. To construct these price level indices, price information is gathered through a variety of sources and surveys for various items such as food, housing, apparel, transportation, health, recreation, and personal services. The FPLI is constructed in much the same fashion as the Consumer Price Index (CPI) which is periodically published by the Bureau of Labor Statistics. Evaluations of the methodology used in Florida indicate that it is probably a fairly well-constructed estimate of the price level differences across counties within the state (see Chambers, Hartman, and Vincent 1980).

The notion behind using such a cost-of-living adjustment is that it will tend to reflect necessary differences in the salaries paid to teachers and other school personnel by local school districts and is therefore a good representation of the difference in the cost of education. The major problem with this notion is that costs of living and costs of education, while related to one another, are not the same thing. The cost of living is but one component in the location and work decision which affects the supply, and hence the salaries, of school personnel. The attractiveness of regions and school districts as places to live and work affects the willingness of individuals to supply teaching or any other labor services and therefore ultimately affects the salaries that have to be paid to attract certain kinds of individuals. Prices of goods and services in the local markets affect the attractiveness of regions, but so does the level of crime, pollution, the climate, and access to consumption opportunities and cultural amenities, just to mention a few additional factors.[1] Moreover, attractiveness also may extend to specific characteristics of school districts as places to work (for instance, high-ability students might tend to attract teachers because they are perhaps regarded as easier and more interesting to teach).

An additional problem with using a cost-of-living adjustment is that it is relevant only to the market basket of goods and services purchased by the average consumer. In order to provide equal purchasing power to local school districts, one must price out the representative market basket of school resources commonly purchased by these districts. That is, such an index must reflect the relative prices paid by local school districts not only for school personnel but also for utility services (natural gas and electricity), bus fuel, books and supplies, and so forth. Thus, a cost-of-living index is not an appropriate method for adjusting for education cost differences.

Teacher Training and Experience Adjustments

Another approach used to adjust for costs of school personnel has been to use indicators of the levels of teacher training and experience as the basis for at least some portion of the distribution of state funds to local districts. Although the details vary from state to state, such formulas usually involve adjustment of the distribution of school funding based on the composition of the teaching staff with respect to the levels of education and experience superimposed on a standardized statewide salary schedule which has been devised specifically for this purpose. Individual districts still maintain their own salary schedule for the actual determination of teacher salaries, but the statewide standardized schedule is used for the purpose of adjusting funding for the differential levels of teacher education and experience.

Such an adjustment may be viewed in two ways. It may be regarded as an encouragement to local districts to hire teachers with greater levels of training and experience. Alternatively, it could be viewed as providing one mechanism through which the state can compensate districts for "excess costs" associated with the higher levels of salaries related to training and experience. This may be particularly relevant during a period such as the last ten years in which many districts have suffered considerable declining enrollments along with declines in turnover rates among staff. In combination, these conditions have resulted in an increase in the average levels of training and experience of the teacher work force and thus in average teacher salaries. Such increases are clearly beyond the control of local school district decisionmakers in the short run.

If one views teacher training and experience adjustments as a way of encouraging the hiring of "more qualified" teachers, then it is likely to be an appropriate mechanism to achieve that goal. If, however, one views these adjustments for training and experience as compensation for differential costs, one could argue that this is contrary to the underlying concept of what a cost adjustment should be. Adjustments for differential costs of education should be based only on factors which are beyond local school district control. At least in the long run, the levels of training and experience of the teaching staff are well within the control of local school officials. Therefore, providing ongoing adjustments to distributions of school funding based on levels of teacher training and experience could be viewed as compensating districts for expenditures that are perceived by local officials as improving the "quality" of educational services they offer. Such adjustments might therefore be disequalizing by offsetting expenses which would have been voluntarily incurred by relatively wealthy school districts.

One difficulty with justifying such compensation for teacher training and experience on the basis of short-run costs associated with declining enrollments is that such adjustments may have the effect of reducing the incentives for local decisionmakers to make the appropriate long-run adjustments in employment practices, since someone else (namely the state) is bearing the burden of the costs. Were such compensation to be contemplated by state officials, however, there are two issues that need to be addressed. First, it will be necessary to determine the target or desired levels of seniority for each district. That is, how much seniority would the district desire if it had complete free choice and could instantaneously alter the staff composition with respect to years of experience? It is the difference between the actual and desired levels of seniority that determine the degree of "excess" seniority which characterizes the teaching force of the school district. Such an analysis requires an examination of the patterns of hiring across local districts.[2]

The second issue is that it will be important that any compensation provided to school districts for excess seniority be phased out automatically over time. The automatic phase-out of such compensation will maintain the incentive for districts to make the necessary adjustment. The time dimension of the phase-out will depend on how quickly districts will be able to make the necessary staff adjustments based on expected levels of staff attrition and enrollment decline. The greater the extent to which schools are funded out of local taxes, the greater the concern over the incentive effects of compensation for short-run cost effects from declining enrollments. Under a system of full state assumption, such incentive problems would not be present for local decisionmakers, and one could more easily justify state intervention and support related to short-run cost effects.

WHAT IS A COST-OF-EDUCATION INDEX?

A cost-of-education index (CEI) is designed to reflect the variations across local school districts in the cost of providing a given level of educational services. Ideally, it would determine how much more or less it costs different school districts to provide the same quality of educational services or the same level of educational outcomes. However, because of the significant difficulties with defining what educational quality is and with determining the relative valuation of particular kinds of educational outcomes for different kinds of children, a CEI is determined on the basis of the cost of service delivery. Service delivery can be defined in terms of the resources (both quantities and kinds) devoted to providing schooling to different kinds of children. For practical purposes then, a CEI is an attempt to cost out some market basket of school resources devoted to the provision of educational services. What underlies the cost variation is a set of resource price indices that reflect the cost of purchasing similar kinds of school resources across local school districts. The key to determining what constitutes a cost difference lies in the ability to sort out the differences in expenditures required to purchase homogeneous units of some particular school resource. What are the differences in price that would be required for different districts to buy the same resource, and what characteristics define a homogeneous unit? In one sense these price indices reflect "quality-adjusted" prices of school resources where quality is defined by the set of valued resource characteristics that differentiate one unit from another. Since no two teachers are exactly alike, it is necessary to determine some method for adjusting the observed differences in salary between any two representative teachers for the differences in personal characteristics. Any remaining difference in salary reflects a difference in cost of homogeneous teacher services.

Because school districts are located in different regions of the state, exhibiting differences along such dimensions as the cost of living, labor market conditions, attractiveness and cultural amenities, climate, and density of populations, these school districts would have to pay different salaries to attract the same kinds of personnel (that is, personnel with similar sets of personal characteristics), spend different amounts of money to heat and cool school buildings, and would have to provide different levels of resources for busing pupils to and from school. For example, districts in regions exhibiting higher costs of living or poorer quality of life (that is, a poor climate or high crime rate or limited access to shopping and medical facilities), or districts serving high proportions of low-ability or disadvantaged student populations may have to pay higher salaries to attract those teachers or personnel who possess the desired sets of abilities and personal characteristics. Districts in colder climates will have to pay more for energy to heat classrooms than districts in warmer areas, while districts located in warmer regions may tend to face relatively higher costs of airconditioning. Furthermore, districts in sparsely populated areas may exhibit higher costs of transportation services.

METHODOLOGICAL ISSUES

Most of the previous work that has been done to date on educational cost differentials has focused on variations in the salaries of teachers and, to some extent, other school personnel. Three basic approaches have been taken in previous studies attempting to develop a CEI: (1) the pure statistical approach; (2) the supply-and-demand approach; and (3) the behavioral approach.

The Pure Statistical Approach

The *pure statistical model* recognizes in only the vaguest way that there is some kind of market operating for school personnel.[3] Empirical analysis is focused on a statistical approach to deriving estimates of teacher costs with no explicit model to guide the organization or selection of data or the empirical formulation of the equations. Explanatory variables are included in the analysis on the basis of ad hoc rationalizations, and virtually no attempt is made to understand the decision processes that underlie the choices being made by the parties involved in these market transactions—namely, the local school district decisionmakers and individual school personnel. There is no effort to conceptualize the process by which observed prices are determined. The value of such a theoretical foundation is that it provides a firm basis upon which the researcher can organize the data; it aids in the appropriate specification of the estimating equations; and it reduces the ambiguity in interpreting the empirical results.

Loatman (1977) has taken this statistical approach in a recent effort to construct a CEI. One of Loatman's objectives in using this approach was to reduce the complexity associated with the development of an educational cost index. He indicated that he had attempted to minimize the number of "demand-side" variables included in the predicting equations in order to simplify the analysis and make it more easily interpretable by policymakers. He also admitted that such an approach would reduce the accuracy of the estimates somewhat, but he never specified how much less accurate the so-called simple estimates might be. Clearly, one needs some standard of comparison for this purpose.

While one has to be sympathetic to the effort to make the cost index more understandable to policymakers, it is not likely to serve anyone's interest to make use of simple indices because they are simple. It is important to understand the nature of the biases involved with the simple estimates and to determine whether the reduced cost that might be associated with estimating and calculating them is worth the reduced accuracy and hence inappropriate adjustments that would be made to local school districts for differences in the costs of services. Clearly, the use of simple and easily understood estimating equations has its advantages for purposes of explanation to state policymakers. However, if the final result of the analysis based on so-called simple models is ambiguity in interpretation and likelihood of significant bias, then the value of such research to policymakers is limited; in fact, such research may do more harm than good.

With all of the problems that were encountered in the Loatman study in explaining the empirical results (for instance, insignificant variables, differences in the effects across states of particular variables, and variables with the "wrong" sign), it appears that the simple approach created more ambiguities than it resolved. This resulted from excluding a number of important variables from the analysis. It is hard to say that this approach involves any simplification and could easily be explained to legislators. With all of the caveats one would have to make, it is doubtful that any thoughtful legislator would place much confidence in such an index. Indeed, what may appear to be a more rigorous and complicated approach on the surface may be more understandable in the end. That is, the inclusion of a larger number of variables that policymakers perceive to be important in determining wage differentials will increase their confidence that the factors within local district control have been neutralized in the estimation of the cost index. Moreover, a more rigorous and comprehensive analysis would allow for better comparison and provide more adequate estimates of the bias associated with any potential simpler alternative. Having the more rigorous and more complete analysis to fall back on, one can then proceed to try simpler alternatives and to estimate more accurately the bias involved. It is then up to policymakers to determine how accurate they want the cost index to be.

The Supply-and-Demand Approach

A second group of studies, which begins with the direct specification of *supply-and-demand models* for teacher services, has attempted to construct estimates of the CEI from estimates of the structural supply equations.[4] While the models generally conform to standard formulations of supply and demand, they are developed in large part in the absence of any explicit formulation of the behavioral models of teacher or school district decisionmaking that underlie the supply-and-demand relationships. While these studies do account for the simultaneous determination of the levels of wages and employment, they often fail to recognize the interrelationships between the determination of wages and employment on the one hand and the quality or characteristics of teachers on the other. Moreover, even though they formally ignore the differences in teacher characteristics in their theoretical formulation, these researchers ultimately include in their regression equations a set of "preference or fiscal variables" that are intended to reflect the demand by local school districts for quantities and qualities of teachers. By failing to specify and provide direct measures of teacher attributes, these researchers find themselves forced to make a variety of assumptions about which variables reflect the variation in district demand, as opposed to supply, factors in the determination of teachers' salaries. This ultimately reduces their ability to divide in any systematic fashion the explanatory variables into the endogenous and exogenous (controllable or uncontrollable) components necessary for the unambiguous computation of a teacher or personnel cost index.

All of this discussion is not to say that the supply-and-demand model is inappropriate. The point of contention arises out of the difficulty of proceeding in the absence of some kind of underlying theoretical foundation. Without this theoretical base, there is a greater likelihood of misspecification of the statistical model which leads to ambiguity and other problems in interpreting the results.

The Behavioral Approach

The final group of studies is those that begin with an explicit theoretical framework around which the empirical analysis of supply and demand is organized and the estimates of personnel costs are derived.[5] This group of studies specifies the behavioral models of school district decisionmaking on the one hand and individual supply of labor on the other. These studies have a solid theoretical foundation upon which to construct estimates of a CEI, and, although data limitations often inhibit the estimation of the desired equations, such models provide a basis upon which one can evaluate the potential biases and ambiguities. Where adequate data have been available, the empirical results have been consistent with intuition about the patterns of cost differences, and results have been remarkably similar across states. However, a further discussion of the empirical results is deferred until later. What follows is a discussion of some of the major methodological issues that have arisen in the theoretical specification and empirical implementation of behavioral models in the analysis of educational costs and particularly the costs of school personnel.

Opportunity Cost as a Determinant of Teacher Costs. One such behavioral study conducted by Frey (1975) raised a significant methodological issue regarding the determinants of teachers' (or school personnel) salaries and the estimation of cost differences. Frey's study demonstrated the importance of opportunity cost (as measured in his study by the wages of industrial nurses) as a determinant of the variation in teacher wages. It has been suggested, based on his results, that the relationship between teacher wages and such an opportunity–cost measure could well be used as a proxy from which teacher–cost differences might be estimated. The underlying notion is a sound one that has a basis in the theory of wage differentials across regions. There are a number of important theoretical and empirical factors, however, that limit the value of this approach. The issue of comparability of labor markets becomes a paramount concern. That is, in order to make comparisons of wage differentials across markets, one must be comparing markets with a good deal of similarity among them in order to ensure that the results do not reflect irrelevant differences between the two market areas. As Hyman (1977) has suggested, the educational preparation for teaching and the selected alternative occupation(s) should permit some transferability across occupations in response to relative wage differences within regions. Moreover, the alternative wage should be market determined, and the structure of the markets for teachers and the alternative occupations should be similar (for instance, in terms of the degree of competitiveness). Finally, there should be a similar extent and success of bargaining between the two markets to ensure compatibility.

Another practical problem with the use of the opportunity–wage approach is that it ignores the possibility of variations in the quality of the alternative labor force across regions. One would expect, for example, that given differences in the elasticities of demands for quantities and qualities of labor between the teachers and alternative occupations, there will be some variation in the quality of the alternative labor force relative to that of teachers across regions.

Underlying the opportunity–cost method is the notion that there is some systematic structure that relates the wages in all markets to one another. Given the amenities that characterize alternative occupations, job assignments, and regions, it is the combination of the choices by workers among alternative occupations, locations, and employers and the choices by employers among alternative workers that determines the equilibrium wage structure. Thus, there is a systematic relation between wages paid to different types of labor across markets. Indeed, this relation between wages in different occupations is reflected in the wage determination models set out in Lucas (1977) and Chambers (1981). However, the resulting estimating equations in the Lucas and Chambers papers relate the equilibrium values of wages to all of the universal factors (regional amenities and costs of living) that affect wages generally in the market as well as those factors that are unique to a specific occupation or job assignment.

This last point raises one further theoretical concern with the opportunity–cost approach. It reveals the fact that there are some factors such as school or district characteristics that affect the wages of teachers, but clearly may not have any relevance to the determination of wages in other markets. Therefore, the opportunity–cost method alone is not sufficient to capture some of the other factors that might affect the variations in the costs of teachers across regions and school districts.

There is one final issue of practical concern for the use of the opportunity–cost method within states. Specifically, there exist only limited data at present on the measures of opportunity cost. First, much of the data that do exist are available only for the years covered by the U.S. Census, which make it of decreasing value in years following each census year. Second, the data that are available often are simply earnings data uncorrected for differences across regions in hours or days worked per period of time and, as suggested before, are likely to reflect variations in the quality of the labor force. Third, where there are better data on opportunity wages (for example, the "Area Wage Surveys" published by the Bureau of Labor Statistics), they are only available for the major metropolitan areas of the country, and within any given state the surveys themselves are not conducted at the same point in time. Data for different metropolitan areas within a state can be as much as two years apart, which limits its compatibility for the purposes of estimating teacher–cost differences.

The Hedonic Wage Model.   Most of the remaining studies of resource price differences in education share the same basic theoretical and empirical specification. These studies include: Antos and Rosen (1975); Augenblick and Adams (1979); Chambers (1978a, 1978b, 1980a, 1981); Chambers, Odden, and Vincent (1976); Kenny, Denslow, and Goffman (1975); and Wendling (1979). The basic theoretical framework for this analysis was perhaps first formally set out in Lucas (1972), was first employed in analysis of teacher salaries in Antos and Rosen (1975), and is elaborated upon for the assessment of the costs of school personnel in Chambers (1981). The basic theoretical structure is that of the "hedonic wage model." The intuitive notion underlying this theoretical structure is that individuals care both about the quality of their work environment as well as the monetary rewards associated with particular employment alternatives, and that they will seek to attain the greatest possible personal satisfaction by selecting a job with the appropriate combination of monetary and nonmonetary rewards. Similarly, employers are not indifferent as to the characteristics of the individuals to whom they offer particular jobs. The result of these simultaneous choices is the matching of individual employees with employers. It is the result of this matching process itself that reveals implicitly the differential rates of pay associated with the attributes of individual employees and the working conditions offered by employers. More formally, it is the supply of, and demand for, individuals with certain personal attributes to any particular kind of job assignment that determines the equilibrium wages of labor as well as the implicit market prices attached to the personal and job characteristics.

The implicit relationship observed between wages and the personal and job characteristics of individuals is referred to as a hedonic wage index. The word hedonic literally refers to the physical and psychic pleasures that one can derive from engaging in certain activities. In the context of labor markets, the word hedonic refers to the satisfactions or utility derived by employees from the characteristics of the work place and the profits or the perceived productive value derived by employers from the characteristics of the employees they assign to certain jobs. The hedonic wage index permits one to decompose the observed variation in the wages paid to labor into the dollar values attached to each unit of the personal and workplace characteristics. For example, one could determine how much more an employer would have to pay in the market to attract individuals with greater verbal proficiencies or greater physical strength to a particular kind of job, or how much less at the margin an employer would have to pay to attract workers to a job in airconditioned office space or to a job with a greater probability of bodily injury attached to it.

Turning attention to markets for school personnel, hedonic wage theory suggests that in estimating the variations in the costs of school personnel, one cannot simply look to the differences in actual sala-ries paid across local school districts. Because of the differences in the attractiveness of local districts or the regions in which they are located, different salary levels will be required to attract the kinds (or qualities) of personnel necessary to provide similar levels of edu-cational services across districts. For the purpose of identifying cost differences, it is essential to decompose salary variations into those that are within as opposed to outside the control of local school deci-sionmakers. The controllable components of salary variation reflect the conscious choices of school decisionmakers in terms of the char-acteristics of the personnel employed and the attributes of the jobs to which they are the estimates of differential personnel costs.

To clarify this argument a bit, consider for a moment which ele-ments of the employment transaction are actually controlled by local school officials. As a school decisionmaker, one can control not only the number of teachers employed but also specifically which teach-ers, in terms of some set of personal characteristics, are employed out of any pool of willing applicants. Moreover, within certain limi-tations, school district officials can control the salary schedule and other aspects of compensation and working conditions. What these decisionmakers do not control is the composition of the willing pool of applicants (with respect to their personal characteristics) who show up to offer their services for any specified salary schedule and working conditions. In essence, what they do not control is the will-ingness of individuals to *supply* their services at any specific levels of monetary and nonmonetary compensation.

Given this context, one can observe the patterns of salaries being paid individual school personnel across local school districts in rela-tion to the particular personal, job, and locational characteristics. Hedonic wage theory offers both a conceptual framework for inter-preting such relationships and a technique for disaggregating the rela-tionship into the component parts. It allows one to determine the dollar weights implicitly placed by the market upon the characteris-tics of individual school personnel and the attributes of the jobs to which they are assigned and the workplace in which they are located.

Unit of Observation and Analysis. The Kenny, Denslow, and Goff-man (1975) study differs from the framework described above pri-marily in the unit of analysis. It focused on the district as the unit of analysis, while the hedonic wage model is in terms of the individual.

There are both strong theoretical and empirical reasons for select-ing the individual, as opposed to the district, as the unit of analysis for examining variations in salaries. At the theoretical level, this approach allows the analyst to capture many of the subtleties of the employment transaction that would not be captured using district salary scales or average salaries. The approach treats the hiring proc-ess as one that occurs on an individual basis and one that reveals the unique combination of characteristics associated with the individual school employee and the job to which they are assigned. It explicitly accounts for potential intra- as well as inter-district choices of teach-ers and school decisionmakers and, hence, may reveal far more about the implicit relationship between salaries and the attributes of per-sonnel, schools, districts, and regions than would be revealed by using district salary scales as the unit of analysis. By capturing these subtleties in the market for school personnel, one is better able to control for the effects of characteristics of school personnel in order to determine the variations in salaries associated with differences in the factors outside district control (that is, the supply factors associ-ated with school personnel).

From the standpoint of the empirical analysis, the advantages of using the individual as the unit of analysis is that it allows for gather-ing more detailed data on personal characteristics and working condi-tions than would be available using the district as the unit of analysis. These detailed data are important for ensuring ability to control for the effects of teacher characteristics in assessing the impact of fac-tors beyond district control. Using the district as the unit of analysis, the analyst would require data on the attributes of virtually every teacher in the district in order to control in the statistical analysis for the impact of teacher attributes on salaries. Using the individual as the unit of analysis, the researcher need only select a sample of teachers from the target population and request more detailed infor-mation regarding individual circumstances than could ever be made available on all teachers. Moreover, by using the individual teacher as the unit of analysis, one avoids the potentially serious problems of aggregation and resulting bias in the empirical estimates that may arise out of using the district as the unit of analysis.

All of this discussion is not to suggest that the district cannot be used as the unit of analysis for some purposes. The point is that the appropriate unit of analysis, based on the underlying theoretical framework and the apparent way in which employment transactions occur, is the individual teacher. If one accepts this formulation of the model, then estimates of the hedonic wage relation based on the individual as the unit of analysis should be estimated as the standard of comparison. To determine whether or not parameter estimates obtained from district data are satisfactory, one should compare these estimates with those obtained from the individual data with respect to both statistical and economic significance. Statistical significance refers to the sample properties of the estimates and involves the determination of the probability that the differences in the estimates were obtained by chance. Economic significance refers to the magnitude of the difference in the estimates and the implications of the alternative calculations for the distribution of dollars. One could, for example, establish that the results obtained from the alternative procedures are statistically different from one another, and yet the magnitudes of the differences in terms of the observed relative wages could be small. Of course, one must establish some criteria for determining economic significance, but this can be left to policymakers if they are provided with additional information about the costs of pursuing the alternative methodologies and other potential benefits from one or the other.

Empirical Specification and Variable Selection.   In addition to suggesting a nonlinear form for the estimating equation, hedonic wage theory indicates that the estimating equation is a reduced form rather than structural equation (see Chambers 1981; Rosen 1974). This reduced form equation reflects the equilibrium achieved by the interaction of the supply-and-demand sides of the market, and one may use ordinary least squares regression to estimate the parameters of the model.

One of the problems with the hedonic wage analysis, whether it is for school personnel or any other type of labor, is in the process of variable selection. The theoretical models of supply and demand for labor take us only part, albeit an important part, of the way in this process of determining which variables should be included in the empirical analysis. In particular, it suggests that at least two classes of variables need to be included—namely, personal and job (including locational) characteristics.

What is needed is a way of conceptualizing the variable selection process: that is, a scheme for classification of variables based on the purpose they serve within the context of the supply-or-demand analysis. Specifically, one needs to determine what kinds of factors will tend to affect perceived productivity (and hence the demand side of the market) on the one hand and teacher preferences (the supply side of the market) on the other. What are the factors that characterize the environment—both that within which production occurs and that within which teachers live and work on a daily basis? Before proceeding with this analysis, it is important to point out that no amount of theory is going to provide an entirely satisfactory method for ensuring that the list of variables selected for the analysis of wage variations is a complete or an adequate representation of reality. It will always be possible to suggest alternative interpretations of particular variables or to speculate about certain missing personal, job, or locational attributes. The purpose of this section, therefore, is to present a modest attempt to develop a conceptual framework that will provide a foundation for variable selection.

As a starting point for this discussion, one may look to a conceptualization of educational production proposed by Levin (1978). He suggested:

> (A)n educational production function need not begin with a basic understanding of the learning process as much as it requires an understanding of the "technology" of that process. For example, studies of agricultural production do not require an understanding of plant biology or physiology. They do not necessitate a knowledge of photosynthesis nor must we know the biochemical processes by which nutrients are converted into plant growth. All that is required is an overall understanding of which nutrients and conditions must be present to stimulate growth (1978: 5).

What Levin proceeds to propose are three dimensions or ingredients necessary in examining the value of personnel inputs into educational production. Specifically, he proposed these dimensions to personnel inputs: (1) capacity, (2) effort, and (3) time. The models of supply and demand which underlie the hedonic wage theory contain counterparts of each of these elements. Capacity is represented by the set of personal characteristics of job assignments (that is, more attractive job assignments tending to elicit greater effort). Time is represented by absolute time allocations to various activities and the proportionate time allocations among assignments.

Table 2-1 sets out the basic framework for the selection of variables to be included in the analysis of the salaries of school personnel. Much of what is specified in the table is self-explanatory. Certain features, however, should be discussed. First, the table reflects an effort

Table 2-1. Framework for Selection of Variables To Be Included in the Analysis of Variations in the Salaries of School Personnel

---

A. *Personal Characteristics*

   1. Capacity to Perform Assigned Tasks

      a. Quantity, quality, and the nature of professional training (for example, degree level, total years of schooling, certification, major field of study, quality of college attended, vintage of degree).

      b. General measures of intellectual ability (for example, undergraduate grade-point average, rank in undergraduate class, verbal and quantitative ability).

      c. Professional experiences (for example, years employed in present district, total years of experience in present job title, years unemployed since entering career as an educator, tenure, years of experience in other careers).

      d. Background characteristics, particularly as they relate to the backgrounds of school clientele (both children and their parents) and co-workers and to personal and emotional maturity and experience.

   2. Attitudes, Preferences, and Characteristics Related to Alternative Job Opportunities

      a. Background characteristics (for example, age, sex, race or ethnic background, and family socioeconomic status).

      b. Personal circumstances (for example, current family status and responsibilities and constraints on labor market mobility related to family status).

B. *Job Characteristics*

   1. Terms and Conditions of Employment

      a. Job classification and scope of responsibilities (for example, hours or weeks of work, job title, class sizes for teachers, or school sizes for principals).

      b. Fringe benefits provided by the district (for example, contributions to insurance plans and paid sick leave).

   2. Quality of the Organizational, Technological, Social, and Physical Environment

      a. Bureaucracy of the organizational unit (for example, as reflected by school or district size).

Table 2-1. continued
_____

B. *Job Characteristics (continued)*

   b. Pupil abilities and special needs (for example, as reflected by test scores or the composition of pupils according to physical or mental handicaps, special abilities, age or grade levels, or cultural background).

   c. Match between the individual's capacity and the requirements of the assignment (for example, the relation between undergraduate training and subject matter being taught, and the match between certain individual background characteristics and the background characteristics of pupils, parents, and other school personnel).

   d. The quality of support services and facilities (for example, access to professional or clerical support, access to instructional materials, and age or condition of school buildings).

   e. Safety of the place of work (for example, as measured by overall crime or assault rates within municipalities connected with school attendance areas).

C. *Regional Characteristics*

  1. Condition and Structure of the Labor Market

   a. Competitiveness of the labor market (for example, density of school districts, proportion of the market accounted for by the largest district in the region, relative market power of the individual district, and size and density of the region as a proxy for competitiveness of other related labor markets).

   b. Availability of labor market opportunities for the individuals or their spouses (for example, as reflected by the rate of unemployment in the region and region size).

   c. Degree of surplus in the market for teachers (for example, as reflected by the ratio of job applications to new hires for teaching personnel in the region or district).

  2. Dimensions of the Quality of Life

   a. Cost-of-living as proxied by region size, density, degree of urbanization, and land and housing costs in the region in which the district is located.

   b. Access to urban areas (for example, commuting distances to local employment centers and travel times from nonmetropolitan counties to the nearest major central city).

Table 2-1. continued

C. *Regional Characteristics (continued)*

    c. Access to consumption opportunities and medical facilities (for example, retail and service trade establishments and hospitals per square mile and per capita in the region).

    d. Access to recreational facilities (for example, acres of state and national parks, historical monuments and related facilities within given driving distances or times).

    e. Climatic conditions and air quality (for example, average or maximum summer or winter temperatures, annual rainfall or snowfall, percent of days with primary or secondary violations of air quality standards in the region).

---

to employ the Capacity–Effort–Time (CET) model suggested by Levin (1978). The framework makes explicit reference to personal capacity variables under the section A1. *Capacity* in this context refers to those characteristics of workers that are perceived by local school decisionmakers to contribute to the equality of the district's educational program. Most of the kinds of variables included are those which may be to greater or lesser degrees observed or assessed indirectly by school decisionmakers and parents. The objective of this exercise is not so much to reveal a full understanding of the nature of the decisionmaking processes that underlie the observed outcomes (that is, assignment of the individual workers to jobs), but rather to identify the ingredients of which that process appears to be composed. One of the ingredients is that the most important of the valued attributes of school employees must be factors which can be assessed or observed either directly or indirectly by local officials. Moreover, these characteristics should be ones which are commonly believed by parents to affect educational quality—even if the decisionmakers themselves have been instrumental in creating the beliefs. Nevertheless, the choices of districts must within limits appear to be reasonable and credible to the local community.

Effort is defined by Levin as "the level of energy used to convert capacity into instruction for each unit of instructional time" (1978: 18). This feature of Levin's model is reflected in at least three places in Table 2-1. Specifically, the conversion of labor power (capacity) into effort (labor services) is proxied by the attitudinal and preference variables included in A2, and potentially all of the job characteristics. That is, one's effort on the job is not only related to certain systematic differences in background characteristics and personal circumstances but is also affected by the satisfactions derived from on-the-job consumption—that is, the satisfactions derived from (1) challenging or interesting work, (2) job assignments which are consonant with one's personal preferences (some of which may be systematically reflected by objective background characteristics), or (3) job assignments for which the burden of work is relatively light or for which the district provides enough support to reduce the difficulty of performing the tasks.

Time allocations may be indirectly reflected in the job assignments. Those individuals who tend to allocate time among work activities (for instance, disciplinary versus instructional activities) in accordance with decisionmaker preferences may tend to get the preferred job assignments. To the extent that current job assignments and their attributes do reflect the individual's patterns of time allocation, there will be some bias in the coefficients. For example, preferred job attributes (those for which teachers or school personnel would normally give up wages) may show up in the analysis with positive coefficients, reflecting the fact that teachers, who employ preferred patterns of time allocations and whose services are therefore valued more highly, will be assigned to these preferred jobs. For purposes of estimating a personnel cost index, this may not raise a significant problem. However, for the purposes of employing estimates of job characteristics in an analysis of personnel cost differences across educational programs, this omitted variable may create some problems of interpretation.

The regional characteristics and some of the district-level job characteristics specified in Table 2-1 go beyond the immediate limits of Levin's conceptual framework. In general, these are the factors reflecting the overall quality of the environment within which the individual works and lives and the condition and structure of the labor market in which equilibrium wages and employment levels are determined. Moreover, these are the dimensions of the model which are essentially outside the control of local school decisionmakers as well as other local employers.

Underlying the selection of these kinds of regional or locational characteristics is a fairly substantial literature in the analysis of regional differences in costs of living and wage rates. Theoretical developments in urban economics have suggested that cost-of-living differences across regions will be related to the cost of producing goods that are not traded (exported) across regions—that is, goods and services which are produced and consumed locally (see Tolley 1974). In general, differences in the cost of producing these local goods will be related to the cost of immobile factors of production such as land. This suggests that a base price of land or, at the very least, some indicator of housing costs would be an appropriate variable to include in analysis of local wage differences. Kenny, Denslow, and Goffman provide a cogent explanation of this relation as follows:

> Let us for the moment assume that the level of amenities is constant. The cost of producing some commodities will vary systematically across geographical regions. Housing-plus-access is an example of such a commodity. Suppose that land in the rural areas surrounding towns costs $X per year per plot. An individual working in the center of town always has the option of living in the urban/rural border and commuting into the center of town every day. Towns with larger populations tend to have greater commuting distances, and thus the total cost of housing-plus-commuting will be greater in large cities than in small towns. Therefore, as the population of a metropolitan area increases or as an area becomes more urbanized, the price of housing-plus-access will increase, increasing the cost of living. Similarly, as the base price of land in rural areas rises, the price of housing-plus-access will increase.
>
> As a simple approximation, wages will adjust such that an hour's work will purchase the same basket of goods across different areas of employment. Thus, real wages are assumed to be constant. Workers will demand more to work in large cities, where the total cost of housing-plus-commuting is greater; the increased wages demanded in large cities will drive the cost of living up still further, and eventually this "multiplier" process will lead to equilibrium increases in wages and in the cost of living. To summarize our results, wages and the cost of living are predicted to rise with increases in urbanization, the population of urban areas, and the base price of land in rural areas (1975:176).

An empirical literature has also developed which is directed toward verifying the relationship between costs of living across regions and such variables as population growth and the city size since such variables reflect differences in demand for, and hence prices of, local goods (see Haworth and Rasmussen 1973; McMahon and Melton 1978). Finally, Rosen (1977) has been instrumental in extending the empirical basis for selecting locational attributes important in the determination of regional wage differentials.

HOW IS A CEI CONSTRUCTED?

With these methodological issues out of the way, let us now consider procedurally how one goes about the construction of a cost-of-education index. The initial phase in the development of a CEI involves identifying the relevant categories of school resources for which individual price or cost indices might be required. This requires division of school personnel into categories amenable to empirical analysis and separating out the various nonpersonnel categories of school resources and services for which cost variations are likely to exist. Previous research on these various budgetary elements has focused on four basic categories of personnel inputs—namely, teachers, school site administrators, district administrators and nonprofessional or support staff—and two categories of nonpersonnel inputs—energy and transportation services. The personnel categories account for about 85 percent of operating school district budgets, while transportation and energy services account for approximately 6 to 8 percent. The remainder of school district budgets accounts for about 7 to 10 percent and includes a variety of miscellaneous items (for instance, textbooks, supplies, and materials) which are either purchased in statewide markets or for other reasons are not likely to exhibit cost variations that would have significant impact on the overall CEI. Other items that might be included, such as insurance costs, do not lend themselves easily to systematic empirical analysis. Nevertheless, such items do not constitute a substantial proportion of school district budgets, and it is unlikely that they would dominate the basic patterns of variation in educational costs across the state.

The second stage in the development of the CEI involves estimation of separate cost indices for each of the relevant categories of school inputs and services identified above. This analysis begins with an examination of the full range of factors that explain variations in the prices of school resources and expenditures on school services. Once a substantial portion of the overall variance in these prices and expenditures have been explained, then that portion of the variation due to factors which are beyond local school district control is isolated. *To the extent that these prices or expenditures for school resources and services are beyond local control, they represent a difference in the cost of educational services. It is this component of* the variation in prices outside local school district control that constitutes the resource price index.

The final phase of the analysis involves combining the individual resource price and service cost indices into a single index that reflects the overall difference in the costs of educational services. This is accomplished by costing out a fixed or standardized market basket of school resources and services across all school districts in the state. This overall index is referred to as the CEI.

Costs of School Personnel

The construction of personnel cost indices begins with the specification of a set of statistical relationships, based on hedonic wage theory, that describe the overall variation in the salaries of the various categories of school personnel. A separate statistical relationship is specified for each relevant category of school personnel. The basic structure of these relationships, however, is derived from standard hedonic wage theory outlined in the previous section. These statistical relationships examine the systematic variation in salaries as they relate to variations in:

1. Personal characteristics (for instance, age, experience, education, sex, race or ethnic background, ability traits);

2. Working conditions, terms of employment, and job assignments (for instance, days and hours of work, types of children served in assignment, class sizes, job title); and

3. District and regional characteristics which are beyond local control (for instance, district size, types of students served throughout district, and factors reflecting variations in costs of living, labor market conditions, and attractiveness of local areas as places to live and work).[1]

It is this third set of factors (district and regional characteristics) that forms the basis for the simulations of the *costs of school personnel* described below. These factors shall subsequently be referred to as the "cost factors."

The general form of the statistical relationship which is used for the analysis of personnel costs may be expressed as follows:

$$\text{Log}_e \text{ SALARY}_{ij} = \alpha + \beta \cdot Q_i + \gamma \cdot X_j + U_{ij} \qquad [1]$$

where

$\text{Log}_e \text{ SALARY}_{ij}$ = the natural log (ln) of the annual salary of individual i employed in district j;

Q_i = a set of variables describing the personal characteristics, working conditions, terms of employment, and job assignment corresponding to individual i;

X_j = a set of district and regional characteristics which are outside district control (that is, the cost factors) corresponding to district j;

α, β, γ = the coefficients or parameters that define the nature of the relationship and which will be estimated using statistical methods;

U_{ij} = the error term in the statistical relationship (that portion of the observed variation in the dependent variable, ln SALARY_{ij}, that cannot be explained by systematic factors but which is determined rather by random factors).

Data on each of these items included in Q and X are collected, the statistical relationship specified in [1] is estimated, and a simulation of the variations in salaries associated only with variations in the cost factors (X) across the state is conducted. The simulation of personnel costs provides an answer to the hypothetical question, "How much more or less would it cost for different school districts across the state to recruit and employ similar kinds of personnel (as defined by their personal characteristics) in similar kinds of jobs (defined by their job assignment characteristics)?" It is important to recognize that even though only the variables representing the cost factors are included in the index of personnel costs, it is essential, nevertheless, to include the personal and job assignment characteristics in order to control adequately for, and ultimately neutralize the impact of, these elements that are within the discretion of local school decisionmakers.

Using the general formulation of the salary equation specified in equation [1], it can be demonstrated how the index of personnel costs is actually computed. The salary "costs" for a given district may be simulated by estimating the salary district i would have to pay if it were to employ personnel with some standardized set of characteristics in specified types of job assignments. Procedurally, this salary cost is simulated using a standardized value of Q (for example, the mean value for the state which is denoted by $\overline{Q}$) while using the actual values of X_j corresponding to district j. This simulated salary cost for district j (SALCOST$_j$) may be represented by the expression:

$$\text{SALCOST}_j = \text{EXP}(\hat{\alpha} + \hat{\beta} \cdot \overline{Q} + \hat{\gamma} \cdot X_j) \qquad [2]$$

The hat ($\char"5E$) over the parameters α, β, γ indicate the use of statistical estimates. Given the salary cost figure in [2], the personnel cost index (PCI$_j$) can be specified as the ratio of SALCOST$_j$ to the standardized salary level $\overline{\text{SALCOST}}$ determined by $\overline{Q}$ and $\overline{X}$. Formally, this may be written

$$\text{PCI}_j = \text{SALCOST}_j / \overline{\text{SALCOST}} \qquad [3]$$

Nonpersonnel Costs

The two elements of nonpersonnel costs that have been analyzed in the previous literature are transportation and energy costs. The basic notion of trying to isolate the uncontrollable portion of the observed variation in expenditures holds here as it does for personnel costs. There are, however, some slight variations in methodological approach because of the differences in the nature of these services. These approaches are briefly described in turn below.

Energy Costs. Differences in energy costs arise from two sources: (1) differences in the energy requirements necessary to compensate for climatic variations across the state, and (2) differences in the prices paid for energy sources such as natural gas and electricity. Variations in climate will necessitate greater levels of energy consumption in order to heat and cool school buildings to "comfort levels." Moreover, districts located in different parts of a state will be served by different suppliers of energy services (natural gas, electricity, liquid propane or heating oil) and will therefore be subject to different rate schedules. An engineering approach has been taken to the determination of energy consumption.

Determination of the variations in energy requirements involves three steps:

1. Specification of a standard building design;

2. Division of the state or region into homogenous climatic zones and preparation of the data representing a "typical" year's weather pattern; and

3. Simulation of the energy (natural gas, electricity, and so on) consumption requirements using the weather data for the various climate zones along with the standard building specifications as input into a computer simulation program designed for this purpose by energy experts.[6]

While it is recognized that school building designs vary across districts, it is generally not practical to gather the kind of detailed data necessary to do a district-by-district analysis of energy requirements. Moreover, the use of standard building design for calculation of energy costs avoids the possibility that the state would become responsible for high costs of energy that might be associated with an inefficient energy design.

All districts within any particular climate zone are assumed to have the same climate and thus the same energy requirements for the standard building. While this is clearly an oversimplification, climatic variations within climate zones would be extremely small by design and would have only small effects on overall energy costs.

The second step in the determination of energy costs involves costing out the energy requirements derived from the simulation described above. Price information can be obtained from the utility companies or from the public utility commissions within each state.

One of the limitations of this approach lies in the assumption of a fixed building design. No account is taken in the estimates of the possibility of differences in building design that might have been stimulated by high prices of energy. Districts facing colder climates or rapidly rising energy prices may well have decided to build schools with better insulation or to provide increased insulation in existing schools in order to reduce the energy requirements necessary to heat buildings to comfort levels. To the extent that these districts have indeed made such capital improvements (that is, increased insulation), estimates using a standard building design may overestimate actual energy costs. However, total energy costs in this case would have to include not only the current consumption costs of energy services but also the amortized cost of the capital investment required to increase building insulation. This complicates the analysis considerably, and whether it has any significant impact on the cost estimates remains to be seen. In general, this is not likely to be of great significance except in the most extreme cases of climatic differences across regions of the state.

Transportation Costs.   The first step in the analysis of transportation costs involves the specification of a transportation cost function that will explain the variations in expenditures for transportation services across local school districts.[7] The basic framework for specifying such a cost relationship may be found in the economic theory of production and cost. With this in mind, the equation has been designed to account for three kinds of variables that are likely to cause variations in transportation expenditures:

1. Outcome measures: levels of transportation services provided by local school districts (for example, numbers of pupils transported between home and school, and miles of transportation services for nonhome-to-school services such as field trips, or athletic events);

2. Input prices: indices of the costs of transportation personnel and the costs of fuel; and

3. Technology and environmental factors: factors that affect the differences in the combinations of resources (transportation inputs) required to provide home-to-school or other transportation services such as numbers of pupils per square mile in the district (that is, student density), or percent urbanization and population density of the country.

The data available from most states for the analysis of transportation costs usually do not include costs of capital equipment such as buses used to provide transportation services. Yearly capital costs would include the estimated depreciation of equipment plus an estimate of the foregone earnings to society resulting from the fact that funds are tied up in school buses. That is, capital cost includes not only an estimate of the wear and tear and general reduction in value of the bus but also the opportunity cost to society of using this money for buses rather than some other social or private investment.

When using expenditure figures that do not include this cost of capital, it is necessary in the cost analysis to predicate the estimates of variations in transportation costs on the existing level of *district-owned* capital equipment (that is, buses) used in the provision of home-to-school transportation services. Therefore, the independent variables used to explain variations in transportation expenditures include: output measures, input price levels, and technology or environmental factors as specified above, plus a measure of the level of capital equipment (that is, number of buses) owned by the district. It is not necessary to include contractor-owned vehicles in this equation since contractors are presumed to charge districts directly for the total costs of transportation (including the current portion of capital costs), and this cost should be reflected in the parameter estimate attached to the variable included in the equation to indicate the cost impact of privately versus district-operated systems.

Given this conceptual framework, one can estimate, using econometric methods, the transportation cost equations and then simulate the average (that is, per pupil transported) costs of home-to-school transportation services.

The CEI. The CEI is a single, overall index designed to reflect the relative differences in the costs of providing the *same level of educational services* across local school districts. These differences in cost are exclusively those that derive from the variations in the component cost indices for the personnel and nonpersonnel school resources and services.

Specifically, the CEI costs out the same quantity of school inputs and services across all districts within the state. Conceptually, this procedure is similar to that used to calculate the Consumer Price Index (CPI) published by the U.S. Bureau of Labor Statistics. The CPI involves pricing out a standard or "fixed" market basket of consumer goods and services at different points in time or in different locations, respectively. Applying this technique to develop a CEI involves using the component indices described previously to price out a standard of fixed market basket of school resources. The one major conceptual difference is that there is an attempt in the CEI analysis to neutralize for the differences in the characteristics of school resources that might be imbedded in the observed variations in prices across districts. These component cost indices for school resources are adjusted to reflect the costs of purchasing a comparable set of inputs or resources across districts. The CEI, therefore, reflects the variations in the overall costs of providing not only the same quantities of school inputs but also inputs exhibiting the same characteristics across all school districts.

To illustrate the technique, consider the following simplified example. Define the following:

$TSALCOST_j^*$ = the salary cost index for the standardized (*) teacher for district "j." (The asterisk is used to indicate the standardization procedure.)

$OSALCOST_j^*$ = the salary cost index for other school personnel (standardized for personal characteristics) in district "j."

$TRAN_j^*$ = the per pupil costs of a standardized level of transportation services for district "j."

$ENERGY_j^*$ = the per pupil costs of a standardized level of energy services for district "j."

Because of the method of determining TRAN and ENERGY, the standardized level of services is already imbedded in these indices. Similarly, the calculation of TSALCOST and OSALCOST already contain the standardized characteristics of these respective sets of school personnel. However, the standardized staff–pupil ratios in each of these two cases must be further specified. Define these standardized input configurations as:

$TPUP^*$ = the standardized ratio of teachers to pupils.

$OPUP^*$ = the standardized ratio of other school personnel to pupils.

It is stressed that the word "standardized" as used above means that the inputs or input characteristics are going to be set at some fixed level for the purpose of pricing or costing out the same educational service levels across all districts in the state. The component price indices are subscripted with a "j" to indicate the costs to district "j" of this standard package of resources, while no subscript is placed on the input configurations represented by TPUP and OPUP as they represent the quantity standard that is to be maintained in the costing technique. The cost (CEDUC*) of a standardized or fixed quantity and characteristics of school resources to a district "j" is then determined by the following equation:

$$CEDUC_j^* = (TSALCOST_j \cdot TPUP^*) + (OSALCOST_j \cdot OPUP)$$

$$+ CTRAN_j^* + CENERGY \qquad [4]$$

The CEI itself is simply a relative index of education costs and may be written as:

$$CEI_j = CEDUC_j^* / CEDUC^*$$

where $CEDUC^*$ is the cost of educational services in the comparison or standardized district.

It can be shown mathematically that an equivalent way of calculating the CEI is to sum the resource cost indices together weighting each by the standardized proportion (for example, the mean value) of school district budgets devoted to the respective category of school resources.

PATTERNS OF COST DIFFERENCES

In general, the results of the CEI studies that have been completed are very encouraging. Based on a casual examination of the results of these studies in five states [Florida—Kenny, Denslow, and Goffman (1975); Missouri—Chambers, Odden, and Vincent (1976); California—Chambers (1978a, 1980b); Texas—Augenblick and Adams (1979); New York—Wendling (1979)], one finds that the patterns of cost differences across different types of districts are quite similar and are generally consistent with intuition about the nature of such differences in cost. Overall variation in educational costs ranged from about 20 percent in California to about 40 percent in Texas. That is, the highest cost districts in these states exhibited about 20 to 40 percent higher costs of education than the lowest cost districts in the states.

The overall pattern of cost differences tends to be dominated by variations in the costs of personnel because of the relative importance of personnel in the budgets of school districts. In particular, one finds that the metropolitan areas exhibit higher costs of education than the nonmetropolitan areas, and the large central cities tend to exhibit, on the average, higher costs than smaller central city and suburban districts. These patterns are offset to a degree by the somewhat higher than average costs of personnel in remote rural areas.

The basic statistical patterns show that the relatively larger and highly urbanized areas with higher population densities have relatively higher costs of education. The relationship, however, is not strictly increasing. That is, the relationship of these variables to personnel costs tends to be U-shaped. As urbanization and population density increase from the lowest levels, there is a decrease in personnel costs until a certain point is reached after which personnel costs tend to increase with increases in urbanization and population density. One might argue that this reflects the notion that the remote rural areas will tend to have some difficulty in recruiting teachers of given characteristics due to the limited accessibility to shopping and all the other amenities of urban life as well as the higher costs of some goods related to transportation costs to rural or remote areas. On the other hand, as one moves into the more highly urbanized areas, housing and other costs of living tend to rise fairly dramatically along with exposure to greater levels of pollution, crime, and so forth, all of which tend to decrease attractiveness and raise costs for school personnel.

One of the most encouraging aspects of all of the empirical results is that although different studies use slightly different combinations of cost factors, the basic pattern of results is similar. That is, the urbanized areas tend to have the highest costs, and remote, rural locations also faced somewhat higher than average costs of personnel. As a way of demonstrating the similarities in the patterns of cost differentials, the regression coefficients of the cost factors estimated in four different states were used to estimate hypothetical personnel cost indices in a single state. Specifically, the coefficients estimated for Texas, Missouri, New York, and California were used to estimate cost indices for California school districts. In essence, the patterns of cost differences (as reflected by the coefficients of these cost factors) observed in Texas, Missouri, and New York were superimposed on data for California school districts, and the personnel cost indices based on these patterns were compared to those obtained from the California estimates. Correlations among these four indices ranged from a low of .71 between Missouri and California to .82 for New York and California to .85 for Texas and California.[8] These results suggest quite strongly that the patterns of cost differentials are very similar across states.

As of this writing, only two studies of energy costs in school districts have been completed, and both studies were conducted in a single state (California) which limits, to some degree, the generalizability of results. Although there are fairly dramatic differences among school districts with respect to climatic patterns in California, utility rate schedules as well as the patterns of usage of various fuel sources (which are partially conditioned on the rate schedules) reduces the generalizability of the results. However, some observations might yield useful insights.

Overall energy costs vary on the order of three to one across California. This implies a 300 percent variation in energy expenditures required to heat and cool school buildings to comfort levels as well as to provide adequate lighting and other sources of energy to carry on school programs (that is, to provide a standardized level of energy services). The predominant source of variation in energy costs results from variations in costs of heating, 90 percent of which is done by natural gas with the remainder from electricity, heating oil, and liquid propane. Cooling costs, while varying considerably over the state, were not as important because of the reduced levels of usage during summer months relative to winter months during which heating is important.

Underlying this three-to-one variation in energy costs is approximately a five-to-one variation in consumption of natural gas and a one and one-half to one variation in electricity consumption each varying in opposite directions (that is, colder areas consume more natural gas for heating while warmer regions consume more electrical power for airconditioning). Moreover, there is an almost two-to-one variation across the state in unit prices of both natural gas and electricity with rates generally being higher in the metropolitan (warmer) areas, although not uniformly so. Government-operated utilities tend to charge the lowest rates.

Despite these rather wide variations in energy costs, overall variations in costs of education tend to be dominated by the variations in costs of school personnel. Energy costs account for only approximately 2 to 3 percent of the average school district budget, while personnel costs generally amount to about 85 percent of the budget.

The highest transportation costs tend to be found in relatively small, rural, sparsely populated school districts. This results in part from the diseconomies of small-scale operation of these systems and in part from the higher costs associated with transporting children to and from school in sparsely populated areas where distances to and from school tend to be quite large.

It is of interest to note that the costs of transportation services provided by private contractors appear to be relatively higher than the cost of district-owned systems (see Chambers 1978a, 1980a). This result, however, may be misleading. The reason for this is that

Table 2-2. Summary Statistics for Cost-of-Education Indices for California School District, 1979-80

City Size in Metro.-Nonmet. Areas (1)	Cost of Education Index (2)	Teacher Cost Index (3)	Sch. Admin. Cost Index (4)	Dist. Admin. Cost Index (5)	Cls. Pers. Cost Index (6)	Energy Cost Index (7)	Avg. Cost Trans. Services (8)
Pop > 500,000							
No. of Districts	4	4	4	4	4	4	3
Mean	1.0506	1.0670	1.1306	1.2911	1.0953	.9415	441.33
Std. Dev.	.0178	.0207	.0338	.0806	.0274	.0719	369.17
Minimum	1.0398	1.0461	1.1002	1.1945	1.0609	.8458	205.90
Maximum	1.0771	1.0947	1.1789	1.3759	1.1219	1.0039	866.81
Pop = 250-500,000							
No. of Districts	3	3	3	3	3	3	2
Mean	1.0241	1.0408	1.1000	1.2353	1.0547	.9474	398.61
Std. Dev.	.0318	.0264	.0454	.0748	.0600	.0361	42.22
Minimum	.9889	1.0142	1.0495	1.1557	.9855	.9257	368.75
Maximum	1.0508	1.0670	1.1375	1.3043	1.0895	.9891	428.46
Pop = 100-250,000							
No. of Districts	14	14	14	14	14	14	8
Mean	1.0291	1.0351	1.0939	1.2327	1.0669	1.0035	304.47
Std. Dev.	.0254	.0310	.0237	.0367	.0166	.0712	95.21
Minimum	.9807	.9753	1.0435	1.1621	1.0390	.9257	186.75
Maximum	1.0719	1.0770	1.1237	1.2811	1.0876	1.1832	466.04

Pop < 100,000, Metr.

No. of Districts	605	605	605	605	605	605	431
Mean	1.0115	1.0181	1.0274	1.0676	1.0181	.9808	225.24
Std. Dev.	.0258	.0309	.0498	.1198	.0375	.1289	175.40
Minimum	.9571	.9352	.9290	.6978	.9144	.8458	64.69
Maximum	1.0782	1.0871	1.1264	1.2767	1.0998	2.2220	3179.56

Nonmetro. Cities

No. of Districts	417	417	417	417	417	417	310
Mean	.9703	.9722	.9587	.9170	.9728	1.0294	227.12
Std. Dev.	.0146	.0228	.0409	.1036	.0286	.1622	113.26
Minimum	.9177	.9066	.8433	.5955	.9021	.7378	74.30
Maximum	1.0038	1.0555	1.0690	1.1866	1.0682	1.7245	874.09

Total State

No. of Districts	1043	1043	1043	1043	1043	1043	754
Mean	.9955	1.0003	1.0015	1.0109	1.0011	1.0003	228.17
Std. Dev.	.0302	.0362	.0587	.1384	.0417	.1442	153.64
Minimum	.9177	.9066	.8433	.5955	.9021	.7378	64.69
Maximum	1.0782	1.0947	1.1789	1.3759	1.1219	2.2220	3179.56

Source: Chambers (1980b:5).

the per pupil transportation expenditures reported by local school districts generally do not reflect current portions of capital costs for district-owned systems, while the expenditures reported by a district that contracts for services would tend to reflect all costs of the private contractor including amortized capital costs. Therefore, the figures between district-owned and privately contracted systems are generally not comparable. One study, however, did attempt to estimate capital costs for district-owned systems in order to develop comparable figures for the costs of transportation services (Chambers 1980a). The statistical analysis was redone using these comparable data, and the results reversed themselves. In particular, all other variables included in the analysis revealed the same basic patterns of variation in transportation costs except the variable indicating the relative cost of contractor versus district-operated services. This variable changed sign from positive to negative, suggesting that privately contracted services were about 6 percent less expensive in per pupil costs than district-operated systems. This does not imply that private services are always cheaper. To draw such a conclusion would be extrapolating far beyond the range of the sample of school districts used in the statistical analysis. Further analysis should be done to improve the crude estimates of capital costs used to make total transportation costs more comparable for the contractor versus district-operated systems. Nevertheless, the results are robust enough that they suggest that there are circumstances when privately contracted services are likely to be cheaper, and more extensive examination of private alternatives to district-operated systems might yield significant savings to taxpayers.

As an example of what cost indices look like and what the patterns of variations in costs are, Table 2-2 presents the results of a recent study of educational cost differences in California (Chambers 1980b). The table reveals the overall patterns of cost differentials for the CEI, the component personnel and energy cost indices as well as the variations in the costs per pupil transported of home to school transportation services. The CEI (column 2) is a weighted combination of the component indices shown in columns 3 through 7 where the weights are the average proportions of school district budgets allocated to these school resources. Column 8 shows the "Average (per pupil transported) Costs of Transportation Services." This component of educational costs has not been included in the overall CEI primarily because transportation services in California are currently funded independently of the remainder of the educational program.

Table 2–2 shows a breakdown of the indices (the mean value, the standard deviation, the minimum and maximum values, as well as the number of districts) by city size and type according to population and location in metropolitan versus nonmetropolitan areas and presents the overall descriptive statistics for the state. The mean value of the CEI is .9955 (approximately 1.0) with the range running from .9177 up to 1.0782. These figures indicate that the highest cost district in the state exhibits over 16 percent higher costs than the lowest cost district in the state. Taking the ratio of the highest to lowest cost index for each component index, this overall variation in the CEI derives from variations of about 1.21 to 1 in teacher costs, 1.40 to 1 in school administrator costs, 2.31 to 1 in district level administrator costs, 1.24 to 1 in classified personnel costs, and 3.01 to 1 in energy costs.

Estimated average per pupil (transported) costs of transportation services run from a low of about $64.69 to a high of $3,179.56, with an average of $228.26.

APPLYING AND IMPLEMENTING THE CEI

State Aid to Education

There are a number of ways in which the CEI might be used by state policymakers to adjust state aid to local school districts for variations in the cost of educational services. One approach is simply to determine the level of general fund aid to which any given school district is entitled under the current formula and then to multiply that state aid level by the CEI so that the distributions of aid would reflect differences in the purchasing power of educational dollars across districts. Thus, the distributions of state aid would reflect "real" differences in access to educational services as reflected in real as opposed to "nominal" differences in local fiscal capacity.

Another approach would be for the state to cost out a standard market basket of school services and to ensure that current arrangements for finance—no matter what the existing contributions from federal, state, and local sources—provide local districst with access to this level of services. This approach would involve the following three steps:

Step 1.   The state would establish some level of general educational services (measured in terms of intensities of school resources such as the kinds and quantities of different school personnel per pupil, levels of per pupil spending on instructional materials, and so on) that policymakers believe should be provided to all children in the state.

Step 2.   The state could then price out these service levels using the component cost indices along with information on actual statewide average salary or cost figures for different categories of school personnel and other school services. This will determine a dollar figure necessary for every individual school district in the state to be able to provide the same educational services.

Step 3.   Compute the level of spending that would occur in the district under the current formula for distributions of state aid prior to any adjustment for cost differences.

Then: (a)   If the spending level under the current arrangements is not sufficient to provide the level of services specified in Step 1 and at the cost determined in Step 2, then adjust the level of state aid in order to provide sufficient funds to compensate for excess costs.

(b)   If the spending level under current arrangements is sufficient (that is, if the spending figure under existing arrangements is greater than or equal to that calculated in Steps 1 and 2), then no additional state aid would be required.

This approach would avoid any short-term disruptions in services that might be caused by sudden adjustments or shifts in the levels of state aid as they relate to costs of educational services. It provides the state policymakers some time to begin to consider ways of phasing in a system of finance that they regard as equitable and which perhaps would include adjustments for cost differences as a standard part of the distribution formula.

In addition to the applications to general fund appropriations, the component indices for school personnel and other resources that go into the construction of the overall CEI could be used to cost out just about any combination of resources that might be used to provide educational services and programs. In particular, policymakers could cost out resources associated with the provision of specific categorical programs for special education, vocational education, bilingual–bicultural education, and so forth, and adjust distributions of categorical aid for differences in resource prices. This would force policymakers to specify, at least for purposes of funding, the resource configurations that would be appropriate for these programs. Then state aid distributions would reflect not only the composition of children served and the differences in resource configurations required to serve them but also differences in the prices of these resources. In concept, similar cost adjustments in federal categorical aid to local districts also could be devised.

Cost Adjustments Over Time

The methodology for constructing a CEI described in this chapter would lend itself nicely to the adjustment of state-aid distributions over time. Salary levels in the respective years may be simulated, assuming no changes in the distribution of teacher characteristics and certain endogenous (controllable) working conditions over time. Such a simulation would isolate the increase in salary levels from one year to the next due to changes in the cost of living and other conditions relevant to the statewide as well as local labor markets. Inflationary trends in energy costs can also be estimated fairly easily. Once given the results of the simulation of energy consumption requirements (that is, to heat and cool buildings located in different climate zones within a state), one need only acquire the necessary information on utility rate schedules to cost out these requirements at different points in time in order to assess the inflationary effects. Only every few years would state officials have to review the building specifications to make sure that they continue to represent the relevant standards of practice used in the construction of energy-efficient school buildings.

Currently, the consumer price index, either for the nation as a whole or for an individual state, is often used as a rationale upon which to base estimates of inflation in the costs of public services and is used as an indicator for necessary budget increases to account for inflation. By simulating changes in educational costs as outlined in the methodological section above, one can obtain a more direct measure of inflation of the cost of educational services provided by local public school districts. Although the changes in consumer price levels over time are likely to be an important source of change in educational costs, it is not necessarily the only source of change and is not designed to reflect the change in prices or costs of the resources purchased by local school districts.

One recent study of educational cost differences in California provides some estimates of the effects of inflation on teachers' salaries across various regions of the state (Chambers 1980b). Differences in teachers' salaries were simulated over a two-year period, while controlling for the distribution of teacher characteristics and the controllable job assignment characteristics, and a yearly rate of inflation was determined. This estimate of inflation is intended to reflect changes in teacher costs which are beyond local control. The average inflation rate of teachers' costs for the state was approximately 11.70 percent per year (for 1978 to 1980). In comparison, the average rate of inflation in consumer prices for the state of California over the two-year period was approximately 13.3 percent. Note that the implication of these differential rates of inflation is a declining real wage for teachers. This decline is precisely what one would expect to find given the alleged surplus supply which has characterized the teacher market since about 1970.

One further advantage of using the cost-of-education approach is that estimates of inflation may be easily broken down according to the regions of the state or even on a district-by-district basis. Currently, consumer price changes are generally available for only a limited number of major metropolitan regions within a state.

Stability of the CEI Over Time

As noted, the CEIs calculated in various states compare favorably with one another. Two studies have also done comparisons of the CEI over time within a single state, and as one might expect, the CEIs for different years compared quite closely (Chambers 1978a, 1980b). In the Missouri study, teachers' salary cost indices were compared for consecutive years (1974–75 and 1975–76), and the correlation was .94. In the California study, the overall CEI as well as the component indices were compared over a two-year period (1977–78 to 1979–80). Despite the passage of Proposition 13 (the Jarvis–Gann property tax limitation measure in California) between these two studies, the overall correlation between the CEIs was .87. The correlations among the 1978 and 1980 personnel cost indices ranged from

.76 for the teachers' cost index to .98 for the district administrators' cost index. Thus, in both states the patterns of cost differentials across local districts appear to be relatively stable, as one would expect, over short periods of time.

The importance of this finding is that it suggests that it may not be necessary to recalculate the CEI on a yearly basis. That is, the parameter estimates obtained in one year might well be used to recalculate the component cost indices for the subsequent year. This is not to suggest that there are not some important changes in patterns of costs for individual districts, and indeed these kinds of changes from one year to the next might warrant the cost of updating the index on a year-to-year basis. In fact, one possibility would be to replicate exactly the base year study for up to three years, and then to conduct a major evaluation and reanalysis of educational cost differentials every third or fourth year. This kind of approach would provide for the subtle changes in patterns of cost from one year to the next at a relatively low cost, while offering the opportunity for a major revision only once every three or four years.

EQUITY AND EFFICIENCY IN SCHOOL FINANCE

This chapter has focused attention on only one aspect of the reform of school finance and the improvement of equity in the distribution of intergovernmental aid to education. However, any single adjustment alone will not accomplish this goal. For too long, the reform of school finance systems and the adjustment of aid for categorical programs have been conceptualized independently of one another. If a more equitable distribution of school funding is to be achieved and services are to be delivered more effectively and efficiently, adjustments to school funding must be conceptualized within a broader context (for example, see Chambers and Hartman 1980). Adjustments of the distributions of state aid for the costs of school resources will have to be integrated with adjustments being considered for additional costs of serving students with special needs. Different districts serve different compositions of children with respect to educational need and therefore have to provide different configurations of resources and services. Policymakers should begin to consider what kinds of systematic differences in resources are required to serve various special need populations and what the differences in costs of these services are. Only by conceptualizing these different sources of educational cost differentials within the context of a common framework (for funding purposes, if no other) will policymakers be able to assess costs to the state and nation of new funding arrangements, administrative and legislative mandates for service delivery, and court mandates for redistribution. Moreover, by integrating these various sources of educational cost differentials, districts serving various student populations can be treated in systematically different ways that reflect perceived educational needs within the context of overall limitations on governmental resources available for education.

NOTES TO CHAPTER 2

1. From the standpoint of the entire local economy, the price level and general attractiveness of a region are interrelated through their mutual effects on wage rates which in turn affect prices. From the standpoint of any individual public service or industry, however, these factors can have independent effects and are regarded as exogenously determined.

2. For a more complete discussion of the issues involved in such an analysis, see Chambers (1979).

3. Loatman (1977) is the primary example of how the pure statistical approach has been applied.

4. Studies using the supply-and-demand approach include Brazer (1974), Brazer and Anderson (1975), and Stiefel and Berne (n.d.).

5. Studies using a behavioral approach include Antos and Rosen (1975), Augenblick and Adams (1979), Chambers (1978a, 1978b, and 1981), Frey (1975), Grubb and Hyman (1975), Kenney, Denslow, and Goffman (1975), and Wendling (1979).

6. For a more elaborate description of the methodology and empirical results, see Chambers (1980a). Energy costs are also analyzed in Chambers (1978a).

7. Studies using this basic kind of approach to analyze transportation costs include Chambers (1978a, 1978b, 1980a) and McKeown (1978).

8. Comparisons with other states were not made because of the difficulty of assembling all the necessary data.

REFERENCES

.

Antos, Joseph R., and Sherwin Rosen. 1975. "Discrimination in the Market for Public School Teachers." *Journal of Econometrics* 3, no. 2 (May): 123-150.

Ashenfelter, O. 1971. "The Effect of Unionization on Wages in the Public Sector." *Industrial and Labor Relations Review* 24, no. 2 (January): 191–202.

Augenblick, John, and Kathleen Adams. 1979. "An Analysis of the Impact of Changes in the Funding of Elementary/Secondary Education in Texas: 1974/75 to 1977/78." Denver, Colo.: Education Commission of the States.

Averch, Harvey A., et al. 1974. *How Effective is Schooling? A Critical Review of Research.* A Rand Educational Policy Study. Englewood Cliffs, N.J.: Educational Technology Publications.

Baird, R.N., and J.H. Landon. 1971. "Monopsony in the Market for Public School Teachers." *American Economic Review* 61, no. 4 (September): 966–971.

_____. 1972. "The Effects of Collective Bargaining on the Public School Teachers' Salaries." *Industrial and Labor Relations Review* 25, no. 3 (April): 410–416.

Barro, S.M. 1974. "The Impact of Intergovernmental Aid on Public School Spending." Ph.D. dissertation, Stanford University.

Brazer, Harvey E. 1974. "Adjusting for Differences Among School Districts in the Costs of Educational Inputs: A Feasibility Report." In *Selected Papers in School Finance 1974*, edited by Esther Tron. Washington, D.C.: Office of Education, U.S. Department of Health, Education, and Welfare.

Brazer, Harvey E., and Ann P. Anderson. 1975. "A Cost Adjustment Index for Michigan School Districts." In *Selected Papers in School Finance 1975*, edited by Esther Tron. Washington, D.C.: Office of Education, U.S. Department of Health, Education, and Welfare.

Chambers, Jay G. 1975. "The Impact of Collective Negotiations for Teachers on Resource Allocation in Public School Districts." Ph.D. dissertation, Stanford University.

_____. 1976. "The Impact of Bargaining on the Earnings of Teachers: A Report on California and Missouri." Paper presented at the U.K.–U.S. Conference on Teacher Markets, University of Chicago, December.

_____. 1977. "The Impact of Collective Bargaining for Teachers on Resource Allocation in Public School Districts." *Journal of Urban Economics* 4 (July): 324–329.

_____. 1978a. "Educational Cost Differentials Across School Districts in California." Report prepared under subcontract to the Education Finance Center of the Education Commission of the States for the School Finance Equalization Project of the California State Department of Education.

_____. 1978b. "Educational Cost Differentials and the Allocation of State Aid for Elementary/Secondary Education." *The Journal of Human Resources* 23, no. 4 (Fall): 459–481.

_____. 1979. "School District Behavior, Markets for Educational Resources and the Implications for Public Policy: A Survey." In *Economic Dimensions of Education*, edited by Douglas Windham. Washington, D.C.: National Academy of Education.

_____. 1980a. "The Development of a Cost of Education Index: Some Empirical Estimates and Policy Issues." *Journal of Education Finance* 5, no. 3 (Winter): 262-281.

_____. 1980b. "The Development of a Cost-of-Education Index for the State of California." Final Report, Parts 1 and 2, prepared for the California State Department of Education.

_____. 1980c. "A Reply to Matthews and Brown, The Development of a Cost of Education Index: Some Empirical Estimates and Policy Issues." *Journal of Education Finance* 6, no. 2 (Fall): 239-245.

_____. 1981. "The Hedonic Wage Technique as a Tool for Estimating the Costs of School Personnel: A Theoretical Exposition with Implications for Empirical Analysis." *Journal of Education Finance* 6, no. 3 (Winter): 330-354.

Chambers, Jay G., and William T. Hartman. 1980. "A Cost Based Approach to the Funding of Educational Programs: An Application to Special Education." Paper presented at the Special Education Collaborative Project Conference, Institute for Research on Educational Finance and Governance, Stanford University, October.

Chambers, Jay G.; William T. Hartman; and Phillip E. Vincent. 1980. "Florida's Price of Living Index and Alternative Cost of Education Adjustments: A Framework and Evaluation." Report No. 2, SRI International, prepared for the Florida Department of Education, February.

Chambers, Jay G.; Allan Odden; and Phillip E. Vincent. 1976. "Cost of Education Indices Among School Districts." Denver, Colo.: Education Commission of the States.

Chambers, Jay G., and Phillip E. Vincent. 1980. "Interim Development and Progress Report on Alternative Cost of Education Models and Indices." Report No. 3., SRI International, prepared for the Florida Department of Education, May.

Cooper, Gary D. 1976. "Spatial Price Indices: The Florida Experience." *Review of Regional Studies* 6 (Winter): 36-47.

Ehrenberg, R.G. 1975. "A Model of Public Sector Wage Determination." *Journal of Urban Economics* 2, no. 3 (July): 223-245.

Ellickson, Bryan, with Barry Fishman and Peter A. Morrison. 1977. *Economic Analysis of Urban Housing Markets: A New Approach.* Santa Monica, Calif.: R-2024-NSF.

Florida Department of Administration. 1977. "Florida Price Level Index, October 1976." Tallahassee, Florida.

Fox, James N. 1975. "Cost-of-Living Adjustments: Right Intent, Wrong Technique." *Phi Delta Kappan* 56 (April): 548-550.

Frey, D.E. 1975. "Wage Determination in Public Schools and the Effects of Unionization." In *Labor in the Non-Profit and Public Sectors*, edited by D.S. Hammermesh. Princeton, N.J.: Princeton University Press.

Griliches, Zvi. 1970. "Notes on the Role of Education in Production Functions." In *Studies in Income and Wealth*, edited by W. Lee Hansen. New York, N.Y.: National Bureau of Economic Research.

_____. 1971a. "Hedonic Price Index for Automobiles: An Econometric Analysis of Quality Change." In *Price Indexes and Quality Change: Studies in New Methods of Measurement*, edited by Zvi Griliches. Cambridge, Mass.: Harvard University Press.

_____. 1971b. "Hedonic Price Indexes Revisited." In *Price Indexes and Quality Change: Studies in New Methods of Measurement*, edited by Zvi Griliches. Cambridge, Mass.: Harvard University Press.

Grubb, W. Norton. 1975. "Identifying Teacher Supply Functions and Constructing Cost Indices: Methodological Explorations with California Unified School Districts." Unpublished paper, Berkeley, Calif.: University of California.

Grubb, W. Norton, and James Hyman. 1975. "Constructing Teacher Cost Indices: Methodological Explorations with California Unified School Districts." In *Selected Papers in School Finance 1975*, edited by Esther Tron. Washington, D.C.: Office of Education, U.S. Department of Health, Education, and Welfare.

Hall, W.C., and N.E. Carroll. 1973. "The Effect of Teachers' Organizations on Salaries and Class Size." *Industrial and Labor Relations Review* 26, no. 2 (January): 834–841.

Haworth, C.T., and D.W. Rasmussen. 1973. "Determinants of Metropolitan Cost of Living Variations." *Southern Economic Journal* 39 (October): 183–201, and J.P. Mattila. 1976. "Comment" (and Reply), *Southern Economic Journal* 42 (April): 744–751.

Hyman, James B. 1977. "Cost of Education Indices: Alternative Methods, Issues and Answers." Ph.D. dissertation, Stanford University.

Johns, Roe L. 1975. "An Index of Extra Costs of Education Due to Sparsity of Population." Gainesville, Fla.: Education Finance and Management Institute.

Johnson, Gary P. 1978. "Cost-of-Education Indices: The State of the Art and Implications for Indiana School Finance Reform." Unpublished paper, State of Indiana, State Department of Public Instruction, Indianapolis, March.

Kasper, H. 1970. "The Effect of Collective Bargaining on Public School Teachers' Salaries." *Industrial and Labor Relations Review* 24, no. 1 (October): 57–72.

_____. 1971. "On the Effects of Collective Bargaining on Resource Allocation in Public Schools." *Economic Business Bulletin* 23, no. 3 (Spring–Summer): 1–9.

_____. 1972. "The Effects of Collective Bargaining on the Public School Teachers' Salaries—Comment." *Industrial and Labor Relations Review* 25, no. 3 (April): 410–416.

Kenny, L.; D. Denslow; and I. Goffman. 1975. "Determination of Teacher Cost Differentials Among School Districts in the State of Florida." In *Selected Papers in School Finance 1975*, edited by Esther Tron. Washington, D.C.: Office of Education, U.S. Department of Health, Education, and Welfare.

Lancaster, K.J. 1966. "A New Approach to Consumer Theory." *Journal of Political Economy* 74 (April): 132–157.

Levin, Henry M. 1978. "Recruiting Teachers for Large City Schools." Unpublished monograph, Brookings Institution, June.

_____. 1970. "A Cost Effectiveness Analysis of Teacher Selection." *Journal of Human Resources* 5 (Winter): 24–33.

_____. 1980. "Educational Production Theory and Teacher Inputs." In *The Analysis of Educational Productivity: Issues in Macroanalysis*, edited by C. Bidwell and D. Windham. Cambridge, Mass.: Ballinger Publishing Company.

Lipsky, D.B., and J.E. Drotning. 1973. "The Influence of Collective Bargaining on Teachers' Salaries in New York State." *Industrial and Labor Relations Review* 27, no. 1 (October): 18–35.

Loatman, Bruce. 1977. "Alternative Cost-of-Education Indices." Unpublished paper, Arlington, Va.: Killalea Associates, Inc.

_____. 1980. "Theory and Development of Education Price Indices for Public School Districts." A Report to the National Institute of Education Under Contract NIE–400–77–0022, March.

Lucas, Robert E.B. 1972. "Working Conditions, Wage-Rates and Human Capital: A Hedonic Study." Ph.D. dissertation, Massachusetts Institute of Technology.

_____. 1974. "The Distribution of Job Characteristics." *Review of Economic Statistics* 56 (November): 530–540.

_____. 1975. "Hedonic Price Functions." *Economic Inquiry* 13 (June): 157–178.

_____. 1977. "Hedonic Wage Equations and Psychic Wages in the Returns to Schooling." *The American Economic Review* 67, no. 4 (September): 549–558.

Matthews, Kenneth M., and Carvin L. Brown. 1980. "Response to: The Development of a Cost of Education Index: Some Empirical Estimates and Policy Issues." *Journal of Education Finance* 6, no. 2 (Fall): 236–238.

Mayer, T. 1969. "The Distribution of Ability and Earnings." *Review of Economics and Statistics* (May): 189–195.

McFadden, D. 1974. "Conditional Logit Analysis of Qualitative Choice Behavior." In *Frontiers in Econometrics*, edited by Paul Zarembka. New York, N.Y.: Academic Press.

McKeown, Mary P. 1978. *Distributing State Aid for Pupil Transportation: An Average Cost Formula*. Springfield, Ill.: Illinois Office of Education.

McMahon, Walter W., and Carroll Melton. 1978. "Differences in the Cost of Living Among States and Within States." Faculty Working Paper No. 459, University of Illinois, Urbana–Champaign.

Muellbauer, J. 1974. "Household Production Theory, Quality, and the 'Hedonic Technique'." *American Economic Review* 64 (December): 977–994.

Nutter, G. Warren, and John H. Moore. 1976. "A Theory of Competition." *The Journal of Law and Economics* 19 (April): 39–65.

Rosen, Sherwin. 1974. "Hedonic Prices and Implicit Markets: Product Differentiation in Pure Competition." *Journal of Political Economy* 82 (January/February): 34–55.

_____. 1977. "Wage-Based Indexes of Urban Quality of Life." Paper presented at CUE Conference on Urban Economics, Academy for Contemporary Problems, Columbus, Ohio, May 5.

Scott, Michael J. 1977. "Alaskan Interregional Cost Differentials." Fairbanks, Al.: Center for Northern Educational Research, University of Alaska–Fairbanks, March. Mimeo.

Simmons, James C. 1975. "Comments on 'Cost-of-Living Adjustments in School Finance'." *Phi Delta Kappan* 57 (October): 120.

Simmons, James C., et al. 1973. "Florida Cost-of-Living Research Study: Florida Counties Price Level Index (FPLI) for October 1972." Tallahassee, Fla.: Florida State University. Mimeo.

Stiefel, Leanna, and Robert Berne. n.d. "Price Indexes for Teachers in Michigan: A Replication and Extension." New York, N.Y.: New York University. Mimeo.

Thornton, R.J. 1971. "The Effects of Collective Negotiations on Teachers' Salaries." *Quarterly Review of Economics and Business* 11, no. 4 (Winter): 37–46.

Toder, Eric Jay. 1971. *The Distribution of Public School Teachers by Race and Income Class in an Urban Metropolitan Area.* Report to the Bureau of Research, Office of Education, U.S. Department of Health, Education, and Welfare. Medford, Mass.: Tufts University.

Tolley, George S. 1974. "The Welfare Economics of City Bigness." *Journal of Urban Economics* 1 (July): 324–345.

Turnbull, D., and Gareth Williams. 1976. "Personal Characteristics and the Earnings of Teachers: An Earnings Function Approach." Paper presented at the U.K.–U.S. Conference on Teacher Markets, University of Chicago, December.

Wasserman, William. 1963. *Education Price and Quantity Indexes.* Syracuse, N.Y.: Syracuse University Press.

Wendling, Wayne. 1979. *Cost-of-Education Indices for New York State School Districts.* Denver, Colo.: Education Commission of the States.

Wood, Norman. 1974. "Survey of Florida Teacher Purchases: Forty-Two Counties, Analysis and Results." Athens, Ga.: University of Georgia. Mimeo.

3 MUNICIPAL OVERBURDEN AND STATE AID FOR EDUCATION

*Jane Sjogren**

INTRODUCTION

Providing equitable and appropriate support to cities for the provision of public education has been a goal in the school finance reform movement. Attainment of the goal, however, has been complicated not only by the special needs of cities for education services and the high costs of providing these services but also by the cities' need to finance and provide a wide variety of other municipal services as well. In the recent case of *Levittown* v. *Nyquist* in New York State, the Court ruled that the evidence presented was "satisfactorily established" in terms of having to provide more noneducation services than other less densely populated municipalities. The implication of this ruling for the state school aid formula was that this "overburden" limits the ability of large urban areas to finance education and that the state aid formula should provide extra funds to such overburdened urban areas as a means of equalizing educational opportunity.

While the *Levittown* decision gave legal recognition to the concept of "municipal overburden," economists, educational administrators, city officials and policymakers have been aware of the idea for some time. Yet there is little agreement on how the concept of municipal

*Jane Sjogren, Assistant Professor of Economics, Wellesley College.

overburden should be defined, whether or not municipal overburden actually exists (and if it does how it should be measured), and how it can be appropriately recognized in state education aid formulas. This chapter explores each of these three concerns. In the first section, the concept of municipal overburden is reviewed along with the issues it incorporates and how it has been defined. The arguments of whether or not municipal overburden actually exists and the major empirical attempts to measure it are explored in the second section. In the final section, how provision for municipal overburden can or has been incorporated into state formulas for aid to education and the potential outcomes of such provision are considered. The objective of this presentation is to provide a comprehensive overview of the issues reflected in the term municipal overburden using current research on the topic, and to provide students of school finance with a realistic idea of how this issue fits into current attempts to improve the equitability and efficiency of state aid to public elementary and secondary education.

DEFINING MUNICIPAL OVERBURDEN

If indeed the concept of municipal overburden has an appropriate place in a formula for state aid to education, a definition of the concept is requisite. While the intent of the *Levittown* v. *Nyquist* ruling, for example, is clear, an applied definition of the concept of municipal overburden is more complicated than it may seem at first glance.

At an intuitive level, the concept of municipal overburden seems straightforward. From the perspective of a policymaker concerned with improving the equity aspects of a state education aid formula, the intuitive argument for municipal overburden goes as follows.

Urban areas (or cities) have particularly high needs for noneducation public services, such as police and fire protection, both per square mile and per capita. This is due in part to the population density which characterizes an urban area but also to other factors such as the characteristics of its population or the composition or size of its tax base. Thus, for example, the costs of fire protection per capita are likely to be higher in urban than in nonurban areas because of the presence of high-rise buildings which require elaborate and expensive fire-fighting equipment. In addition, fire protection has to be provided for many public and private facilities in addition to resident taxpayers' homes, even if the owners or users of those buildings are not city residents. Police costs may be high because crime rates are often higher in densely populated areas. In addition, other services which are not necessary in nonurban municipalities are needed in cities. For example, a citywide public sewage system (as opposed to individual responsibility for waste disposal) is necessary for health reasons. Or a mass public transit system is necessary because a built-up city can only accommodate limited numbers of private vehicles. Other services may be necessary because of the characteristics of a city's population. Large ethnic groups or a large elderly population, both of which are often found in cities, frequently require specialized social services, such as job counseling or special transportation. Or, large populations of poor people may need a range of social services while drawing heavily on regular municipal services, such as hospitals, as well.

Overall, it is argued, cities simply need both more and a wider range of public services. In addition to high needs for services in urban areas, it is argued that locally financed public services often are more expensive in cities than in nonurban areas. Municipal employee unions and collective bargaining may result in relatively high salaries for municipal employees. Also, both the amounts of non-personnel resources found in cities and their unit costs are likely to be high. For example, repairing or renovating a public facility such as a sewage system is likely to be necessary because many urban facilities are old and expensive because they are complex. All of these considerations represent claims on the city's tax revenue. Yet that tax revenue also may be limited by factors beyond the city's control. For example, the tax base may be limited by the presence of nonprofit institutions like churches or universities which do not pay property taxes but are covered by city services. Or users of city services such as public transport may not pay municipal taxes which are commensurate with their use of those services. And per capita property values may be low, especially if the urban economy is weak.

Thus, the argument goes, cities need more municipal services, those services are more expensive, and cities may have less capacity to support those services than nonurban areas. As a result, one very important municipal service, public elementary and secondary education, may not be adequately provided by the cities because education must compete with other locally provided services for local revenues. In other words, the relatively heavy demands for noneducation services result in a substitution of municipal funds away from education, even when a city is taxing itself relatively heavily. It cannot "afford" to provide educational services because it must provide other noneducational services. From the state's perspective, the non-education burden on local revenues in urban areas can be interpreted as a reduction in local capacity to finance education. And if this is the case, insofar as the state wishes to support equal educational opportunity, it is appropriate for the state to step in with additional funding in order to insure that students living in the cities have access to adequate educational services.

While this view of municipal overburden may seem reasonable, formulating a more rigorous definition of it in order to determine the extent to which it exists for a particular urban area is much more complex. Before reviewing the formal definitions of municipal overburden used by economists and others in attempts to ascertain its existence, it is helpful to review some of the terms which are commonly used in discussing municipal overburden and some of the issues they represent.

Related Concepts and Issues

As noted earlier, the concept of municipal overburden implies that urban areas must provide above-average amounts of noneducation municipal services which result in the substitution of municipal funds away from education, limiting cities' abilities to provide educational services. In order to define and identify municipal overburden for purposes of improving education finance systems, it is necessary to separate fiscal effort for noneducation services from that made to provide education services. This distinction is necessary because the fundamental issue behind municipal overburden is how the noneducation tax burden affects the financing of education. While the extent to which a municipality furnishes education and noneducation services can be identified in terms of the amounts it spends for various types of services, such as fire and police protection, waste disposal, social welfare services, and public elementary and secondary education, expenditures do not provide a clear picture of the *fiscal effort* a municipality makes to provide these services. Nor do they take into account the municipality's *fiscal capacity*, the extent to which *fiscal stress* exists, the relative *costs* it faces, and its *need* for these services. All of these considerations are directly related to municipal overburden.

Fiscal capacity describes the wealth a municipality has available for taxation purposes. That is, it represents the size of the local tax base. Because the main source of tax revenue for municipalities is the property tax, fiscal capacity is most often described in terms of the equalized value of taxable property in a municipality's jurisdiction. Equalized rather than assessed values are used because assessment practices vary among municipalities; equalized values are comparable across a state. While measures of fiscal capacity generally include only taxable real estate property, sometimes measures of fiscal capacity are adjusted to reflect residents' incomes either as an alternative to real estate values or in combination with them.[1] (This is done in part on the theory that resident income is a better measure of local wealth because it reflects residents' lifetime incomes.) Fiscal capacity is usually described as a total dollar amount or on a per capita basis. Fiscal capacity relates to municipal overburden in that it indicates the size of the local tax base or the amount of wealth a municipality has at its disposal for taxation.

Fiscal effort represents the level at which a municipality taxes itself. Typically, fiscal effort is measured in terms of the dollars (or mills of dollars) charged in taxes by the municipality as a proportion of equalized property value (fiscal capacity). This measure is often used because property taxes represent the largest share of local revenue from local sources. However, because some municipalities, cities in particular, may receive local revenue from nonproperty taxes such as local sales, users, or excise taxes, sometimes fiscal effort includes these when estimates of effective local tax rates are made. However, some measure of tax rate per dollar of equalized property values is usually used to represent local fiscal effort. Fiscal effort is important for estimating municipal overburden as it indicates how heavily a municipality is taxing itself to provide current levels of local public services.

Fiscal stress reflects the relationship between fiscal capacity and fiscal effort when tax rates draw heavily upon local wealth, that is, when unusually large demands are placed on a local tax base. Fiscal stress characterizes a municipality when it places a significant tax burden on its full fiscal capacity in order to provide some minimum level of municipal services. The term municipal overburden is usually employed to denote the effects of high tax-revenue spending for noneducation services on the level of educational services, while fiscal stress refers more generally to situations in which a municipality taxes itself at rates which bear heavily on its full fiscal capacity even though it is not providing a commensurately high level of all (education and noneducation) services. Thus, fiscal stress is likely to be related to the existence of municipal overburden, though, it is difficult to measure. What one viewer may regard as a municipality under fiscal stress, another may not. Some of the reasons for this discrepancy are discussed below.

Costs of providing municipal services (both education and noneducation) are likely to be related to fiscal stress. A municipality which faces high costs for the resources it needs to provide its municipal services is more likely to have fiscal stress than one which faces lower costs. To the extent that an urban municipality must pay higher costs for its noneducation services, the level of costs for these services may not only increase fiscal stress but also may influence educational spending, as the argument for municipal overburden suggests.

Need for noneducation services also may be related to fiscal stress and, accordingly, municipal overburden. A municipality may have particular needs for certain locally provided services. For example, it may have a large elderly population which requires increased public medical services, or it may have a large low-income population which requires increased social services such as low-cost housing administration or other welfare-related services. High crime rates may necessitate increased use of police and fire services. Additionally, many cities need to provide extraordinary services such as increased maintenance of public areas or special services to accommodate visitors or businesses. However, the need factor in municipal expenditures is a complex one because it is difficult to make a distinction between real (nondiscretionary) need and local preference for certain types or amounts of services. For example, while many would agree that certain publicly supported services such as refuse systems which meet public health standards are necessary, needs for other locally funded services such as special transportation for the elderly may not be as obvious. In addition, some local services such as health inspections, or facilities such as those modified for the access of the handicapped, may either be mandated (by the state or federal government) or may require local contribution. However, it is difficult at best to distinguish what is discretionary versus nondiscretionary in terms of local expenditures. While the notion that there is some "minimum bundle" of services which a city must provide seems reasonable, defining that bundle in specific terms not only for cities in general but for a specific city necessarily involves subjective judgment. Yet, it is important to distinguish discretionary expenditures from nondiscretionary ones in order to determine whether a city must operate in fiscal stress to provide basic services or whether the voters or the city government actually prefer large amounts of public municipal services and tax themselves accordingly.

The *separation of education versus noneducation tax burdens* is a continuing concern among all of these issues. In order to ascertain how the level of tax burden for noneducation services affects the provision of education services, it is necessary to determine what the extent of fiscal effort, fiscal capacity, and fiscal stress is for noneducational services. While the need for this distinction is clear, distinguishing between education and noneducation tax burdens is not simply a matter of applying the ratio of education-to-noneducation expenditures to current levels of fiscal effort and fiscal capacity. The accuracy of this approach is inhibited by several factors. First, school district jurisdictions are frequently not coterminous with municipal boundaries, making separation of tax bases and tax rates for education and noneducation services difficult for measurement purposes. Second, factors affecting fiscal effort are likely to influence both education and noneducation expenditures. In a city which has many low-income students who need supplementary educational services, demand for other (noneducational) services for this group will be high as well. Or, a city with a large elderly population is likely to have a low demand for educational services but higher demands for other types of services. This is related to the third factor, which is that fiscal effort and fiscal capacity for noneducation services are likely to be only partially substitutable for that for education, and the extent of the substitutability is difficult to identify. For example, if it is determined by some means that a certain proportion of a municipality's fiscal effort is for education and the remainder is for all noneducation locally funded services, it is likely that only a portion of the effort for the noneducation services could be reallocated to education. Fixed expenses such as maintenance of facilities or local debt service may exist or certain minimum levels may be mandated; for example, as by health standards. Again, both costs and need must be taken into account in separating education from noneducation fiscal effort.

A final issue concerning the identification concept and measurement of municipal overburden is *the extent to which burden is considered to be a relative or absolute concept.* Like the idea of fiscal stress, the existence of municipal burden can be viewed either as exceeding some predefined level of fiscal effort in relation to fiscal capacity for a set of education or noneducation services, or it can be viewed as applying to the municipalities which have higher degrees of fiscal stress, either overall or for just education or noneducation services. Clearly, defining and identifying the existence of a tax burden has a great deal to do with which of these approaches is used. While using a definition based on a relative measure takes into account the context in which municipalities are being compared, it necessarily means that at least one municipality will be viewed as burdened. Whereas, an absolute measure provides a standard which can be consistently applied; but at the same time, it abstracts from the context in which the fiscal efforts of municipalities are being evaluated.

While fiscal effort, fiscal capacity, fiscal stress, costs, and needs for services all have some relation to the concept of municipal overburden, they often are defined, used, or measured differently by various researchers who have studied the existence of municipal overburden and attempted to estimate it.

Defining Municipal Overburden

While the notion of municipal overburden is not new, most of the applied definitions of it have been developed within the last decade. Early recognition of the concept is attributed to Paul Mort who suggested that urban areas should receive more state aid for education because they had to provide larger amounts of noneducation services than did smaller sized communities. Subsequently, Guthrie and others (1971) and Coons and others (1970) viewed municipal overburden in terms of fiscal stress, looking primarily at the level of noneducation taxes levied. Sacks (1972) viewed municipal overburden somewhat differently, defining it as an above-state-average ratio of local school expenditures to total expenditures. Netzer (1974) focused more directly on local tax capacity, viewing municipal overburden as excess large city tax burdens which are identified in terms of higher percentages of personal income absorbed by "locally borne" taxes. More recently, Miner and Sacks (1980b) and Knickman and Reschovsky (1980b) have tried to apply working definitions of municipal overburden to the education finance systems in New York and New Jersey, respectively. Miner and Sacks defined municipal overburden as systematic fiscal stress in providing noneducation services which reduces local effort for education, viewing fiscal stress as above-normal use of fiscal capacity. Knickman and Reschovsky focused on the relationship between fiscal stress incurred in providing a "minimum bundle" of noneducation services and the level of local spending on education. At a less theoretical level, one state school aid formula (Michigan) simply identifies municipal overburden as existing in urban areas when millage rates exceed 125 percent of the state average.

These and other definitions of municipal overburden vary in the extents to which they focus on cities versus all municipalities, the general aspect of tax burdens as opposed to the separation of education from other municipal services, and applied versus theoretical approaches to defining municipal overburden.

In light of previous approaches to identifying municipal overburden and given that most of the current interest in municipal overburden is focused on determining how it should be incorporated into state education aid formulas, its definition should directly reflect its relation to financing education. Accordingly, an operational definition of municipal overburden has two components:

- First, municipal overburden reflects the relative tax burdens of a community for education and noneducation services. Thus, it takes into account both the fiscal capacity and the fiscal effort of a municipality with regard to each of these groups of local services;

- Second, municipal overburden reflects the *relationship* between the level of the noneducation tax burden in a municipality and the level of education services it provides. Thus, municipal overburden exists in proportion to the extent to which a large tax burden for noneducation services is systematically accompanied by a low level of educational services.

In applying this two-part definition of municipal overburden to the municipalities in a state, it is important to keep several considerations in mind. First, whether the existence of municipal overburden is determined according to an absolute or relative (among districts in a state) measure, it is based on a normative view of equity. That is, it is assumed that municipal overburden represents a disadvantage for a local education system and that that disadvantage should be recognized and compensated in the state aid formula. While this assumption is not at question here, it should be recognized as a normative assumption, given that political priorities and other aspects of policymakers' perspectives are subject to change.

Second, the working definition of municipal overburden suggested above (as well as most others) has been developed with specific reference to state education aid formulas. The general concept of overburden in local governments could be applied to any subset of locally provided services, not just education. It is used in the remainder of this chapter, however, to look only at the impact of local financing for noneducation services on local provision of education. Accordingly, it is viewed specifically from the perspective of altering state education aid formulas rather than altering other aspects of state and local public finance systems.

Finally, while municipal overburden is generally perceived as a characteristic of urban situations, it also may apply to nonurban municipalities, depending on their characteristics and on how overburden is defined and measured.

DOES MUNICIPAL OVERBURDEN REALLY EXIST?

While the concept of municipal overburden may be intuitively appealing and its implication for state school aid formulas clear, a number of issues which are related to its definition and measurement must be confronted before it can be reasonably recognized in a state aid formula. Most of the difficulties determining its existence and magnitude are directly related to the issues reviewed in the preceding section: fiscal capacity, fiscal effort, fiscal stress, costs, need, the separation of education from noneducation effort and capacity, and relative versus absolute definitions of burden.

Conceptual Considerations

There are several conceptual considerations which suggest either that municipal overburden does not exist or that it is limited by other factors. From an economist's perspective, an often-cited model of local expenditures, known as "Tiebout Theory" (Tiebout 1956), suggests that municipal overburden cannot exist. Simply stated, the theory postulates that an individual will live in a municipality which offers the types and amounts of public services (in combination with other characteristics such as size or location) which he values, and that he will accordingly pay the level of taxes needed to support his preferences. If one views the costs of living in a municipality (in particular, the local taxes) as too high for the benefits received, he will move to another municipality which provides the services he prefers at a cost (or tax) he is willing to pay. That is, the local taxpayer "votes with his feet." If this is true, it implies that people who live in areas such as cities which have high taxes value the amenities or services received enough to pay those taxes. If this is the case, their tax burden supports the types and amounts of services they prefer, and they would not necessarily spend more for education if they did not have to provide for other noneducation services. This theory suggests that municipal overburden cannot exist because local taxpayers, represented by their local governments, prefer to spend local funds on noneducation services rather than increase their taxes or shift funds from noneducation to education services in "overburdened" cities. Funds are not being substituted away from education in order to provide noneducation services. If a taxpayer prefers to have more education services, he will move to a community that shares his preferences and spends its local revenues accordingly.

This theory, however, does not take into account two important constraints. First, and most importantly, it assumes that people can move freely from one community to another. Yet, an individual's mobility often is limited by employment or by the costs of moving. Second, it relies on community residents having preferences for services which are both homogeneous and consistent over time, so that the mix of services and the tax rates do not have to change quickly or drastically. Often these conditions are not met, thus allowing for the disequilibrium implied by municipal overburden to exist.

Other considerations are related to the costs of providing public services in cities. Part of the argument for municipal overburden rests on the premise that costs are higher in urban areas and are therefore a contributing factor to municipal overburden. The three cost-related considerations discussed below are introduced here because they enter the argument for the existence of municipal overburden and because they do so on a largely conceptual rather than an empirical level. In general, they lack substantial empirical measurement.

The first deals with the effects of two potentially offsetting factors affecting the costs of providing public services in cities—congestion effects and economies of scale. Because of the population density which characterizes cities, congestion effects make the provision of municipal services more expensive in urban areas than in other municipalities. For example, because high population density precludes natural disposal of refuse, cities must provide and maintain large and elaborate public waste disposal facilities. At a certain size, however, these systems may realize economies of scale which make the per capita operation costs lower than those for another system in a smaller municipality. While the existence of congestion effects and economies of scale is often disputable, it is difficult to estimate their net effects for the entire range of public services provided in cities. That is, it is difficult not only to determine each of their effects on the level of costs of aggregated public services in cities as compared to other types of municipalities but also to determine the extent to which they offset one another.

A second consideration addresses the effects of tax importing or exporting in cities. It has been suggested that cities in particular are able to "export" their taxes by having some proportion of the total tax burden borne by nonresidents. For example, if a city has a local sales tax, nonresidents who come to shop in the city bear part of that tax burden. Or, nonresidents who pay property taxes on an office in the city bear part of the local tax burden. If there is substantial tax exporting, it is expected that it would decrease municipal overburden. There is little agreement, however, as to how to measure tax exporting or its net effects.

A third consideration is the effects of nonlocal revenues. Many municipalities and cities in particular receive substantial amounts of revenues for education and other services from state and federal sources. Some of these funds are categorical and must be used for special services, such as housing or compensatory education. Other nonlocal funds, such as federal revenue-sharing, are general aid and can be used as the municipality prefers. While it is reasonably easy to observe the different types and amounts of nonlocal revenue received by municipalities, it is often difficult to distinguish the use of total revenues from how local revenues would be spent in the absence of nonlocal funds. That is, it is difficult to determine how local revenues would be allocated among education and noneducation services if no other funding were available. Thus, while the availability of nonlocal revenues would appear at least in principle to alleviate municipal overburden, the mix of categorical and noncategorical funds, and the very presence of such funds, obscures the extent to which local revenues are substituted away from a particular public service like education.

These considerations add to the complexity of making empirical estimates of the existence and extent of municipal overburden in cities or other municipalities. Difficulty in defining and measuring fiscal effort, fiscal capacity, and fiscal stress abound in the public finance literature. Other work has been done on estimating educational and noneducational costs in general and for cities in particular. Much of this work also seeks to distinguish need from preference in the provision of public services, and for education in particular. The separation of fiscal effort and fiscal capacity into education and noneducation spheres, however, has been dealt with only in those studies which focus directly on the estimation of municipal overburden, and these are relatively few.

Empirical Attempts to Measure Municipal Overburdens

Most of the empirical work on the measurement of municipal overburden has been in response to legally mandated state school finance reforms. The two major efforts to date were conducted by Miner and Sacks for New York (1980b) and Knickman and Reschovsky for New Jersey (1976, 1980b), two states which have large urban municipalities. The conceptual approaches, measurement techniques, and the conclusions of these studies are reviewed here and their implications assessed for the working definition of this chapter. In addition, an earlier and more general study by Netzer (1974) which examines municipal overburden in a more general context also is reviewed. Descriptions of these studies are presented not only to review evidence about the existence and magnitude of municipal overburden but also to show current thinking on how municipal overburden is appropriately measured for purposes of incorporating a municipal overburden factor into state aid formulas.

Netzer's study (1974) deals specifically with the existence of municipal overburden and how it affects general approaches to school finance, such as district power equalizing or full state funding. He viewed municipal overburden as existing in a situation in which large-city nonschool fiscal difficulties effectively sterilize part of their taxpaying capacity that might be otherwise available to finance schools. Using broad-based data for eight large cities, he suggested that although urban municipalities may have high property values per pupil (a measure of fiscal capacity commonly used in school aid formulas), the fiscal capacity of cities is low relative to other municipalities in terms of per capita income, per capita property values, and total and residential property values. At the same time, fiscal effort as measured in per capita local tax collection, local taxes as a proportion of income, nonproperty taxes, and effective property taxes is high. He suggested that, despite some tax exportation, urban areas are disadvantaged by municipal overburden when their residents have higher proportions of their personal incomes absorbed by locally borne taxes, and that this exists to varying extents in the cities he studied, especially as they experienced economic decline. In general, he concluded that cities have serious excess tax burdens when tax burdens are identified in terms other than the standard property value per student and local property tax rate. He noted that because most forms of state aid to education use these measures of fiscal capacity and fiscal effort, they will not be particularly effective in compensating for the extra burdens which cities face simply by dint of their size and complexity.

In interpreting these conclusions, it is important to bear several considerations in mind. First, the study involved cities in a number of states, rather than urban areas within a single state. Thus, its conclusions only apply in a general sense rather than to a particular state approach to financing education in light of municipal overburden. Second, while the study used a range of definitions of fiscal capacity and fiscal effort, it did not directly address tax burdens for education as opposed to those for noneducation services. Rather, it dealt with the fiscal stress on the urban local public finance system as a whole; it dealt more with general fiscal stress than with the particular effects of noneducation fiscal stress on education. In addition, it gave little attention to the distinctions between needed versus discretionary spending or to the level of costs. It provided, however, a very logical second step to the intuitive argument for municipal overburden by offering a general appraisal of how municipal overburden can be viewed and how it relates to general schemes for state aid to education.

As part of the research for the court-mandated reform of New Jersey's school finance system, Knickman and Reschovsky (1980b, 1980c) looked for specific evidence of municipal overburden in New Jersey. In many respects, their analysis was substantially more elaborate than Netzer's, both conceptually and in terms of the detail of data collected and analyzed. New Jersey is a particularly appropriate state in which to investigate municipal overburden. As a developed Northeastern state with a substantial urban population in several older cities and with a school finance system which was found to favor wealthier municipalities, New Jersey would seem like an obvious place for municipal overburden to exist.

In designing their original study for the state of New Jersey, Reschovsky and Knickman (1976) viewed municipal overburden in terms of the fiscal effort necessary for communities to provide necessary or "needed" public services. By taking this approach, the researchers intended to capture the distinction between need and preference for services and, to some extent, account for differences in costs. They did not, however, distinguish between education and noneducation services, but rather identified municipal overburden simply in terms of relative fiscal effort for all needed services. Using a large sample of New Jersey communities, they found that this form of overburden did exist in the state's poorer cities and that it tended to be proportional to the degree of urbanization of a community and to the socioeconomic status of its residents. In addition, overall municipal taxes were higher in urban areas than in nonurban areas, and school expenditures were a larger proportion of total municipal taxes in those municipalities as well. They also found evidence of overburden, thus defined, in several rural communities.

In subsequent work, Knickman and Reschovsky (1980a) refined their approach, redefining municipal overburden as the relation between general fiscal stress and the level of spending on education. Again, estimating revenue needs based on a "minimum bundle" of needed services, the researchers suggested the construction of an index to measure fiscal stress by estimating the difference between the tax effort necessary for needed services, using some "appropriate" measure of fiscal capacity, and a municipality's observed tax effort. To the extent that fiscal stress varies systematically with local spending for education, municipal overburden could be identified. This approach has not been tested empirically, however, and other research on the relationship between education and noneducation spending has been inconclusive.[2]

While this research offers evidence that some form of municipal overburden exists in New Jersey, the approach used by the authors included some arbitrary decisions on their part as to what constitutes need and how fiscal capacity should be measured. Because both of these factors include subjective elements, as noted earlier, the researchers' choices are open to dispute.

The third major source of empirical information on municipal overburden is found in the work of Miner and Sacks (1980a, 1980b) in the state of New York. Like New Jersey, New York with its sizable urban areas seems a likely place for municipal overburden to occur. The approach taken by Miner and Sacks differed significantly from that of Reschovsky and Knickman. They viewed municipal overburden in New York in terms of the relative fiscal burdens imposed by revenues used to finance education and noneducation public services. Accordingly, they developed a measure of "net fiscal burden" which was adjusted for tax exportation, divided into taxes paid for education and those paid for noneducation services, and reflected the relative burdensomeness of those taxes on a school district (as opposed to municipal) basis. Using this measure, they considered relatively high district ratios of noneducation local revenue to fiscal capacity as indicators of overburden. Rather than attempting to separate need from preference, they assumed that choice (or local preference) is not the explanation when the average burden measure for a category or type of school district (such as urban districts) is significantly higher than for other types of districts. Thus, their approach was quite different from that used by Reschovsky and Knickman in that they did not attempt to separate local need from preference but did distinguish between effort and capacity for education and noneducation services. Like Reschovsky and Knickman, they assessed the use of alternative measures of fiscal capacity, and included resident income as well as property values (both total and residential) as measures of local wealth. Fiscal stress was defined in relative terms, as the "above-normal" use of fiscal capacity.

Using these approaches in combination with detailed data from the universe of municipalities in New York, they found substantial evidence of municipal overburden, particularly in urban areas when adjustments were made for tax exporting. In particular, they found that urban areas were characterized by high noneducation tax rates and had approximately average education tax rates, making the cities' total tax burden large relative to other municipalities. In addition, the cities had relatively higher noneducation-to-education revenues. They also found, however, that a number of suburbs, particularly those around New York City, had high education tax rates, especially in respect to an income-based measure of fiscal capacity.

Summary of Current Research

A strong conceptual argument can be made against the long-run existence of municipal overburden. However, given the realities of limited mobility and limited responsiveness of local governments to local preferences, in combination with the fact that cities operate their public systems in substantially different circumstances from smaller municipalities, the idea that some amount of municipal overburden exists in cities does not seem unreasonable. But, measuring it so that it can be accommodated through a state education aid formula or by some other form of local aid is a particularly difficult and complex task which is full of both conceptual and measurement problems.

As indicated by the three studies reviewed here, municipal overburden can be and has been measured in substantially different ways. Yet despite differing methodologies and conceptual limitations, all three of these studies found evidence that municipal overburden does exist in urban areas.

Returning, however, to the two-part definition of municipal overburden, which views it as first the relative fiscal effort among districts for education and noneducation public services, taking relative fiscal capacity into account, and second as the effects of noneducation effort and expenditure levels on the level of expenditures for education, real evidence on municipal overburden is still unclear. Netzer indicated only that urban areas face generally greater tax burdens in relation to their fiscal capacities than do other types of municipalities and that this ultimately affects the level of spending for education in cities. Knickman and Reschovsky offered evidence showing that fiscal stress is greater in cities just for providing for needed services like education. While they suggested a means of determining the effects of this stress on local spending for education, the empirical evidence is currently undeveloped. Miner and Sacks, in comparing tax effort for education and noneducation services, obtained somewhat mixed results, although there is general indication that cities face larger relative tax burdens for noneducation than education services. The extent to which these higher tax burdens affect spending for education, however, is not clear.

Thus, while all of this evidence indicates that municipal overburden, broadly defined, exists, its magnitude in terms of its effect on spending for education is generally undetermined.

FORMULAS FOR STATE AID TO EDUCATION

One of the fundamental reasons for providing state aid to education is to equalize access to educational services for all residents of the state. Most of the reforms in the structure of state aid to education which are currently underway are specific attempts to improve this aspect of equality. As part of this effort, many states are considering adding factors to their formulas which reflect specific characteristics of districts affecting their abilities to provide at least some minimum level of educational services. Thus, a formula factor reflecting municipal overburden ideally would provide extra aid to districts in proportion to the magnitude of their overburden.

The form of a factor in state aid formulas to compensate districts which have municipal overburden would depend on a number of considerations, including:

- the extent to which current aid formulas focus on equalization of educational expenditures or equalization of local tax effort;
- the extent to which municipal overburden is defined in terms of fiscal effort, fiscal capacity, or fiscal stress;
- the extent to which fiscal effort and fiscal capacity for education can be separated from that for noneducation services.

Each of these is discussed below and followed by an assessment of the potential effects of incorporating various forms of municipal overburden factors in state aid formulas.

Alternative Forms

A number of viable options exist for incorporating a municipal over-burden factor into a state aid formula. This discussion of alternative forms is based not only on the previous discussion of municipal over-burden but also on currently used forms and those presently being considered by several state legislatures.

Most attempts at equalization of local education through state aid have focused either on equalizing expenditures per student through-out a state or on equalizing local tax effort for education among a state's districts. If a state's primary approach to equalization is through equalizing tax efforts, a municipal overburden factor should be designed to take into account differences in tax effort among districts for noneducation services. That is, because municipal over-burden represents the extent to which noneducation tax effort im-poses a burden on local spending for education, a tax effort equali-zation approach to school finance reform which includes recognition of municipal overburden should logically adjust for the noneducation inequalities in order to ensure comparable fiscal positions for financ-ing education. This, to a certain extent, means including noneduca-tion aid in education aid formulas.

If, on the other hand, equalization efforts are focused on limiting disparities in expenditures per student across the state, and municipal overburden in some districts reduces their levels of expenditures for education, the formula factor should be designed to increase aid, perhaps on a per student basis, to compensate directly for spending on noneducation services which has been substituted away from edu-cation. To do this, however, would involve specific estimates of the amount by which current local expenditures are depressed because of noneducation spending. In addition, it would have to take into account not only relative need for and cost of noneducation services, as discussed earlier, but also the effects of need and costs on current educational expenditures in a district. The information needs for such treatment would be prodigious.

Whether tax or expenditure equalization is the primary focus of a state aid formula, the translation of a municipal overburden is de-fined. Specifically, it can be viewed in terms of fiscal effort, fiscal capacity, or fiscal stress, and measured accordingly. As discussed ear-lier, fiscal stress combines fiscal effort and fiscal capacity to form a more complete estimation of the local tax burden than either descriptor can do on its own. As a measure of local tax burden either for education and noneducation services separately, or for all local services, it is generally preferred to local fiscal effort as a more comprehensive measure of local tax burden. A fiscal stress index similar to the one suggested by Knickman and Reschovsky (1980a) could be used. From a pragmatic point of view, however, fiscal stress indicators are difficult to use in aid formulas because of their complexity and their substantial data requirements, especially when they are separated into education and noneducation components. In addition, the concept of fiscal stress is not universally recognized by researchers or by policymakers. Standard measures of fiscal effort, such as millage rates, do not fully describe local tax effort, even when separated into fiscal effort for education and noneducation services (a task which can be empirically difficult especially when districts and municipalities are not coterminous as evidenced by the efforts of Miner and Sacks). However, a measure such as tax rates does have the advantage of simplicity and relative ease of estimation. In Michigan, one of the few states which currently has a municipal overburden factor in its education aid formula, additional state aid is allocated to those districts whose education tax rate (as distinguished from noneducation) is greater than 125 percent of the statewide average. The amount of the aid is directly proportionate to the amount by which it exceeds that average. (The bulk of the funds set aside for this factor goes to Detroit, the state's largest urban municipality.)

These considerations emphasize the importance of separating tax burdens for education and noneducation services. If a municipal overburden factor is incorporated into an education aid formula, it becomes, at least in principle, part of financial aid for education received from the state by those districts which have municipal overburden. That is, it is translated into aid for education. As such, it should be based on some measure of the effects of municipal overburden on local spending for education. And in order to do this, it is necessary to know how local spending for education is affected by noneducation tax burdens. The construction of the factor thus should take both education and noneducation tax burdens into account, not only to determine if a district qualifies for municipal overburden aid but also to determine the appropriate amount of aid. To do this, in a manner which takes both education and noneducation burdens into account as well as the relationship between them, is a complex task, particularly when there are aspects of need and costs which are interrelated among education and noneducation services. Given this complexity, the formula factors actually used may perhaps be proxies for the existence of the relationship. For example, if it can be shown that the size of a municipality's low-income population is directly related to both education and noneducation tax burdens, a count of Aid to Families with Dependent Children (AFDC) households could perhaps be used to represent the existence and extent of municipal overburden. Use of a proxy factor, however, while perhaps a simpler means of factoring in municipal overburden, necessitates the calculation of its relation to education and noneducation tax burdens in order to determine the extent to which the proxy accurately represents the presence and extent of municipal overburden. In addition, it may tend to obfuscate both the purpose and the form of the aid in the eyes of policymakers and district officials. That is, if municipal overburden aid were allocated according to a proxy factor representing degree of urbanicity, it would be difficult to distinguish it in the public view and in practice from additional education aid to cities. Similarly, if it were based on district poverty, it would be difficult to distinguish from an educational need factor. In sum, if a municipal overburden aid factor were to be introduced into a state education aid formula, it should directly reflect the relationship between education and noneducation local tax burdens in a district and should be distinguished from other forms of educational factors (such as need or cost factors) for both policy and operational purposes.

Consequences of a Municipal Overburden Factor

In considering the use of a factor to reflect municipal overburden in state education aid formulas, policymakers and others should take into account a number of potential consequences and assumptions inherent in its use. First, this normative assumption underlies the use of such a factor: that municipalities which have relatively or absolutely high tax burdens either in general or for noneducation services should receive additional state aid in the name of equalization. While this may not appear to be an issue worthy of dispute, it is important not to lose sight of the fact that it does represent a point of view and therefore has an element of subjectivity which may make it politically vulnerable and susceptible to changes in political or other views.

Second, it is important to clarify whether such aid is intended primarily for all districts which meet some established criteria or if it is intended to be a form of aid to education in urban areas only. Although evidence to date suggests that municipal overburden exists primarily in cities, it is not limited only to urban areas. In addition, if a municipal overburden factor is defined so that it results in the allocation of aid for education to cities only, some consideration should be given as to whether it substitutes for other forms of aid expressly designed to reflect cities' particular characteristics (such as additional aid to meet high educational needs or costs in cities) or if it acts to mitigate other aspects of the aid system.[3]

This is directly related to a third and very important consideration: because municipal overburden is a sort of "half-breed" education concern (that is, it originates outside the system in which education operates), its effects may either be felt directly in the system which produces educational services or they may have more of an impact outside that system. From a perspective which focuses on financing education (rather than noneducation) services, the effect of a municipal overburden factor may be either additive or substitutive. Additional education aid to municipalities which have municipal overburden may either increase educational expenditures or it may be used to substitute for current expenditures so that more local funds can be spent for noneducation services or local tax burdens can be reduced. Because of the complexity of the concept of municipal overburden in which education and noneducation local tax burdens interact to depress educational spending, and because there is little real evidence about the precise nature of the relationship of education to noneducation tax burdens, it is not entirely clear whether municipal overburden should be in the form of aid to education or as general tax relief for certain municipalities. That is, because of the possibility of aid to compensate for municipal overburden being used for substituting rather than for increasing educational spending and of the close relationship to noneducation factors, it is not entirely clear that compensating for the effects of municipal overburden should be considered purely within the education finance context. Perhaps it more appropriately belongs within the context of general state aid to municipalities. Broadening the context in which municipal overburden is recognized and treated seems even more appropriate given the consideration that municipalities whose school districts qualify for municipal overburden aid in an education aid formula may regard it as an incentive to substitute local funds away from education in order to qualify for increased state aid for education and to increase their total municipal budgets.

Another more pragmatic consideration is that providing aid for municipal overburden is potentially quite costly for a state education aid system. Since the real extent of municipal overburden is unclear and the possibility exists of districts decreasing education tax burdens relative to those for noneducation services to qualify for increased state funds, the potential costs of such a factor to a state could be quite sizable. If the state imposed a limit on the amount of funding available for municipal overburden aid, as Michigan currently does, the costs could be contained but only at the expense of providing half-hearted and perhaps ineffective treatment of a potentially widespread problem.

Overall, the difficulties of compensating for the effects of municipal overburden through the state education aid formula are formidable. If the basic objective of a state aid formula is to increase statewide equality in financing education, it may be more appropriate and more politically expedient to recognize municipal overburden in a more general sense by providing a general form of additional aid to urban districts. This aid could be provided through general tax relief to districts which have high levels of both education and noneducation tax efforts, or to simply provide additional education aid on a per student basis to districts which have particularly large overall tax burdens. Until a general, accepted definition and measure of municipal overburden are available, treating municipal overburden through state education aid formulas, even when its existence is legally recognized, is likely to remain a thorny problem.

NOTES TO CHAPTER 3

1. Gurwitz (1980) has suggested that fiscal capacity should be estimated on the basis of the capitalized value of taxable property. This approach, however, has not been tried. Odden (1976) provides a discussion of various measures of local taxable wealth.
2. See, for example, Ladd (1975) and Grubb and Michaelson (1974).

3. There is some indication that municipal overburden aid in Michigan may offset the effects of Michigan's district power equalizing approach because the high noneducation tax rates which qualify urban areas like Detroit for municipal overburden aid are sometimes accompanied by high education tax rates as well, so that these municipalities are not recognized as needing state aid under district power equalizing. The validity of this argument is currently being studied by M. Addonizio in the Michigan State Department of Education.

REFERENCES

Coons, John, et al. 1970. *Private Wealth and Public Education.* Cambridge, Mass.: Harvard University Press.

Grubb, W. Norton, and Stephen Michaelson. 1974. *States and Schools: The Political Economy of Fiscal Federalism.* Lexington, Mass.: Lexington Books.

Gurwitz, Aaron. 1980. "The Capitalization of School Finance Reform." *Journal of Education Finance* 5, no. 3 (Winter): 297–319.

Guthrie, James, et al. 1971. *Schools and Inequality.* Cambridge, Mass.: MIT Press.

Knickman, James R., and Andrew Reschovsky. 1980a. "Fiscal Stress and School District Responses to Intergovernmental Aid." *Proceedings of the 72nd Annual Conference on Taxation.* Columbus, Ohio: National Tax Association Tax Institute of America.

_____. 1980b. "The Measurement and Use of Municipal Overburden Indices in School Finance Formulas." Unpublished paper, Tufts University, Medford, Mass.

_____. 1981. "Municipal Overburden: Its Measurement and Role in School Finance Reform." In *Selected Papers in School Finance*, edited by Esther Tron, Washington, D.C.: U.S. Department of Education.

Ladd, Helen. 1975. "Local Education Expenditures, Fiscal Capacity, and the Composition of the Property Tax Base." *National Tax Journal* 28, no. 2 (June): 145–158.

Miner, Jerry, and Seymour Sacks. 1980a. "Municipal Overburden and School Finance in New York State Revisited." Unpublished paper, Syracuse University, New York.

_____. 1980b. "Study of Adjustments of New York State School Aid Formula to Take Account of Municipal Overburden." Unpublished paper, Syracuse, N.Y.: Maxwell School, Syracuse University.

Netzer, Dick. 1974. "State Education Aid and School Tax Efforts in Large Cities." In *Selected Papers in School Finance 1974*, edited by Esther Tron. Washington, D.C.: U.S. Department of Health, Education, and Welfare.

Odden, Allan. 1976. *Alternative Measures of School District Wealth.* Report no. F76-6. Denver, Colo.: Education Finance Center, Education Commission of the States.

Reschovsky, Andrew, and James Knickman. 1976. "Municipal Overburden in New Jersey: An Assessment." *Urban Observatory Research Reports.* Newark, N.J.: New Jersey Department of Education.

Sacks, Seymour. 1972. *City Schools/Suburban Schools: A History of Fiscal Conflict.* Syracuse, N.Y.: Syracuse University Press.

Tiebout, Charles M. 1956. "A Pure Theory of Local Expenditures." *Journal of Political Economy* 64 (October): 416-424.

4 SCHOOL FINANCE REFORM AND THE CITIES

Margaret Goertz *

On June 23, 1978, a trial court invalidated New York State's system of financing elementary and secondary education. This decision, *Levittown* v. *Nyquist* (1978), was the first in the country to address specifically the unique educational finance problems of large cities. The suit was a dual challenge to the state aid statute. Levittown and twenty-six other low-property wealth districts claimed that the existing school finance system failed to equalize the wealth-related ability of districts to spend for education. The urban intervenors charged that the formula failed to recognize four overburdening conditions in the state's four largest cities—municipal overburden, educational overburden, cost differentials, and absenteeism overburden—resulting in "an overstatement of the city districts' capacity to finance public education and an arbitrary and irrational deprivation of state aid" (*Levittown* 1978: 4–5).[1] The court responded by establishing a dual equity standard, requiring both greater equalization of wealth-related spending variations (fiscal neutrality) and recognition of the special educational and fiscal needs of the state's large urban school districts.

The *Levittown* decision highlights the fiscal and educational problems of city school districts throughout the country. Cities face

*Margaret Goertz, Policy Research Scientist, Education Policy Research Institute, Education Testing Service.

113

higher costs of educating disproportionate numbers of low-achieving, bilingual and other high-cost students, greater demands for municipal services, and higher prices for purchasing goods and services. Yet state aid formulas often overstate cities' wealth and understate their educational needs, school tax effort, and higher costs. In this chapter, the dimensions of the urban school finance problem are outlined; current urban-oriented adjustments in state aid formulas are summarized; and policy questions related to implementing urban provisions in state school finance systems are raised.

THE URBAN SCHOOL FINANCE PROBLEM

Research in the mid–1960s documented the decline of the urban tax base; the changing composition of the urban population in general, and school population in particular; and the disparities in education expenditures between the cities and their suburbs. In the early 1970s scholars linked these demographic and fiscal patterns to the deficiencies of state education aid formulas. They showed that the large cities, especially those in the Northeast and Midwest, faced a growing mismatch between educational resources and educational and fiscal demands on those resources, and argued for new state and federal funding programs which would direct additional dollars to urban school districts.[2] As a new decade begins, it is important that the problems of large urban school districts be reexamined in light of recent demographic and fiscal trends.

The urban school finance problem, as it has been defined, has four dimensions. First, the cities have a resource base (fiscal capacity) that is insufficient to meet increasing educational costs. Second, education costs are greater in the cities due to the large number of students requiring special educational services (educational overburden) and to the higher prices paid for all goods and services. Third, the far greater demand for noneducation services in cities places a disproportionately higher drain on the urban tax dollar than in nonurban areas (municipal overburden). Finally, state aid formulas are generally insensitive to these problems and therefore fail to compensate for the unique fiscal disadvantages of large urban school districts.

Fiscal Capacity [3]

A primary cause of the fiscal problems of urban school districts has been the movement of business and people out of the central cities, leaving these communities with a concentration of lower income and minority-group residents and, in many cases, with a deteriorating tax base. While the nation's largest cities have been losing population since 1950, this phenomenon became more widespread in the 1970s. Central cities in fifty-two of the eighty-five largest metropolitan areas experienced absolute population losses between 1970 and 1976. Yet, in this latter period of time, the proportion of black households increased from 17.9 to 20.4 percent in the central cities, but only from 4.0 to 5.2 percent in the suburbs.

Central cities generally have lower income levels than their suburbs. The first column of Table 4–1 shows central city per capita income as a percent of the average income of its suburbs for thirty major metropolitan areas. In 1976, suburban income exceeded that of the central city in all but eight metropolitan areas. Five of the eight exceptions are located in the West. The cities look even poorer when income is measured on a household basis. In the Northeast, for example, central city per capita income was on average 83.4 percent of suburban per capita income. The proportion dropped to 66.7 percent, however, when a household income measure was used. This difference reflects both the larger number of poor households and the smaller number of earners per household in the central cities.

Many central cities also suffered from a decline in economic activity in the 1970s. Central city retail sales declined in real terms in half of the country's eighty-five largest metropolitan areas, while thirty-one cities showed an absolute decrease in real total income. These losses were particularly evident in the Northeast and Midwest. Only sixteen central cities had increases in retail sales which surpassed the national increase in real income; fifteen were located in the South and West.

One major consequence of these economic trends is a decreased capacity to raise local revenues for education and other public services in the cities. Column 2 of Table 4–1 shows 1976 per pupil property valuations—the traditional measure of fiscal capacity in state education aid formulas—for central cities as a percent of their state average valuations. This ratio ranged from a low of 29 percent in

Table 4–1. Socioeconomic and Fiscal Characteristics of Thirty Major Metropolitan Areas

Region	Percent of Per Capita Income, 1976 $CC^a \div OCC^b$	Percent of Per Pupil Property Value, 1976 $CC \div$ State Average	Percent of Households with Children, with Poverty Income, 1976[c] CC	OCC	Education Expenditures as a Percent of Total Expenditures, 1977 CC	OCC
Northeast						
Washington, D.C.	84	—	15.0	2.8	22	45
Baltimore, Md.	78	57	22.8	3.5	26	61
Boston, Mass.	81	78	24.7	6.2	34	52
Newark, N.J.	54	29	NA	NA	30	45
Buffalo, N.Y.	79	71	20.0	5.4	28	35
New York, N.Y.	84	111	18.0	4.2	25	46
Philadelphia, Pa.	83	102	16.7	6.7	32	50
Pittsburgh, Pa.	95	138	17.5	7.1	31	57
Midwest						
Chicago, Ill.	79	61	19.2	3.9	39	52
Indianapolis, Ind.	99	105	8.8	3.3	42	56
Detroit, Mich.	80	89	19.5	4.1	32	48
Minneapolis, Minn.	94	—	8.9	2.8	24	46
Kansas City, Mo.	92	177	NA	NA	36	47
St. Louis, Mo.	80	109	23.3	6.5	34	57
Cincinnati, Ohio	97	128	NA	NA	22	47
Cleveland, Ohio	68	91	27.1	3.9	36	49
Milwaukee, Wisc.	82	90	NA	NA	35	45

South						
Miami, Fla.	79	123	NA	NA	32	39
Atlanta, Ga.	82	162	NA	NA	28	46
New Orleans, La.	91	192	NA	NA	31	36
Memphis, Tenn.	118	112	17.0	6.3	35	39
Dallas, Texas	108	111	10.5	4.1	41	50
Houston, Texas	102	104	10.2	4.8	41	48
San Antonio, Texas	75	46	NA	NA	48	55
West						
Phoenix, Ariz.	103	234	10.7	4.7	45	54
Los Angeles, Calif.	103	78	12.3	7.8	34	42
San Diego, Calif.	107	83	NA	NA	43	50
San Francisco, Calif.	94	183	16.7	6.9	27	39
Denver, Colo.	107	171	12.6	4.4	28	57
Seattle, Wash.	108	176	10.7	4.6	25	53

a. CC = Central city.

b. OCC = Outside central city (suburbs).

c. Of those households with children under eighteen, percent with incomes less than $5,000 in 1976.

NA: Not available. Data not broken down by categories of central city and outside central city.

Sources: 1976–77 Merged Federal Data File as compiled by AUI Policy Research, Washington, D.C.; Advisory Commission on Intergovernmental Relations, *Central City–Suburban Fiscal Disparity and City Distress, 1977*, M–119 (Washington, D.C.: U.S. Government Printing Office, 1980); and U.S. Department of Housing and Urban Development, *Annual Housing Survey, Housing Characteristics for Selected Metropolitan Areas, 1975, 1976, 1977* (Washington, D.C.: U.S. Government Printing Office, 1980).

Newark to a high of 234 percent in Phoenix. In spite of the economic declines just noted, seventeen of the cities had above-average property valuations, including seven communities located in the East and Midwest. In short, these relatively high property valuations mask underlying economic characteristics that can undercut the capacity of cities to raise revenues from their tax bases.

Educational Overburden

Despite deteriorating tax bases, cities are faced with escalating education costs. Although most urban school districts are losing pupils, those who remain are disproportionately in need of costly special educational services. New York City, for example, has 32 percent of the state's enrollment, but 79 percent of its bilingual, 51 percent of its handicapped, and 53 percent of its low-achieving (compensatory education) students. The impact on New York City schools is substantial; 60 percent of their enrollment falls into these special categories. For its suburbs, the comparable figure is 20 percent. Similarly, more than half of Newark, New Jersey, students required remedial education programs in 1979–80, while 12 percent were enrolled in bilingual education classes.

Although comparable data are not readily available on the concentrations of handicapped, bilingual, and educationally disadvantaged pupils in all thirty major metropolitan areas, some proxy measures exist. In 1976, twenty-four of these districts had a minority enrollment of 50 percent or more; in eight, the minority enrollment exceeded 75 percent of total enrollment. As shown in Columns 3 and 4 of Table 4–1, the cities also educate large numbers of students from poverty households. In central cities in the Northeast and Midwest, an average of 20 percent of households with children under the age of eighteen had incomes less than $5,000 in 1976. This percentage was generally four to five times larger than that of their surrounding suburbs. Although the percentage of poor households is smaller in the central cities in the South and West, the concentration of poverty is still two to three times greater than in the suburban areas.

Programs tailored to meet the special needs of these children are expensive, and these costs are compounded due to the heavy concentration of these children in city school districts. The federal government was the first to respond to those problems associated with the incidence of poverty, and with the concentration of disadvantaged students in urban and rural school districts. Since the mid–1960s, federal aid has flowed through the Elementary and Secondary Education Act (ESEA) in highest proportions to the central city and poor rural districts, and to districts with large proportions of minority pupils.

In 1978, Congress added a provision to ESEA, the largest of its education programs, recognizing that school districts with high numbers or high concentrations of children eligible for compensatory education incur higher per pupil costs and should receive additional federal aid. The basic rationale underlying this authorization was (1) that pupils in schools and districts with higher numbers and concentrations of pupils needing remedial programs have more severe need for compensatory services than other compensatory education pupils; (2) that districts characterized by high numbers or concentrations of such pupils tend to have more severe fiscal problems; and (3) that a fixed statewide sum per pupil for serving such students is not adequate to recognize "the extra needs associated with urban and rural concentrations of poor children" (U.S. Congress 1978).[4] Chapter 1 presented a more comprehensive discussion of financial issues associated with special pupil populations.

Municipal Overburden

A third problem affecting the finances of urban school districts is municipal overburden. As described in the *Levittown* decision, municipal overburden exists when the available local tax base must support a greater than average level of nonschool public services because of the dependent character of urban populations (for example, greater than average proportions of poor and aged), other higher than average service needs of densely populated areas (for example, fire, police, sanitation), and more extensive state-imposed service responsibilities. This pressure for municipal services often leaves the large city districts less able to meet the unusually high educational needs of their students.

In 1977, as in the twenty preceding years, per capita local government expenditures for all services in the central cities exceeded those in suburban areas, the difference rising steadily from 27 percent in 1957 to 39 percent in 1977. These disparities resulted largely from the high level of noneducational expenditures in the cities: average per capita noneducational expenditures in the central cities were 74 percent higher than those in their suburbs in 1977. The suburbs continued to devote larger shares of their budgets to education. In 1977, education expenditures represented 34 percent of city budgets, and 50 percent of suburban budgets (ACIR 1980: Table 5). Table 4–1 shows these relationships for the thirty selected metropolitan areas.

Urban school districts spent an average of $25 per capita less on education in 1977 than other districts in their metropolitan areas, and they raised fewer dollars per capita for education from local taxes. Yet, total taxes in central cities were 25 percent higher than those in the suburbs. Despite their relatively deteriorating tax bases and lower income levels, central cities raised $80 per capita more in local revenues for all services than did their neighboring communities (ACIR 1980: Table 8).

The competition for funds among public services will most likely intensify in cities as their financial positions grow more precarious. The late 1970s saw a dampened rate of growth in intergovernmental aid to municipal governments, an upsurge in the growth rate of local revenues, and a considerable slowing of growth in expenditures.[5] This period of fiscal restraint has left its mark on city expenditure patterns. Between 1973–74 and 1977–78, social welfare functions (education, public welfare, and health and hospitals) declined in their relative importance (from 32.2 to 27.5 percent of city spending), while urban services (police, fire, and sanitation), infrastructure (highways, sewers, and so on) and debt service remained relatively stable. Education's share of the municipal budget decreased by 13 percent in fiscally dependent districts during this period (Merget 1981).[6] For a fuller discussion of municipal overburden, see Chapter 3.

Higher Costs

Many cities also face a higher cost of doing business. Studies of educational price differentials in California, Missouri, and New York have shown that cities must spend more than other districts in their states to purchase equivalent educational services (Chambers 1980; Chambers et al. 1976; Wendling 1979). For example, it has been estimated that the price of educational services is 25 percent above average in New York City, while prices in St. Louis and Kansas City are 15 percent and 13 percent above average, respectively. In California, costs in the largest metropolitan areas have been estimated to be 110 percent of the state average, compared to an average of 97 percent for districts located in nonmetropolitan areas. A detailed discussion of this issue can be found in Chapter 2.

State Aid to Education

The final element in the urban school finance problem is the failure of most state aid systems to respond adequately to the problems described above. Early state aid formulas were aimed at redistributing resources from wealthy urban centers, with their high-quality school systems, to assist impoverished outlying school districts which had a lower level of most educational resources. As the school finance reform movement was to demonstrate, however, the low level of funding and structural imperfections, such as flat grants and minimum aid, minimized the impact of these state equalization aid programs.

After the first *Serrano* decision in 1971, many states began to direct more state aid to school districts with low property valuations. State support of education increased from 44 percent of state and local revenues in 1970–71 to 53 percent in 1979–80. Yet analysts warned that property tax base equalization alone was no longer an adequate answer to all school finance inequities. It would not resolve the contemporary problems of the large cities, and might in fact exacerbate their condition (Berke 1974; Berke and Callahan 1972; Callahan et al. 1973). These scholars argued that, by and large, the central city fiscal difficulties were not attributable to low property values, and the lower level of education effort in cities would place them at a disadvantage under "power-equalizing" formulas, despite their higher overall tax effort.

How have recent changes in school finance systems affected the finances of urban school districts? Only imperfect answers exist. Studies have looked at the impact of reform in a number of individual states. Most have evaluated school finance reforms against the statewide goals of fiscal neutrality, expenditure equality, and tax effort equality; none has looked *directly* at the distribution of aid to city school districts or examined their new expenditure and tax rate

Table 4–2. Per Capita Education Aid and Education Expenditures for Thirty Major Metropolitan Areas, Central City ÷ Outside Central City Ratios, 1970, 1977

Region	Per Capita Education Aid[a]		Per Capita Education Expenditures[a]	
	$CC^b \div OCC^c$ 1970	$CC^b \div OCC^c$ 1977	$CC^b \div OCC^c$ 1970	$CC^b \div OCC^c$ 1977
Northeast				
Washington, D.C.	59	57	106	107
Baltimore, Md.	92	277	103	111
Boston, Mass.	61	159	78	113
Newark, N.J.	215	393	105	118
Buffalo, N.Y.	68	82	63	84
New York, N.Y.	73	78	64	66
Philadelphia, Pa.	148	142	85	78
Pittsburgh, Pa.	84	89	85	100
Midwest				
Chicago, Ill.	112	164	79	95
Indianapolis, Ind.	75	81	74	94
Detroit, Mich.	106	121	67	75
Minneapolis, Minn.	43	70	54	89
Kansas City, Mo.	63	70	87	92
St. Louis, Mo.	71	118	94	97
Cincinnati, Ohio	51	72	116	82
Cleveland, Ohio	109	108	107	111
Milwaukee, Wisc.	70	116	73	100

South

Dade County, Fla.	—	—	—	—
Atlanta, Ga.	87	112	114	108
New Orleans, La.	78	96	104	85
Memphis, Tenn.	70	80	—	92
Dallas, Texas	70	56	91	79
Houston, Texas	80	78	75	85
San Antonio, Texas	89	105	62	121

West

Phoenix, Ariz.	56	78		87
Los Angeles, Calif.	69	84	85	105
San Diego, Calif.	102	83	81	100
San Francisco, Calif.	75	88	79	98
Denver, Colo.	73	57	87	69
Seattle, Wash.	42	65	54	80

a. Education aid and expenditure data include federal aid.

b. CC = Central city.

c. OCC = Outside central city (suburbs).

Source: Advisory Commission on Intergovernmental Relations, *Central City–Suburban Disparity and City Distress, 1977* (Washington, D.C.: U.S. Government Printing Office, 1980), Tables 5, A–11, and A–18.

levels. The Advisory Commission on Intergovernmental Relations (ACIR) provided some data for a preliminary assessment of the fiscal status of urban school districts in 1977 but did not distinguish state from federal assistance. Nonetheless, these data, as presented in Table 4–2, permit some generalizations.

First, in most sections of the country, cities still lag behind their suburbs in intergovernmental aid to education, although the gap is narrowing. In 1970, twenty-three of the cities shown in Table 4–2 received less per capita education aid than their outside areas; by 1977 this number had dropped to eighteen. In those cities which remained at a relative disadvantage, thirteen saw a reduction in the aid disparity; in five cases, however, the gap widened.

Second, changes in the state and local system for funding education have had a marginal impact on the relative expenditure levels of city school systems. In 1970, only six of twenty-seven central cities spent more per capita than their suburbs; in 1977 this number had increased only by two. Stated another way, in 1977, two-thirds of the largest urban school districts still had fewer resources to commit to education than their surrounding areas. These disparities would appear larger if the expenditure figures excluded federal aid which is concentrated in the central cities.

It appears, then, that reforms in school funding have not gone far in redressing the imbalance in education resources which face most central cities. Most of the improvement in the financial status of cities has resulted from the increased allocation of aid through equalization aid formulas designed to offset wide disparities in per pupil property valuations. Nearly all of the cities which showed substantial gains in aid were districts with below-average property wealth (see Table 4–1).

URBAN-ORIENTED ADJUSTMENTS[7]

A number of states have components in their school finance formulas which directly or indirectly allocate additional aid to urban school districts. In Table 4–3 the urban-oriented adjustments to state school finance systems in effect in 1978–79 are summarized. These adjustments are grouped according to the problems addressed: fiscal capacity, educational overburden, municipal overburden, and cost of education.

Adjustments to Fiscal Capacity

Three types of adjustments to the traditional measure of fiscal capacity which have recognized the problems of the cities are: (1) modifying property wealth measures by income; (2) measuring fiscal capacity on a per capita, rather than on a per pupil, basis; and (3) adjusting the per pupil denominator in the wealth measure to reflect the extra educational needs of a school district.

Income Factors. Seven states included an income adjustment in their equalization aid formulas in 1978–79. Chapter 5 describes many of these approaches. In some cases, this adjustment makes the fiscal capacity of cities appear significantly lower than under a straight property wealth measure. For example, Hartford, Connecticut's 1977 property valuation per pupil was $84,890; its income-adjusted valuation under the state's new finance formula is $29,750 per pupil. This dramatic change results from two factors: Hartford's per capita income is low compared to the state average, and the income adjustment is the ratio of a district's per capita income to that of the *highest* income district in the state.

In other cases, an income adjustment may make a low-income district look relatively wealthier. For example, fiscal capacity is defined in the Maryland state aid formula as the sum of one-half of aggregate property wealth and total income wealth. Although Baltimore has below-average per pupil income (75 percent of the state average), its per pupil property wealth is even lower relative to the state average (51 percent). By summing the two wealth measures, the city's relative fiscal capacity becomes 60 percent of the state average, a figure higher than its relative per pupil property wealth.

Connecticut's formula is unique in that it includes an income factor in the measure of tax effort, as well as fiscal capacity. The calculated school tax rate in the Guaranteed Tax Base (GTB) formula is locally raised revenues divided by property valuation modified by the income ratio described above.[8] This adjustment has the effect of making the tax effort of low-income districts look relatively higher, thus generating more state aid.

Per Capita Wealth Measures. Three states, Connecticut, Massachusetts, and Virginia, measure fiscal capacity on a per capita basis. The

Table 4-3. Summary of Urban Adjustments in State School Finance Systems, 1978-79

| State | Fiscal Capacity | | | Educational Overburden | |
	Income Adjustment	Per Capita	Pupil Needs Adjustment[a]	Poverty[b]	Density
Alabama					
Alaska					
Arizona					
Arkansas					
California				X[c]	
Colorado				X	X[d]
Connecticut (1979-80)	X	X		X	
Delaware					
Florida			X		
Georgia					
Hawaii					
Idaho			X		
Illinois				X[e]	
Indiana			X		
Iowa			X		
Kansas	X				
Kentucky					
Louisiana					
Maine			X		
Maryland	X				X[f]
Massachusetts		X		X	
Michigan					
Minnesota			X	X	
Mississippi					
Missouri	X		X	X	
Montana			X		
Nebraska			X		
Nevada			X		
New Hampshire					
New Jersey					

Table 4-3. continued

| Educational Overburden (cont'd.) | | | | Education |
Disadvantaged Pupils[b]	Bilingual Pupils	Concentration Factor	Municipal Overburden	Price Differentials
	X			X
	X			
X	X			
	X			
X	X			
X				X
X				
X				
(X)[e]	X	X		
X				
(X)[f]				
	X			
X	X		X	
		X		
X				
X	X			

(Table 4-3. continued overleaf)

Table 4-3. continued

	Fiscal Capacity			Educational Overburden	
State	Income Adjustment	Per Capita	Pupil Needs Adjustment[a]	Poverty[b]	Density
New Mexico			X		
New York			X		
North Carolina					
North Dakota					
Ohio				X	
Oklahoma					
Oregon					
Pennsylvania	X			X	X
Rhode Island	X				
South Carolina			X		
South Dakota					
Tennessee			X		
Texas			X		
Utah			X		
Vermont					
Virginia	X	X[g]			
Washington					
West Virginia					
Wisconsin[h]					
Wyoming			X		

a. Includes states which apply weightings for special needs pupils to expenditure guarantees. Does not include states that weight only for grade-level differentials. (See note 9.).

b. "Poverty" includes only those aid programs not earmarked for low-income or educationally disadvantaged children. "Disadvantaged Pupils" includes only those aid programs targeted to these types of students, regardless of criteria used to distribute aid.

c. Includes Urban Impact Aid.

d. This provision does not give eligible districts more actual dollars to spend, but provides them more state aid relative to local property taxes.

Table 4-3. continued

Educational Overburden (cont'd.)

Disadvantaged Pupils[b]	Bilingual Pupils	Concentration Factor	Municipal Overburden	Education Price Differentials
	X			
X	X			
X		X		
X				
X		X		
X	X			
X	X			
X	X			
X				X
X	X			

e. The 1978 Amendments require that school districts with a concentration of Title I pupils above the state average must submit a plan for expenditure of these funds on disadvantaged children.

f. Two-thirds of Density Aid must be used for compensatory education programs. The state established the separate compensatory education program in 1979–80.

g. Fiscal capacity is defined one-third on a per capita basis and two-thirds on a per pupil basis.

h. State also funds Integration Aid in 14 school districts.

Sources: Tron (1980) and author's survey of selected state departments of education.

first two states use a straight per capita approach, while Virginia defines district wealth partially (one-third) on a per capita basis and partially (two-thirds) on a per average daily membership (ADM) basis. Changing the denominator in the fiscal capacity component of the formula from pupils to population better reflects the capacity of a school district to raise revenues for all public services, not just education. This approach directs more aid to cities because they generally have below-average enrollment ratios.

Pupil–Needs Adjustments. Finally, a number of states adjust the fiscal capacity measure to reflect the higher level of educational needs in urban and other school districts (see Column 3, Table 4–3). For example, New York State's aid formula incorporates a weighted pupil count in the denominator of the wealth measure which gives extra weight to educationally disadvantaged and handicapped students. Similarly, the per pupil wealth measure in Illinois's formula includes an extra weighting for Title I eligible children. Most of the states noted in the table, however, recognize only the higher costs of special education and vocational education in the fiscal capacity measure; only six include measures of poverty or educational disadvantage.[9] Since the cities contain disproportionate numbers of students with extraordinary educational needs, applying weightings to the denominator of the fiscal capacity measure can make these school districts look relatively poorer.

Educational Overburden Adjustments

A major focus of the school finance reform movement has been a concern with relating state education aid to individual student needs. Prior to *Serrano*, the only student needs recognized in most state aid formulas were grade-level differentials. Since this time, states have been active in developing new aid programs for special education, vocational education, and compensatory education. In 1978–79, all fifty states provided special education aid, and forty-four states provided funds for vocational education. Twenty-four states appropriated funds for compensatory education programs or provided additional aid on the basis of a poverty count or district density; six states used more than one approach. States have been slower to fund bilingual education programs, however, with only fifteen providing aid in this area.

Cities benefit from formulas which target aid to students requiring special education and vocational education programs. However, while cities generally do not have disproportionate numbers of these types of students, they are heavily burdened by the needs of low-income or disadvantaged students, and of bilingual students. Therefore, state aid programs which recognize poverty or low-achievement levels are often more beneficial to urban districts. States use a variety of approaches in distributing funds to meet these needs: aid to disadvantaged students; poverty adjustments; concentration factors; and density factors.

Targeted Aid for Disadvantaged Pupils. In 1978–79, eighteen states provided categorical aid for compensatory education programs. Some of these states used socioeconomic measures to determine the allocation of funds; others, such as New York and Michigan, used test scores. New Jersey implemented a formula combining both of these measures.

Poverty Adjustments. Nine states allocate additional funds to districts based on the number of students from low-income families *but do not require districts to spend the entitlement on these students.* California, Colorado, Ohio, and Pennsylvania use a flat grant approach. Illinois, Minnesota, Massachusetts, and Missouri incorporate additional weightings for poverty students in their equalization formulas, while Connecticut uses an Aid to Families with Dependent Children (AFDC) count in calculating the number of pupils on which the payment of aid is based.

Concentration Factors. Four of these states have recognized the additional costs facing school districts that educate large numbers of impoverished students by including *concentration* provisions in their "poverty adjustments." In Illinois, districts using the "resource equalizer" formula receive an additional weight of up to 0.675 for each Title I eligible; the weight is based on the concentration of Title I pupils in the district relative to the state average concentration. Similarly the AFDC weighting in Minnesota's foundation aid program, 0.5, is increased for districts with concentrations of AFDC children greater than 6 percent; districts receive an additional 0.1 pupil unit for each percent of concentration greater than 6 percent, up to a maximum weighting of 1.1.

Ohio's Disadvantaged Pupil Impact Aid (DPIA) is distributed to districts based on their concentration of AFDC pupils. In 1979–80, districts with concentrations of less than 18.5 percent received between $10.00 and $30.00 per pupil (in total ADM) of aid, while districts with concentrations greater than 18.5 percent received grants ranging from $112.00 per pupil (18.5 to 22 percent) to $176.50 per pupil (concentration of 38.5 percent or more). In Pennsylvania, districts receive $200 per poverty pupil in "regular" poverty aid, and an additional payment of $30 to $200 per poverty pupil in "super" poverty aid, based on the district's concentration of poverty students.[10]

Density Factors. Two states allocate aid through density factors. Maryland grants an additional $100 per student in aid to school districts having a population density greater than 8,000 per square mile. Currently only Baltimore City qualifies, and two-thirds of these funds must be used for compensatory education purposes. Pennsylvania provides two levels of density aid: districts with a population of 10,000 or more per square mile are allowed a higher reimbursable expenditure limit under the state's percentage-equalizing formula (density aid); districts with this density and a larger student population (in excess of 35,000 weighted pupils) receive the equivalent of 21 percent of their instructional expenditures times their aid ratio (super density aid).

Aid for Bilingual and Bicultural Education. Fifteen states shown in Table 4–3 provided funds to support bilingual or bicultural education programs in 1978–79. Several urban states, notably, Pennsylvania and Ohio, did not aid these programs.

Municipal Overburden Adjustments

Only one state in the country, Michigan, includes direct municipal overburden aid in its state aid program. This program is designed to reduce the level of local taxation required for schools in districts where local nonschool operating tax rates exceed the state average by more than 25 percent. Adjustments are made to the district's per pupil dollar guarantee so that a given level of school tax effort can raise more dollars of state education aid than in nonmunicipally overburdened districts.

Policymakers in Connecticut considered incorporating a direct noneducation tax overburden adjustment into their school aid formula in 1979. This factor would have adjusted each district's effort measure in the state's GTB formula by the ratio of a town's total tax rate (municipal and education) to the state average town total tax rate, if this ratio exceeded 1.0.

Several of the adjustments discussed earlier in this chapter provide indirect municipal overburden aid: per capita fiscal capacity measures; density aid; and, in some states, poverty aid. As noted, the use of a per capita wealth measure in an education aid formula recognizes the high nonschool service demands in cities which can limit the resources available for education. In Pennsylvania and to some extent in Maryland, population density aid programs are designed to provide urban districts with extra funds not directly related to the educational needs of the districts. The density factor in Colorado's formula allows Denver to participate in the state's equalization program with a lower local tax rate than is required of other, less densely populated, districts. This approach is similar to that used in the Michigan municipal overburden adjustment. Finally, some poverty adjustments, such as Ohio's DPIA and Pennsylvania's poverty aid, have been considered municipal overburden aid. The funds are not earmarked, and in both states they supplement categorical aid programs for educationally disadvantaged students.

Cost of Education Differential Adjustments

Three states currently recognize price differentials in their state aid formulas. Florida's district cost differential, which is probably the best known of the three, is applied to each district's total program cost before local effort is subtracted to determine state aid. The index, which is based on the Florida Price Level Index, ranged from a low of 0.9412 to a high of 1.0716 in 1978–79. In Alaska, the number of instructional unit allotments allowed a district under its foundation program range to 155 percent of the basic allotment according to the geographical region in which the district falls. Finally, under Washington's recent reform law, the "guarantee level" for each district varies in part due to differences in salary levels for both certificated and classified personnel. However, the legislation also included provisions intended to equalize these salaries across districts over a period of time.

The Impact of Urban Adjustments

It is difficult to quantify how much additional state aid is generated by the urban adjustments noted in Table 4–3. Many of the fiscal capacity and cost adjustments were part of larger finance reforms which substantially increased state support of education apart from these specific factors. And many states which distribute "education overburden" aid through weightings in their general aid formulas do not report how much of this aid is generated by each category of special needs students. One can look, however, at the proportion of state aid earmarked for educationally disadvantaged and bilingual students in those states that use categorical aid programs. In most cases, these funds represented no more than 5 percent of state current operating aid in 1978–79.[11] New York State, which provides additional weights for educationally disadvantaged students in its general aid formula, also distributed only 4.4 percent of its operating aid through this weighting. In Pennsylvania, however, poverty and density aid represented nearly 17 percent of the state's 1980–81 basic instruction subsidy. It is reported that nearly 20 percent of Illinois's equalization aid is generated by the Title I weightings in the formula (Lundeen et al. 1980).

Although these programs represent a small fraction of general state aid to education, they can have a more substantial impact on the cities' state aid revenues. In Maryland, for example, density aid and compensatory education aid represented only 3 percent of the state's education aid payments but provided 11 percent of Baltimore City's state funds. Similarly, 14 percent of Newark's state aid in 1979–80 was for special-needs pupils, while New York State's PSEN weightings generated 8 percent of New York City's state aid dollars. In Pennsylvania, however, density and poverty aid account for nearly 60 percent of Pittsburgh's and 45 percent of Philadelphia's state aid payments.

In summary, states have developed a variety of adjustments to their state aid formulas which are designed to address the special educational problems of urban school districts, and of districts with similar characteristics: inadequate definitions of fiscal capacity; educational overburden; municipal overburden; and cost of education differentials. In most cases, these adjustments account for only a small proportion of state education aid allocated to all districts. These funds are generally inadequate to compensate for either the greater educational or fiscal needs of large city school systems, or for the insufficient flow of equalization aid to those urban districts with above-average property valuations.

POLICY QUESTIONS

States employ a variety of adjustments, with widely differing price tags, to direct additional state aid into urban school districts. How does a policymaker decide which of these approaches is the most suitable for a state? There are three basic questions one must address: (1) Will the cities in the state receive more aid under a particular adjustment? This is largely a function of the relative fiscal capacity of the urban districts and the way in which the adjustment is structured. (2) Are the data required to calculate the adjustment readily available by school district boundaries, or do suitable proxies for these data exist? (3) Will the distribution of aid under the adjustment be politically acceptable?

Will Cities Benefit?

A number of factors can limit the extent to which urban-oriented adjustments help cities. First, there are many situations where cities will not benefit from an income adjustment to a per pupil property wealth measure. If the adjustment modifies property wealth by a ratio of district income to state average income, districts with *above*-average incomes will not receive more aid, unless that adjustment is keyed to a higher income level—often an expensive proposition. (Of the thirty major urban districts shown in Table 4–1, eighteen had per capita incomes which exceeded the state average in 1976.) Adding two wealth measures together, as is done in Maryland, can sometimes hurt low-income cities like Baltimore. Also, cities can appear relatively wealthier or poorer on an income measure, depending upon the definition of income used. Urban districts will generally look wealthiest on a per pupil income measure and poorest using a household denominator.

An adjustment which does not penalize cities with above-average incomes is to modify property wealth by a measure of poverty, thus recognizing the *distribution* of income in cities. As noted earlier, although many cities appear relatively wealthy on an average income measure (such as per capita income), they have large concentrations of poor households. For example, New York City's per capita income was 101 percent of the state average in 1976, yet 25 percent of its households had incomes of less than $5,000 that year (see Ciano 1980).

Second, if a city's state aid ratio is already high due to its low relative wealth, any modification to that district's fiscal capacity will yield only marginal increases in state aid. For example, the large cities in New Jersey have such low property valuations that they receive, on the average, more than three-quarters of their aidable expenditures in state aid. Adjusting the fiscal capacity measure to reflect low incomes, poverty, or even adopting per capita measures, would only incrementally increase the states' share of these districts' expenditures. In this case, a more profitable approach would be to increase categorical aid rather than reduce fiscal capacity.

Third, adjustments to the denominator of the fiscal capacity measure which reflect special educational needs also can have their pitfalls. For example, it is argued in New York State that the inclusion of weightings for handicapped and educationally disadvantaged students reduces New York City's wealth measure, thus generating more state aid. Yet these weightings also reduce the state average per pupil wealth against which New York City's fiscal capacity is compared. Therefore, although weightings drop the city's wealth measure by $20,000 per pupil, its relative wealth decreases only 2 percent, from 114 to 112 percent. This occurs for two reasons: with nearly one-third of the state's students, New York City "drives" the state average; and most of the students who receive weightings (high school students and special education students) are equally distributed throughout the state. The use of weightings in the denominator of Illinois's fiscal capacity measure is more successful (from the urban perspective) because the primary weighting is for Title I students (who are concentrated in the cities), and the guaranteed tax base level is fixed by legislation rather than representing the statewide average wealth.

Finally, even categorical aid programs designed to aid special student populations concentrated in urban areas can have differential effects on the cities. For example, in many states this aid is allocated through the equalization aid formula using weightings. If a city has a high per pupil property valuation, however, it will receive only limited amounts of special needs aid, generally less per pupil than districts with less of an educational overburden. Another issue concerns the criteria used to distribute aid to educationally disadvantaged pupils. Cities generally have a larger proportion of their state's impoverished students than of their low-achieving students. Thus an aid formula which allocates aid based on test scores will generally provide less aid to the cities than one based on poverty.

Are the Necessary Data Available?

One common complaint among policymakers is: "We can't use this adjustment because we don't have the data for calculating it." Some states do not have a state income tax; many of those that do, do not collect income data by school district boundaries. Other states have not implemented statewide testing programs. Most cannot collect corresponding figures on school and nonschool expenditures. In most states, these are reasons enough to drop the notion of an income adjustment, a municipal overburden adjustment, or aid to educationally or economically disadvantaged students. However, Connecticut has used an income adjustment in its state aid formula for several years without levying a state income tax. Michigan's formula includes an adjustment for high nonschool tax rates; yet school district and municipal boundaries are not coterminous.

Often states can draw on alternative sources of data, or develop proxies for data which are not available. For example, those states in the Northeast and in the South, where school district boundaries are coterminous with municipal or county jurisdictions, can use income data published by the U.S. Bureau of the Census, as does Connecticut (see Coley 1978). In Michigan, school districts apply for municipal overburden aid and are responsible for reaggregating the necessary data along school district lines. Other states use population density as a proxy for municipal overburden; current population figures for most districts with high densities (cities) are available from the U.S. Bureau of Census on a regular basis. Other proxies for high urban service needs could be poverty, size, or property density (see Berke et al. 1981).

Is the Adjustment Politically Feasible?

A third issue that policymakers must address is which, if any, of the proposed urban adjustments is the most politically acceptable. In some states, such as Florida and Connecticut, urban legislators are well organized and influential in the development of school finance policies. In others, such as New Jersey, representatives from the cities are greatly outnumbered by their suburban and rural colleagues. Each adjustment yields a different distribution of aid, benefiting different types of districts. The choice of an adjustment will reflect the type of political coalition needed to support the change.

Some adjustments, such as density aid, provide additional funds only to a small number of urban districts. Per capita fiscal capacity measures can benefit not only cities but other districts with below-average enrollment ratios. Income factors and poverty adjustments generally help rural districts, as well as cities. Cost-of-education indices tend to have a regional impact; that is, suburbs usually share the same higher prices as the central city that they surround. Categorical aid for special education and vocational education programs will be distributed more evenly around a state than aid for economically disadvantaged students. Compensatory education aid distributed on the basis of the socioeconomic status of students will be more concentrated in cities than aid distributed on the basis of low test scores.

Sometimes an adjustment which initially benefits cities is revised in order to provide a broader distribution of aid. For example, the original weighting for Title I students in Illinois's resource equalizer formula ranged from 0 to .75. Districts with average concentrations of Title I students received an additional weight of 0.375; Chicago, with more than twice the average concentration, was allowed a weight of 0.75. The 1978 amendments to the formula increased the weighting for the district with an average concentration to 0.45 (and then to 0.50 in 1979) and reduced the maximum weighting to 0.675. This change effectively shifted poverty aid away from Chicago and the poorest rural districts into those districts with lower concentrations of impoverished students.

In other cases, cities may have the political leverage to manipulate factors in the existing formula to their benefit. For example, in some states urban school districts are helped by declining enrollment relief, as well as no loss provisions, and lobby for these provisions to meet changing demographic conditions.

In short, urban adjustments to school finance formulas are not directly transferable from one state to another. The applicability of any particular approach to a state's finance system will be determined by the interaction of a number of factors: the socioeconomic characteristics of the state's cities; the structure of the adjustment; the availability of pertinent data; and the political environment in which school finance policies are developed.

CONCLUSION

The urban school finance problem persists, in spite of a more active role by state government in the funding of elementary and secondary education.

> Central cities continue to be high tax, high expenditure jurisdictions that are receiving increasing amounts of external aid for their public service needs. Suburbs are facing more tax pressures and expenditure demands than formerly, but they still exhibit relatively low effective tax levels (though the CC/OCC disparity is narrowing) and thus far have avoided extreme noneducational expenditure demands. . . . In short, fiscal disparities continue to be a problem for the nation's largest central cities, despite the greater levels of state and federal aid . . . directed to cities between 1970 and 1977 (ACIR 1980: 17).

Reforms in state school funding programs have benefited urban school districts which have low per pupil property valuations, primarily those in the Northeast and Midwest. Yet the use in some of these states of district power-equalizing formulas, which relate aid to the level of school effort as well as relative property wealth, have restricted the flow of aid to many poor urban centers. Several states have adjusted their education finance formulas to recognize the diminished fiscal capacity, education overburden, municipal overburden, and higher education costs facing the cities. These adjustments, however, generally represent only a small portion of total state education aid and, when coupled with deficient equalization aid programs, are inadequate to meet the problems outlined in this chapter.

Recognizing that traditional school finance remedies do not go far enough in addressing their fiscal problems, cities are now turning to the courts for relief. Following in the footsteps of New York's largest cities, Baltimore filed suit in 1979 and Newark in 1980. It may well be that as *Serrano* set the stage for the school finance reforms of the 1970s, urban court cases will dictate the education finance agenda of the 1980s.

NOTES TO CHAPTER 4

1. For a summary of the intervenors' case, see Scheuer (1979).
2. For information on the urban finance problem generally, see Campbell and Sacks (1967). For applications to state and federal aid, see Riles (1970), Sacks (1972), Berke and Kirst (1972), and Levin and others (1973).
3. Data for this section are drawn from ACIR (1980). For parallel trends in the 1960s, see Riles (1970).
4. The concentration provision in Title I of ESEA is found in P.L. 95–561, Sec. 117 — Grants for Local Education Agencies in Counties with Especially High Concentrations of Children from Low Income Families.
5. See Merget (1981) for data on the period FY 1974 through FY 1978, and U.S. Congress, Joint Economic Committee (April 20, 1980) for data on the period FY 1978 through FY 1980.
6. These figures do not include education expenditures for city school districts that are fiscally independent.
7. Much of the information contained in this section is drawn from Tron (1980). For more detailed information on a state, contact the "state authority" who prepared that state's report for that volume.
8. For a description of Connecticut's education finance formula, see Connecticut State Board of Education (1979).
9. These states are Illinois, Indiana, Minnesota, Missouri, Nebraska, and New York. They include states with foundation programs that apply weightings for poverty or educationally disadvantaged students to foundation guarantees, but not directly to fiscal capacity measures. This approach yields the same results mathematically as using an unweighted foundation guarantee, but applying a weighted pupil count to the wealth measure.

10. Philadelphia and Pittsburgh are limited to $165 per poverty pupil in regular poverty aid and $150 per poverty pupil in super poverty aid.
11. Current operating aid is defined here as total state aid minus aid for teacher pensions and capital outlay and debt service. Figures are drawn from Tron (1980: Table 2).

REFERENCES

Advisory Commission on Intergovernmental Relations (ACIR). 1980. *Central City-Suburban Fiscal Disparity and City Distress, 1977.* Washington, D.C.: U.S. Government Printing Office.

Berke, Joel S. 1974. *Answers to Inequity: An Analysis of the New School Finance.* Berkeley, Calif.: McCutchan Publishing Corporation.

Berke, Joel S., and John J. Callahan. 1972. "*Serrano v. Priest:* Milestone or Millstone for School Finance." *Journal of Public Law* 21 (April): 23-71.

Berke, Joel S., et al. 1981. "Implementing the Urban Mandate of *Levittown v. Nyquist:* An Analysis of Alternative Approaches to Compensating for Municipal Overburden in the New York State Aid Formula." Washington, D.C.: Educational Testing Service. Mimeo.

Berke, Joel S., and Michael W. Kirst. 1972. *Federal Aid to Education: Who Benefits? Who Governs?* Lexington, Mass.: Lexington Books.

Callahan, John J., et al. 1973. *Urban Schools and School Finance Reform: Promise and Reality.* Washington, D.C.: The Urban Coalition.

Campbell, Alan K., and Seymour Sacks. 1967. *Metropolitan America: Fiscal Patterns and Governmental Systems.* New York: Free Press.

Chambers, Jay G. 1980. "The Development of a Cost of Education Index." *Journal of Education Finance* 5, no. 3 (Winter): 262-281.

Chambers, Jay G., et al. 1976. *Cost of Education Indices Among School Districts: An Application to the State of Missouri.* Denver, Colo.: Education Commission of the States.

Ciano, Thomas, et al. 1980. "Measuring Fiscal Capacity in Urban School Districts: Meeting the Urban Mandate of *Levittown v. Nyquist.*" Washington, D.C.: Education Policy Research Institute of Educational Testing Service. Mimeo.

Coley, Richard J. 1978. "A School Finance Researchers' Guide to Personal Income Data for the 50 States." Washington, D.C.: Educational Testing Service. Mimeo.

Connecticut State Board of Education. 1979. *Equity and Excellence in Education.* Hartford, Connecticut.

Levin, Betsy, et al. 1973. *The Higher Cost of Education in Cities.* Washington, D.C.: The Urban Institute.

Levittown v. Nyquist, 408 N.Y.S.2d 606 (Nassau County Supreme Court, 1978).

Lundeen, Virginia, et al. 1980. *The Illinois General Purpose Grant-in-Aid System 1979–80.* Normal, Ill.: Illinois State University.

Merget, Astrid E. 1981. *Coping with the Budget Crunch.* Washington, D.C.: International City Management Association.

Riles, Wilson C. 1970. *The Urban Education Task Force Report: Final Report of the Task Force on Urban Education to the Department of HEW.* New York: Praeger Publishing Company.

Sacks, Seymour. 1972. *City Schools/Suburban Schools: A History of Fiscal Conflict.* Syracuse, N.Y.: Syracuse University Press.

Scheuer, Joan. 1979. "*Levittown v. Nyquist*: A Dual Challenge." *Phi Delta Kappan* 60 (February): 432–436.

Tron, Esther O. 1980. *Public School Finance Programs, 1978–79.* Washington, D.C.: U.S. Government Printing Office.

U.S. Congress, House Committee on Education and Labor. May 11, 1978. *Report No. 95–1137.* Washington, D.C.: 95th Cong., 2d Sess.

U.S. Congress, Joint Economic Committee. April 20, 1980. *Trends in the Fiscal Condition of Cities: 1978–1980.* Washington, D.C.: 96th Cong., 2d Sess.

Wendling, Wayne. 1979. *Cost-of-Education Indices for New York State School Districts.* Denver, Colo.: Education Commission of the States.

5 ALTERNATIVE WEALTH MEASURES

E. Kathleen Adams *
Allan Odden **

INTRODUCTION

The measurement of the fiscal capacity of local school districts is both an elusive and necessary endeavor. It is elusive because, ultimately, these government units have the potential to raise more revenues than they presently do: their capacity, at least in the short run, exceeds their actual efforts. It is necessary because the intent of intergovernmental grants, particularly in education, is to equalize that fiscal capacity. Much thought has been given, therefore, to what constitutes the fiscal capacity, or wealth, of a school district.

Conceptually, fiscal capacity refers to the ability of a government unit to raise tax revenues for a particular public service. Empirically, it is generally measured in relation to the need for the particular service, such as the number of pupils attending public schools. The fiscal capacity of school districts historically has been a measure of property wealth per pupil, which is in juxtaposition to measures of per capita income that are usually used for measuring state fiscal capacity.

Since property taxes are the predominant source of revenue for schools, this measure of local wealth has been readily accepted by

---

* E. Kathleen Adams, Economist, Education Finance Center.

** Allan Odden, Director, Education Programs Division, Education Commission of the States.

143

legislators and used in the design of virtually all school aid programs. Using this sole component to measure fiscal capacity of districts, however, has recently been scrutinized by legislators and researchers, and intensified by the intent and impact of recent court decisions. The result has been a broadened view of what constitutes the fiscal capacity, or ability to raise revenues, of local school districts.

In a sense, the public policy issue of school finance is unique in the attention received from researchers on the issue of fiscal capacity. Growing significance of the states' intergovernmental aid programs for school districts and an explicit goal of reducing spending disparities have induced researchers to develop broadened measures of fiscal capacity by relying on behavioral analyses of school district taxing and spending.

In this chapter, a historical development of this research covering measures of state as well as school district and city fiscal capacity is presented. The approach and research specific to school districts in the many states analyzed are then presented. Two different uses of the research results are discussed. The first is altering present wealth measures either by developing broad indices of fiscal capacity or, more simply, by developing "income factors" to modify property wealth. The second is the simulated impact of the use of broadened wealth measures in alternative school finance formulas. The simulation impacts allow discussion of the policy implications of broadened fiscal capacity measures in terms of the additional costs to the state, the types of districts and pupils affected, and the impact on student and taxpayer equity. A final section includes a speculative discussion on the direction of future research on these issues.

CONCEPTUAL APPROACHES

Most conceptual approaches to defining fiscal capacity are behavioral in nature. In other words, they view the taxing behavior of states, cities, and school districts, and infer from this behavior something about their ability to raise revenues.

An historical view of this work must recognize the importance of the "representative tax system" approach used to measure the fiscal capacity of states by the Advisory Commission on Intergovernmental Relations (ACIR 1971). ACIR noted that "fiscal capacity measures are concerned with the ability of governments to obtain resources for public purposes," but that their potential is different than their actual behavior. The variation in tax sources actually used and the state's relative dependence on each one led ACIR to define fiscal capacity for the states in a way that viewed states "as if" they behaved similarly. ACIR first derived a national average tax rate for each kind of state and local tax used, then estimated the revenue which would be generated from a particular state's tax base at the average rate. The aggregation of these potential tax yields constituted the estimate of each state's total tax capacity.

There are obviously many refinements that can and have been applied to this approach. Adjustments have been made for the actual relative importance of each tax source within a state. Since this approach is specific to one point in time, adjustments also have been made in some measures to account for time trends which create different tax pressures (ACIR 1977). The ACIR study in 1977 reported indices based on rates of change in tax effort, on the premise that residents perceive taxes as more burdensome when they are increasing than when they are stable or falling.

Current approaches to measuring school district wealth are similar to the ACIR approach in two respects: they abstract from the tax sources actually used by school districts and they examine the behavior of those school districts. These approaches can be described as both short-run and long-run in nature. The short-run approaches are specific to one particular time period, whereas the long-run approaches are more dynamic in nature and analyze cumulative impacts.

Under the short-run approach, all factors which are believed to affect the ability and willingness of school districts to raise local tax revenues at one point in time are examined. The researchers of two of the first significant studies of this type (Feldstein 1975; Ladd 1975) used their results to argue for a broadened measure of school district fiscal capacity. The policy focus of Ladd's study was the potential for developing indices of school district wealth that accounted for not only total property wealth but also the composition of the property tax base (residential, commercial, and industrial property), as well as household income.

While, as noted above, the time dimension has been included in the ACIR (1977) measures of fiscal capacity and pressure, this issue is only beginning to be addressed for school districts. Research on city school districts in particular (Aiken and Auten 1976) suggests that the time dimension is important for localities: "fiscal capacity would then be reached when further increases in tax rates gives rise to sufficient evasion, avoidance and emigration by people, wealth and economic activity so that the reduction in tax bases would offset or more than offset rate increases."

In addition to school finance research over a multiple time period, some beginning work to quantify a long-run concept of fiscal capacity has been done for major cities (Gurwitz 1977). Gurwitz's work, moreover, represents another step forward in measuring fiscal capacity in that it attempts to define an absolute rather than relative measure of the fiscal capacity of cities. Gurwitz defined the "maximum sustainable revenue" as that amount of tax revenues a city can raise over an indefinitely long time period, without reducing the level of the tax base. From this, the author defined the "optimal" tax rate in one time period as that which allows the city to obtain this maximum.

Although the ACIR approach to defining fiscal capacity is the most comprehensive, it is difficult to apply to jurisdictions below the state level. For local jurisdictions, such as school districts, which are legally constrained to rely on property tax revenues, the representative tax system may not accurately reflect their ability to raise revenues. Gurwitz further argued that the economic impact of the same institutional tax may be different in different jurisdictional areas. The remainder of this chapter, therefore, covers the research and use of broadened local wealth measures specific to local school districts.

APPROACHES SPECIFIC TO SCHOOL FINANCE

The concern of policymakers and school finance experts for broadening district wealth measures originally grew out of several issues. First, it was argued that low-income persons located in districts with high property wealth were inequitably treated by equalization formulas that focused solely on property wealth. Second, in many states the correlation between median family income and assessed property valuation was found to be low and sometimes negative (Odden 1976). Third, income was considered a comprehensive measure of ability to pay that linked taxes raised to the actual burden placed on school district residents. Ultimately, it was argued, property taxes were paid out of current income.

On the other hand, assessed property was and is the legal tax source for school districts. Second, it is an immobile asset which, given certain market conditions, reflects the value of the rental income that could be obtained from it. Current interests in alternative wealth measures, noted by Odden (1976), were the potential use of per capita, as opposed to per pupil, wealth measures and some kind of "income factor." Some type of combination of property wealth and income was viewed as the way to broaden the district wealth measure.

This thinking and the court decisions in the early seventies gave impetus to much of the research done on the fiscal response of school districts. Economists began to redefine the fiscal capacity of school districts based on results from fiscal response research. This research was based on a model that hypothesized that education expenditures per pupil were a function of

- Property wealth;
- Composition of property wealth or the ability to export property taxes;
- Household income;
- Need as measured by the number of students needing special services;
- Intergovernmental aid from state and federal levels;
- Price differences for education resources;
- Community preferences for education; and
- Differences related to technology, such as scale of district operation.

Feldstein (1975) conducted one of the pioneering studies. He interpreted the *Serrano v. Priest* decision in the most technical sense possible.[1] He felt the decision called for "categorical equity," that is, particular categories of services, such as education, were deemed as "fundamental interests" whose consumption could not be allowed to differ substantially or bear a strong relation to an individual's ability to pay. Feldstein's analysis was on local property wealth adjusted by the statistical relationship between it and *all* other factors, economic as well as noneconomic, that affect spending[2]: income; percent residential property; state and federal aid; measures of public and private enrollments; and a pupil growth rate. This use of all explanatory factors in developing a broadened wealth measure is unique to Feldstein.

Feldstein's work gave rise to additional research (Adams 1979a, 1980a; Carroll and Park 1979; Ladd 1975; Lovell 1978; Vincent and Adams 1978) and comment (Black, Lewis, and Link 1979, 1980; Wentzler 1980). These studies analyzed data in nearly one-third of the fifty states.

Approaches somewhat different from Feldstein's which also use the research results to develop a fiscal capacity measure involve a focus only on the major economic factors affecting local fiscal behavior. These include some measure of property wealth per pupil household income, and tax base composition (Adams 1979a; Ladd 1975).[3] While these factors are only a subset of all the factors included in the analyses, as Aiken and Auten (1976) noted, income, wealth, and the potential for tax exporting are the primary variables that affect community budget constraints. The potential for residents of local school districts to export taxes is determined primarily by the amount of nonresidential property value located within the district.

The results of the studies which focus on the impact of these three variables are consistent in regard to their impact. Both household income and residential property value have positive and significant impacts on variations in expenditures per pupil. The impact of the ability to export taxes, as measured by the percentage of nonresidential property (Adams 1979a, 1980a; Vincent and Adams 1978), also has a positive impact on expenditures. Although the relative importance of these factors differs somewhat among the states studied, the presence and direction of the impact have been confirmed by studies in all states.

In general, the studies have found that property wealth per pupil is the most important factor in causing variations in expenditures per pupil, with household income being the second most important. This was true for Colorado, Minnesota, Wisconsin, Maryland, and Kansas. In New York, however, the impact of residential property wealth and income were fairly equal on a dollar basis; differences in $100 of wealth and income led to approximately $1 in expenditure per pupil differences. The overall variation in property wealth among districts is significantly greater, however, than the variation in income.

In a study of Connecticut districts, however, Lovell (1978) found that median family income was more important than the per pupil property tax base in explaining the variation in education expenditures per pupil. His study also included a measure of the distribution of income within the community. The more unequal the distribution, the higher the expenditures per pupil since the median voter faces a lower tax price in such communities (Lovell 1978: 493).

The impact of the ability to export taxes estimated by these studies is as expected: the greater the relative portion of a district's tax base held by nonresident voters[4] (that is, the greater the ability to export local taxes to persons outside the school district), the greater the expenditures on public education, all other characteristics held constant. The best treatment of this factor and its relation to defining measures of school district fiscal capacity is provided by Ladd (1975). Her major contribution is the identification of the separate and individual impact on expenditures of the residential, commercial, and industrial components of a district's property tax base.

The results of these studies have been used to develop indices that adjust the property wealth measure by the separate but independent effects of the other two variables. As Ladd (1975) noted, the method used by herself and others "can only be justified in relation to the purpose for which the fiscal capacity concept is used"—the equalization of expenditure levels among districts.

Since Ladd separated the impacts of each component of the property tax base, she developed the most comprehensive index. Rather than simply measuring a district's wealth in terms of total property valuation, she argued for a measure which weights the components according to their actual impact on spending. Income is also included in her analysis. An abbreviated algebraic description of the index developed by her for Massachusetts school districts follows:

$$FC_i = \left(\frac{Y_i}{Y_a}\right)^{\gamma} \left(\frac{R_i}{R_a}\right)^{\beta} \left(\frac{r_a}{r_i}\right)^{\delta}$$

where

Y_i = measure of household income in ith district,

Y_a = statewide average household income,

R_i = residential market value per pupil in ith district,

R_a = statewide average residential market value,

r_a = statewide average percent residential property,

r_i = percent residential property in ith district, and

γ, β, δ are regression coefficients from the analysis of expenditure variations.

Such an index combines the three primary fiscal capacity factors and weights them according to their relative impact on expenditure variations. The higher the district's residential property wealth and income, the higher its index value. Conversely, the higher the percentage residential property, the lower its index.

Although this is a technical measure, derived from a one-year statistical analysis, Ladd's findings for Massachusetts school districts are informative. When the behavioral index is compared to an index using total market value per pupil, the usual measure used in school finance equalization formulas, Ladd concludes that the latter may overstate fiscal capacity in low-income, highly industrialized communites and in communities with a high incidence of poverty. While the weighting scheme suggested by her statistical approach is difficult to translate into actual usage, the direction for relative weightings could be helpful to policymakers.

Whether the index or adjustment to property wealth is additive or multiplicative depends on the type of statistical analysis used to analyze the behavior of school districts. A linear statistical analysis provides results that can be best used to develop an additive factor. A log–linear statistical analysis, on the other hand, provides results that can be best used to develop a multiplicative factor. Log–linear analysis has proved more robust statistically (Adams 1980a) and is used by most researchers.

The work by Ladd and most others suggest a combination of factors in a multiplicative manner. Several states, including Connecticut, Missouri, and Rhode Island, presently combine property wealth and income in this manner. Analyses similar to Ladd's, but using linear statistical tests, have been used to suggest additive adjustments to property wealth measures (Adams 1979b; Vincent and Adams 1978). Kansas, Maryland, and Pennsylvania presently combine property and income in an additive manner. In the former two, wealth and income have equal weights; in Pennsylvania, property is weighted more than income.

Although most of the studies mentioned above focus on property wealth and current household income as two important explanatory variables, those two variables are not considered equal from a conceptual economic basis. Using a nonbehavioral approach, McMahon (1978) developed a conceptual basis for combining property wealth and current income which, it turns out, is additive in nature. Since property wealth reflects the value of a stream of income over the lifetime of an asset, and current income is only a measure of monies received from human or other capital in a one-year period, McMahon developed a method for combining property wealth and current income in one time period by converting current income to a permanent income measure.

His formula for district wealth at time t is

$$W_t = Y_{pt} + Y^e_{pt} + kA_t$$

where

Y_{pt} = current personal income from human capital and financial assets,

Y^e_{pt} = the present value of expected future income from these,

A_t = net assets, and

k = factor to convert property to market value where under assessed.

When he estimated the factor which would convert personal income[5] to an estimated lifetime stream, the following equation emerged:

$$W_t = (1 + 13.9) Y_{pt} + kA_t$$

This equation is not dissimilar to that derived by Vincent and Adams (1978). Both approaches combine property wealth and income in an additive manner, with a heavy weighting on the current income measure.

Three of the states that use "income factors" or have considered them, add income and property wealth. In so doing, they have faced the issue of their relative weighting. In most instances, the weighting with the strongest political acceptance was finally used. However, both the McMahon (1978) and Vincent and Adams (1978) research approaches can provide substantive justifications for the relative weightings. Indeed, in a study of Maryland, Adams (1979a) found that current income could be weighted eleven times that of property, based on their respective behavioral roles. This weighting was derived from the analysis of fiscal response of Maryland school districts, using the regression coefficients on Maryland household income and state equalization aid. The purpose of using these coefficients is to set aid differences among districts in relation to their differences in household income so as to neutralize exactly for the impact of household income on expenditures (Vincent and Adams 1978: 20-21). The adjustment suggested from this analysis of historical behavior is consistent with McMahon's 1978) conceptual approach in the relative weighting given to current income.

APPLICATION TO SCHOOL FINANCE PROGRAMS

The use of the behavioral approach in analyzing school district fiscal response or capacity has, in general, resulted in the recommendation of an income factor in a school aid formula. This adjustment, as noted, can be made in several ways, each having different effects and evoking different political reactions. In this section, the operational and political problems that a state faces when incorporating an income factor are discussed. An example of an operational problem is what divisor of income to use. Should it be per household or per pupil? An illustration of the political considerations is the number and type of state aid "losers" that result when an income factor is adopted. Also, the actual experience of those states that have implemented an income factor, as well as a state that is considering one, is discussed.

Operational and Political Considerations

Any state that considers the use of an income factor has a number of operational decisions to make. The appropriate divisor and weighting for the income factor are relevant operational problems.

While a median family income measure is the best indicator of the income level of households, some argue that an income per pupil measure reflects the capacity side, or income of the school district, as well as the need side, or number of pupils. A median family income measure has been used by those using a behavioral approach to defining fiscal response and capacity (Adams 1979a; Ladd 1975), on the rationale that if one purpose of state aid is to counteract the ability and preferences of the median voter to spend on education, median family income is the appropriate measure. The use of a per pupil or a per capita income measure, therefore, is misleading in that it would not describe the budget constraint of this median voter. State aid may not be effective, therefore, in reducing expenditure variation. Moreover, a variable which measures family income is usually the variable which performs best, statistically. In New York, for example, per pupil and per capita measures were tested for comparison, but the household income figure was the strongest statistically (Adams 1979b).

Comparisons of the impact of the various divisors for property wealth are well known (see Odden 1976). Many of these effects also hold for income measures. Per capita income measures decrease the apparent relative wealth of a district when it is a large populous area. Alternatively, per pupil measures increase the apparent wealth or capacity of a district when there is a lower proportion of the population in public schools. This is true in areas with small family size and a large proportion of pupils in private schools, often characteristics of large urban areas. The relative standings of school districts, obviously, can be significantly altered simply by using a different divisor for the income measure.

The weighting of income versus property is another issue that emerges when a broadened fiscal capacity measure is developed. In those states that have adopted income factors, an equal weighting usually has been given to the two measures. While research results can also guide this decision, the implied weight for income can be so large, such as was the case for Maryland, that the adjustment may cause a shift in the distribution of state aid that is too radical.

Whatever the particular type of change, a state will encounter political pressures from districts whose wealth is seemingly altered overnight by the adoption of an income factor. The strongest political aversion to altering wealth measures in a formula involves dealing with aid losers. The effect of an income factor on the relative fiscal capacity of districts may be predictable but that does not necessarily make it appealing.

One method of dealing with this political dilemma of losers is to create an index of fiscal capacity relative to the highest income district. All districts below the highest income are deemed less wealthy, their capacity is adjusted accordingly, and they are eligible for more state aid.

A recent change in Connecticut's income factor took this latter approach. It was felt that the previous income adjustment, which compared a district's median family income to the state average, had too large an impact on school aid. As a consequence, the state now uses the ratio of each district's per capita income to the highest district's income. This approach, however, costs the state significantly more money to fund the formula. In a sense, the political problem of aid losers has been translated into a fiscal problem, an increase in costs.

In New York, a special task force studying school finance has considered a number of income factors. Originally, the factors were defined relative to the statewide average, but in present simulations the income adjustment is defined relative to the income of the district at the 75th percentile.

A final concern which evokes political interest is that of individual versus district equity. Many people expect school finance equity on a district basis to result in individual taxpayer equity. This is not necessarily the case. The fact is that there are low-income persons located in districts of both high property wealth and low property wealth. An income factor in the school aid formula adjusts aid to a school district on the basis of some measures of average income for the district. For districts with high property wealth and high average income, the loss in aid would mean relatively higher school taxes and lower education services. Opponents of income factors argue that low-income persons located in this type of district are adversely affected by such a policy. In addition, horizontal equity among individual taxpayers is not achieved by such a policy.[6]

The counterpoint to such reasoning is that a policy tool directed at the district level is not intended to, nor can it, address individual issues. A policy tool which impacts individuals equally with respect to income, regardless of location, is needed to solve such a problem. Many states have resorted to circuit breaker programs of property tax relief in conjunction with changes in school finance in order to ameliorate individual inequities. Circuit breakers are generally targeted on low-income individuals overburdened by property taxes.

General Impacts of Income Factors

The three states of Missouri, Rhode Island, and Connecticut use multiplicative income factors which modify some part of their formula, either the measure of property wealth, or the required tax rate, for example. Three other states, Maryland, Pennsylvania, and Kansas, use additive combinations of wealth and income. The impact, of course, is to alter the aid distribution so that higher income districts receive less aid than would otherwise be distributed to them. This is the basic intent of any such adjustment, but its total impact on the system of state aid can vary greatly depending on a number of details, such as to what the factor is applied, whether it is additive or multiplicative, what denominator is used for the income measure, and so forth, as well as the formula's actual structure.

Most of the states that presently use income factors in their formula implemented them at the same time other changes were made in the school aid formula. It is therefore difficult to decipher the specific impact of the income factor alone on the school aid system. In the late 1960s, Rhode Island was one of the first states to modify the property wealth figure by an income factor. The state used U.S. Census data and multiplied a district's property wealth per pupil by the ratio of its median family income to the state average. In 1975 Connecticut adopted a similar income adjustment but applied it to a measure of property wealth per capita.

Missouri introduced a multiplicative income factor into its formula along with other changes in a 1977 reform. That decision was aided by a simulation model which described the expected impact on the school aid system. The Missouri income factor adjusts the deduction tax rate by the districts' adjusted gross income per return relative to the statewide average.[7] The simulated impact of the income factor at the time of its creation and other changes indicated that it would only marginally reduce expenditure inequalities but significantly impact the fiscal neutrality of the system with respect to both property wealth and income (Odden 1978). A recent study showed that this expected impact did occur; the simple correlation and elasticity of expenditures per pupil and income decreased over the three years studied, 1977 to 1980 (Adams and Odden 1980).

Simulation analyses for Wisconsin make simple assumptions about the fiscal response of school districts to changes in state aid (Nelson 1980). The results are presented "as if" districts use all aid increases for higher school spending and "as if" they used aid increases entirely for tax relief. The income factor analyzed is the ratio of a district's income *per pupil* to the statewide average, multiplied by property wealth per pupil. When districts are categorized by this income measure, 68 percent lose or have little change in aid. However, both the lowest income and the lowest spending, as well as the wealthiest and highest spending districts, have aid increases. Unfortunately, the author does not give measures of the extent to which the income factor affects wealth or income neutrality.

Another impact of this particular income factor is that state aid to Milwaukee, a city of about average property wealth, drops from $513 to $200 per pupil. This results primarily because the income measure is divided by pupils, which tends to increase the relative income standing of an urban area with a low percentage of its total population of school age and in public schools.

THE CASE OF NEW YORK

Although simulated impacts of broadened fiscal capacity measures have been developed before (see Odden 1976) and in a number of states (see Nelson 1980), recent work for a school finance task force appointed by the governor and board of regents in New York provides some of the most comprehensive examples of the use of simulations in a policy reform context. They are used to address some of the major issues related to the use of broadened measures of school district fiscal capacity such as: how the patterns of state aid distribution are altered; how the share of financing education is changed between the local and state levels; and how the broadened measures impact the equity of the structure, both in terms of reducing overall spending disparities and enhancing fiscal capacity neutrality.

Beginning With Policy Research

The process of investigating the potential need for a broadened fiscal capacity measure in a school aid formula can be significantly informed by policy research on the role of economic factors not currently used in an equalization formula, such as income and the ability to export local taxes. This helps to determine the nature and extent of their role in causing disparities in educational expenditures. The results of such research provide the new pieces of knowledge from which a policy debate can proceed.

In New York State, such research was conducted both for one particular school year (Adams 1979b) and for school years over time (Adams 1980b). The results of this research showed that both property wealth and income played major roles in creating disparities in expenditures per pupil among New York school districts both in any one year and over multiple time periods. Furthermore, the research results were stronger when the model was analyzed in log form rather than in linear form, indicating that a multiplicative rather than an additive income factor was appropriate.

While the research model suggested that household income was the conceptually appropriate income factor to analyze, the research also tested the impact of an income per capita, an income per pupil, and a poverty measure. The statistical results indicated that the household income factor, as measured by New York gross income per state income tax return, was the most powerful. Indeed, an income per pupil figure was statistically insignificant in most analyses. Finally, the research results provided information that indicated how each school district would respond to a change in aid received under the formula. In simulating changes in the New York equalization formula, an individualized fiscal response for each district was used rather than a simple assumption that all districts would use the aid in the same manner, either to increase spending or to decrease tax rates or some combination of the two.

The Impact of an Income Factor

The income factor simulated in New York was a multiplicative adjustment that modified a property wealth per pupil measure by a ratio of the district's household income to the income of the district at the 75th percentile.[8] The use of that broadened fiscal capacity measure had three major effects (Odden 1979):

1. The distribution of state aid was changed. Relatively more aid was allocated to low-income districts, most of which were either rural or large city school districts. Relatively less aid was allocated to higher income districts, which tended to be suburban.

2. The cost to the state increased. The decrease in aid to the higher income areas was more than offset by the increase in state aid to the lower income areas. In general, state aid increased statewide by about 10 percent with the addition of the income factor.

3. The equity of the school finance system improved. Not only was the relationship between expenditures per pupil and household income reduced but also the relationship between expenditures per pupil and property wealth was reduced. Furthermore, expenditure disparities themselves were reduced.

Other Policy Concerns

Even though the results of policy research on the role of income can be used initially to design broadened fiscal capacity measures, other measures not indicated by the research results but nevertheless raised in the policy arena can also be analyzed by the simulation process. Previous work by Odden (1976) and Nelson (1980) are examples of this type of analysis. The impact of a variety of other income factors in New York was requested and the results presented in detail (Palaich 1980). Both multiplicative and additive income factors, as well as per capita income and per pupil income adjustments, were analyzed. The results indicated that each adjustment had impacts quite different from one another, both in terms of the distribution of state aid, cost to the state, and impact on the equity of the system. In some cases the differences were dramatic and contradictory. For example, while a household income factor increased aid to the large cities and decreased aid to suburban districts, the per pupil income factor had just the opposite impact. Without research on the impact of various income measures, it would be difficult to select a particular factor on other than political grounds. The research results can be used to make a substantive justification for a particular adjustment, household income in the case of New York. Political considerations, however, can lead to a "fine tuning" of any particular income adjustment.

Simple or Comprehensive

The fiscal response model used to predict local district response to changes in aid is also important in determining the impact of a broadened capacity measure. The common assumption in most simulation activity is that districts will use half the state aid increase to increase spending and half to reduce local taxes. Other assumptions, usually used to provide boundaries of the impact, are that districts will use all the state aid increase for higher spending or all for lower taxes. The fact is that each school district, depending on its socio-demographic characteristics, will have an individual response to a structural change in a school aid formula, including the use of a broadened measure of fiscal capacity.

In New York, the results of using the simple fiscal response assumption of one-half spending increase and one-half tax rate decrease were compared to the results of an individual fiscal response designed from the fiscal response research on data over a multiple time period (Adams 1980b). There were significant differences. As compared to the simple fiscal response assumption, the results for the individual fiscal response showed that:

1. The state cost increased, which means the simple assumptions are inaccurate in measuring the behavior of local school districts.

2. The use and distribution of state aid differs by school district fiscal characteristics. Low-income and low-spending districts tend to respond more strongly to the revised formula, increasing their spending with more local funds and using nearly all state aid increases to increase spending. A fifty-fifty pattern holds for only the districts in the middle income and wealth ranges, while the use of aid for more spending rises above the 50 percent level in the upper income and wealth ranges.

3. As a result of these patterns, the simulated impact indicates that the equity of the overall structure is further enhanced.

Conclusions

The issue of broadened fiscal capacity measures for state public school equalization aid formulas has received substantial attention over the past five years. Research results from nearly one-third of the states indicate that, whether taxed locally or not, household income, property wealth, as well as the composition of the property tax base, have important and separate roles in creating disparities in expenditures per pupil among school districts. Applied policy research, preferably using data from a number of school years, can estimate the particular roles played by these three variables in a state. The results of such research then can be used to develop broadened fiscal capacity measures that reflect the role of property wealth, the composition of property wealth, and household income. The effect of such a change in measuring school district fiscal capacity can then be identified through simulating alternative uses of such a broadened measure, again using the research results to estimate an individual fiscal response to a structured change in the aid formula. Such simulations usually indicate that broadened wealth measures improve the equity of the system along three lines: (1) reducing disparities in expenditures per pupil themselves; (2) reducing property-wealth-related expenditure disparities; and (3) reducing disparities related to family income.

FUTURE DIRECTIONS

The state-of-the-art in developing alternative fiscal capacity measures for school districts has progressed significantly in the last decade. The index approach to calculating a broadened wealth measure offered by Ladd (1975) is perhaps the most operational use of the results of fiscal response research. Her index combines residential, commercial, and industrial property with a measure of household income, using weights derived from a regression analysis.

Another way to use her results would be to weight the value of commercial, industrial, and residential property and determine a weighted property value figure. For example, if the weight for residential property were set at 1.0, the weights for commercial and industrial property suggested by her research would be 1.26 and .55, respectively. This weighted value of property could then be adjusted by an income factor. This approach may be used in future school finance research and policy reform efforts.

While this approach is a viable one in the context of desired equity goals and the use of property taxes to fund public schools, it has a weakness, but one inherent in using the results of any behavioral approach. The weightings are statistical estimates of the average behavior of all school districts, which is usually not indicative of the behavior of any one particular district. The weightings may, therefore, under- or overestimate the actual impact of these fiscal factors on any one district.

This problem is one reason why Gurwitz (1977) developed a measure of city fiscal capacity that accounts for the unique *local* impact of all sectors of the economy. In other words, the sources of income to firms and households that determine the revenues that a school district can raise are of a different type and weighting in large urban economies than in suburban and small rural areas. The Gurwitz approach to fiscal capacity should constitute one component of future developments in fiscal capacity research, although its highly technical nature makes it difficult to operationalize.

Further, the Gurwitz approach to measuring capacity should be evaluated by its intended use. The policy focus of Gurwitz's specific work is the growth of the economic activity of major cities. Gurwitz's policy objective is to determine the optimal tax rate for a city area, one which does not retard the growth of its economic base. This approach, therefore, is limited in its application to school districts as jurisdictions, since schools constitute just one use of the local property tax. Moreover, this policy focus, to determine optimal tax rates, is different from that of most school finance reform, which is the reduction of differences in expenditures per pupil caused by economic or fiscal capacity factors.

In a sense, the research on school district fiscal capacity to date has been influenced by litigation and state-level policy issues. The research has responded by providing needed analysis and information. One might ask whether the emergence of additional issues will alter its conceptual and operational approaches.

One particular issue is the potential use of other local taxes, such as sales or income, in financing schools. Several states presently allow school districts in urban areas to use nonproperty tax sources of revenue. If all districts begin to use other taxes, should this lead to a new measure of local wealth? Not necessarily, if the major components of a school district's ability to raise revenues are viewed as its residents' wealth, income, and ability to export taxes. The wealth and income of a school district resident obviously affects the district's ability to raise local tax revenues, whatever the source. The ability to export taxes, if property and sales taxes were levied, would need to include the sales tax as well as property tax component; the concern would be to measure the ability to export sales taxes, as well as property taxes. Sales taxes can be exported, for example to nonresident consumers. A measure of this ability and its relative impact then would be a needed factor in the measure of local district fiscal capacity. Resident property wealth, income, and the ability to export taxes constitute a fiscal capacity measure, regardless of the particular tax handle used.

In summary, the consideration of alternative school district wealth measures is extensive. It includes significant research, simulation modeling, and state involvement. Most states, however, have not acted on this issue, partially because of the difficulty in translating the complicated research work into understandable policy terms, and partially because changes in fiscal capacity measures significantly alter the pattern of state aid distribution. The research on fiscal capacity is expanding and produces results that can be used to make more comprehensive evaluations of the wealth neutrality of state school finance structures. In the future, states likely will continue to examine this issue and strike a balance among the conceptual, operational, and political concerns.

NOTES TO CHAPTER 5

1. Feldstein focused on the court's mandate for fiscal neutrality between expenditures per pupil and local wealth. Complete wealth neutrality would mean

$$\alpha_1 = 0$$

where $\alpha_1 = B_w + B_p \, \gamma_{pw}$

and B_w = adjusted wealth elasticity,

B_p = price elasticity,

γ_{pw} = elasticity in price with wealth inherent in DPE formula.

2. Technically, the adjusted wealth elasticity B_w is defined as:

$$B_w = B_1 + \Sigma B_j \, \gamma_{xjw}$$

and B_1 = elasticity of expenditures with respect to property wealth,

B_j = elasticity of expenditures with respect to the jth independent variable,

γ_{xjw} = elasticity of the jth independent variable with respect to property wealth.

3. Only residential property wealth is used in this research as opposed to total property wealth. The nonresidential component reflects the ability to export taxes and enters the analysis as a price variable. For a thorough treatment on this distinction, see Ladd (1975).

4. This is generally approximated by a measure of the amount of commercial and industrial tax base located within the school districts (see Ladd 1975: 147–149), and requires an assumption about the distribution of housing values within the community.

5. McMahon used estimates of the present value of lifetime earnings from the U.S. Bureau of the Census for males by age, race, and educational level. He used these figures, adjusted for percentage of whites versus blacks in the population, to convert average annual current income into estimates of future income.

6. Horizontal equity requires that taxpayers with equal ability be treated equally by a given tax structure.

7. $$t_m = t_s * \left(\frac{\text{AGI}_i}{\text{AGI}_a} + 1 \right) * .05$$

where t_m = modified deduction tax rate,

t_s = standard deduction tax rate,

AGI_i = adjusted gross income per return in the ith district, and

AGI_a = statewide average adjusted gross income per return.

8. The simulated changes included more than just an income factor. Others were changes in the pupil weights for students needing special services and a geographic cost of education index, both developed on the basis of additional policy research (see New York State Special Task Force on Equity and Excellence in Education 1980).

REFERENCES

Adams, Kathleen E. 1979a. *Analysis and Comparison of Fiscal Response in Four States*. Report No. F79-13. Denver: Education Finance Center, Education Commission of the States.

_____. 1979b. "Fiscal Response and Capacity of New York School Districts." Report to the Special Task Force on Equity and Excellence in Education. Denver: Education Finance Center, Education Commission of the States. Unpublished paper.

_____. 1980a. *Fiscal Response and School Finance Simulations: A Policy Perspective*. Report No. F80-3. Denver: Education Finance Center, Education Commission of the States.

_____. 1980b. "Fiscal Response in the New York Simulations." Report to the Special Task Force on Equity and Excellence in Education. Denver: Education Finance Center, Education Commission of the States.

Adams, Kathleen E., and Allan Odden. 1980. "The Relationship Between Property Tax Assessments, Tax Burdens and Missouri School Finance and the Equity Impacts of the 1977 Reform." Report to the School Finance Study

Committee of the State Board of Education. Denver: Education Finance Center, Education Commission of the States.

Advisory Commission on Intergovernmental Relations. 1971. *Measuring the Fiscal Capacity and Effort of State and Local Areas.* Washington, D.C.: ACIR.

_____. 1977. *Measuring the Fiscal "Blood Pressure" of the States 1964–75.* Washington, D.C.: ACIR.

Aiken, John S., and Gerald E. Auten. 1976. "City Schools and Suburban Schools: A Fiscal Comparison." *Land Economics* 54, no. 4 (November): 452–466.

Black, David E.; Kenneth A. Lewis; and Charles K. Link. 1979. "Wealth Neutrality and the Demand for Education." *National Tax Journal* 32, no. 2 (June): 157–164.

_____. 1980. "Wealth Neutrality and the Demand for Education, a Response." *National Tax Journal* 33, no. 2 (June): 239–241.

Carroll, Stephen J., and Rolla Edward Park. 1979. "The Search for Equity in School Finance: Michigan School District Response to a Guaranteed Tax Base." R–2393–NIE/HEW. Santa Monica, Calif.: The Rand Corporation.

Feldstein, Martin S. 1975. "Wealth Neutrality and Local Choice in Public Education." *American Economic Review* 64 (March): 75–89.

Gurwitz, Aaron. 1977. *The Financial Condition of Urban School Districts: A Federal Policy Perspective.* Santa Monica, Calif.: The Rand Corporation.

Ladd, Helen F. 1975. "Local Education Expenditures, Fiscal Capacity and the Composition of the Property Tax Base." *National Tax Journal* 28 (June): 145–158.

Lovell, Michael C. 1978. "Spending for Education: The Exercise of Public Choice." *The Review of Economics and Statistics* 60, no. 4 (November): 487–495.

McMahon, Walter W. 1978. "A Broader Measure of Wealth and Effort for Educational Equality and Tax Equity." *Journal of Education Finance* 4, no. 1 (Summer): 65–88.

Nelson, F. Howard. 1980. "The Distribution Equity of an Income Factor in the State Aid Formula." *Journal of Education Finance* 6, no. 2 (Fall): 201–225.

New York Special Task Force on Equity and Excellence in Education. 1980. "Research Findings and Policy Alternatives: A Second Interim Report." Albany, New York.

Odden Allan. 1976. *Alternative Measures of School District Wealth.* Report No. F76-6. Denver, Colo.: Education Finance Center, Education Commission of the States.

_____. 1978. "Missouri's New School Finance Structure." *Journal of Education Finance* 3, no. 4 (Spring): 465–475.

_____. 1979. "Simulation Results: Third Round." Report to the Special Task Force on Equity and Excellence in Education. Denver: Education Finance Center, Education Commission of the States.

Palaich, Robert. 1980. "Fiscal Capacity Alternatives." Denver: Education Finance Center, Education Commission of the States.

Slack, Enid. 1980. "Local Fiscal Response to Intergovernmental Transfers." *The Review of Economics and Statistics* 62, no. 2 (August): 364–370.

Vincent, Phillip E., and E. Kathleen Adams. 1978. *Fiscal Response of School Districts: A Study of Two States, Colorado and Minnesota.* Denver: Education Finance Center, Education Commission of the States.

Wentzler, Nancy. 1980. "Wealth Neutrality and the Demand for Education: A Comment." *National Tax Journal* 33, no. 2 (June): 237–238.

▌▌ CURRENT STATE SCHOOL SUPPORT PROGRAMS

To provide a context within which to consider the chapters on educational need and fiscal capacity and those on accountability and adequacy, three chapters discuss various aspects of existing state school support programs. The first chapter reviews the range of alternatives in possible programs and summarizes existing state programs for school operation. Selected aspects are discussed and issues identified that may merit consideration.

The other two chapters in Part II provide background information on existing state programs for financing pupil transportation and school facilities. The transportation chapter includes a comprehensive historical discussion of the development of pupil transportation formulas. Both chapters discuss alternative approaches, the present status of state efforts, and policy concerns that should be of interest to fiscal planners.

6 AN ANALYSIS OF STATE SCHOOL SUPPORT PROGRAMS

Orlando F. Furno*
Dexter A. Magers**

INTRODUCTION

For a century various forces have converged to bring about the development of present state school finance programs. These forces represented not only the theories of past school finance greats but also their hopes and dreams. Rather than resulting in a single model for financing schools, state school financing programs have been shaped and molded in diverse ways. The forces reflect the evolving values of a society, for they include political, social, economic, psychological, educational, constitutional, and legislative developments and pressures.

This chapter contains an overview discussion of current state school support plans and also includes material on the evaluation of state school finance plans. To set the stage for the chapter, a brief description has been included of the evolution of state school finance plans, including the contributions of some early school finance pioneers. Next, the discussion focuses on the relative revenue contributions of local, state, and federal levels of government, including the sources of revenue at these three governmental levels. Because of the

---

*Orlando F. Furno, School Finance Specialist, School Finance Branch, U.S. Department of Education.

**Dexter A. Magers, Chief, School Finance Branch, U.S. Department of Education.

importance of taxation on real property to school finance, trends in real property taxation are examined in some detail.

From the selected guiding principles for evaluating state school finance programs, conclusions have been formulated about existing programs. Lastly, issues have been identified that will likely face school finance revisionists in future years.

Portions of the chapter have been drawn from materials prepared by the states in their response to section 842 of Public Law 93–380, and other statements are based on materials in *School Finance Programs 1978–79* published by the U.S. Department of Education.

EVOLUTION OF STATE SUPPORT SYSTEMS

The state–local relationship in school fiscal matters as it is known today evolved from more than a century of debate. The dramatic beginnings of the theoretical basis of the relationship in financing education may be traced to Ellwood P. Cubberley (1905), who first documented the great disparities in the financing of local school programs. Cubberley inferred that these discrepancies resulted from the states' heavy dependence on local property taxes to support education. In his 1905 study, he recommended that the state ensure a minimum program of instruction to all children and also advocated that the state reward the effort of districts aspiring to exceed this minimum. The reward for effort aspect of his program was controversial then and remains so today.

Although Cubberley's (1905) theory was dominant in the early part of the century, other theories were evolving. Harlan Updegraff (1919, 1922) expanded on Cubberley's reward for effort policy and proposed rewarding district effort in terms of local tax rates. Updegraff's plan made it possible, through state aid, for a community of less than average wealth to raise as much money for a given tax rate as would be raised in a community of greater than average wealth. This plan received little or no recognition in 1922 but had a far-reaching impact as can be seen in present aid formulas such as district power-equalizing, guaranteed yield, and percentage-equalizing.

The conceptual basis for current equalization schemes has been credited to George I. Strayer and Robert M. Haig (Mort, Reusser, and Polley 1960). In 1923 Strayer and Haig gave recognition to the fact that the state not only had the right but also the duty to mandate a minimum program. They broke away from Cubberley's "doles to the needy" and placed on the state the responsibility to equalize the financial burden of a foundation program. Strayer and Haig were dealing principally with inequalities of educational opportunities and school support burdens. The unequal burdens resulted from state decisions to operate numerous school districts rather than a single district. By placing the major responsibility for the support of public education at the local level, the state created (1) school districts with varying abilities to support education and (2) school districts varying in the degree to which they would tax themselves to support education. This development created the need for the state to equalize the financial burden to support education and to equalize the educational opportunities afforded children. Strayer and Haig proposed to equalize these burdens through their foundation plan. This equalization was to be achieved by the following plan:

1. A local school tax in support of the satisfactory minimum program would be levied in each district at a rate which would provide the necessary funds in the richest district.

2. The richest district then might raise all of its monies by means of this local tax, assuming that a satisfactory tax, capable of being locally administered, could be devised.

3. Every other district could be permitted to levy a local tax at this same rate and apply the proceeds toward the cost of schools, but—

4. Since the rate is uniform, this tax would be sufficient to meet the costs only in the richest district and the deficiencies would be made up by state subventions (Strayer and Haig 1923: 174–75).

The Strayer–Haig principles were readily used to evaluate state finance plans. Accordingly, early opportunities were provided to find the shortcomings in the Strayer–Haig foundation plan. First, most states lacked the revenue to equalize expenditures up to its richest district. Thus, the foundation program became a minimum rather than a maximum program, or at most an average program of education depending upon where the level of funding was set in relation to the richest district. For poor communities, the foundation level soon became the maximum educational program. Equality of educational opportunities for all children in the state was not realized.

The richer districts were permitted to tax themselves above the foundation level rate and keep the proceeds. The result was the creation of expenditure disparities of such magnitude as to seriously erode the equalization of educational opportunities concept. Moreover, some state aid plans provided large amounts of monies on a flat per pupil basis so that more money was distributed than was required for equalization purposes. These funds went to the richer school districts for "political reasons." Without such grants to these districts, it was reasoned that the state legislatures would not adopt foundation programs or needed revisions to them. Such basic conflicts in the foundation program plan are still not fully resolved today.

Even though the foundation program theory is still dominant today, some states have enacted finance plans which distribute funds based upon guaranteed yield formulas, aid ratio formulas, millage formulas, guaranteed tax base formulas, or combinations thereof. The foundation program theory has many dynamic facets whose implications are still being studied, such as the following:

1. There is clear economic justification for complete equalization of an "adequate" educational program and not just a minimum one.

2. The concept of equalization of the burden of educational support has been expanded to include equalization of tax bases among school districts.

3. The method of computing the cost of the foundation program in terms of weighted pupil units has benefitted from the research of many investigators.

4. The justification for permitting communities to spend beyond the foundation program is being stated not only in terms of its implications for local control but also for its contributions to educational experimentation and change.

5. The adequacy of the level of support for which the state shares responsibility must be sufficiently high to secure a reasonable degree of equality of educational opportunity for all students.

6. Attempts have been made to secure more adequate measures of the relative ability of communities to support education.

7. There is a growing realization that any state aid plan must be analyzed and evaluated in terms of its effects—short- and long-term—upon all school districts against a backdrop of critical

principles such as equalization of educational opportunity, efficiency and effectiveness, economic stability, equalization of support burdens and tax bases, adequacy and comprehensiveness of the educational program, and the establishment of educational goals and objectives.

TRENDS

Revenue for public education comes from local, state, and federal governments. These funds for education are derived primarily from taxes on property, sales, and income. In 1900 of the $214 million spent for public elementary and secondary education, local governments contributed 80 percent, state governments 17 percent, and the federal government 4 percent. Of the $83.0 billion spent for education in fiscal year 1979, local governments contributed $36.8 billion, or 44.3 percent; state governments $38.6 billion, or 46.6 percent; and the federal government $7.5 billion, or 9.1 percent. This trend toward a greater percent from state contributions has been steady during eight decades. The state is now the major contributor and is expected to continue as such.

Local Taxation

Property taxation accounts for over 97 percent of all local revenue for public education. Of the numerous nonproperty taxes available to local jurisdictions, only the sales and income taxes are large revenue producers, but their collection at the local level in most states is not easy. In the future, property taxes will continue to be the mainstay of local revenue for school districts with nonproperty taxes providing only minor support.

Trends in the Property Tax Base. The U.S. Bureau of the Census estimated that the total gross assessed value of taxable property in the United States for 1978 was $1.509 trillion. In comparison, the amount for 1966 was $0.498 trillion—an increase of 203 percent. Although there is considerable lack of agreement concerning procedures to use to develop ratios to convert assessed values to fair market values, the use of a "size weighted or sales-price ratios" method indicated the approximate market value of ordinary taxable realty was $1.277 trillion in 1966 and $3.171 trillion a decade later, a 150 percent increase. It is doubtful that the taxable property base will continue this rate of increase in real value because of preferential use laws, property exemptions, limitations in growth, circuit breakers, and other restrictions.

Trends in Property Tax Base Composition. In 1976 the distribution of total assessed value of locally assessed taxable realty was as follows: (1) single family, 49.9 percent; (2) multifamily, 9.3 percent; (3) acreage, 11.9 percent; (4) vacant platted lots, 3.8 percent; (5) commercial, 16.7 percent; and (6) industrial, 7.4 percent. The percentages in 1976 varied little from those in 1966 for the nation as a whole. However, the composition of the property tax base varied greatly when individual states were compared. The data do not support any inferences for supporting predictions that widespread changes will or will not occur in the property tax base composition. Many influences operate on the composition of the property tax base. Inflation is surely one such factor, but so are legislative prescriptions and proscriptions, reassessment cycle policy, past assessment practices, and value estimation mechanics.

Trends in Property Tax Limitations. In many instances, the attention given to property yields, tax base, burden, assessment performance, and property composition reflects the taxpayer's concerns to limit local taxing and spending. Although the most famous of these limitation endeavors has been California's Proposition 13, limitations on property taxation can be noted in documents in colonial times. Generally, limits on local governments can take many forms. California has limited property taxation to 1 percent of the basic cash value of property. New Jersey limits increases in spending appropriations, subject to certain exemptions, to 5 percent of the previous year's total in the absence of voter approval. Limits related to property taxes are commonly applied to assessments, rates, and levies. For example, Minnesota and Maryland limit assessment increases to specified levels. About thirty-eight states have constitutional or statutory tax rate limits. In the future, it is expected that limitations on assessment increases and tax rates will continue, though the numerical values of these limits will probably change in both directions in accordance with need and the political times.

State Revenue

At the turn of the century, state taxes on property produced over 50 percent of all the revenue needed to operate state governments. Seven decades later, property taxes accounted for slightly over 2 percent of all revenue raised by state governments. In 1970, state governments derived 29.5 percent of their revenue from general sales, use, or gross receipts taxes; 13.1 percent from motor fuel sales; 4.8 percent from tobacco products sales; 3.2 percent from alcoholic beverage sales and licenses; 6.2 percent from motor vehicles and operators licenses; 2.3 percent from state property taxes; 1.4 percent from severance taxes; 27.0 percent from income taxes from individuals and corporations; 10.4 percent from a myriad of other state taxes; and 2.1 percent from death and gift taxes.

As may be deduced from these statistics on state taxes, the three largest sources of revenue for state governments are those from income, general sales, and motor vehicle fuel taxes. Such taxes provide state governments with the revenue they need to support public elementary and secondary education. Of course, another important revenue source for state and local government is the federal government. For example, in 1902 state and local governments received about $7 million from the federal government (Bicentennial 1978: 125–126); in 1970 they received $21.8 billion, and in 1980 they will receive approximately $91 billion (Special Analyses 1981: 241).

Federal Revenue

In 1900, about 44 percent of all federal revenue was derived from customs taxes. In 1971, federal revenues were derived from the following sources: (1) individual income taxes, 46 percent; (2) corporate income and profit taxes, 15 percent; (3) excise taxes, 10 percent; (4) estate and gift taxes, 2 percent; (5) employment taxes, 25 percent; and (6) all other taxes, 2 percent. These statistics indicate that the federal government derives the majority of its revenues from income taxes, employment taxes, and excise taxes. These funds are distributed for public education through numerous grants and other programs.

It is not expected that the federal government will increase its share of financing public education in the near future. Instead, it is more likely that it will decrease its share. Moreover, the grants to public schools will probably be in the form of general block grants and less in the form of specific categorical grants.

CRITERIA FOR EVALUATION

The people of the various states have had a long history of concern for effective public education which began long before the constitutional convention was held during the Revolutionary War. Throughout the past two centuries, the concern for effective public education could be discerned in various ways. For instance, the states' numerous commissions would convene and, within a large array of mandates, laws, regulations, and statutory provisions, would study and reform school finance programs. As complex as these arrangements seem today, their roots were firmly grounded in participatory democracy and the well-being of the individual.

Guidelines for Evaluation

The reform or evaluation of a state school finance program should meet several fundamental tests: (1) funds should not be distributed by the state in such a way that the education of a pupil is dependent upon the wealth of a district rather than the wealth of the state; (2) the state should recognize that equal dollars per pupil does not ensure equal educational opportunity; (3) the burden of supporting educational programs should not fall unequally upon different groups of taxpayers; and (4) the burden of supporting educational programs should not fall solely or unequally upon one class of wealth. Meeting these conditions does not necessarily require state legislatures to spend more money for education. In light of these concerns for equity, some guiding principles were published in connection with Section 842, "Assistance to the States for State Equalization Plans," which can be used in the evaluation of state finance plans and programs. These equity guidelines and references to similar items in other literature are discussed below.

Program Neutrality.[1]   This principle embodies the concept that state funds should not be distributed in such a way that financial support shifts from one educational program to another unless so designed.

Program neutrality can often be violated through program mandates not purposely incorporated into the distribution formula. Low expenditure limitations with low foundation program levels often have this effect. For example, program weights should not be designed so that aid for the regular instructional program is diverted to operate special programs or vice versa.

Fiscal Neutrality.[2]   This principle has two aspects associated with it. The first refers to taxpaying equity; the second, to per pupil expenditure equity. State school finance programs should be developed so that the formulas result in equal tax burdens and in foundation program expenditure levels within predetermined tolerances. This implies equalization of both tax burdens and tax efforts.

Local Control.[3]   Local control refers to the principle that the financing program should place the authority over educational programs and expenditures as close to the pupils and their parents as possible. It also presumes an efficient school district and regional organization.

Equality of Educational Opportunity.[4]   Reflected in this principle is the concept that each child have equal access to an instructional program suited to his or her own learning potential and that such programs be of similar quality and breadth within reasonable tolerances. It does not necessarily mean equal dollars per pupil nor equal dollars per program. A state school finance program should not favor one child at the expense of another nor deny any child an opportunity available to another.

Justice (Financial Equity).[5]   This principle applies to the first aspect of fiscal neutrality, namely taxpaying equity, but among individuals rather than among school districts. It also implies that the burden of taxation for public education should not fall excessively upon one class of individual taxpayers.

Fiscal Variability.[6]   This principle recognizes that a state school finance program can embody both general equalization formulas, categorical equalization formulas, and nonequalization categorical formulas. However, recognition of this principle does not imply that the other guidelines may be greatly violated.

Political Feasibility. [7] This principle can probably best be communicated by a quote from *The Wall Street Journal* (1977) "... it's a general rule of administration that if you organize any enterprise on the basis of a single principle, like equality, you create an absurd situation for all other principles. ... Balancing contradictory principles is the job of the state legislatures" ("Review and Outlook" 1977: 16).

Criteria for Evaluating Formulas

These criteria are neither new nor novel, nor are they the result of critical analysis of the authors. In the main, these are criteria of effectiveness. Over the years, these criteria appear to have gained the general approval of specialists in school finance (see Furno 1961; Woollatt 1952).

Objectivity. All data entering the various state school finance program formulas should be uniform, accurate, and objective to the degree that is necessary for yielding only one correct answer to any person who calculates the value of state aid for each formula.

Data Availability. The data needed in the state's school finance program formulas should be easily obtainable from the local school districts and at a reasonable cost.

Practicality. The time and money required first to compute state aid for each formula and, second, to maintain and audit the data should be commensurate with the results. Local school districts should know with certainty what their state aid for each formula will be at the time such districts are required to submit their budgets for voter, town, or city approval. This objective implies that the state legislature will enact state aid legislation upon a timely basis each year.

Simplicity. Each formula in the state school finance program should be constructed in the simplest possible terms consistent with validity and objectivity. The state aid formula should be easily understood.

Flexibility. The formula should be developed in such a way that adequate provisions are made for accommodating major program cost variations due to changes in price and not changes in the quality and quantity of the program.

Economy and Efficiency.   The distribution of state funds should not require an excessive number of persons, equipment, or money. State funds should be distributed in such a way that neither local districts nor state departments of education are overly burdened.

As stated earlier, state school finance specialists have been echoing these principles and criteria for evaluating school finance programs for years. Johns (1977) proposed such goals as follows: (1) the finance program should result in substantial equalization of educational opportunities throughout the state; (2) the finance program should be fiscally neutral; (3) the school program should be financed by an equitable taxation system; (4) the school finance program should promote the efficient use of school funds; and (5) the finance plan should preserve local control of education and promote local initiative for improvement of the educational program.

Charles Benson (1977), speaking on state school finance reform, discussed a procedure for automatically adjusting a state's foundation program (the principle of adjustability), equalizing tax bases (the principles of tax equity and fiscal justice), and instituting local control over expenditures at the building level by principals (the principle of local control).

The Phi Delta Kappa Commission on Alternative Designs for Funding Education (1973) proposed a school finance model encompassing fiscal neutrality and equalization of educational opportunity. The proposed model was assumed to meet most of the criteria and guidelines enumerated here. A primary assumption was that the model would be "properly developed and implemented."

The Association of Flat Grant School Districts of New York State (1977) also advocated adherence to a number of principles in the distribution of state funds to local districts. The Association called for local control of education and for "changing the present New York State financing system, but in ways that are fair, just, equitable, and efficient." The Association also called for equal educational opportunities and equitable treatment of all taxpayers in the state, defining this treatment as follows: (1) the financial ability and needs of districts should be measured more fairly and more comprehensively; and (2) each district should make a reasonable effort in taxing itself.

As noted earlier, to develop and implement a state school finance plan based upon one or two principles will ultimately lead to chaos. The state's plan should be based upon balanced judgment. Interestingly, not until Strayer, Haig, and Mort meshed together the principles of justice, equality of educational opportunity, fiscal neutrality, adaptability, taxpayer equity, and political feasibility was great progress made in financing the public schools by the various state legislatures. Consideration of all these principles was not just a compromise but a judicious application of balanced judgment. Alexis de Tocqueville, the distinguished observer and commentator on early American life and democracy, although obsessed with the principle of equality, recognized the potency of balancing many forces and principles in making decisions to resolve human problems. Such must be the case for state school finance reform.

ANALYSIS OF CURRENT PROGRAMS

The purpose of this analysis is not to describe each state's current school finance program. To do so would require a compendium of hundreds of pages. Instead, some of the salient elements in state school finance programs are discussed with references, in some instances, to specific states. These elements are then evaluated in terms of previously discussed criteria, principles, and objectives.

Principal Features

There are numerous ways to analyze state school finance programs, with no best way or right way to do so. The programs are too complex to capture the essence of fifty diverse programs under a few headings. For this analysis, only a few basic features are examined to provide a cursory overview of state school finance programs.

Weighted Versus Unweighted Programs. Fifteen states weight pupils in their basic support programs. Eighteen states weight pupils in broad categories, whereas seven states weight pupils in specific programs. Ten states weight teacher units, and five states weight classroom units in their basic support programs. Because some states report weighting their basic support programs under several features, the categories of weighting are not mutually exclusive.

Whether or not a state weights pupils results in shifts of state funds to various districts. As important as weighting is to dollar distribution, how pupils are counted also provides for large shifts in dollars distributed to districts. Some states, like Michigan and Arizona, distribute funds on an average daily membership (ADM) pupil count. Such a distribution formula favors large urban centers which have low attendance ratios. Other states, such as New York and Arkansas, distribute funds on an average daily attendance (ADA) pupil count. These formulas favor rural and suburban centers over low-attendance, large city areas. Some states distribute funds on a per resident capita basis, whereas others distribute on an attendance basis. In the former, funds go to areas which have a high private school enrollment, whereas in the latter example the reverse is true.

Another source of inequality regarding equality of educational opportunities occurs when pupil programmatic weights do not accurately reflect the relative instructional costs of such programs. For example, some states weight certain special eduation programs at a fraction of their true costs and enact stringent requirements. The result is a shift of funds from regular programs to special education programs. A similar result is produced when secondary programs are inadequately cost weighted. Funds then are shifted from the elementary to the secondary education programs.

Minimum Foundation Programs. Today twenty-nine states utilize a foundation program concept to distribute state aid. Of these states, only Maryland, Virginia, and West Virginia have foundation programs without some type of pupil weighting. Indiana, Nebraska, New Mexico, Tennessee, and Utah adjust their foundation program allowances for teacher degree status or experience in each district.

The typical foundation program is defined as a dollar per pupil support level less the proceeds of an equalized required tax rate on full property valuations. If the expenditure level in the foundation program is set too low, the principle becomes less meaningful and the result is a minimum program. Some writers on school finance have argued that most states with foundation programs have not kept up with inflation, resulting in guarantees much below that needed to support an adequate educational program in poor school districts.

For example, even in the wealthy state of New York a study showed that only 3 to 5 percent of the districts in the lowest wealth decile had expenditure levels 1.25 times the minimum guarantee (Furno 1978). This indicates that for poor school districts the level of the state's foundation program is their maximum educational program.

In states with foundation programs, most legislatures are reluctant to provide for automatic increases in formulas, whether based on an index of price changes or on improvements made in the average educational program provided. They have preferred to adjust formulas with current evidence before them. Reluctance to automatic formula adjustments has come about because of the notion that automatic adjustments automatically increase costs. The result is an annual or biennial legislative battle to adjust state aid, consuming an inordinate amount of legislators' time. Recent techniques in some states, such as Oregon and Kansas, provide the state legislature with the options of increasing state aid or of keeping state aid at a previous year's level (Daicoff 1976). One look at the Consumer Price Index and Cost of Education Index should convince even the most skeptical individual that formulas need to be adjusted because of the effects of inflation on the purchasing power of the school dollar.

Variable Guarantee Programs.   The principal alternatives to the minimum foundation program are the variable guarantee programs. These programs have variations such as percentage-equalizing, guaranteed yield, guaranteed tax base and guaranteed budget. Though these programs have received considerable thought and attention, they are not new or novel. As noted earlier, these programs are based upon Updegraff's 1922 proposal. He generalized Cubberley's "reward for effort and doles to the needy" approach and built a system of state aid on the policy of rewarding effort in terms of tax rates.

Presently, the states of Alaska, Delaware, Massachusetts, Vermont, Pennsylvania, and Rhode Island utilize to some degree a percentage-equalizing provision in their basic support formulas. The states of Colorado, Maine, Michigan, Montana, Ohio, Oklahoma, and Utah utilize a guaranteed yield formula in their basic support programs. The six states of Connecticut, Illinois, Kentucky, Missouri, New Jersey, and Wisconsin distribute funds on a guaranteed tax base basis. Seven states distribute basic school support on the basis of a guaranteed budget: Arkansas, Iowa, Kansas, Missouri, New Jersey, Oregon, and Washington.

In the main, variable guarantee programs are based on spending level and tax effort decisions made at the local school district level. This is unlike the foundation program where a state sets the spending and tax requirement levels. It should be remembered that for any given year there is a precise mathematical equivalent between foundation programs and variable guarantee programs. However, the results upon spending levels, tax efforts, and curricula are not the same over the years. In almost all instances, variable guarantee programs contain tax rate, tax base, or spending level constraints. For example, in Michigan a poor district cannot spend as much per pupil as a wealthy district since the state only guarantees spending levels up to a specified tax rate.

One of the serious drawbacks of variable guarantee programs is that they result in wide divergence in spending levels. Since cost per pupil is highly correlated with school quality, the effect is a violation of the principle of equality of educational opportunities. Some advocates maintain that such programs provide local freedom of choice, and the decision to provide a high or low spending level rests with the local people. The fact remains that variable guarantee programs result in large differences in spending levels and thereby in educational program offerings.

Guaranteed Minimums. Both foundation and variable guarantee programs contain minimum spending level provisions. They need not, but most do. In fact, in the past some states, such as Connecticut, distributed all basic support funds on a flat grant or guaranteed minimum basis. The decision to do so was generally defended on the property tax relief concept or on the political concept of "every district should receive some state aid or else the state legislature will not pass the school finance program, that is, the political feasibility principle."

Approximately seventeen states still distribute some funds to local districts on the basis of flat grants regardless of district wealth or basic support programs. For example, Connecticut, Illinois, Missouri, and Virginia distribute some state aid on a flat grant per pupil formula. These provisions violate the equalizing effects of the basic school support formula so that funds are not distributed inversely to district wealth.

Some states provide minimum guarantees in the form of save-harmless provisions, decreasing enrollment, and so forth. In 1978–79, fifteen states were identified with such provisions. An original purpose of save-harmless aid was to protect districts from the extreme effects of rapidly declining state support. Save-harmless aid generally benefits districts which have had large increases in property valuations and declining enrollments. A high relationship exists between district wealth and save-harmless aid (Furno 1978). In fact, in one year the state of New York distributed state aid on the basis of its support formula to only a very few districts (NYSDE 1977). All of the other districts received state aid on the basis of save-harmless provisions. Minimum guarantees operate in a disequalizing manner, and their use will probably continue to increase the expenditure level gap between poor and rich school districts and to disequalize state aid.

State Share of School Expenditures. Various writers have commented on the relationship between the state share of total costs and the adequacy of programs supported by the state. Hickrod (1973) found a high positive relationship as he studied the programs of various states, both at a fixed date and over a period of time. He found that the expenditure level gap between rich and poor districts was the least when the state's share of the foundation programs was the most; when the expenditure level gap was the greatest, the state share of the foundation program was the least.

One of the first theorists to address the importance of the state's share of the cost of education was Swift (1922). He called for the establishment of a percentage of the cost of education that should be paid by the state. The hope was that there was a justifiable set percentage applicable to all states—a conclusion which ignored the economic roots of the need for state aid. For example, he ignored the level of state aid as an important variable. Clearly, 50 percent of a $2,000 per pupil support level is much better for a district's educational program than 90 percent of a $1,000 per pupil support level.

In 1978–79, the median state share of state and local school expenditures was 53 percent. In twenty-six states only narrow percentage changes occurred over the past decade. Hawaii still supports 100 percent of school expenditures. Alaska, Kentucky, New Mexico, Alabama, and Delaware are the five highest support states, excluding

Hawaii. The lowest five states are Oregon, New Hampshire, South Dakota, Nebraska, and Connecticut. Over the past decade, the states of New Mexico, New York, Wyoming, and Massachusetts decreased their share the most—minus 9 percent.

Selected Programs and Purposes.   It is important not only to evaluate state school finance programs in terms of formula distributions but also to evaluate them in terms of aid for selected programs and purposes. State comparisons are difficult, if not almost impossible, because states do not report mutually exclusive categories. For example, many states provide aid for various programs through their basic support programs. Other states provide aid for the same programs and purposes but through categorical programs. States are reluctant to report aid by standardized categories, opting instead to report data in accordance with their own state's definitions of categories and programs.

Nevertheless, basic support programs provide the major part of state funds to local districts. Some states have provided estimates of aid for various purposes which may be subsumed under the rubric "pupil targeted instructional programs." Thus, aid would be identified under purposes such as special education, vocational education, compensatory education, bilingual or bicultural education, and adult education. Almost all states report aid for special education and vocational education. However, many states either do not support or cannot separate out aid for such programs as compensatory and bilingual education programs. State comparisons and evaluations to be effected in accordance with the proposed principles, goal, and objectives enunciated earlier would require more detailed uniform reporting than has occurred to date.

Pupil Transportation.   Only three states report no separate state aid for pupil transportation (Iowa, New Hampshire, and Vermont). In these states districts must fund their pupil transportation programs out of their state's basic support program. Iowa, however, does have a separate and distinct funding program for the transportation of nonpublic pupils.

Although pupil transportation costs represent a relatively minor portion of state school aid, much attention has been paid to funding such programs. A review of the transportation literature reveals that certain criteria with regard to the formation of formulas are repeated over and over again (see Melcher 1981). Paul R. Mort (1933) reported these criteria. Featherstone and Culp (1965) reiterated them. Mort (1933) stressed the need for a minimal number of factors and the importance of objectivity.

In the debate over what the relative shares of the state and local districts should be in pupil transportation, the two concepts of equalization and economy are often raised. Some states completely run the pupil transportation system. Other states support 100 percent of its costs. Some states reimburse districts a flat percentage of their pupil transportation costs regardless of wealth. This procedure is highly disequalizing. It often results in poor districts shifting funds from educational programs in order to pay for transportation. Yet too high a reimbursement percentage of cost creates little incentive to economize and operate efficient and effective transportation systems.

State Programs for Capital Outlay.   Not all states provide funds for capital outlay projects (see Wilkerson 1981). Twenty-nine states distribute funds on a formula or project basis to local school districts. Three states provide funds for capital outlay projects, not through separate formulas but through their basic support programs. Alabama provides about $65 per teacher unit and requires that the amount be spent for capital outlay purposes. Kentucky allocates $1,800 per classroom unit for capital outlay. Maine provides funds on the basis of approved construction costs. In twenty-two states, either the local districts support capital outlay projects completely or the states periodically float a state bond issue for these projects.

Of all the state funding programs, the capital outlay program is the least equalizing. Only a few states have capital outlay programs which are reasonably equalizing. In most states, local funding of capital outlay projects results in less funds being available for the current instructional program. Both the principles of fiscal equalization and equal educational opportunity are violated.

CONCLUSIONS

As long as a state's public education consists of pupils regularly meeting in one place with teachers, and as long as the operational and support units are subdivisions of the state, the structure of school financing programs is likely to remain the same for many years to come. Changes will result from an almost permanent set of school finance issues. In evaluating a state school financing program, or in attempting to reform it, one must confront issues which have been debated by previous generations of reformers. They remain issues because they are, in essence, values deeply felt by citizens of our nation.

Issues in Financing Education

As America enters the 1980s, public education policymakers will continue to be confronted with a series of issues related to the financing of education. Major concerns will be related to equity and to quality or efficiency in funding public elementary and secondary education.

Equity Issues. From the earliest efforts to develop state school support programs, the challenge has been to develop school financing programs that will contribute to attaining the goal of equal educational opportunity for all students. In this seemingly endless search, several questions have continued to plague policymakers. Are equal educational results required to demonstrate the existence of equal educational opportunity? Will equal resources result in equal opportunity? If one accepts the premise that true equality results from the unequal treatment of unequal students, does equal educational opportunity then require that differential funding levels be provided for students on the basis of their physical or mental condition, cultural background, or occupational aspiration? What features should be included in a state school finance program to assure that equal educational opportunities are given children with racial, ethnic, cultural, and linguistic differences? Should service and support activities be recognized in the allocation of state funds? To what extent should local choice influence disparities in educational expenditures among local school districts in a state? Should the state school support program encourage and reward local school districts in their efforts to increase the spending beyond the basic state program? To what extent should the state school financing program be adjusted to account for a state's different demographic and economic conditions? Several of these questions are discussed in detail in other chapters of this yearbook.

A parallel concern in the quest for equity has been equal treatment of taxpayers. Concerns about equal treatment of equals and unequal treatment of unequals also apply to taxpayers. A basic question is whether equal state and local funding should be the result of equal tax effort irrespective of the wealth of the local school district. From the policy perspective, a further concern is related to the degree to which differences in local tax effort should be permitted. In addition to the previous concerns about tax effort exerted in local school districts, a related issue is the measure of local wealth or the factors other than real property that should be used in determining the relative fiscal capacity, or wealth, of local school districts. Typically, this discussion also leads to the question of whether or not a measure of wealth should be used in computing fiscal capacity when that measure cannot be taxed directly by local school districts. The chapters in this yearbook contain discussions of this concern and others related to the specific problems of urban areas as well as the relationships between the tax burden for schools and the total tax burden for all governmental services.

Issues of Quality and Efficiency. The continuing goal in financing and operating public elementary and secondary schools has been to secure educational quality in the most efficient manner. Educational advocates have always contended that education was underfunded; therefore, the question of the funding level necessary to provide the desired level of educational quality has gone unanswered. Educational productivity research has failed to provide the information needed to guide the policymaker on these two broad questions: (1) Will more funds improve the quality of education? (2) What aspects of educational expenditures can be curtailed with the least loss in quality? Issues such as the components of an adequate educational program, the required level of support, and optimal school and school district size also remain unresolved.

NOTES TO CHAPTER 6

1. See Guthrie and others (1971).
2. See Reischauer and others (1973).

3. See Mort and Ross (1957).
4. See Berke (1974).
5. See Johns and others (1971).
6. See Coons and others (1970).
7. See Rossmiller (1977).

REFERENCES

Association of Flat Grant Districts of New York State. 1977. "How Local Schools Should be Financed." New York. Mimeo.

Berke, Joel S. 1974. *Answers to Inequality: An Analysis of the New School Finance*. Berkeley, Calif.: McCuchan Publishing Corporation.

Benson, Charles. 1977. "Recent National Trends and Their Relationship to the New York State Situation." Paper presented at New York State Conference on Equalization of Educational Opportunity, Albany, New York, February 17–18.

Bicentennial Edition. 1978. *Historical Statistics of the United States. Colonial Times to 1970*. Washington: U.S. Department of Commerce, Bureau of the Census.

Coons, John E., et al. 1970. *Private Wealth and Public Education*. Cambridge, Mass.: Harvard University Press.

Cubberley, Ellwood P. 1905. *School Funds and Their Apportionment*. New York: Teachers College, Columbia University.

Daicoff, Darvin W. 1976. "An Analysis of the Kansas School District Equalization Act of 1973." In *Selected Papers in School Finance*, edited by Esther O. Tron. Washington, D.C.: U.S. Office of Education.

Featherstone, E. Glenn, and D.P. Culp. 1965. *Pupil Transportation*. New York: Harper & Row.

Furno, Orlando F. 1961. "A Statistical Look at the Cost of Education Index." *School Management* 5 (January): 140–56.

_____. 1978. "An Analysis of the Impact of State Aid on Local School Districts in New York State." Albany, New York: New York State Finance Project. Mimeo.

Guthrie, James W., et al. 1971. *Schools and Inequality*. Cambridge, Mass.: MIT Press.

Hickrod, Alan. 1973. *The 1973 Reform of the Illinois General Purpose Educational Grants in Aid*. Normal, Ill.: Illinois State University.

Johns, Roe L. 1977. "Equity in Public School Finance." Paper presented at New York State Conference on Equalization of Educational Opportunity, Albany, New York, February 17–18.

Johns, Roe L., et al. 1971. *Alternative Programs for Financing Education*. Gainesville, Fla.: National Educational Finance Project.

Melcher, Thomas. 1981. "State Pupil Transportation Finance Programs." In *Perspectives in State School Support Programs*, edited by K. Forbis Jordan and Nelda H. Cambron–McCabe. Cambridge, Mass.: Ballinger Publishing Company.

Mort, Paul R. 1933. *State Support for Public Education.* Washington, D.C.: The American Council on Education.

Mort, Paul R.; Walter C. Reusser; and John W. Polley. 1960. *Public School Finance.* New York: McGraw–Hill.

Mort, Paul R., and Donald H. Ross. 1957. *Principles of School Administration.* New York: McGraw–Hill.

New York State Department of Education. 1977. "Analysis of 1976–77 Save-Harmless Provisions of State Aid to New York State School Districts." Albany, N.Y.: Bureau of Educational Research. Mimeo.

Phi Delta Kappa Commission on Alternative Designs for Funding Education. 1973. *Financing the Public Schools—A Search for Equality.* Bloomington, Ind.: Phi Delta Kappa.

Reischauer, Robert D., et al. 1973. *Reforming School Finance.* Washington, D.C.: The Brookings Institution.

"Review and Outlook, Sons of *Serrano*." 1977. *The Wall Street Journal.* (May 12): 16.

Rossmiller, Richard A. 1977. "Full State Funding: An Analysis and Critique." In *Constitutional Reform of School Finance*, edited by Kern Alexander and K. Forbis Jordan. Lexington, Mass.: D.C. Heath and Company.

Special Analyses Budget of the United States Government Fiscal Year 1982. 1981. Washington, D.C.: Executive Office of the President, Office of Management and Budget.

Strayer, George D., and Robert M. Haig. 1923. *The Financing of Education in New York.* New York: Macmillan Company.

Swift, Fletcher. 1922. *State Policies in Public School Finance.* Washington, D.C.: Department of Interior.

Updegraff, Harlan. 1919. *Applications of State Funds to the Aid of Local Schools.* Philadelphia: University of Pennsylvania.

_____. 1922. *Rural School Survey of New York State: Financial Support.* Ithaca, N.Y.: Joint Committee on Rural Schools.

Wilkerson, William. 1981. "State Participation in Financing School Facilities." In *Perspectives in State School Support Programs*, edited by K. Forbis Jordan and Nelda H. Cambron–McCabe. Cambridge, Mass.: Ballinger Publishing Company.

Woollatt, Lorne H. 1952. *A National Cost of Education Index.* New York: Columbia University.

7 STATE PARTICIPATION IN FINANCING SCHOOL FACILITIES

William R. Wilkerson *

INTRODUCTION

In spite of a general enrollment decline in the nation's public schools, school construction dollar needs have not diminished greatly. Price inflation has heavily influenced school construction costs; much of the school plant built in the 1950s and early 1960s now needs major renovations; the increased cost of energy has caused expenditures for retrofitting for energy efficiency; and the requirements for accessibility for the handicapped have resulted in remodeling projects.

Most school construction funds are obtained by borrowing through bond sales. Interest rates on tax-exempt bonds reached historic highs in 1980 and will require substantially higher debt service payments than would have been expected only a year ago. To illustrate, the range in interest rates for all Indiana long-term school bonds in 1979 was 5.5 to 6.5 percent. In 1980, interest rates of up to 9.6 percent were incurred on high quality bonds. The average annual debt service on $5 million borrowed at 6 percent for twenty years is approximately $440,000 compared to $575,000 for the same length of term at 9.6 percent.

*William R. Wilkerson, Professor of School Administration, Indiana University.

Public elementary and secondary schools in 1978–79 spent $90.6 billion, of which $4.5 billion was for construction, $2 billion for other capital outlay, and $1.9 billion for interest on debt (Bureau of the Census 1980). These data probably understate the case since they exclude construction and equipment financed by quasi-governmental authorities and also exclude lease payments to such entities. Thus it is likely that expenditures for sites, construction, equipment, and interest were at least 10 percent of the total expended for all purposes by public schools.

Long-term debt of all public schools at the end of the 1978–79 fiscal year stood at $35 billion, not including debt incurred by school building authorities and by certain municipalities for school construction. Long-term debt retired in 1978–79 amounted to $2.9 billion while $3.3 billion in new long-term debt was issued (Bureau of the Census 1980). Thus built-in impetus for increased debt service payments exists since most of the old debt retired probably required much lower interest payments than the new debt incurred.

While much of the funds for current operation of public schools are derived from state grants, major responsibility for financing school construction resides with local school districts. Thus local tax-paying capacity frequently is the major determinant of ability to build schools.

None of the many legal attacks brought against the methods which the states use to finance education has focused directly on school facilities. This fact is somewhat surprising since the basic thrust of the rule of "fiscal neutrality"—financial capacity must be a function of the wealth of the state as a whole rather than of the local district's tax base—was so obviously violated in instances where little or no state aid for school construction existed. An Arizona court had this pertinent comment on the matter (*Hollins* v. *Schoffstall* 1972): "However, funds for capital improvement are even more closely tied to district wealth than are funds for operating expenses. The state and county make no contribution whatever to the costs of capital improvements. The capability of a school district to raise money by bond issues is a function of its total assessed valuation."

The focus of this chapter is state programs to assist local school districts in financing school construction projects. In the first section, a review is presented of the recent trends in state participation in financing school facilities. Representative state grant programs are briefly described in the second section with a discussion of current programs in selected states. State loan programs are discussed in the third section, and existing state school facility aid programs are evaluated in the fourth. Each of these sections assumes that aid to local school districts for school facilities will be in the form of financial assistance, but state assistance can also be provided in planning projects and arranging the financing package. These other types of assistance are discussed in the fifth section. The concluding section consists of a brief discussion of important issues in implementing a well designed state assistance program.

BACKGROUND

The movement toward more state participation in financing of school facilities has been slow. In 1950-51, nineteen states were granting funds for that purpose; the twenty-five states making grants in 1956-57 was reduced to twenty-four in 1962-63; and the twenty-six states granting funds in 1968-69 and 1975-76 increased to twenty-nine by 1978-79 (Tron 1980; Wilkerson 1976). Table 7-1 shows the nature of state participation in funding local school construction or debt service in 1978-79.

Typically, once a state commences granting or loaning school construction or debt service funds to local districts, the practice tends to continue. Notable exceptions are California and Ohio, both of which had massive combination loan and grant programs during the 1950s and 1960s and provided no aid in 1978-79.

Table 7-2 shows amounts available for state grants for 1950-51 and selected later years. Grants increased substartially until 1975-76, then declined in 1978-79. States' methods used to appropriate funds may explain part of the variance from year to year in that an appropriation made in a given year may not be drawn upon until subsequent years as construction progresses.

Ten of the twenty-nine states had appropriated in excess of $50 million for school construction or debt service grants in 1978-79. Eight of the twenty-nine made available less than $10 million, which is less than required to construct and equip a single new high school facility for 1,500 pupils in most locations in the United States.

Table 7-3 places the state appropriations for capital outlay or debt service in perspective as related to all state grants for education. For all granting states, school facility-related grants amounted to 6.6 percent of all grants. When compared to all education appropriations

Table 7-1. Type of State Participation in School Facility Financing, 1978-79

States with Operative Grant Programs (29)	States with Loan Programs (10)	States with Neither Grant nor Loan Programs (16)
Alabama	Arkansas	Arizona
Alaska	Indiana	California
Connecticut	Michigan	Colorado
Delaware	Minnesota	Idaho
Florida	North Carolina	Iowa
Georgia	North Dakota	Kansas
Hawaii	Utah	Louisiana
Illinois	Virginia	Montana
Indiana	Wisconsin	Nebraska
Kentucky	Wyoming	Nevada
Maine		Ohio
Maryland		Oklahoma
Massachusetts		Oregon
Michigan		South Dakota
Mississippi		Texas
Missouri		West Virginia
New Hampshire		
New Jersey		
New Mexico		
New York		
Pennsylvania		
Rhode Island		
South Carolina		
Tennessee		
Utah		
Vermont		
Washington		
Wisconsin		
Wyoming		

Source: Tron (1980: 330).

for the fifty states, facility-related grants amounted to only 3.7 percent of the total.

A 1977 report from the Education Commission of the States (Augenblick 1977) included a discussion of the major issues in state aid for capital projects. Among the issues identified are:

1. Population and enrollment changes affect interdistrict and intra-district facilities needs.

2. Requirements to comply with changing health and safety codes and to assure accessibility for the handicapped have required costly renovations and have added to new construction costs.

3. Facility needs are not uniform among districts within a state and facility costs vary much more than current operating costs.

4. Construction costs vary within a state by geographic location due to material, labor, and site acquisition costs.

5. While facility needs are not related to tax capacity of districts, ability to obtain construction and the burden of paying for facilities are largely dependent upon taxable wealth.

6. Targeting state aid for new construction discriminates against districts (particularly urban) which need funds for renovation rather than new construction.

7. Percentage-sharing grant schemes discriminate against districts which have difficulty raising local matching funds.

8. Debt and tax rate ceilings imposed by the state may unduly restrict local ability.

9. Lack of uniform assessment procedures and state tolerance of systematic underassessing adversely and inequitably affects the capacity of local districts to obtain construction and debt service funds.

10. Low-wealth districts typically incur relatively high interest costs on building funds obtained by bond issues.

11. The common requirement for electorate approval of bond issues may prevent construction or renovations even when need can be demonstrated convincingly.

12. Failure of the state to equalize funds for capital purposes may negate equalization of current operation programs in terms of total local tax burdens.

13. Prior effort (or lack thereof) of local districts to finance school facilities is sometimes ignored in state efforts to provide equity for new capital projects.

Table 7-2. Amount of State Funds Available for Grants to Local School Districts for Capital Outlay and Debt Service, Selected Years (in $ millions)

State	1950-51	1956-57	1962-63	1968-69	1975-76	1978-79
Alabama	$ 1.5	$ 2.0	$ 2.0	$ 2.0	$ 1.9	$32.1
Alaska	.5	1.5	.8	1.6	28.8	131.3
California	7.1	–	–	–	–	–
Connecticut	.5	3.0	8.7	16.0	22.8	18.0
Delaware	2.9	7.1	12.2	15.7	30.5	19.6
Florida	6.0	11.8	17.9	56.5	145.3	83.6
Georgia	–	14.3	20.0	28.3	33.7	63.3
Hawaii	M^a	.4	6.6	30.3	64.9	32.5
Illinois	–	–	–	1.9	362.3	10.0
Indiana	–	–	–	46.6	43.0	41.5
Kentucky	–	8.6	11.2	20.8	50.4	59.9
Maine	–	–	.9	4.0	30.4	13.8
Maryland	7.0	4.0	11.2	50.5	92.4	134.5
Massachusetts	1.2	9.8	16.2	23.7	114.7	113.2
Michigan	3.0	7.3	–	–	14.6	20.8
Mississippi	1.0	5.0	7.5	6.6	8.7	9.0
Missouri	.6	1.8	1.1	1.8	M^a	2.4
New Hampshire	–	.3	1.1	2.9	5.3	6.1
New Jersey	–	10.7	15.9	28.6	34.7	68.9
New Mexico	–	–	–	–	13.2	6.6
New York	2.0	10.0	116.2	184.0	226.0	220.0
North Carolina	23.3	14.2	.2	8.4	–	–

Ohio	1.9	8.7	—	—	—	—
Pennsylvania	.4	13.2	35.0	50.0	159.9	167.0
Rhode Island	Mᵃ	Mᵃ	1.6	4.1	7.4	6.0
South Carolina	—	25.5	2.3	16.4	19.1	22.7
Tennessee	6.3	7.7	8.8	10.4	13.4	26.9
Utah	—	1.4	3.4	4.2	3.6	11.7
Vermont	—	1.2	4.4	4.6	3.3	4.6
Virginia	6.9	1.4	—	—	—	—
Washington	3.2	17.3	20.0	13.0	61.5	83.9
West Virginia	3.1	Mᵃ	—	—	—	—
Wisconsin	—	—	—	—	—	20.0
Wyoming	—	—	—	—	—	5.5
Totals	$78.1	$187.0	$325.3	$632.9	$1,591.8	$1,435.4

a. M indicates that grants of less than $100,000 were made.

Sources: 1975–76 and 1978–79 data obtained from Tron (1980). Data for other years from Barr and Jordan (1971:142–143).

Table 7-3. State Grants for School Building Purposes, 1978–79, and Relationship to Total State Grants for K–12 Education (*in $ millions*)

State	Total Appropriation for Public K–12 Schools	Appropriation for Construction or Debt Service	Percent of Appropriation for School Facilities Purposes
Alabama	$ 666.4	$ 32.1	4.8
Alaska	367.7	131.3	35.7
Connecticut	295.3	18.0	6.1
Delaware	184.3	19.6	10.6
Florida	1,368.2	83.6	6.1
Georgia	859.5	63.3	7.4
Hawaii	269.8	32.5	12.0
Illinois	1,933.2	10.0	.5
Indiana	777.2	41.5	5.3
Kentucky	647.0	59.9	9.3
Maine	171.6	13.8	8.0
Maryland	773.4	134.5	17.4
Massachusetts	859.3	113.2	13.2
Michigan	1,450.9	20.8	1.4
Mississippi	372.5	9.0	2.4
Missouri	569.3	2.4	.4
New Hampshire	15.1	6.1	40.4
New Jersey	1,378.9	68.9	5.0
New Mexico	339.3	6.6	1.9
New York	3,353.0	220.0	6.6
Pennsylvania	1,848.5	167.0	9.0
Rhode Island	117.7	6.0	5.1
South Carolina	509.9	22.7	4.5
Tennessee	480.9	26.9	5.6
Utah	307.7	11.7	3.8
Vermont	58.9	4.6	7.8
Washington	976.4	83.9	8.6
Wisconsin	725.3	20.0	2.8
Wyoming	69.1	5.5	8.0
Totals	$21,746.3	$1,435.4	6.6
Add other 21 states	16,848.7	–0–	–0–
	$38,595.0	$1,435.4	3.7

Source: Tron (1980:14–15).

REPRESENTATIVE STATE GRANT PROGRAMS

By 1978–79, legislation providing for state financial assistance for local school facility projects had been enacted in twenty-nine states. The four types of programs were complete state support, equalized grants, percentage-matching grants, and flat grants. As shown in Table 7–4, the most prevalent approach was the equalized grant. Percentage-matching and flat grants were each used in six states. Only three states had a complete state support program. In the following discussion, brief descriptions will be presented of each approach in selected states.

Table 7–4. Types of State Capital Outlay and Debt Service Grant Programs in the United States, 1978–79[a]

| | Grants-in-Aid | | |
Complete State Support	Equalization	Percentage-Matching	Flat
Florida	Illinois	Alaska	Alabama
Hawaii	Maine	Connecticut	Georgia
Maryland	Massachusetts	Delaware	Indiana
	Michigan	Missouri	Kentucky
	New Jersey	New Hampshire	Mississippi
	New Mexico	Vermont	South Carolina
	New York		
	Pennsylvania		
	Rhode Island		
	Tennessee		
	Utah		
	Washington		
	Wisconsin		
	Wyoming		

a. Placement in categories based upon grant program with largest appropriation for 1978–79 to avoid double-counting of states with more than one grant program.

Source: Tron (1980).

Full State Assumption

Under a full state assumption program, the state finances either the full cost of the project or a portion of the project, typically referred to as the approved cost. Distinctions between approved and unapproved costs are usually based on criteria or standards that prohibit the state funds from being used for certain types of construction or identified phases of a total project. Local funds are typically used to construct the portions of the total construction project that are not included in the approval. Of the three states that have full state assumption programs, only Florida and Maryland can be considered typical, for Hawaii is a single state system and has no local school districts. For illustrative purposes, Maryland's program is discussed here.

Maryland began paying 100 percent of approved costs of construction projects on February 1, 1971. Site purchases are the obligation of the local school district. All costs of debt service for obligations created prior to June 30, 1967, are also paid by the state. For 1978–79, $134.5 million was appropriated for these purposes. Since Maryland provides approximately 34 percent of all state–local revenues for all school purposes, its program runs counter to the general national trend of relatively heavy support for current operation and modest or no support for facilities.

Equalization

Some states desire to participate in financing school facilities, but consider that financing facilities is a joint responsibility and that differences in local fiscal capacity should be recognized. In these instances, school facility construction projects or capital outlay debt is financed on a sharing basis with the state payment being in an inverse relationship to local wealth. Of the twenty-nine states that participate in financing local school district facilities, fourteen states use this equalization approach.

New Jersey uses payments of principal and interest on outstanding debt added to budgeted capital outlays as the needs measure for an equalization grant with the current expenses to state support ratio as a multiplier to provide equalization. Another debt service grant of up to $25 per pupil is made for those districts with exceptional need and who are making high effort.

Part of the basic state aid program of Maine is allocated for local debt service payments and a state sharing ratio from 0 to 90 percent is established for each district depending upon local valuation.

In New Mexico, an equal tax yield program guarantees $35 per mill levied on real property for capital purposes. Maximum levy equalized is two mills for a period of three years.

Pennsylvania made available $169 million in 1978–79 to approximately 500 districts for lease–rental payments and bond sinking funds. The need measure is differentiated on the basis of elementary and secondary facilities, and is contingent upon justification of need by a local ten-year capital improvement plan and approval of building by the state department of education. Allocations are equalized according to an aid ratio based on market value of property and personal income data or a previously utilized capital reimbursement fraction, whichever is larger.

Utah provides equalized aid based on bond principal requirements and uniform local effort of 13.5 mills. A second tier of the program provides additional funds based upon an 18 mill chargeable levy for what is termed "critical formula amount."

Washington makes equalized grants based on approved project costs with the state percentage determined by relationship of local assessed valuation per pupil to the state average. Upper limit of the state grant is 90 percent.

Percentage-Matching Grants

Six states have enacted a percentage-matching program that requires a fixed percentage of funds from local school districts. Typically, the percentage is computed as a portion of the approved project with the local school district paying the balance.

Delaware pays 60 percent of debt service for approved projects for all districts and 60 percent of costs for minor capital improvements. Construction of special education and vocational facilities is borne entirely by the state. Approved project costs are based upon formulas for square footage and costs that are related to the client utilization of the facility.

New Hampshire grants from 30 to 55 percent of principal payments on debt, with the differentiation based upon reorganization status of the recipient districts. Principal payment on debt for approved projects is the primary need measure that may be increased by capital reserve funds used on the project.

Vermont reimburses districts for 30 percent of all approved costs for construction, alterations or acquisitions and 20 percent of yearly debt service payments on bond issues approved for construction.

Flat Grants

Payments under flat grant programs normally are made on the basis of either pupils or classroom units. In contrast to the other programs under which funds are not paid until projects are approved or debt has been incurred, flat grants are normally disbursed on an annual basis or the funds are held in escrow by the state. Statutory provisions typically place restrictions on the uses of funds by local school districts to assure that funds are used for school facility purposes such as capital construction or debt and interest payments.

Georgia grants $28 per square feet on the basis of seventy-eight square feet per pupil increase since the last capital outlay allotment to the district. Grants are restricted for specified instructional and support facilities, and remodeling is also included. Recipient districts must have bonds outstanding on at least 14 percent of potential.

Indiana grants $40 per pupil in average daily attendance (ADA) which must first be used for debt service purposes. If not needed for debt service, districts have the option of using the funds for current operation or for capital reserve purposes.

Kentucky grants $1,800 per classroom unit for capital outlay or debt service uses. Long a part of the state's equalization program, this grant program is now considered a flat grant since there is no requirement for any local contribution which is ability-related.

Alabama has two grant programs. The larger of the two for 1978–79 distributed $100,000 to each district, and another $17.3 million was granted on a uniform per pupil amount to all districts. The other grant was based upon $68 per classroom unit and was part of the basic support program.

South Carolina appropriates $30 per pupil to be used for approved project construction costs or debt service payments. Funds undistributed to local districts are held in reserve by the state and granted when projects are approved.

Critique of Typical Programs

Full state assumption undoubtedly solves interdistrict equity problems. However, unless extremely careful state monitoring of local aspirations is maintained, it is probable that perceived local needs will escalate to the point that insufficient state funding capability soon results. If that occurs, then capacity to satisfy clearly demonstrated construction needs is impaired.

Equalization programs must be evaluated in terms of whether the measure of need is appropriate and the extent to which disparities in local ability are considered. If a uniform unit of need is applied to all districts, then the many conditions that cause need to be nonuniform are ignored. If the unit of need for the formula is not consistent with actual cost requirements, the goal of equalization of access and tax burden is not attained. The same result occurs if the sharing ratios have unrealistic upper limits or floors.

Programs which include current construction dollar needs along with prior effort considerations and which distribute funds in inverse relation to local ability are rare but are recommended.

Percentage-matching grants have one basic flaw even if based on realistic measures of need. Districts with low fiscal ability may have insurmountable problems in raising the required local match, while high ability districts can do so with relative ease.

Flat grants for school construction or debt service purposes do not attack adequately the problems of uneven need among districts—some districts may receive a windfall each year while others remain impoverished.

STATE LOANS

Loans to local school districts by the state can provide valuable assistance in situations where a local district might have difficulty in marketing bonds at favorable interest rates or where statutory, constitutional, or practical debt limitations may have been reached. State loan plans were utilized as early as 1810 in Virginia and 1844 in Wisconsin (Barr and Wilkerson 1973). Permanent school funds have been a major funding source used by the states, along with retirement programs, appropriations, and borrowing by the state.

If states borrow and loan bond proceeds to local districts, the effect is to substitute the credit of the state for that of the school district. To the extent that interest rates are less than available to the district in the competitive market, the difference has the same effect as an outright grant from the state.

Usual practice is for the loan to be used for capital purposes only except for Michigan and Minnesota which make loans for debt service payments. Indiana makes loans which may be used for remodeling, thus alleviating a problem where local districts have little difficulty obtaining funds for new construction but cannot raise adequate monies for work on existing buildings.

Two exemplary state loan programs of the past are nonfunctioning at this time. Ohio and California had loan programs where local districts were required to exert a specified uniform local effort for repayment. If the yield of the prescribed levy was insufficient to amortize the debt, the balance was forgiven by the state and thus became a grant. California's program was of exceptional significance, for approximately $2 billion was advanced to local school districts since 1949.

State loan funds now in existence usually have relatively small amounts available for any one district and may not provide significant tax relief to recipient districts if repayment is required.

The primary advantages of state loans are:

1. Funds are made available when needed without the necessity of marketing bonds.
2. Interest rate subsidies may have the effect of a grant.
3. Loans may provide a means to circumvent arbitrary bonded debt limits.

While state loans by themselves are probably not a good solution to the equity problems inherent in school construction activities, if they are accompanied by equalizing grants or forgiveness features, they may be desirable components of a comprehensive state assistance program.

EXISTING PROGRAMS

A 1976 study for the U.S. Office of Education sought to gather and analyze relevant data concerning equalization of local school districts' ability to finance their school construction and related debt service requirements (Wilkerson 1976). Data were sought from at least fifteen districts of each state (except Hawaii), five for each with high, average, and low fiscal ability. Usable responses were obtained from 519 districts from forty-three states. Total enrollment of the respondents was 7.1 million.

Wide variation was found for all of the variables of the study, both within and among states. Major findings and conclusions included:

1. Many of the factors connected with school construction finance simply are not systematically related to simple measures of need, burden, or ability. Prior effort (or lack thereof) and timing of construction and bond issues are major causes of distortion.

2. The influence of full valuation of property per pupil, the ability measure used in the study, was pervasive. Richer districts had much more debt per pupil, made considerably higher debt service payments per pupil and yet had effective tax rates of only 40 percent of the low ability districts. Per pupil receipts for capital reserve funds were nearly twice as great as for the low ability group, and the high ability group's average effective tax rate for that purpose was only half as much. Debt potential for the high ability group was more than four times as great as for the low group.

   Where state grants were made, more state funds flowed to the more able districts. Need for an effective system of state support, based on equalization, was evident.

3. Expenditures for school building purposes fell unevenly across the school districts of a state. Debt service payments per pupil ranged from zero for forty-four of the responding districts to $1,908 per pupil for the district ranking highest.

4. Given that the predominant method for financing school construction has been borrowing, the best single measure of need for a state grant program is debt service costs per pupil. This measure takes into consideration prior effort and relative fiscal strength of

districts in the bond market. Where reserve funds are used, per pupil collections for a stipulated time period might be added to debt service requirements to obtain a more appropriate measure of prior effort.

The study concluded with guidelines for a feasible state program which could bring about a reasonably high degree of equalization of burden and effort.

Significant federal grants to the states were made available in the late 1970s from Public Law 93–380, Section 842. The focus of the $12.7 million program was "Assistance to States for State Equalization Plans." All but four of the fifty states were successful applicants, and the recipient states used the funds for comprehensive studies or in some cases as reimbursement for state-initiated studies that were in process or had already been completed.

State equalization plans were to be evaluated in terms of conformance with eight "equity guidelines." Four of the guidelines that specifically mentioned school facilities were:

1.   Adequacy of educational programs;

2.   Cost variations;

3.   Comprehensiveness of program (here capital outlay and debt service were explicitly recognized); and

4.   Equalizing financial ability.

The other four guidelines dealt with equity of the tax support system, educational efficiency, decisionmaking, and evaluation. A summary of the plans developed by thirty-five of the states was recently completed (Furno 1980), and several of the proposals dealt with school construction and debt service funding.

Representative *recommendations* regarding state aid for school buildings follow.

States with no aid at present:

Arizona—provide state aid on an equalized basis with all districts to participate; funds could be accumulated for future needs.

Colorado—equalize funding of debt service.

Montana—equalize debt service tax levies.

Nebraska—support capital outlay and debt service by state in same ratio as current operation.

Ohio—base funds on need for facilities.

Oklahoma—participate in construction and debt service on an equalized basis.

Wyoming—increase state mill levy for construction aid.

States with loan programs only:

Arkansas—equalize state grants for debt service payments and issue state bonds to be backed by dedicated state tax funds (available funds to be allocated by formula based on need, ability, and effort).

Minnesota—power-equalize current levies for construction and debt service.

North Dakota—increase amount of loan fund and create "new funding mechanisms."

States with grants:

Alabama—develop a mechanism to gather data on school buildings to enable funding on "need" basis.

Delaware—move from 60 to 100 percent funding of capital projects and state assumption of all existing indebtedness.

Indiana—increase support level from $40 per pupil in ADA and change grant to equalize, using debt service requirements as a needs measure.

Kentucky—move to 100 percent state funding.

Missouri—repeal two minor existing programs and secure state participation in construction; also change two-third affirmative vote for bond issue to simple majority.

New York—establish higher per pupil allowances and calculate aid ratio same as for current operation.

Tennessee—develop a new means of determining need to replace per pupil flat amount.

OTHER STATE ASSISTANCE

States may render valuable assistance to local school districts in several ways in addition to granting or loaning construction or debt service funds. Some of these devices may require no direct cash outlays, while others may require staffing relevant state agencies with qualified personnel to render technical assistance.

Assistance with Planning

Proper planning of facilities is a task which requires expertise ordinarily found only on the administrative staff of large school districts. School districts with infrequent capital projects often rely upon outside architects and planners whose first obligation may not be the fiscal welfare of the state or the local school district. Staffing a state agency with competent planners to provide assistance to local schools could result in facilities that are appropriate for educational needs and are economically designed.

A long-range capital need study is required by some states as a condition to state approval of capital projects. State agencies frequently have qualified staff who can provide leadership, render assistance on specific components of a school facility survey, or make the complete study. Such studies can result in the proper facility delivered when and where needed.

Assistance with Financing

Most school facilities are financed by borrowing through bond issues. This is a complex task for the school district, particularly since needs for bond issues may not occur frequently. Technical personnel from state agency staffs can render valuable service on structure and timing of bond issues to accomplish favorable interest rates.

Several states market bonds on behalf of local districts. Credit of the state thus may be substituted for weaker local credits, and the expense of several small offerings can be avoided.

Local school districts frequently do not have the capacity to arrange interim financing while waiting for downward trends in interest rates. Temporary loans from state funds would be a valuable adjunct to other state participation if permanent financing remains as a local responsibility.

Use of such state sources as pension funds to purchase local district capital obligations is another form of assistance with financing that could benefit local districts with no impairment of the state's fiscal position. In such cases the negotiated interest rate should approximate the market at the time to avoid damage to the investment return for the pension fund.

Facilitation of Competition

Several states have statutory or regulatory deterrents to the competitive market place—related both to construction and financing costs. Requirements that discriminate in favor of local architects, engineers, and contractors or that mandate wage scales can cause building project costs to be higher than necessary. Permitting permanent financing to be arranged by negotiations of interest rates instead of competitive bidding may negate any construction cost savings attained through competition. Where such situations exist, sound public policy requires that corrections be achieved.

Several states have laws which prevent use of modern construction delivery systems. Construction management, value engineering, fast-tracking, and design-build are examples of newer techniques which may save time and money over the traditional method of bidding by general contractors on plans and specifications prepared by architects and engineers. When it can be demonstrated that more efficiency and greater economy can be attained, legislation permitting the newer delivery systems is desirable.

Provisions for Debt Refunding

The credit markets recently have been experiencing wide variations in interest rates, particularly for long-term securities. School districts, as well as states, frequently have been faced with the undesirable choice of arranging long-term financing at comparatively high interest costs or postponing financing while inflation caused project costs to soar. Several states have enacted legal provisions to allow refunding of bond issues when interest rates fall. When this is permitted, capital projects can be built when needed, construction costs can be fixed, and financing costs may be reduced at a later time. All states should permit this, and their laws should be structured so that only one of the bond issues is charged against whatever limitations on debt apply.

State Guarantees of Local District Debt

Investors in municipal obligations are concerned with the safety of the investment. Any action which the state can take to add a further measure of security should positively affect interest rates on local school bonds. A provision in the state constitution or in statutes explicitly stating that the state will make bond principal or interest payments in the event of a local default at least partially substitutes state for local credit. To illustrate, Indiana has such a statutory provision, and one of the major bond rating agencies assigns a credit rating of at least "A" for all Indiana school bonds as a result. Making such a provision is not likely to have a fiscal impact on any state, but should result in lower interest rates for its subdivisions.

Removal of Unrealistic Debt or Tax Rate Limitations

While the trend in school finance is for lowered reliance on property taxes, many states have retained limits on debt which are related solely to the property tax base. Need for school buildings is a function of pupils unhoused or improperly accommodated rather than a function of property valuation. Relating debt service funds to a maximum tax rate for such purposes may severely restrict marketability of bonds.

The logical consequences of obsolete limitations are substandard facilities for property-poor districts or costly alternative financing arrangements devised to evade the limitations. Corrective action in this matter is needed in several states, and such action need not have adverse fiscal consequences on the states.

Codes and Standards

Building codes and space standards should be evaluated periodically to make necessary changes that coincide with existing and expected conditions. Antiquated and irrelevant building codes have become evident as the nation faces energy problems. Space requirements for school facilities in many states were developed in an era of general expansion of the schools, cheap energy, and the move to suburbia. Such codes and space standards which are now counterproductive should be updated.

A need for reasonable space standards and for codes to assure the health and safety of building occupants does exist. Where no state space standards are present, buildings which are obsolete when constructed may result. Standards need to be flexible enough to permit adaptation to local needs and permit some experimentation. On the other hand, standards should not require such large sites or so many specialized facilities that maintenance of both urban and rural neighborhood schools is precluded.

Alternative Revenue Sources

The property tax appears to have fallen out of favor as the major revenue source for local schools. For those states wishing to continue to regard school facility construction as a local obligation, consideration should be given to permit local access to nonproperty taxes. Such action may do little toward solving equity problems, but it would permit utilization of revenue sources which are responsive to the economy.

DESIGNING A STATE ASSISTANCE PROGRAM

For states to adopt sound programs for financial assistance to local school districts, several issues need to be addressed if a well-designed, responsive program is to result. Following are some of the more dominant policy questions and implications.

1. Is some local financial contribution desirable? If so, then the sharing ratio should be designed to achieve equity of access to dollars for capital purposes and equity in the resulting local tax burden.

2. If local financial participation is included, what should local revenue sources be? The typical practice of sole reliance upon the property tax may be outmoded and incongruent with wishes of taxpayers, and consideration could be given to nonproperty revenues as well.

3. Should local school building funds be raised only by the traditional bond issue method? Accumulation of capital funds which are kept invested may be a valuable adjunct to or replacement of borrowing, particularly to obtain front-end planning and site costs, for relatively minor projects, and for purchase of equipment.

4. Should state funds be allocated for remodeling as well as for new construction? For many districts, remodeling of existing structures in established neighborhoods may be more desirable than building replacement facilities. Grant programs frequently are only for new facilities and thus do not address the needs of all districts.

5. What should be the need measure for grant programs? Approved project costs based on square footage standards and cost per square foot may be an appropriate measure if based on objective standards related to educational program requirements and if cost allowances are adjusted periodically. Flat per pupil annual allowances may reward some districts while seriously hampering others faced with substantial need. Reimbursements based on locally determined project costs may result in local irresponsibility and waste of state funds.

6. Should the grant program recognize prior effort made by districts? If so, then consideration must be given to granting funds for debt service purposes. An additional complication is present if capital reserve or current funds have been used by some districts to construct facilities. If these factors are not considered, then those districts which have not faced up to their capital needs are favored compared to those which have.

7. Should local districts have the option of supplementing approved project costs used for the state grant program with additional locally derived funds? If so, the result is equity problems in terms of features included in facilities; if not, local aspirations may be ignored.

8. Should state loans be used to provide initial funds for local districts' construction and remodeling needs? States may be able to obtain funds at lower interest costs than local districts would incur.

However, if repayment is solely a local burden, little or no equity results except to the extent that any interest subsidy may be regarded as a grant.

9. Should intrastate price differentials be considered in calculating local district entitlements? Remote rural locations, urbanized areas, and specific geographic locations may encouter building costs higher than in other locations in a state; if equity of access is a policy goal, then adjustments for such deviations should be made.

These and other policy questions should be answered before an exemplary state assistance program can be created. Assumption of financial responsibility by a state should be accompanied by a prominent role of appropriate state agencies to assure that state funds are used to build only proper facilities when and where they are needed.

REFERENCES

Augenblick, J. 1977. *Systems of State Support for School District Capital Expenditures.* Denver, Colo.: Education Commission of the States.

Barr, W.M., and K.F. Jordan. 1971. *Financing Public Elementary and Secondary School Facilities in the United States.* Bloomington, Ind.: National Education Finance Project Special Study No. 7, Indiana University.

Barr, W.M., and William R. Wilkerson. 1973. *Innovative Financing of Public School Facilities.* Danville, Ill.: Interstate Printers and Publishers, Inc.

Bureau of the Census. 1980. *Finances of Public School Systems in 1978-79.* Washington, D.C.

Furno, Orlando F. 1980. *Section 842, Equalization Plans.* Washington, D.C.: U.S. Department of Education.

Hollins v. Schoffstall, Superior Court of Arizona, Maricopa County, No. C-253652 (June 1, 1972).

Tron, Esther O. 1980. *Public School Finance Programs, 1978-79.* Washington, D.C.: U.S. Government Printing Office.

Wilkerson, William R. 1973. "Problems and Issues of Fiscal Neutrality in Financing School Construction." Washington, D.C.: School Finance Task Force, U.S. Office of Education. Mimeo.

——. 1976. "Equalization of School Construction Finance." In *Selected Papers in School Finance, 1976,* edited by Esther O. Tron. Washington, D.C.: U.S. Government Printing Office.

8 STATE PUPIL TRANSPORTATION PROGRAMS

*Thomas R. Melcher**

Pupil transportation is an essential element in all state educational systems. Transportation service plays an important role in assuring that educational opportunities are equally available to all children within a state. Because transportation need and local wealth vary widely among districts, state support is necessary if adequate transportation service is to be provided in all districts with a reasonable level of local effort.

The importance of pupil transportation in state educational systems has grown rapidly during the past half-century as the magnitude and cost of the service have increased. In 1929–30, 1.9 million pupils, or 7.4 percent of total enrollment, were transported in the United States at a cost of $54.8 million. Pupil transportation was significant primarily in consolidated rural schools, and the scope of service was essentially limited to transportation to and from school. The school district consolidation movement, the growth of secondary education, improvements in motor vehicles and road conditions, and the increased availability of state support contributed to the growth of pupil transportation during the ensuing decades. By 1949–50, 6.9 million pupils, or 27.7 percent of total enrollment, were transported at a cost of $214.5 million (Grant and Lind 1980).

*Thomas R. Melcher, State Aid Section, Minnesota Department of Education.

The magnitude and cost of pupil transportation have continued to increase during the past three decades. In 1969–70, 18.2 million pupils, or 43.4 percent of total average daily attendance (ADA), were transported at a cost of $1.2 billion. By 1978–79, the number of pupils transported had increased to 22.9 million, 58 percent of total ADA, while transportation costs reached $3.3 billion (NASDPT 1980). Factors accounting for the increases included the expansion of transportation service in urban and suburban areas, increased utilization of transportation for instructional purposes, introduction of busing for desegregation, and rapidly escalating energy costs.

The growth of pupil transportation service and cost has been accompanied by a growing recognition of the need for equitable state support programs. Based on research findings and the results of experimentation by the states, a number of alternative transportation funding approaches have been developed and implemented. In this chapter the pupil transportation finance research is reviewed, the present status of transportation support in the states is examined, and the alternative methods available to the states for financing pupil transportation are analyzed.

REVIEW OF RESEARCH

Most pupil transportation finance research since the 1920s has been directed at the development of alternative methods for measuring school district transportation need. Related literature has dealt largely with the classification and evaluation of funding models based on these methods, and with the review of state pupil transportation finance programs.

Measuring the Need

Early research in pupil transportation finance was stimulated during the 1920s and 1930s by the development of the state minimum foundation program. Strayer and Haig (1923) developed a conceptual model for such a program but did not specify how it could be operationalized. Mort (1924) established a procedure for defining the state minimum foundation program and divided the costs of the program into two groups. Group one consisted of costs that are equal for all classrooms or teacher units throughout the state. Included in group two were the costs of special provisions, such as pupil transportation, which are not uniformly required in all communities. Mort's research focused primarily on the measurement of group one costs and did not attempt "to arrive at a fundamental solution of the problem of measuring the educational need represented by transportation costs" (1924: 60). The actual pupil transportation expenditures of rural districts were taken as a proxy measure of transportation need, and a method was developed for relating transportation costs to group one costs based on density. In 1926, Mort called for an index of transportation costs which could be utilized in the state minimum foundation program:

> There is need for the development of an adequate index for measuring the cost of transportation of pupils. In some communities transportation of pupils is necessary in order that the state's minimum program may be offered. The costs of such transportation are legitimate responsibilities of the state as a whole. . . . Up to this time, however, no adequate index of transportation cost has been developed. States that are seriously attempting to assume the responsibility for a satisfactory minimum program are handicapped for the lack of such an index (1926: 99).

Responding to the need specified by Mort, Burns (1927) developed a transportation index based on two major concepts: (1) the transportation component of the state minimum foundation program for a given community should reflect the average level of transportation service and cost in communities with similar conditions, and (2) the factors used to measure transportation needs and costs should not be subject to local control. Reasoning that transportation need depends on the number of pupils transported and the average distance between home and school, Burns defined transportation need per pupil as the proportion of average daily attendance (ADA) transported, multiplied by the square root of the geographic area per school building.

Analyzing data for New Jersey counties, Burns found a curvilinear relationship between transportation need per pupil and school population density, where density was defined as average daily attendance per square mile. Regression equations of the form $Y = be^{ax}$ were developed to predict transportation need based on school population density. To determine the predicted transportation need for a county in dollars per pupil, the number of need units obtained from the regression equation was multiplied by the state average transportation cost per need unit.

Burns evaluated his transportation need index by examining the factors associated with variations between predicted and actual transportation need. It was found that "variability from the curve of transportation need, for places of like density, was caused by local policy with respect to type of school buildings and educational program" (1927: 40). Burns concluded that "the density of school population is a valid and reliable criterion by which the transportation need of a community may be predicted (1927: 19).

Johns (1928) reviewed the work of Burns and developed a refined procedure for measuring transportation need based on school population density. Like Burns, Johns sought to develop a measure of transportation need which would reflect the average service level and cost in communities with similar conditions, based on factors not subject to local control. Johns's chief criticism of the procedure developed by Burns was that it relied on area per school building as a weighting factor for measuring variations among communities in cost per pupil transported. Johns observed that a strong relationship between cost and area per school building had not been established, and noted that "it is unsafe to use any weighting factor for cost whose influence is not known" (1928: 12).

Johns divided the problem of measuring transportation need into two components. First, the community's need for transportation, in terms of number of students to be transported, was determined by analyzing the relationship between percent of ADA transported and school population density. Using regression analysis, equations of the form $Y = A/(X + K)$ were used to predict percent of ADA transported based on density. Second, the cost per pupil transported to be recognized in the state minimum program was determined using regression analysis, with actual cost per pupil transported as the dependent variable and density as the independent variable. The state-recognized transportation cost for each district was then determined by multiplying the predicted cost per pupil transported from the second step by the number of students to be transported from the first step. Analyzing data for five states, Johns concluded that "the density of school population is a valid, independent variable for the prediction of per pupil costs of transportation because the two variables are highly associated" (1928: 30).

The early pupil transportation studies of Burns and Johns measured pupil transportation need by estimating the proportion of students to be transported and determining an appropriate state-recognized cost for the transportation of these pupils. As walking distance requirements were established for determining state transportation aid eligibility, the number of pupils to be transported became a given, and pupil transportation finance studies focused more specifically on defining and measuring pupil transportation costs.

During the 1930s, alternative methods were developed for determining the transportation cost to be recognized in the state minimum foundation program. One alternative was to define transportation need based on cost per bus route rather than cost per pupil. Evans (1930), in a California study, used multiple regression analysis to predict the cost per bus route based on a daily route mileage and seating capacity, and developed a table of predicted costs for bus routes having various combinations of mileage and seating capacity. Mort (Mort and Reusser 1941: 417–419) applied the method developed by Evans in school finance studies in New Jersey and Maine. In the Maine study, separate equations were developed for routes on paved and unpaved roads.

Reusser (1932) developed a similar approach in a Wyoming study. Observing that the number of children transported and route length were the two chief factors affecting the cost of transportation routes, Reusser calculated a pupil-mile measure by multiplying the number of pupils transported by route length. Regression equations were then developed for predicting the cost per route based on pupil miles. The predicted costs for all routes in a district were summed to determine the state-recognized transportation cost for the district.

Evans and Reusser both considered the use of density in measuring transportation need but found it unsuited to the conditions in their respective states. In California, Evans found that a density measure could be applied with favorable results in counties having a fairly uniform population distribution, but that same measure was inappropriate for counties having significant uninhabited areas. He commented that "in order to establish any definite relationship between density of population and the requirements in the way of transportation, it would be necessary to consider not the total areas of districts or counties under consideration, but that part of the area which is inhabited" (1930: 33). Reusser found little relationship between density and transportation need in Wyoming, concluding that "density of school population means little in Wyoming counties because of the vast regions which are unpopulated" (1932: 76). Johns addressed this problem in an Alabama study by deducting the area not served by transportation routes from the total area of the county (Mort and Reusser 1941).

A second alternative method for determining the state-recognized pupil transportation cost for each district was to predict cost per pupil based on several independent variables. In an Ohio study, Hutchins and Holy (1938) identified thirty factors affecting transportation cost, including fourteen beyond the control of local school boards and sixteen subject to local control. Of the fourteen factors not subject to local control, number of pupils transported, density (pupils per square mile), and road conditions were found to be the most significant in determining the cost of pupil transportation. A regression equation was developed to predict cost per pupil transported based on these three factors; the resulting predicted costs correlated .66 with actual costs.

To determine the impact of managerial factors on transportation costs, the sixteen factors subject to local control were correlated with the residuals from the regression equation. Managerial factors found to be significantly associated with the variations between predicted and actual cost per pupil included pupils transported per bus, average number of trips per bus, percent of bus capacity used, average number of bids per route, and percent of buses owned by the school district.

A third alternative, recommended by Lambert (1938), was the use of a detailed budget model. Under this method, the specific quantities of labor, materials, and equipment necessary to convey pupils in a district to and from school would be determined. The state-recognized pupil transportation cost would then be calculated by applying appropriate unit costs to the quantities of inputs required by the district. The unit costs would be developed through statewide cost analysis. Lambert contended that the budget model was preferable to formula-based funding methods because it provided for a comprehensive review of all factors affecting transportation costs, while the formula-based methods could not. He was particularly critical of methods based on density alone, arguing that such methods oversimplify the problem, ignoring the impact of such factors as topography, climate, road conditions, population distribution, and the presence of uninhabited areas.

By the late 1930s, a substantial body of pupil transportation finance research was established. The three methods most commonly proposed for determining state-recognized pupil transportation costs were: (1) determination of cost per pupil based on area density, or area density plus other factors not subject to local control; (2) determination of cost per bus route based on route length and bus size; and (3) the use of a detailed budget model.

Between 1940 and 1970, there were few published reports of pupil transportation finance research. Most of the studies conducted during this period were aimed at refining the methods developed during the 1920s and 1930s, and applying them in selected states. In the late 1940s, Johns (1949) reviewed the development of a refined method for predicting cost per pupil transported based on area density and road conditions. Barr, in a 1955 study, reported on a formula utilized in Indiana for predicting transportation costs based on linear density. Linear density was defined as the number of pupils transported per mile of bus route.

During the 1970s, the school finance reform movement and rapidly escalating transportation costs combined to create a renewed interest in pupil transportation finance. Transportation analyses were included as a component of comprehensive school finance studies in several states. Responding to the problem of limited resource availability for education coupled with rising transportation costs, most of these analyses sought to develop transportation finance methods which would provide an equitable distribution of state aid among districts and a strong incentive for efficient operation.

National Education Finance Project (NEFP) studies conducted during the early 1970s included an analysis and assessment of pupil transportation finance methods in selected states. Farley, Alexander, and Bowen (1973) analyzed the Kentucky pupil transportation finance program. They recommended that the state-recognized cost per pupil transported be determined based on the relationship between cost per pupil and net area density, using a regression equation of the form $Y = aX^b$. Net area density was defined as the number of pupils transported divided by the square mile area of the district served by school bus routes. In addition to the basic state allotment, a supplementary allotment was recommended for the cost of transporting exceptional children.

In a South Dakota study conducted by the NEFP, Frohreich (1973) recommended that the relationship between cost per pupil transported and linear density be used to determine the formula-adjusted cost per pupil transported, based on a regression equation of the form $Y = aX^b$. A weighting factor of 5.0 was suggested to provide supplemental financing for the transportation of exceptional children who could not be transported on regular transportation equipment.

Jordan and Alexander, in a 1975 Indiana study, recommended the adoption of a similar linear density formula, with a weighting of 5.0 for severely handicapped children. Area density and district versus contract operation were considered for the formula but were rejected. It was observed that area density has the advantage of being fixed and not subject to local control, while linear density is dependent upon district routing decisions. Linear density, however, was preferred because it provides a more accurate measure of transportation need, particularly in districts with an uneven population distribution, natural barriers to transportation, or a necessity to provide busing for desegregation. District versus contract operation was rejected in order to promote efficiency through the use of a uniform formula for all districts. It was emphasized that the formula should be recomputed annually to adjust for changing cost and density patterns.

During the late 1970s, a number of state school finance studies funded under P.L. 93-380, Section 842, included substantial transportation components. State-funded transportation research projects also were conducted in several states.

Frequently, these studies recommended the refinement or adoption of an area density or linear density formula. In Arkansas, Alexander and others (1978a) concluded that the state area density formula should be adjusted annually using a curve of best fit between area density and cost per pupil transported to correct for changing cost-density relationships. It was also suggested that an adjustment factor be developed for the excess cost of transporting exceptional pupils, and that consideration be given to modifying the existing density measure by deleting areas not primarily served, or adopting a linear density measure. Stollar and Tanner (1978) recommended that the Indiana linear density formula be refined to (1) reflect current cost-density relationships, (2) include a correction factor for inflation, (3) adjust for local wealth variations when aid reductions are necessary to match entitlements with appropriations, and (4) provide depreciation aid for district-owned vehicles.

An area density formula was recommended in a Maryland study conducted by Price Waterhouse & Company (1980), while researchers in Colorado (Gallay and Grady 1978), Louisiana (Alexander 1980), Tennessee (Johns 1978), Texas (Briggs and Venhuizen 1976), and West Virginia (Alexander 1978b) recommended the adoption of linear density formulas. Alternative methods utilizing several independent variables were also analyzed in the West Virginia and Colorado studies. In West Virginia, Alexander and others (1978b: 177–192) developed multiple regression equations for predicting cost per pupil transported based on thirteen factors reflecting area and linear density, road conditions, prevailing wage rates, dispersion of school buildings, and economies of scale. Linear density entered the equation first, accounting for 63 percent of the variance among districts in cost per pupil transported. A road conditions index entered the equation next, increasing the R^2 statistic to .66. The full thirteen variable prediction equation accounted for approximately 84 percent of the variance. As an alternative to the multiple regression approach, linear density alone was used to predict cost per pupil transported, based on a curvilinear equation of the form $Y = aX^b$. The alternative procedure was found to explain 66 percent of the variance in cost per pupil transported, and was recommended because it provided a reasonably high level of accuracy with a much simpler formula.

In Colorado, Gallay and Grady (1978) used seventeen independent variables to predict cost per mile and cost per pupil transported. Included among the independent variables were area density, linear density, highway density, average teacher salary, income per pupil, number of pupils transported, total miles, number of conventional and small buses, and several geographic factors. The combination of linear density, highway density, and average teacher salary was found to account for 70 percent of the variation in cost per mile. Linear density accounted for 84 percent of the variation in the cost per pupil, when both factors were expressed in logarithm form. It was concluded that cost per pupil transported is preferable to cost per mile as a unit of comparison, and that linear density is an appropriate independent variable for predicting variations among districts in cost per pupil transported. In a separate Colorado study, Bernd (1975) recommended that state funding of pupil transportation be based on a line of best fit between cost per pupil transported and miles per pupil, the inverse of linear density.

Hennigan, Furno, and Gaughan (1978), in a New York study, considered a predicted cost formula but rejected it in favor of a two-tier aid ratio formula. Area density, number of pupils transported, and number of schools to which transportation was provided were used in a linear regression formula to predict district total pupil transportation cost. The predicted cost formula was not recommended because large deviations were produced between predicted and actual cost and because of the complex statistical procedures involved. In the first tier of the recommended formula, each district was provided with 95 percent of actual cost per pupil transported or 95 percent of the ninety dollars, whichever was less. The second tier provided for actual cost per pupil transported minus ninety dollars, multiplied by the following aid ratio: 1 - (.4 district wealth divided by state wealth). To adjust for cost variations among transportation categories, handicapped pupils were assigned a weighting factor of 6.0, and nonpublic pupils a factor of 2.0.

In an Illinois study, McKeown (1978) developed a formula for predicting cost per pupil transported based on area density, linear density, mode of operation (district-owned, contractor-owned, or mixed), and district type (elementary, high school, or unit district). Eight dummy variables were used to control for mode of operation within district type, and eighteen additional dummy variables were used to account for mode of operation and district type within area density and linear density. The full twenty-six variable model was found to explain 56 percent of the variation in cost per pupil transported. Based on analysis of state average transportation costs for regular, special, and vocational education pupils, special education pupils and vocational education pupils were weighted, respectively, at 4.294 and 1.347.

Alternative Funding Models

Based on the findings of pupil transportation research and on the results of experimentation by the states, a wide variety of pupil transportation finance methods have been developed during the past half-century. Writers in the field of school finance have periodically classified these methods into major categories or funding models. Mort, in a national school finance study conducted in 1933, identified five such models. In the first model, transportation funding was based on a measure of transportation need such as the density approach developed by Burns and Johns. Objective measures of transportation workload, such as pupil miles, were used in the second model. In the third model, state authorities reviewed local transportation budgets to determine state-recognized costs. The fourth model was based on the actual expenditures of school districts, while the fifth model provided flat grants for pupil transportation.

Chase and Morphet (1949: 103–104) classified state transportation support methods based on provisions for equalizing fiscal capacity and on methods used to determine transportation need. Where transportation aid is provided within the basic state support program or as a special-purpose equalization grant, variations in local fiscal capacity are recognized in allocating state aid. Special-purpose flat grants do not adjust for variations in local fiscal capacity. Methods used to determine transportation need include (1) density formulas, (2) percentage reimbursement formulas, (3) approved budgets, and (4) allowable cost reimbursements based on standard unit costs.

Featherston and Culp (1965: 63–64) grouped state transportation aid formulas into four general categories. A flat grant per pupil transported was provided by states in the first category. Included in the second category were state provisions to reimburse districts for part or all of the cost of transportation, usually with certain limitations. The limitations could take the form of a percentage reimbursement, a ceiling on reimbursible unit costs, or a procedure for determining allowable costs. In the third category, approved transportation costs were determined based on the average unit costs for districts with similar characteristics, such as density of transported population. The fourth category included states in which approved transportation costs were calculated based on a formula composed of factors found to bear a relationship to variations in transportation costs, such as density, road conditions, number of buses, bus miles, and pupil miles.

State pupil transportation finance methods were classified by Stollar (1971) into six basic funding models: (1) no state aid for transportation; (2) state flat grant per pupil transported; (3) full recognition of transportation cost variations beyond district control due to factors such as density and wage levels; (4) state ownership and operation of the transportation system; (5) state payment of the approved cost of transportation; and (6) state payment of a fixed percentage of actual costs.

Skloot (1978) suggested that state funding formulas for pupil transportation may be divided into two basic groups. Formulas included in the first group are based on individual district experience, while those in the second group are based on fixed cost units or average costs. The experience—based model provides a reimbursement to districts for a portion of actual or approved costs; the level of funding is based on the workload and expenditures of the individual district. In the fixed unit cost model, districts with similar unit characteristics receive similar funding, irrespective of workload and expenditure variations due to differences in local policies and management practices. The experience-based model is attractive from a local perspective in that funding levels reflect actual costs; however, the fixed unit cost model is preferable from a state perspective because it provides an incentive for efficient operation and provides comparable funding for districts with comparable unit characteristics.

Criteria for Evaluation

Several criteria for evaluating state pupil transportation funding programs have been suggested in the school finance literature. In an early study, Mort (1933: 111-112) proposed two basic criteria. First, the funding method should be based on the cost of providing a transportation program of uniform quality throughout the state. Cost variations due merely to differences in local policy should not be recognized. Second, "the additional cost involved in transporting atypical children" should be fully recognized (1933: 112).

Johns, in a 1949 study, concluded that no method of state support for pupil transportation is fully satisfactory unless it:

1. Provides adequate transportation services for all pupils who need it;

2. Encourages efficiency and discourages extravagance in local transportation management;

3. Is based on a completely objective formula, leaving nothing to the subjective judgment of state officials;

4. Is based on an equitable formula which takes into consideration all substantial variations in necessary transportation costs resulting from factors beyond the control of local boards; and

5. Is part of a balanced comprehensive foundation program of education financed by an equitable taxing system (1949: 49).

Featherston and Culp (1965: 64–67) recommended that the state pupil transportation support program: (1) take into account the factors which cause substantial variation in justifiable costs, such as density, road conditions, and prevailing wage levels; (2) be as simple as possible while retaining accuracy; (3) exclude factors subject to local manipulation, which may encourage inefficiency; (4) be based on past experience so as not to depart radically from established practice; (5) be as objective as possible; and (6) encourage efficiency in local transportation management. Similar criteria have been suggested by Stollar (1971), Bernd, Dickey, and Jordan (1976), and Jordan and Hanes (1978).

Evolution of State Support Programs

While the history of pupil transportation in the United States is as long as that of the nation itself, state support for pupil transportation was not widely established until the 1920s. Prior to the mid-nineteenth century, the transportation of pupils was considered a parental responsibility, and no public funding was provided. With the advent of compulsory attendance legislation and the school consolidation movement, the need for public financing of pupil transportation became widely recognized. In 1869, Massachusetts became the first state to authorize the expenditure of public funds for this purpose (Abel 1923). By 1900, eighteen states had enacted pupil transportation laws, and by 1919 the transportation of pupils at public expense was authorized in all forty-eight states.

Most of these early laws authorized local expenditures for pupil transportation, but did not provide state aid. Only four states provided aid for pupil transportation prior to 1910 (Burke 1957). New Jersey and Wisconsin provided a flat amount per pupil transported, while Connecticut and Vermont based state aid allocations on a percentage of actual cost, not to exceed a certain amount per pupil. In other states, the financing of pupil transportation was generally regarded as a local matter.

With the development of the state minimum foundation program during the 1920s and 1930s, state participation in pupil transportation finance increased substantially. In 1933, Mort reported that thirty-two states participated to some degree in funding pupil transportation. Fourteen states included approved transportation cost in the basic state school support program, eight states provided flat grants, and six states reimbursed a percentage of district expenditures. Delaware and North Carolina provided full state funding of transportation costs. Two states provided for the transportation of pupils from unorganized territory or districts unable to maintain schools to other districts.

In general, however, the level of state support was low, often requiring a substantial unequalized local contribution. Mort concluded that "less than one-third of the states are rated as having provisions for the transportation of pupils which are sufficiently adequate to guarantee educational opportunities to children not living within walking distance of school" (1933: 112).

After 1933, the number of states providing aid for pupil transportation and the level of state support gradually increased. The methods used to allocate transportation aid grew more refined and complex as the procedures developed through research were adopted in several states. By 1948, all but eight states provided aid for pupil transportation. Sixteen states distributed transportation aid as a component of the basic state support program, eighteen through special purpose flat grants, two through special purpose equalization grants, and four through some combination of these methods (Chase and Morphet 1949).

Procedures used to determine the transportation aid allocation varied widely among the states. Eleven states reimbursed districts for a percentage of costs, eight states employed a density formula, and four states based aid allowances on approved budgets. Seventeen states provided allocations for a portion of authorized costs based on a variety of standards or limitations, such as a maximum amount per bus, per pupil or per mile, or a unit cost schedule for various budget items (Chase and Morphet 1949).

In 1965, Featherston and Culp reported that forty-four states provided aid for pupil transportation. Transportation aid was included in the basic support programs of twenty states, while twenty-two states funded pupil transportation through categorical aid programs, and two provided transportation funding in both basic support and categorical programs. Procedures used to determine the allocation of transportation aid among districts varied widely. Two states provided a flat grant per pupil transported, nine states reimbursed districts for a percentage of transportation costs, ten states provided funding for approved expenditures, and twenty-three states employed formulas composed of factors associated with variations in transportation costs. Most of the formulas were used to determine allowable cost per pupil transported. Density of transported population was a primary factor in the formulas of ten states, while mileage was a major factor in eleven state formulas. Road conditions were used in the aid calculation process in six states. In general, more than half of the funding for pupil transportation was obtained from local sources.

Jordan and Hanes, in a 1978 survey, reviewed several aspects of state pupil transportation finance programs, including the level of state support in relation to total expenditures, travel distance eligibility requirements, and factors used in distributing state aid. The level of state support could not be identified for six states providing transportation funding as an element in the basic state support program. Of the remaining forty-four states, fourteen provided less than 50 percent of total transportation expenditures from state sources, fourteen provided between 50 and 70 percent, and sixteen provided more than 70 percent. This level of support reflected a significant increase in state funding of pupil transportation since the mid–1960s.

Statutory requirements specifying minimum travel distances from home to school as a precondition for state aid were found in thirty-one states. Twenty-four of these states specified a single minimum distance; one mile was used in five states, one and a half miles in eleven states, and two or more miles in eight states. In seven states, travel distance requirements for state aid eligibility varied by grade level, with longer distances required for secondary pupils than for elementary pupils.

Considerable differences were found among states in the factors used in distributing state transportation aid. Expenditure per pupil transported was used as a principal criterion in determining the aid allocation in eleven states, while seven based the state aid allocation primarily on a density measure; six utilized bus capacity; and two provided flat grants. In several states, a combination of factors was used; the set of factors employed in nineteen states suggested that an efficiency or average cost concept was used in the allocation of funds.

THE PROGRAMS

At present, considerable diversity exists in state provisions for financing pupil transportation. State aid as a percentage of total transportation expenditure ranges from zero to one hundred. State support is provided for the transportation of nonpublic school pupils in approximately one-third of the states, predominantly in the Northeast and Midwest. A majority of the states have established minimum travel distances from home to school as a requirement for state aid eligibility, ranging from less than one mile to four miles. Factors used in allocating state aid among districts vary widely: some states base aid allocations on individual district expenditures, while others use detailed budget models, density formulas, or fixed unit cost formulas.

Detailed information concerning present state support programs was obtained for this study from a questionnaire submitted to each state department of education. Additional data regarding expenditures and state aids for pupil transportation were obtained from reports of the National Association of State Directors of Pupil Transportation and the U.S. Office of Education.

State Aid

In 1978-79, total public expenditures for pupil transportation in the United States amounted to $3,341 million (NASDPT 1980). Identifiable state aid for pupil transportation totaled $1,835 million, or approximately 55 percent of expenditures (Tron 1980). This figure underestimates the level of state support for pupil transportation in that transportation funding provided through basic state support programs was excluded for at least five states in which amounts specifically for transportation could not be identified. Adding estimated state transportation funding of $80 million for these states, the total level of state support for pupil transportation in 1978-79 was approximately $1,915 million, or 57 percent of total expenditures.

Among the states, the amount of state aid as a percentage of transportation expenditures varied substantially in 1978-79. New Hampshire was the only state providing no support for pupil transportation. In Hawaii and South Carolina, on the other hand, the pupil transportation systems were state-owned and -operated; actual expenditures were paid directly by the states with no local contribution. Of the remaining forty-seven states, seven provided state aid for less than 40 percent of expenditures, eighteen for between 40 and 60 percent, fifteen for between 60 and 80 percent, and seven for more than 80 percent. In twenty-three states, the local contribution to pupil transportation funding was equalized by the state, either by including the transportation entitlement within the basic state support program or through an equalized levy within the categorical transportation aid program. In the remaining states, local levies for pupil transportation were not equalized by the state.

Travel Distance Requirements

Minimum travel distances from home to school have been established as a requirement for state aid eligibility in at least thirty-seven states. Twenty-eight of these states specified a uniform distance for all grade levels in 1980–81, while nine specified longer distances for secondary pupils than for elementary pupils. Of the states specifying a single distance for all pupils, seven set the minimum distance at one mile, eleven at one and a half miles, six at two miles, and four at greater than two miles. The longest distance requirements were found in the sparsely settled plains states: Kansas and South Dakota established a minimum of two and a half miles, while Montana employed a three-mile minimum, and Nebraska used a four-mile minimum. Travel distance requirements were generally not applied to handicapped pupil transportation; several states also waived distance requirements where hazardous traffic conditions were present.

Factors Included

In 1980–81, a variety of factors were used in state transportation aid programs to determine school district transportation need. Programs based primarily on actual or approved district expenditures were utilized in seventeen states, while seven employed detailed budget models, twelve used density formulas, and eleven employed fixed unit cost formulas.

Among the states using an actual or approved district expenditure approach, several different methods were used to limit or control the state portion of total costs. In nine states, the state share was limited to a fixed percentage of actual or approved expenditures. South Dakota provided funding for 50 percent of actual cost, not to exceed a certain amount per mile. In Oregon, school districts were reimbursed for 60 percent of approved costs for the second prior year. Wyoming included 75 percent of actual transportation costs in the state foundation program, while Michigan provided categorical funding for up to 75 percent of approved transportation costs. West Virginia provided funding for 80 percent of nonsalary operating costs, plus a flat amount per bus driver and a bus depreciation allowance. Idaho and Nevada included 85 percent of authorized transportation costs in the state foundation aid program. New Jersey supplied categorical funding for 90 percent of the cost of approved bus routes, while New York included 90 percent of approved transportation costs in the basic state support program.

Eight states determined the state share of pupil transportation expenditures by deducting a certain amount from total actual or approved costs. In Maine, 100 percent of transportation costs for the second prior year were included in the state foundation program. Massachusetts provided a categorical reimbursement for 100 percent of authorized costs less five dollars per pupil in average daily membership. In Illinois, districts were reimbursed for the cost of transporting eligible pupils less a qualifying amount, or sixteen dollars per eligible pupil, whichever was greater. Pennsylvania provided funding for approved costs less a qualifying amount, with the approved cost equal to the lesser of actual cost for authorized transportation or a formula providing standard unit rates for various cost components. In California, state aid was provided for approved prior year expenses less a qualifying amount; approved expenses were limited to state-wide median expense per bus day, plus 25 percent, based on sixteen bus classifications reflecting bus capacity and hours of operation.

In Connecticut, Rhode Island, and Vermont, state funding for pupil transportation was provided through percentage-equalizing or guaranteed tax base formulas. By including transportation expenditures in the state's basic percentage-equalizing formula, Rhode Island and Vermont provided funding for a percentage of transportation cost varying inversely with district wealth per pupil. In Connecticut, a categorical guaranteed tax base program was used to reimburse districts for between 20 and 60 percent of transportation cost, depending on local wealth.

Seven states provided full state funding for approved pupil transportation services through detailed budget models: Alaska, Delaware, Georgia, Louisiana, Maryland, New Mexico, and North Carolina. In this method, transportation need is defined in terms of the quantities of labor, materials, and equipment necessary to provide appropriate transportation service in each district. Generally, state administrators closely monitor the level of inputs requested by the districts to assure that a transportation program of uniform quality is maintained throughout the state. After defining the transportation program for each district, the state funding level is calculated by applying standard unit costs to the approved quantity of inputs. District costs which exceed the approved state funding level are paid with local funds. Budgetary models used in selected states are described below.

In Delaware, separate reimbursement formulas were used for districts providing transportation service by contract and through district operation. For contracted districts, formula components included a return of capital allowance, a fixed cost allowance, an attendant wage rate, and a layover rate. The return of capital allowance provided a certain amount per vehicle, based on seating capacity and model year. The fixed cost allowance provided for the cost of wages, supervision, profit, and operation for a standard thirty-mile minimum route: a variable amount was provided based on bus capacity and geographic region. In addition to the basic fixed cost allowance, additional allowances were provided for each mile in excess of thirty and for midday routes. The attendant wage rate and the layover rate were computed on an hourly basis. Buses for district-operated transportation systems were provided by the state. Operating costs were reimbursed through a fixed cost allowance, an attendant wage rate, and a layover rate similar to but slightly lower than that provided for contracted districts. The standard rates for both district and contract operations were adjusted for inflation based on the private transportation subsection of the Consumer Price Index for the Philadelphia region.

The Georgia transportation funding model included five line items. First, a uniform amount was allocated per bus driver for all districts. Second, a standard allowance was provided per vehicle for bus insurance. Third, a bus replacement allowance was calculated based on the prior year average cost by bus size. Fourth, an operating expense allowance was determined using the average cost per mile by size of bus within four geographic regions of the state. Finally, an adjustment was made for increased fuel costs.

In Louisiana, the transportation aid allocation included a fixed amount per bus driver plus a bus operation allowance based on bus length and route mileage. The level of funding for bus driver salaries was based on a state minimum salary schedule. For each bus length, the bus operation allowance provided a certain rate per mile for the first six daily route miles, with reduced rates for additional mileage.

The Maryland transportation aid formula consisted of a series of allowances for various transportation budget categories. For each approved route vehicle, a replacement allotment was provided which varied with vehicle capacity and year placed in service. Additional allotments were provided for approved spare vehicles and for the cost of special equipment such as lift gates. An allowance for driver and aide salaries was computed based on a fixed hourly rate plus 15 percent for fringe benefits. Salary allowances for uncertified drivers and aides were 15 percent lower than those for certified drivers and aides. For operation and maintenance costs, a per mile allowance was provided which varied with vehicle capacity; miles travelled on unpaved roads were doubled for funding purposes. Based on the number of pupils transported, each district was allowed a certain number of administrative personnel at specified salary rates. Additional allowances were made for other budget items including administrative travel, training costs, driver physical examinations, and bus inspections.

In New Mexico, an allowance was computed for each vehicle which included amounts for bus depreciation, operation and maintenance, contractor profit, fuel, driver's salary, and employee benefits. A certain amount was allowed for bus depreciation on each contractor-owned vehicle, depending on vehicle size and model year. For district-owned buses, a capital outlay allowance was made. Funding for operation and maintenance and for fuel was determined using a rate per mile which varied based on vehicle size and road conditions. Special adjustments to the rate per mile were made for routes with frequent stops, heavy grades, and altitudes over 6,000 feet. For contractor-owned vehicles, a profit on operational revenue was calculated at 10 percent of the operation and maintenance allowance. Bus drivers salaries were funded at a base amount depending on total daily reimbursable miles, plus an increment for attending a driver training institute. Employee benefits were calculated at 16 percent of authorized salaries.

Twelve states allocated 1980–81 transportation aid among districts based on an area or linear density formula. Area density formulas were used to determine the transportation aid allocation in six states: Alabama, Arkansas, Kansas, Kentucky, Mississippi, and Oklahoma. Additionally, area density was one of several factors included in the Minnesota transportation aid formula. Area density is calculated by dividing the number of pupils transported by the square mile area of the district. In Kentucky and Oklahoma, the area density measure was adjusted by deleting areas not primarily served; these are areas located more than a certain distance from an approved bus route.

Under the area density approach, an allowable cost per transported pupil is determined based on analysis of the relationship between density and cost. Procedures used to establish the allowable cost include (1) use of a curve of best fit between density and cost per transported pupil based on regression analysis, and (2) calculation of an average cost per pupil transported within specified density groupings. After the allowable cost is established, the transportation funding for a district is calculated by multiplying the allowable cost per pupil by the number of pupils transported. In some states, a district may receive funding greater than its actual cost by keeping its cost below the allowable level; in other states, the level of funding for a district is limited to actual cost.

In Minnesota, transportation aid was allocated among districts through a complex formula in which cost per weighted pupil transported was predicted based on: area density; average daily membership; certain geographic factors such as terrain, road conditions, and regional location; and proportion of students transported in regular, vocational, and special education categories. Weighting factors were assigned to the pupil count for each transportation category based on the average cost per pupil transported in that category in relation to the average cost per pupil transported in the regular category.

Using multiple regression analysis, a predicted cost per weighted pupil transported was determined for each district for the second prior year. The predicted cost was increased by an inflationary cost escalator to establish the allowable cost per weighted pupil for the current year. The allowable cost was then compared with the district's actual cost, and a state aid adjustment was made for a portion of the difference. If the district's actual cost was greater than the allowable cost, the state allocation was increased by 20 percent the first ten-dollar difference per pupil, 40 percent the next ten-dollar difference, 60 percent of the next ten-dollar difference, and 75 percent of the difference exceeding thirty dollars per pupil; the remaining excess cost was paid by the district. If the district's actual cost was less than the allowable cost, the state aid allocation was reduced under a similar schedule, and the district retained a portion of the difference as an incentive for efficient operation.

Five states employed linear density formulas in allocating transportation aid: Florida, Indiana, Missouri, Texas, and Utah. Linear density is calculated by dividing the number of pupils transported by the number of bus route miles. In Florida, Indiana, and Utah, linear density formulas were used to determine the allowable cost per transported pupil. Reflecting the inverse relationship between linear density and cost per pupil, the allowable cost per pupil increases as linear density decreases. In Texas, the allowable cost per bus mile was determined based on the average cost for districts within seven linear density groupings.

In Missouri, the inverse of linear density, bus miles per pupil, was used in adjusting the allowable cost per pupil mile for each district. Based on simple curvilinear regression analysis, cost per pupil mile was predicted from miles per pupil using an equation of the form $Y = ax^b$. A percentage variance factor based on the standard error was calculated to allow for error in the regression equation. If the actual district cost per pupil mile was less than the predicted cost plus the variance factor, the state aid allocation for the district was equal to 80 percent of eligible cost. If the actual cost per pupil mile was greater than the predicted cost plus the variance factor, the state aid allowance was reduced from the 80 percent level: a 1 percent reduction in the state reimbursement percentage was made for each percent that the actual cost exceeded the predicted cost plus the variance factor. For example, if the variance factor was 4 percent, and the district cost per pupil mile was 6 percent greater than the predicted cost, the state reimbursement percentage was reduced to 78 percent, a 2 percent reduction. The maximum reduction in the state reimbursement percentage under this provision was 25 percent; a minimum reimbursement rate of 60 percent was guaranteed.

In eleven states, pupil transportation aid was allocated through formulas providing a flat rate per unit of transportation need, where need was defined in terms of pupils, miles, or buses. In Arizona, the transportation support level was equal to the lesser of a flat amount per transported pupil or per approved route mile, adjusted for district enrollment size. Colorado provided a fixed rate per bus mile, plus 25 percent of district operating cost in excess of this rate. Iowa did not categorically fund pupil transportation but included the state average transportation cost per pupil in the basic state support program. In Montana, a certain amount per mile was allocated for each bus, depending on bus capacity. The Nebraska foundation program included a weighting factor of 1.25 for pupils residing more than four miles from school; this was equivalent to a flat amount per transported pupil. North Dakota provided a flat amount per pupil plus a flat amount per mile. In Ohio, a flat amount was provided per pupil or per mile, whichever was greater; different rates were specified for district, contractor, and public carrier operations. The Tennessee formula allocated 60 percent of the transportation appropriation based on number of pupils transported and 40 percent based on district square mile area. In Virginia, 40 percent of the transportation allocation was distributed based on pupils transported, 40 percent on mileage, and 20 percent on number of buses in daily use. Factors used in the Washington transportation aid formula included number of bus miles, number of logged hours, and a recognized rate of pay for school bus drivers. Wisconsin provided a variable amount per transported pupil, depending on the distance from home to school; transportation costs not reimbursed through this formula were included in the basic state support formula.

Financing Special Education Transportation

Considerable variation may also be found in provisions for state support of special education transportation. More than half of the states fund special education transportation through the basic state transportation formula, without special adjustments except the deletion of minimum distance requirements for state aid eligibility. This approach is commonly used in states employing an actual or approved district expenditure formula or a detailed budget model. Where a certain percentage of actual or approved costs is reimbursed, the reported costs generally include special education transportation costs. Where a detailed budget model is employed, the allocations for vehicles, personnel, and miles usually include the inputs necessary for transporting special education students.

Alternatively, several states make identifiable allocations for special education transportation by (1) providing an adjustment for this service within the transportation aid program, (2) specifying a separate calculation procedure within the transportation aid program, or (3) funding special education transportation through the state special education aid formula. In Kentucky, transportation funding for handicapped pupils is provided through the basic transportation formula by applying a weighting of 5.0 to the count of handicapped pupils transported. Minnesota employs a similar weighted pupil approach, and also provides a supplemental allocation for a percentage of excess special education transportation costs. Several states which fund regular transportation through an average cost formula provide funding for special education transportation through a separate calculation based on approved or actual district cost. For example, Kansas combines a density formula for regular transportation, with an 80 percent reimbursement formula for special education transportation. In other states, the special education aid formula includes a component for the transportation of handicapped pupils. Wisconsin, for example, pays 70 percent of special education transportation costs through the state handicapped aid formula. In addition to state and local funding, federal P.L. 94–142 funds are used for special education transportation finance in some nineteen states ("States Paying Cost . . ." 1980).

ANALYSIS OF ALTERNATIVE PROGRAMS

Because transportation need and local wealth vary widely among districts, state support is necessary to facilitate the provision of adequate pupil transportation services in all districts with reasonable local effort. State programs for financing pupil transportation have two basic elements: (1) the measurement of needs and costs, and (2) the determination of state and local contributions to overall funding. Four major approaches are employed by the states for measuring district transportation need: expenditure reimbursement formulas, detailed budget models, density formulas, and fixed unit cost formulas. After establishing the state-recognized transportation need for each district, state aid may be allocated on a fiscally equalized or unequalized basis. The strengths and weaknesses of alternative transportation funding programs may be analyzed using four general evaluative criteria: (1) recognition of necessary cost variations, (2) use of simple, objective calculation procedures, (3) promotion of efficiency, and (4) adequacy of funding.

Recognition of necessary cost variations is a basic criterion for evaluating state pupil transportation finance programs. The cost of pupil transportation varies considerably among districts, due partially to social, economic, and geographic factors which are beyond district control, and partially to district policies and procedures which affect transportation program quality and efficiency. To ensure that adequate financing is provided for each district, the state funding method should adjust for significant cost variations resulting from factors beyond district control. These factors include topography, road conditions, dispersion of population, prevailing wage rates, enrollment size, incidence of special and vocational education pupils, and density of transported population.

Alternative transportation funding methods differ substantially with regard to procedures for recognizing necessary cost variations. Expenditure reimbursement formulas based on actual costs shift the task of defining transportation need and necessary costs from the state to the local district. The state reimburses all costs at the same rate; no distinction is made between cost differences due to factors beyond district control, and cost differences resulting from district policies and procedures. While this method is appealing from a district perspective, it may result in an inefficient and inequitable funding distribution from the viewpoint of the state. Limited state dollars for pupil transportation are not allocated among districts based on the cost of providing a transportation program of uniform quality throughout the state. Instead, districts which have high costs due to unusually high quality of service or to inefficient operations receive a disproportionate share of available funding at the expense of districts with a lower quality of service or more efficient operations. To address this problem, several states using an expenditure reimbursement method base aid allocations on approved costs rather than actual costs. Through the cost approval process, reimbursable costs for various expenditure components are limited to a state-specified level.

In contrast to the expenditure reimbursement method, the detailed budget model establishes the responsibility for determining necessary costs of pupil transportation at the state level. Transportation need is defined in terms of the quantities of labor, materials, and equipment necessary for the provision of adequate transportation in each district. State officials actively monitor and approve input quantities requested by each district to ensure that transportation services of uniform quality are provided throughout the state. Necessary costs are calculated by applying standard rates to the approved input levels. To the extent that the inputs included in the budget model and the rates applied to approved input levels reflect the actual cost experience of the districts, the detailed budget model provides a thorough method for determining necessary cost variations among districts.

Density formulas provide recognition of necessary cost variations through the application of an average cost concept. Density is generally regarded as the principal factor not subject to local control which affects transportation costs. In states using this funding method, state-recognized costs for each district reflect the average cost for districts with similar density. Within a particular state, the validity of this approach depends on the strength and stability of the relationship between density and unit cost. Where density and cost are closely related, a formula based on density alone will provide an accurate measure of necessary cost variations. Where other factors not subject to district control have a significant independent impact on transportation costs, additional variables may be included in the average cost formula.

Fixed unit cost formulas vary widely in the degree to which necessary cost variations are recognized. Formulas providing a flat amount per transported pupil fail to recognize cost variations resulting from density of transported population, road conditions, prevailing wage rates, incidence of special education pupils, and other factors beyond school district control. Since density is generally the most significant factor contributing to variations in cost per transported pupil, such formulas tend to underfund districts in sparsely populated areas. Where a flat amount is provided per mile, cost variations due to road conditions, frequency of stops, traffic congestion, and vehicle size are not accounted for, placing an undue burden on urban districts. In general, fixed unit cost formulas based on a single factor do not adequately measure district transportation need, and provide an unnecessary bonus to districts with low unit costs at the expense of districts with high unit costs. Formulas utilizing multiple criteria, such as a flat amount per pupil or per mile, eliminate some of the major inequities inherent in the formulas based on a single factor, but may still provide only a rough measure of transportation need. In most cases, fixed unit cost formulas result in larger differences between formula funding and actual transportation cost than the three major alternatives do.

A second criterion is that the procedures for calculating state aid should be as simple and objective as possible while retaining accuracy. Simplicity and objectivity facilitate district planning and budgeting by enabling local administrators to make fairly accurate calculations of state aid entitlements. Administrative costs are lowered at the state and local levels as requirements for detailed record-keeping are reduced, extensive statistical analyses are avoided, and audit procedures are simplified. Additionally, simplicity and objectivity enhance the understanding and acceptance of the funding method by state and local policymakers.

Simplicity and objectivity, while important, should not take precedence over accurate measurement of district transportation needs. Unfortunately, the goals of simplicity and accuracy may conflict: the simpler the formula, the greater the likelihood that some of the factors contributing to necessary cost variations will not be adequately recognized. Fixed unit cost formulas based on a single factor and expenditure reimbursement formulas based on actual costs are probably the simplest methods employed by the states for financing pupil transportation, but they are also the least accurate in measuring necessary cost variations. Fixed unit cost formulas based on multiple criteria may provide greater accuracy, but require additional calculations, more detailed record-keeping, and more extensive audits.

Where a close relationship exists between density and unit costs, density formulas combine moderately simple calculation procedures with a reasonably accurate measurement of necessary cost variations. The data necessary for density formulas are readily available and easily audited. Complex statistical procedures are required at the state level, but the aid calculations may be completed quickly and inexpensively through the use of computers. While the administrative costs of density formulas are quite low, the use of an average cost concept based on complex statistical procedures may hinder understanding and acceptance of the funding method. Particularly where formula-generated costs are recomputed annually, district administrators may have difficulty in projecting state aid entitlements. Average cost formulas using more than one factor may permit more accurate recognition of necessary cost variations, but they are more complex and less understandable than formulas using density alone.

Detailed budget models and expenditure reimbursement formulas based on approved costs are generally more complex than other funding methods. Due to the large volume of data included in the aid calculations, the costs of record-keeping, reporting, and auditing are increased at both the state and local levels. To monitor and approve district programs and funding requests, a state bureaucracy of considerable size may be necessary. Formula adjustments to correct for inflation and changing cost patterns may require changes in several budget categories, rather than one overall rate. Subjective judgments of state officials regarding required services and reimbursement rates may conflict with local preferences, creating difficulties in planning and budgeting, and reducing local understanding and acceptance of the funding method.

Third, the state pupil transportation support program should promote efficiency in local transportation operations. State approval and monitoring of local programs is the most direct method of promoting efficiency. The effectiveness of this approach depends upon the availability and expertise of state administrators working cooperatively with local transportation managers to establish and maintain efficient transportation operations. As an alternative to direct state supervision, efficiency may be promoted by including incentives for efficient operation in the state aid formula. Two types of incentives have been widely suggested: (1) the use of average unit costs in calculating state aid, and (2) cost-sharing between the state and school districts. When efficiency is promoted through the use of incentives, information and assistance should be available from the state department to assist districts in developing more efficient operations. To avoid disincentives for efficiency, factors subject to local manipulation should either be excluded from the funding formula or be closely monitored to minimize potential abuses.

Detailed budget models promote efficiency through state approval and monitoring of district transportation programs, and by applying standard unit costs to approved inputs of labor, materials, and equipment. Expenditure reimbursement formulas based on approved costs also promote efficiency to a certain extent through the program approval process and by limiting reimbursable costs for various expenditure categories. Expenditure reimbursement programs based on actual costs do little to promote efficiency and may provide an incentive for inefficient program operation. The cost-sharing feature of programs that reimburse districts for a percentage of costs may provide some incentive for efficiency; however, since the majority of costs are paid by the state, cost increases are paid primarily from state sources, while cost savings reduce the local contribution only slightly.

Density formulas provide an incentive for efficiency by allocating state aid based on average unit costs adjusted for density. If the actual cost is less than the formula-predicted cost, the district receives funding greater than actual cost as a bonus for efficient operation. If the actual cost is greater than the formula-predicted cost, the district must provide the balance of funding from local sources. Since funding is based on average costs, district administrators are encouraged to compare their transportation operations with similar districts to identify possible cost savings. Districts with costs varying substantially from the norm are clearly identified and may be analyzed to determine what factors have contributed to unusually high or low unit costs.

Fixed unit cost formulas provide efficiency incentives by allowing a flat rate per unit of service and by requiring a substantial local contribution. Given a flat rate of state support per pupil or per mile, districts are encouraged to keep unit costs down so as to minimize the local contribution. Fixed unit cost formulas based on factors beyond district control establish a stronger efficiency incentive than formulas based on factors subject to district control. For example, a formula providing a flat amount per pupil will provide a stronger incentive for efficient bus routing and scheduling than a formula providing a flat amount per mile. Where funding is based on factors subject to district control, state monitoring may be necessary to minimize potential disincentives.

Funding adequacy is the fourth and final criterion for evaluating pupil transportation finance programs. No program of state support is fully satisfactory unless it supplies sufficient funding to enable each district, with reasonable local effort, to provide safe and timely transportation for all pupils needing the service. Funding adequacy requires that the state support program be comprehensive, fully funded, and fiscally equalized. State funding should be provided for all categories of authorized service such as regular, vocational, and special education transportation. All legitimate costs of the transportation program should be recognized in the formula, including capital outlay as well as operating expenses. State appropriations for pupil transportation, in combination with a reasonable local contribution, should fully fund transportation costs. Adjustment factors should be included for inflation and escalating energy costs to ensure that the intended level of state support is maintained. Finally, any local contribution required to support the state-recognized program should be fiscally equalized to provide an equitable distribution of local tax effort.

POLICY ISSUES

In conclusion, at least four basic policy issues must be resolved in designing a state pupil transportation finance program. First, what transportation services will be funded, and for whom? Will the state program be limited to transportation to and from school, or will it include transportation for instructional purposes during the day? Will transportation services for vocational and special education pupils be funded through the basic transportation finance formula or through a separate mechanism? Will minimum travel distances from home to school be established as a requirement for state aid eligibility? If travel distance eligibility requirements are used, will a uniform distance be specified for all grades, or will longer distances be specified for secondary pupils than for elementary pupils? What exceptions to minimum distance eligibility requirements will be provided for hazardous traffic conditions or other special circumstances? Will the state program be limited to public school pupils, or will nonpublic school pupils be included?

Second, how will the cost of pupil transportation be shared by the state and local school districts? What proportion of pupil transportation revenue will be provided from state sources and what proportion from local sources? How will the level of state support be adjusted for inflation and rising energy costs? Will state support be provided for operating costs only, or will bus depreciation be included in the state program? Will state funds be allocated on a flat grant basis or an equalized basis?

Third, how will necessary unit cost variations be recognized? Will greater emphasis be placed on accuracy or simplicity in the measurement of needs and costs? Will the funding method be based on individual district experience or on average unit costs? Will an expenditure reimbursement formula, a detailed budget model, a density formula, a fixed unit cost formula, or some combination of these approaches be employed?

Finally, will the state program be designed to promote efficiency in school district transportation operations? If so, will efficiency be promoted through state approval and monitoring of programs, average cost-funding formulas, cost-sharing between the state and school districts, or some combination of these methods? If an average cost formula is used, will districts with actual unit costs below formula-predicted costs be permitted to retain all or part of the difference as an incentive for efficient operation?

As transportation costs continue to escalate during the 1980s, state policymakers will be challenged to maintain adequate support for the service, and to develop new, efficiency-oriented funding formulas.

REFERENCES

Abel, J.F. 1923. *Consolidation of Schools and Transportation of Pupils.* Washington, D.C.: U.S. Bureau of Education Bulletin No. 41.

Alexander, Kern, et al. 1978a. *Educational Equity: Improving School Finance in Arkansas.* Gainesville, Fla.: Institute for Educational Finance.

_____. 1978b. *Our Children's Educational Needs: Reforming School Finance in West Virginia.* Gainesville, Fla.: Educational Finance and Research Institute.

Alexander, M. David. 1980. "Financing School Transportation." In *Improving School Finance in Louisiana,* edited by Kern Alexander. Gainesville, Fla.: Economics and Education Institute and Gulf South Research Institute.

Barr, W. Monfort. 1955. "State Support of Transportation." *The School Executive* 75 (November): 56–57.

Bernd, Cloyde M. 1975. "A Study of State Aided Pupil Transportation Programs for Colorado." Ph.D. Dissertation, University of Colorado.

Bernd, C.M.; William K. Dickey; and K. Forbis Jordan. 1976. "Revenue Requirements for School Transportation Programs and School Facilities." In *Educationla Need in the Public Economy,* edited by Kern Alexander and K. Forbis Jordan. Gainesville, Fla.: University Presses of Florida.

Briggs, Ronald, and David Venhuizen. 1976. "Characteristics and Costs of Pupil Transportation." *Traffic Quarterly* 30 (April): 303–323.

Burke, Arvid J. 1957. *Financing Public Schools in the United States.* New York: Teachers College, Columbia University.

Burns, Robert L. 1927. *Measurement of the Need for Transporting Pupils.* New York: Teachers College, Columbia University.

Chase, Francis S., and Edgar L. Morphet. 1949. *The Forty-Eight State School Systems.* Chicago: The Council of State Governments.

Evans, Frank O. 1930. *Factors Affecting the Cost of School Transportation in California.* Washington, D.C.: U.S. Bureau of Education.

Farley, Gene C.; M. David Alexander; and Gayle B. Bowen. 1973. "Foundation Program Transportation Study." In *Financing the Public Schools of Kentucky*, edited by Kern Alexander and K. Forbis Jordan. Gainesville, Fla.: National Educational Finance Project.

Featherston, E. Glenn, and D.P. Culp. 1965. *Pupil Transportation.* New York: Harper & Row.

Frohreich, Lloyd E. 1973. "An Analysis and Assessment of South Dakota's Pupil Transportation Program." In *Financing the Public Schools of South Dakota*, edited by Kern Alexander and K. Forbis Jordan. Gainesville, Fla.: National Educational Finance Project.

Gallay, Deborah, and Michael Grady. 1978. *Colorado School Transportation Study.* Denver, Colo.: Colorado Department of Education.

Grant, W. Vance, and C. George Lind. 1980. *Digest of Education Statistics 1979.* Washington, D.C.: U.S. Government Printing Office.

Hennigan, Robert; Orlando F. Furno; and James M. Gaughan. 1978. *Occasional Paper #33: An Analysis of the Pupil Transportation Program in New York State.* Albany, N.Y.: P.L. 93–380, Section 842 Project.

Hutchins, C.D., and T.C. Holy. 1938. "Pupil Transportation in Ohio." *American School and University* (May): 593–599.

Johns, R.L. 1928. *State and Local Administration of School Transportation.* New York: Teachers College, Columbia University.

_____. 1949. "Determining Pupil Transportation Costs." *Nation's Schools* 43, no. 2 (February): 48–49.

_____. 1978. *The Funding of School Transportation in Tennessee.* Gainesville, Fla.: Educational Finance and Management Institute.

Jordan, K. Forbis, and Kern Alexander. 1975. *Financing the Public Schools of Indiana.* Gainesville, Fla.: Institute for Educational Finance.

Jordan, K. Forbis, and Carol E. Hanes. 1978. "A Survey of State Pupil Transportation Programs." *School Business Affairs* 44 (May): 133–134.

Lambert, Asael C. 1938. *School Transportation.* Palo Alto, Calif.: Stanford University Press.

McKeown, Mary P. 1978. "An Efficiency-Oriented Funding Formula for Pupil Transportation." *Journal of Education Finance* 4, no. 2 (Fall): 225–233.

Mort, Paul R. 1924. *The Measurement of Educational Need.* New York: Teachers College, Columbia University.

_____. 1926. *State Support for Public Schools.* New York: Teachers College, Columbia University.

_____. 1933. *State Support for Public Education.* Washington, D.C.: American Council on Education.

Mort, Paul R., and Walter C. Reusser. 1941. *Public School Finance.* New York: McGraw-Hill.

National Association of State Directors of Pupil Transportation (NASDPT). 1980. *Statistics on Pupil Transportation 1978-79.* Redondo Beach, Calif.: Bobbitt Publishing Co.

Price Waterhouse and Company. 1980. "Analyzing Financial Management of a Pupil Transportation System." *School Bus Fleet* (June/July): 18-20.

Reusser, Walter C. 1932. "A Method of Measuring the Need for Transporting School Children." *American School Board Journal* 85 (September): 47, 76.

Skloot, Floyd. 1978. "The Road is Long—Problems in State Funding of Pupil Transportation Programs." *Planning and Changing* 9 (Spring): 34-41.

"States Paying Cost of Transporting Handicapped Students." 1980. *Education Daily* (September 24): 5-6.

Stollar, Dewey H. 1971. "Pupil Transportation." In *Planning to Finance Education,* edited by R. L. Johns, Kern Alexander, and K. Forbis Jordan. Gainesville, Fla.: National Educational Finance Project.

Stollar, Dewey H., and Kenneth Tanner. 1978. *Student Transportation Study for the State of Indiana.* Knoxville: University of Tennessee.

Strayer, George D., and Robert M. Haig. 1923. *The Financing of Education in the State of New York.* New York: MacMillan Company.

Tron, Esther O. 1980. *Public School Finance Programs, 1978-79.* Washington, D.C.: U.S. Government Printing Office.

III ACCOUNTABILITY AND ADEQUACY

The decade of the 1970s has been characterized by a concern for equity in state school finance programs. Through litigation and legislative reform, extensive efforts have been exerted to reduce the incidence of unfair treatment of pupils and taxpayers in terms of unequal, or inadequate, levels of fiscal effort required to fund education among local school districts. As indicated in Chapter 1, these efforts have not resulted in equality of educational opportunity for all pupils.

One of the continuing concerns in the reform effort has been to ensure that particular pupils who generate funds, or their proxies, actually benefit from the funding differentials. This issue and other aspects of fiscal accountability that relate to budgetary review and fiscal accounting procedures are reviewed in the discussion of such procedures and the challenge of developing a responsive policy.

Other accountability issues are related to student performance standards and minimum competency requirements. The second chapter focuses on the interaction of educational needs and various accountability efforts that have been implemented at the state level. Attention is given to the various issues and implications related to the educational accountability efforts.

The concept of adequate educational programs for students has been given increasing attention during the reform movement. Results of reform efforts have indicated that equity in funding does not necessarily result in adequate levels of fiscal support or adequate educational programs and services. In the concluding chapter, the concept of educational adequacy is examined through a discussion of different local, state, and federal efforts to ensure adequacy through voluntary actions, court decisions, regulations, and statutes.

9 FISCAL ACCOUNTABILITY
The Challenge of Formulating Responsive Policy

*Walter G. Hack**
*Carla Edlefson***
*Rodney T. Ogawa****

Fiscal accountability for public school systems: the legislator tirelessly pursues it; the academic passionately embraces it; and the practitioner skeptically regards it. But in so doing, each displays a Don Quixote posture—acting on one's own idealistic perception rather than on a concrete and commonly understood concept. Research and literature on the concept of fiscal accountability, if it has been done, has made no visible penetration into the body of knowledge of school finance.

Not only is there little written about fiscal accountability but to date, no significant or at least readily discernible programs of an explicit or comprehensive nature have been developed in any of the fifty states. It does appear, however, that there is fragmentary evidence of the presence of the concept of fiscal accountability in the research and literature, in specific and scattered legislative provisions, and in an underlying and implicit premise demonstrated in the development of school financing policy in a given state.

The three major sections of this chapter deal with three kinds of manifestations of fiscal accountability. In the first section, the state

*Walter G. Hack, Professor of Educational Administration, The Ohio State University.

**Carla Edlefson, Assistant Professor of Educational Administration, The Ohio State University.

***Rodney T. Ogawa, Assistant Professor of Educational Administration, The University of Utah.

251

of knowledge on fiscal accountability is described in terms of both what is known and what is not known through the research and literature. The second section, legislative provisions and applications, provides a description of how three states provide for their own unique versions of fiscal accountability. These are not meant to be representative state provisions and applications, but they probably are not atypical. In the final section, a case study of Ohio provides a look at the dynamics as well as the substance of a state school financing policy that has fiscal accountability as an underlying and implicit premise.

Before the evidence supporting the concept of fiscal accountability is assessed, it is appropriate to spell out how the authors view this un- or ill-defined notion. It is too early in the development of the concept to formulate a generalizable or universally applicable definition. Instead, in this chapter, fiscal accountability is characterized as school finance policy that specifies accountability for the results or outcomes derived from the exercise of discretionary authority by school policymakers or administrators in fiscal matters including revenue and taxation, budgeting and appropriation, and expenditure and resource management.

THE RESEARCH AND LITERATURE

Paucity is the most accurate descriptor of the body of knowledge pertaining to fiscal accountability. The Education Commission of the States (ECS), a broadly focused organization well positioned to monitor fiscal accountability developments, did not identify fiscal accountability as one of the seven major themes that characterized the numerous and divergent school finance reforms enacted during the decade of the 1970s (Odden and Augenblick 1980). However, tax and expenditure limitations which may be subsumed in the fiscal accountability concept, were mentioned. The concept of fiscal accountability was not brought up either as an issue related to school finance in the 1970s and projected into the 1980s or as an education finance policy issue for the 1980s as seen by state policymakers.

Those few writings that were uncovered are of two types: (1) studies of fiscal limitations and control, and (2) normative discussions of the purposes served by fiscal accountability. In the following section each type is discussed in turn.

Studies of Fiscal Limitations and Controls

Beyond published descriptions of individual states' school financing policies, research efforts have been almost exclusively devoted to descriptions and analyses of tax and expenditure limitations and controls. Tron (1976), in surveying states as to constraints on the ability of school districts to raise revenues and expend money, indicated that the most common form of restriction is the imposition of tax ceilings. She also concluded that states exert fiscal control of local school systems through the imposition of revenue or expenditure limits, fiscal authority review, and voter controls. Tron closed by raising a series of questions which her findings begged. In each case, the questions focused on the effects of the various control mechanisms identified in the study. To date, the literature provides no answers.

The Advisory Commission on Intergovernmental Relations (ACIR 1977) identified two types of fiscal limits: those that limit expenditures directly and those that limit revenues—especially taxes—and thus indirectly control expenditures. Expenditure limits usually provide for a proportional increase over the previous year's level. Referenda may be permitted to override the established limit.

Tax limits are more frequently imposed among the fifty states than are expenditure limits. These limits are of two types: those that restrict the types of taxes available to local governments and those that restrict the use of allowed taxes. Specific limitations include rate limits (mills per dollar of assessed valuation or dollars per $100 of assessed valuation), levy limits (the amount of revenue generated by levying rate on the assessed valuation), assessment ratio rules that specify the percentage of full market value that constitutes the assessed valuation of the property, and full disclosure laws that provide for reduction of tax rates in the event of increases in assessed valuation so as to maintain property tax revenues at or near the previous year's revenue.

The ACIR identified the following factors that have led to greater state control over local taxing powers:

- Public demanding for property tax relief;
- Courts mandating the upgrading of assessment practices;

- States assuming larger proportions of the state-local expenditures;

- States attempting to control the increase in school expenditures; and

- State legislators' contending that state restrictions are needed on local tax and spending powers to withstand the pressure for additional spending in general and employee wages and fringe benefits in particular (1977: 1-2).

The Education Commission of the States (ECS 1978) summarized the tax and expenditure limitation efforts made in the fifty states. As of July 25, 1978, some relevant effort had been initiated in thirty-eight states. The study also analyzed school district budget and tax rate procedures. These included (1) whether a vote is required for budget increases or tax increases, (2) what percentage of vote is required for approval, (3) what percentage of voter turnout is required in this election, and (4) what number of elections can be held in one year. Procedures for approving capital outlay bond issues were also analyzed.

Data from the ACIR (Shannon and Wallin 1978) disclosed state limitations on revenue and expenditure. Four major types of limitations were identified among the fifty states and the District of Columbia. The initial limitation, full disclosure,[1] was in practice in only one state, Florida. Property tax rate limitations,[2] the predominant limitation, were in effect in thirty states. Property tax levy limitations[3] (levy = rate × tax base) were being applied in Colorado, Indiana, Kansas, and Oregon. Of these four states, Indiana and Kansas also were subject to property tax rate limitations. Expenditure limitations were in force in Kansas, Maine, and Arizona. Fifteen states and the District of Columbia had none of the four types of limitations.

Since the passage of Proposition 13 in California in June 1978, a developing literature on tax and expenditure limitations has emerged. Much of it does not center specifically on schools. ECS conducted a study of the politics of the tax and expenditure limitation referenda in four states (Palaich, Kloss, and Williams 1980). They concluded that there was no monolithic "tax revolt" sweeping the country, and that it was impossible to predict the outcome of a containment referendum strictly on the basis of past experience of the state. They did find the state's political culture and current voter attitude to be important determinants of the outcome of such elections.

An important study of the *effects* of tax expenditure limits on the provision of services was conducted by the Rand Corporation (Menchik and Pascal 1980; Pascal et al. 1979). The Rand study pointed out that long-term effects of the fiscal containment movement may be a more regressive tax structure, reduced service levels, arbitrary cuts in public payrolls, fewer opportunies for minority employment, and loss of local control.

Referenda on tax and expenditure issues that were voted on in seventeen states in 1978 were analyzed in terms of origin, legal status, primary focus, and outcome (Mikesell n.d.). Eleven of the issues passed (including California's Proposition 13). Eight of the issues had originated in the legislature, eight by initiative, and one by constitutional convention. Of the seventeen issues, sixteen were constitutional amendments, while the remaining one was enacted as a statute. Property tax controls were the primary focus of eight of the issues, spending was the primary focus of six issues, both property tax and spending were the focus on two of the issues, and tax increases were the focus on one issue. Of the ten property tax control issues, six were passed; and of the eight spending control issues, five were passed.

A three-city study—Chicago, Cleveland, and New York—of the phenomenon of big city school bankruptcy (Cronin 1980) revealed that primary remediation approaches included the imposition of severe fiscal controls and the adoption of drastic retrenchment measures. Cronin considered the causes of the crises; the responses of local, state, and federal government as well as the lending community, the teachers, and the public; and the possible effects of the solutions—especially those related to the inroads made on local autonomy as financial control boards are set up to monitor processes and expenditures.

Discussions of Purpose

Even with the little that has been written about state fiscal accountability practices, there is even less written about the rationale for such practices. This is not to say, however, that the general concept has not received the attention of students of educational finance. In fact, fiscal accountability rests at the assumptive foundation of educational finance thought in the United States. This is evidenced by the consistent recitation in school finance texts of the need for school systems to record and disclose revenues and expenditures to the public. Note, for example, the tone and theme of the following excerpt from a 1956 text:

> The taxpayers have the right to know not only how their moneys have been spent but also how they have been cared for and how they are to be spent. This requires a broad program of financial publicity (Burke 1956:135).

Discussions concerning the functions served by fiscal accountability practices, however, have been entirely focused at the local school district level. The school finance literature has long emphasized the need for school systems to record and publicly disclose their financial operations. This, of course, is the essence of what is now referred to as fiscal accountability. The basic, underlying rationale for such financial recording and reporting, then, is to ensure that the public is informed about or, at a minimum, has access to information about their schools' financial transactions. This access is rooted in the ethos of public ownership and interest that pervades American thinking about education. As social institutions, public schools serve the general public good (Bidwell 1965) and are supported by revenues which in one form or another are provided by the citizenry. Whether funds are generated by local property tax, come from a central state fund, or are allocated by federal legislation, the source is the taxpayers' pocketbook. Fiscal accountability is thus aimed at informing the public about the status of its investment in public education.

The educational finance literature suggests that public disclosure of school systems' financial operations can serve two purposes. The first is a protective function. Fiscal accountability practices protect: (1) the consumer, the public at large; and (2) the producer, the public schools. In the first case, carefully and accurately compiled records of revenues and expenditures can serve to protect the public interest by providing data by which it can be determined if monies have been embezzled, squandered, or otherwise illegally or irresponsibly expended (Lessinger 1973:4).

Sound accounting and reporting practices can also serve to protect the public schools themselves from unsubstantiated accusations of illegal or unethical financial practices. This consideration can be important in these times of scarce monetary resources and public distrust of its institutions and officials.

Careful and systematic accounting practices can be an invaluable asset to both educators and the public in their efforts to develop measures of cost-benefit or cost-effectiveness (Candoli et al. 1978: 185). While professional educators may feel that public schools today face unprecedented levels of public scrutiny, a well-documented tradition exists in this country of public dissatisfaction about the effectiveness and efficiency of public educational institutions (Callahan 1962). Both critics and advocates of public education have proposed cost accounting practices and subsequent cost-benefit and cost-effectiveness analyses as contemporary responses to this long-standing issue. It is argued that such analyses can inform the public about the financial implications of program decisions (Candoli et al. 1978:185).

Reservations have been voiced, however, about the adequacy of both methods of analysis. First, the results of cost-benefit analysis are affected by the choice of the discount rate, a choice that has been argued to be arbitrary. In addition, this method of analysis utilizes market criteria when unmeasured educational outputs may actually be more important in determining the relative value of an educational program (Benson 1978:218).

The major drawback to cost-effectiveness analysis, on the other hand, lies not with the method itself but, as Benson argued: "When there are experiments and programs to evaluate, there is often little gain in effectiveness of educational activities to report upon" (1978: 218).

As shown in the previous discussion, the educational finance and policy literatures are relatively mute on the subject of fiscal accountability of public education at the state level. Beyond the studies of states' constraints on the ability of local school systems to raise revenues and expend money, the literature is devoid of investigations of state fiscal accountability practices. Naturally, then, there is a similar absence of works concerning the effects of such practices. Consequently, about all that can be said for the extant literature on fiscal accountability is that its paucity indicates a wide-open field for future research. For example, answers could be sought to such basic questions as: What mechanisms do state educational agencies employ to hold local school systems fiscally accountable? What patterns exist in fiscal accountability practices across states? To what extent do state fiscal accountability practices weaken the structure of local governance (Burke 1956:129)? What effects do various state fiscal accountability mechanisms have upon curbing school expenditures, narrowing the gap between high- and low-spending districts, or reducing property tax burdens (Tron 1976:282)?

CONVENTIONAL APPLICATIONS

Among the unresolved issues are to what extent and through what mechanisms should state school support programs through state governments hold local school systems fiscally accountable? For these issues as well as the above questions, there are, at this time, no conclusive answers. As noted in the previous section, no comprehensive survey of state fiscal accountability practices has been published. Further, despite some evidence that involvement in federal programs has influenced state educational accounting procedures (Milstein 1976:40), common wisdom holds that fiscal accountability practices vary widely among the nation's educational agencies.

In the absence of a comprehensive description of state fiscal accountability practices, brief descriptions of selected accountability practices are utilized to illustrate a range of alternative strategies employed by states. In the discussion three such strategies are described—uniform budgeting, accounting, and auditing practices; controls on taxation; and state categorical aid. The particulars of each strategy are described as implemented in a selected state. The states examined are Utah, Pennsylvania, and Florida, respectively.

Each description is structured around three dimensions of school systems' financial operations upon which fiscal accountability practices focus. These foci are *revenue accountability, allocation and management accountability*, and *expenditure accountability*. These three purposes of fiscal accountability provide a point of departure for discussions of fiscal accountability at the state level.

Revenue accountability concerns the matter of how school systems are held accountable for decisions concerning the determination of sources and amounts of revenue. With funds being available from numerous potential sources (for instance, several federal programs, local taxes, and a variety of general and categorical state aids), the problem of ensuring that school systems tap sources appropriate to their situations has become a very real one. Similarly, in the face of increasingly limited public funds and the emergence of equity issues, it has become necessary to ensure that school systems seek and receive those allocations that are relatively equitable and meet their particular needs.

Allocation and management accountability, the second focus of fiscal accountability, involves the matter of how school systems are held accountable for decisions concerning the allocation of funds as well as the implementation of those allocation decisions. Once revenues are determined, then local school officials must decide how to spend them. Since typically school systems have not had sufficient resources to fund everything to maximum levels, they must prioritize their needs, explicitly or implicitly, and make allocation decisions on that basis. Furthermore, allocations must be made according to state uniform budgeting standards. Thus, in order to account for the financial operations of any given system, it is necessary to establish how it allocated its funds and the manner in which those decisions were carried out.

The third focus of fiscal accountability, expenditure accountability, relates to how school systems are accountable for decisions to expend funds. This dimension of fiscal accountability receives the most popular attention since it represents what some would term "the bottom line." Fiscal accountability deals with three questions: How much was spent? On what was it spent? Was it legitimate and effective?

Together, these three foci—revenue, allocation and management, and expenditure—provide an "aerial photograph of the school system and its setting" (DeYoung 1956: 140).

Utah

The 1979 Utah State Board of Education's *Budgeting, Accounting, and Auditing Handbook* describes, in detail, the uniform budgeting, accounting, and auditing procedures with which, by state law, all Utah school systems must conform. The intent of implementing such uniform procedures is clearly one of accountability; the handbook stipulates that the new system will support direct delegation of the responsibility for results of educational programs. The question that must be answered in this discussion, however, is: How do these procedures contribute to fiscal accountability?

It is apparent that the budgeting, accounting, and auditing procedures adopted by Utah do address in varying degrees all three foci of fiscal accountability. All school systems are required by law to submit a proposed budget to the state board of education and the state auditor. In preparing a budget, school district officials must show revenues and expenditures of the preceding fiscal year, the estimated revenues and expenditures of the current year, and an estimate of revenues for the next year. This last estimate is based upon the lowest rate of tax levy that, in the opinion of district officials, will raise the amount of revenues required to operate the school system. After a public hearing and school board approval, the budget must be submitted to the state board of education and state auditor.

In terms of appropriations, state law prevents a local board of education from making appropriations in excess of estimated expendable revenue. Further, no increase can be made to any approved appropriation except in the case of emergencies. In such cases, the local superintendent is required to make a written request describing the emergency. The request must then be published, and a public hearing must be held to consider the request.

By law, Utah school systems must also utilize an accrual accounting procedure to record both revenues and expenditures. This means that revenues and expenditures are located when specific transactions occur. In addition, school systems must record revenues and expenditures according to over a hundred revenue classifications and several hundred expenditure classifications published in the handbook. While school districts are encouraged to utilize "individual minimum" expenditure accounts, the broad diversity of revenue and expenditure classifications is intended to accommodate the variations among the state's school systems and provide them with a wide variety of classifications from which they can select in terms of their specific accounting needs. Annual financial reports must be submitted by each school system to the state superintendent of instruction.

Finally, annual audits of a school system's financial accounting are required by Utah law. These audits are performed by independent auditors familiar with school accounting practices who are either independent certified public accountants or independent public accountants licensed to practice in Utah.

That the annual audits attend to all three foci of fiscal accountability is evident in the minimum requirements for financial audits outlined in the handbook published by the state board of education:

1. The school district's system of internal control must be assessed to determine its reliability and the applicable audit tests.

2. All sources of income, including nonrevenue generating, must be examined. Income must be separated by source, and "the propriety of the allocation of tax receipt between the different funds" must be assessed.

3. Disbursements of any funds must be examined. This would include the study of various documents (for instance, checks, warrants, invoices, requisitions, board minutes) to determine the authenticity of disbursements.

4. Actual receipts and expenditures must be compared with the budget to determine effectiveness of financial planning.

5. The legal authorization of expenditures must be checked.

6. Board minutes, insurance policies, contracts, and real estate deeds must be examined "insofar as they affect the financial transactions of the district."

7. The total bonded indebtedness of a school system must be determined, and the details for each bond issue should be recorded.

8. All revenue including those uncollected must be included in the determination of accounts receivable and compared to the official budget.

9. Total expenditures, and accounts payable, must be determined and compared with the year's official budget.

10. The accounting system employed by a district must be evaluated in terms of the accuracy with which it represents the school district's financial affairs.

11. It must be determined if the district is complying with its official salary schedule.

The completed audit, containing the above information, must be submitted to the Utah State Board of Education and the Utah State Auditor.

The annual audit of a school system's financial affairs, then, focuses upon revenue accountability in that all sources of revenue are examined and compared to the official budget for that year. Similarly, the audit examines all expenditures to determine their "authenticity and the legality of their authorization," and to compare actual expenditures with those projected in the annual budget. Finally, allocation and management accountability is established by auditing the "propriety of the allocation of tax receipts" and by assessing the adequacy of financial planning practices through the comparison of actual revenues and expenditures with the official budget.

Pennsylvania

The state of Pennsylvania takes several approaches to hold its local school systems fiscally accountable. In this discussion, the focus is on one particular approach—state controls on taxation at the local level for the support of public schools. By its very nature, control of taxation focuses on the revenue dimension of fiscal accountability. Its importance is underscored by the fact that 46 percent of all funds spent by Pennsylvania's public schools in 1977–78 were generated by local taxes.[4]

The Pennsylvania public schools are divided into five classes based upon population. Class 1 districts are those with 1,500,000 or more in population; class 1A districts have populations between 500,000 and 1,500,000; class 2 districts have between 30,000 and 500,000 inhabitants; class 3 districts have a population between 5,000 and 30,000; and class 4 districts have fewer than 5,000 inhabitants. Classes 1 and 1A consist of only one district each. This point is noted because Pennsylvania laws governing local taxes are uniform for all districts in classes 2 through 4. Since laws are specifically tailored to the situations peculiar to the state's two largest systems, Philadelphia (class 1) and Pittsburgh (class 1A), these two exceptions are discussed separately following a description of tax controls exerted on the state's other 503 systems.

Revenues accrued from local taxes on real property accounted for 35.1 percent of all money spent on public schools in 1977–78. Taxes for general school purposes must not exceed 25 mills. However, school districts may levy an additional tax, on which the state places no ceilings, to raise funds for the following purposes: salaries, rent due municipal authorities or the State Public School Building Authority, sinking fund charges, and amortization of a bond issue which provided a building before the first Monday of July 1959. This has the practical effect of removing any ceiling on the levying of real property taxes to raise revenues for legal and justifiable purposes (Castetter, Ferguson, and Heisler 1980: 64).

As of March 10, 1970, public utility real property in Pennsylvania became subject to taxation by local school districts and municipal governments. Each year public utilities are required to pay a tax at the rate of 30 mills on each dollar of the state taxable value of their real property. Each school district receives a share of these taxes paid by public utilities based upon information submitted to the department of revenue.

School districts also may levy a per capita tax of up to a total of fifteen dollars. This tax is levied on each individual in the school district who is eighteen years of age or older.

Under Act 11 of December 31, 1965, school districts along with other political subdivisions of the state were authorized to collect a wide range of taxes. These include taxes levied on wage and income, real estate transfer, occupation, assessment, amusement, house trailers, and mechanical devices. Act 11 also places a number of controls on the taxes it authorizes. First, in cases where the state general assembly imposes a tax on any subject specified in Act 11, any political subdivision that, at that time, levies a tax on the same subject must cease to do so by the end of the fiscal year. In this same spirit is the stipulation that when two political subdivisions impose a tax on any subjects authorized in Act 11 upon an individual located within both subdivisions, then the tax levied will be one-half of the rate of each subdivision while such duplication exists.

Furthermore, the total taxes levied under Act 11 must not exceed the product of 12 mills times the assessed market value of real property in a given school district. This does not hold for class 3 or class 4 districts in which one hundred or more homes are constructed in a given year.

Act 11 also specified the nature of the process by which tax resolutions must be adopted. First, a notice of intention to adopt a tax resolution must be advertised once a week for three weeks prior to formal adoption. Such a notice must include information regarding the nature of the tax, the reasons for levying the tax, and the estimated revenues that it will generate. Upon final adoption, a certified copy of the resolution must be filed with the state's department of community affairs within fifteen days after its effective date.

As already noted, tax laws have been tailored to the specific situations in Philadelphia and Pittsburgh. Both school districts may levy a real property tax not in excess of 11.75 mills to pay minimum salaries and increments of teaching and supervisory staff, both principal and interest on indebtedness, rentals due to municipal or state authorities, and all other expenses and requirements. Also both Philadelphia and Pittsburgh have been authorized by a series of public laws to collect an additional 17.25 mills of real property tax for general purposes. Both districts currently tax real property to the maximum levels allowed.

State laws also authorize the Philadelphia school district to levy the following taxes: a general business tax of up to 2 mills but not more than 20 mills on net income; a 40 mill tax on pari-mutuel betting; a 12.5 mill tax on the use of real estate for business purposes; as well as a 43.1 mill tax on each resident on income resulting from ownership, lease, and sale of real property and tangible and intangible personal property.

In the case of the Pittsburgh school district, state laws authorize the levying of the following taxes: a tax of 1 to 4 mills on intangible personal property; license fees of two dollars to operate a place of business; a tax of .5 mill on each dollar of business of wholesale vendors; a mill on each dollar of business of retail vendors; and a 10 mill tax on the income of residents and on net profits of businesses and professions.

The above descriptions illustrate that the state of Pennsylvania provides wide ranges on school revenue sources but at the same time places important constraints on the sources and amounts of locally generated revenues which school systems can tap. While it might be argued that in light of the broad discretion provided to local school officials, these constraints are not highly restrictive, they nonetheless designate the legitimate range of revenue sources as well as the relative amount of resources which can be generated from each source. Such constraints thus provide standards to which school districts can be held accountable.

Florida

Like the other forty-nine states (Tron 1980), Florida's school support program specifies categories of programs toward which revenues are allocated. Such specifications impact upon the revenue, allocation, and expenditure foci of fiscal accountability. In the case of Florida, there are three general types of categories. The first is the state's basic aid formula. The second is special categorical aid. Third, there are programs that fall under the rubric of "special allocations." The particulars of each type will be discussed separately.[5]

The program of basic aid accounts for the bulk of revenues provided by the state of Florida to its school districts. The specific amount of funding provided to each district is determined through a three-step calculation process aimed at compensating for different revenue requirements across districts and programs. The state legislature establishes the base student allocation; that is, a basal per student funding level is determined. Having recognized that various instructional programs require different relative levels of funding, Florida has differentially weighted twenty-six instructional programs in its basic aid funding. For example, the basic program for grades four to nine has a cost factor of 1.00, while the program for hospital and homebound students has been assigned a factor of 14.14. These factors represent the low and high extremes of the cost-weighting scale. The other program types specified by the state are kindergarten through grade three; grades ten to twelve; educational alternatives; fourteen types of special education programs, adult basic education and adult high school; and six categories for vocational education.

The second type of program category in Florida's state school support program is specified in terms of allocation of special categorical program funds. Special categorical programs encompass a broad range of instructional and noninstructional services: community schools, instructional materials, school lunch programs, student development services, student transportation, comprehensive health education program, and regional diagnostic-resource centers. Funds allocated for any of these categorical programs are added to the basic aid provided to a school system.

The final type of program category is designated as special allocations of funds for the following: environmental education, compensatory education, and instructional materials for the visually handicapped. School districts must submit written proposals to receive funds for the first two of these special allocation programs. The third category supports an instruction materials center which provides materials for visually handicapped students throughout Florida.

Florida's state school support funding program identifies, to varying levels of specificity, the sorts of programs for which the expenditure of its three revenue categories—basic aid, categorical aid, and special allocations—is appropriate. Such specification of programs reflects each of the three foci of fiscal accountability. First, it determines the levels of *revenue* that a given school system will receive in general, and for designated program areas specifically. Second, it tends to define, at least on the programmatic dimension, what *allocations* are appropriate. Finally, as it defines legitimate allocations it also establishes a standard against which the appropriateness of actual *expenditures* can be judged.

These three descriptions of various elements of state school support programs suggest that alternative strategies are available and are being employed by state agencies to hold local school systems fiscally accountable. These alternative strategies fit into the taxonomy of the three dimensions of fiscal accountability as suggested in the literature: revenue accountability, allocation and management accountability, and expenditure accountability. Pennsylvania's control over local taxation determines both the sources and amounts of revenue which school systems are able to raise locally. Finally, the various program categories enumerated in Florida's school support program determine revenues, define what allocations are appropriate, and establish a standard against which the appropriateness of expenditures can be gauged.

INCREASED FISCAL ACCOUNTABILITY
REQUIREMENTS: OHIO'S RESPONSE

Ohio

Compared with other states, Ohio is a low-tax, low-expenditure, low-public service state, with a long tradition of fiscal conservatism. Of all the states and the District of Columbia, Ohio ranks 50th in state and local revenues per $1,000 of per capita personal income

(Bureau of the Census 1980: 94). Per pupil expenditures for elementary and secondary education are 9 percent below the national average (Ohio Department of Education 1980).

During the 1970s, the state's contribution to school funds rose from about 33 percent to about 45 percent, but the system is still based on property taxes and, particularly, the necessity for voters to approve additional property taxes at frequent intervals. Ohio is a strong "local control" state; thus, its 1975 school finance reform attempt was a guaranteed tax base type. Local expenditures and local tax rates are determined by local approval of property tax levies; therefore, no departure from tradition was required.

Since 1925, Ohio has had a law requiring property reappraisals, and additional progress was made in the 1960s and 1970s in this area. Ohio probably does a better job of conducting current, uniform appraisals than many other states; however, when property is reappraised, only the first 10 mills (called "inside millage") of tax are applied to the new value. Millage above 10 is effectively rolled back to yield the same amount of revenue as it did before reappraisal. Therefore, growth in property tax revenues comes only from inside millage and additions to the tax duplicate unless voters approve increases. This kind of control on the growth of property taxes is not new, for it has existed in some form in Ohio since 1831 (Levin 1977:1).

Public elementary and secondary schools, of course, depend very heavily on property taxes and are most affected by the rollbacks. They typically receive less than half of their revenues from the inside millage; other local governments receive the remainder. Thus, the growth of local revenue in many school districts is less than 5 percent per year.

A considerable amount of national media attention focused on schools closing for lack of money in Ohio in 1977 and 1978. Several legal constraints are worthy of note. Neither the state nor local governments may show deficits in operating funds at the end of the fiscal year. The prohibitions on borrowing from other funds are also very tight. School districts run on a calendar year, so the ones that anticipated coming up short on December 31 would close down for a few days in late fall to save operating costs and make up the days in spring. Schools that did this were required to have a certificate of the estimated deficit from the state auditor. In the ten years from 1967 to 1976, 37 of 617 school districts temporarily closed for financial reasons. The usual length of time of closure was ten to fifteen days. Of the fifteen districts that closed in the fall of 1977, eight were successful in passing levies while the doors were closed. One of the eight was the Toledo city school district, which had closed in 1976. It took two closures for Toledo to pass a levy.

Ohio had a relatively strong set of fiscal controls on school districts in 1977. Some that have been alluded to are:

1. There was very little growth in local revenue without voter approval.

2. School district operating funds were required to show a cash balance of at least zero, and short-term notes had to be paid by December 31.

3. Transfers from other funds to the operating fund, even temporarily for cash-flow purposes, were restricted.

4. Schools needed permission from the state auditor to alter the school calendar because of financial difficulties.

In a state that already had fairly tight fiscal controls on school districts and a low expenditure for education, one might have predicted that the 1977–78 crisis in school finance would have brought an increase in state funds for schools. But the chief response in Ohio was to impose more fiscal accountability.

Problems and Legislative Responses

Table 9–1 shows a classification of the reforms enacted by the Ohio General Assembly in 1978 and 1979. In the areas of revenue accountability and expenditure accountability, few changes were made, although the Ohio legislators tightened up many aspects of allocation or management accountability. Generally speaking, school districts were not exacting great amounts of revenues from overburdened taxpayers; strict controls on revenue growth already existed. Likewise, expenditures were closely regulated. The Ohio legislature concentrated on state oversight of financial management—anticipating revenue shortfalls, cutting budgets to allow living within means, and requiring cutbacks in programs instead of school system shutdowns when funds were short.

Table 9-1. Changes in Ohio Law Affecting Revenue Accountability, Allocation and Management Accountability, and Expenditure Accountability, 1978-79

A. *Revenue Accountability*

Under certain very limited conditions, school districts could ask voters to approve a local income tax levy for the purpose of paying back a state loan (Formula Law).

B. *Allocation and Management Accountability*

1. The state auditor has the specific responsibility to review district finances to look for illegal fund transfers or borrowing (Management Act).

2. A procedure was established for financial takeover of local district by the state board of education (Management Act).

3. The state superintendent must audit the district's educational programs and recommend cuts that could be made before the district is allowed to close for financial reasons (Management Act, prior to passage of No Closing Act).

4. The state board must provide yearly inservice programs on financial management for board members, superintendents, treasurers, and business managers, whose attendance would be required (Management Act).

5. The state board must provide districts with technical assistance in financial management (Management Act).

6. The title of school board "clerk" was changed to "treasurer," and the state requirements for holders of the position were upgraded (Management Act).

7. Recommendations for budget-cutting and fiscal management must be made by the state superintendent and approved by the controlling board before a district may receive a state loan (Loan Fund Act).

8. A state loan was created to give districts another borrowing option and to prevent closing (Loan Fund Act).

9. Additional responsibilities were given to the state superintendent and the county auditor to monitor the budgets of local school districts and to take certain actions if they anticipated a problem (No Closing Act).

10. The state superintendent's authority was increased with regard to the takeover of the finances of a local district (No Closing Act).

(Table 9-1. continued overleaf)

Table 9-1. continued

B. *Allocation and Management Accountability (continued)*

11. School closings were prohibited; districts that run out of money must seek a state loan. The state superintendent must ask the attorney general to seek an injunction to stop a school district from closing (No Closing Act).

12. A subsidy was created for local districts who joined the computer network to implement the Ohio new accounting system (Budget Act).

C. *Expenditure Accountability*

1. A school district budget does not become effective without a certification by the county auditor to the state superintendent that appropriations do not exceed estimated available resources. This strengthened an existing law (Management Act).

2. Every school board must adopt a spending plan to be submitted every year as part of its budget to the state superintendent (Management Act).

3. The school board president, treasurer, and superintendent can be held personally liable for up to $20,000 each if they approve the appropriation of funds for which revenues are not available. This strengthened an existing law (Management Act).

During 1978 and 1979 the Ohio General Assembly passed five bills that contained fiscal accountability measures for local school districts. The first one, the School Management Act (HB 1285), was the result of a House Finance Committee study of the problems behind the record number of school closings in late 1977. As Table 9-1 shows, most of the provisions of the Management Act were in the area of allocation or management accountability.

The second piece of fiscal accountability legislation, the Loan Fund Act (SB 493), was passed in response to the probability that Cleveland and Columbus, as well as some smaller districts, would not have sufficient funds to finish the calendar year. This legislation imposed additional allocation accountability restrictions (see B7 and B8 in Table 9-1) in addition to setting up a state loan fund for bankrupt districts.

The third new bill (SB 59) was the 1979 Foundation Formula Law. It contained additional revenue raising possibilities for districts that had received state loans (see A in Table 9-1). This new provision, allowing state-loan districts to attempt to obtain voter approval of a personal income tax for schools, was enacted because of a concern that some districts might not be able to repay their state loans unless new revenues were available to them.

The 1979–81 State Budget Act (HB 204) contained subsidies for districts who joined a computerized accounting and budget network (see Table 9–1, B12).

Finally, the No Closing Act (HB 44) passed in the fall of 1979, outlawed the practice of closing schools for lack of funds and required districts that were out of funds to use the state loan fund. Previously, the loan fund had been optional. Part of the impetus for the passage of this law came from the Cincinnati schools' inability to pass a levy and their resolve to close in fall 1979. Legislators had believed in 1978 that the loan fund would be a temporary solution to school funding problems in the state. In 1979, they realized more districts would be needing loans, so they decided to make the loan fund permanent and require districts to use it.

Responding to Ohio's Problems

In late 1977 and early 1978 there were clearly some strong political pressures for the Ohio General Assembly to do something about the financial problems of the schools. The large city school systems were in particular difficulty, and the major newspapers in the state made sure that the public was well aware of that fact. The possibility of the large city districts running out of money and shutting their doors to tens of thousands of students in an election year was a strong impetus for state action. (Many rural school districts were also in great difficulty, but their plight was not material for headlines in the big city newspapers.)

There really were only two choices the Ohio General Assembly could make in responding to the schools' financial problems: (1) give the schools enough money to allow them to continue their programs without disruption; or (2) figure out a way to make them get by on available funds.

In 1971 when a similar set of choices confronted the Ohio General Assembly, they chose the first solution (Siegel 1976); in 1978 and 1979 they chose the second.

More Money. There is some evidence that in 1978 and 1979 the governor and the Ohio General Assembly recognized that schools needed more money. Both in the Loan Fund Act of 1978 (SB 493) and the State Budget Act of 1979 (HB 204), the legislative leaders and the governor supported giving a very large proportion of new state money to schools. If more money had been available, more might have gone to schools. However, the state leaders were not willing to raise state taxes for schools (or for anything else). Governor Rhodes had stated many times for the public record that no new state taxes were needed, and he built his 1978 re-election campaign around that pledge. Politicians remembered the political casualties that had resulted from the enactment of the state personal income tax in 1971, and they believed they could not be re-elected if they raised taxes in an election year. The re-election of the governor on a no-new-taxes platform confirmed their belief that the electorate opposed a tax increase.

Without the Governor's support it was unlikely that an increase in funds for schools or a major change in the tax structure supporting schools could be accomplished (Fuhrman 1978; Fuhrman, Berke, Kirst, and Usdan 1979; LWVEF 1978; Siegel 1976). Unlike the Ohio situation in 1971 reported by Siegel (1976), there were no strong forces that favored raising taxes to increase school funds in 1978. Finally, school districts in Ohio had unlimited authority to propose property tax increases for schools. It was relatively easy for state legislators and the governor to rationalize that if people wanted to spend more money on schools, they could vote to increase their local property taxes.

Making Schools Live with Available Revenue. Since the pressure was there to do something about school finance problems, and the political climate and the inclination of the governor ruled out raising taxes, the Ohio General Assembly in 1978 and 1979 responded by enacting more financial accountability measures. There were at least two other factors that explain this kind of response from the legislature.

1. The first factor was a belief that many local school boards were too weak in the face of pressures from interest groups asking for more esoteric programs to be offered in the schools and from em-

ployee groups asking for more wages and fringes. The legislators were afraid that school boards were unable to say "no" to these pressures and then were asking the state for the money to pay for what the local districts had promised but could not afford. This feeling was enhanced by a declining propensity among legislators to favor the positions of organized labor, including the Ohio Education Association (OEA). The governor and the OEA prided themselves as being on opposite sides of most issues, as well. Lobbyists for the Ohio School Boards Association and the school administrators' organizations did not refute the argument that school boards needed to say "no." They tended instead to argue that schools were being required to do too much, and that the general assembly should allow the schools to narrow their mission.

2. A second major factor in explaining the legislature's turning to new financial accountability requirements was the resentment, distrust, and exasperation toward the big city school districts. These feelings were not only prevalent among the rural delegates and the rural leadership but extended even to the legislators who represented the large cities whose schools were in trouble. The clear evidence that there was actual mismanagement existed only for Cleveland (Parham 1977; Senate Education Committee 1978), but Cleveland's errors caused a souring of attitudes toward all the large city districts. Of course there was also resentment against Cincinnati, since that city was the source of a lawsuit against the state's school finance system. Court-ordered desegregation in Cleveland, Columbus, and Dayton complicated matters because state legislators did not want to be politically accountable for bailing out these districts and thus indirectly funding the desegregation efforts.

The behavior of the state policy process in this period could be described as a series of reactions to political pressures caused by local school districts' financial problems. The policies represent incremental changes rather than a total restructuring of the school finance and tax systems. Restructuring is always hard to do, but leaders in the Ohio General Assembly did not want to restructure until they knew what the resolution of the *Cincinnati* v. *Walter* (1979) case would be. Apparently, they did not feel that there was sufficient public support for major tax policy changes without the impetus of a court order. The governor was interested neither in school finance reform nor in tax changes.

Neither education interest groups nor the state superintendent led the policymaking charge during this period. Most of the legislative committee work on these bills was done in finance, not education, committees. Policies contained in the bills passed in 1978 and 1979 were political responses to political pressures. Rather than being education policies, the changes were designed by politicians attempting to be responsive to their constituents' concerns about management of public funds.

The Ohio case suggests that legislative response to school districts' financial problems depends in some part on a number of factors—analysis of the problems, political climate with regard to taxes, timing of elections, the leadership of the governor, pending court decisions, and previous experience with fiscal control.

Effectiveness of the Ohio Measures

A few comments should be made about the effectiveness of the fiscal accountability measures enacted by the Ohio General Assembly in 1978 and 1979. A number of school districts have been helped by the loan funds and management assistance from the department of education, resulting in a more stable financial position for the districts. Some districts may have needed to go through a temporary austerity period to adjust to enrollment decline and inflation or to change poor management procedures (Cronin 1980). As of the end of 1980, 20 districts had received loans, and more than 150 had received some type of management assistance from the state department of education. In general, the property tax referenda passage rate seemed better after people realized that the 1979–81 state budget was not going to result in great new revenues from the state.

Even after the legislative and state department of education efforts, the Cleveland school system continues to suffer in 1981 from myriad violations of state minimum standards, questionable financial management procedures, a 1981 deficit of $46 million, and continual unrest among the employees. A new round of political pressures and legislative responses is beginning.

SUMMARY

As we consider the state-of-the-art of fiscal accountability, what is considered an emerging school of thought appears to be in the process of seeking its own character. A rationale for fiscal accountability appears to be well accepted by many groups concerned with school finance policy. A discrete and comprehensive concept has not yet been developed. However, in exploration of the topic, several characterizations did emerge.

The concept has not yet been defined in a formal and generally accepted terminology. References to fiscal accountability are typically generic and are normative in character—whatever it is, it is good and a goal to be sought. Rather than proposing a definition, the authors instead developed their own characterization of the concept: fiscal accountability is a school finance policy that specifies accountability for results or outcomes derived from the exercise of discretionary authority by school policymakers or administrators in fiscal matters including revenue and taxation, budgeting and appropriation, and expenditure and resource management.

There is no identifiable or comprehensive body of fiscal accountability research and literature. However, isolated studies—many times found in the literature of related fields such as public finance—appear to contribute to an emerging pattern of knowledge suggesting a general concept of fiscal accountability. Typical of these kinds of work are studies of fiscal controls on revenue increases, tax limitations, budgetary procedures and limitations, and expenditure limitations and controls.

Among the fifty states there is limited and fragmentary evidence of the implementation of discrete and idiosyncratic policies that constitute parts or aspects of a concept of fiscal accountability. The patterns of such policies among the states seem to be so varied that few generalizations of fiscal accountability can be drawn at this time. Some states have developed complex patterns of options and controls on revenue increases, some have patterns of options on revenue or tax sources and limitations, while others have established accounting and budgetary mandates or cash flow management controls.

Evidence drawn from the case study in Ohio suggests the presence of an underlying and implicit premise of fiscal accountability. A series of state responses to severe school district financial problems implies a unifying concept that tends to suggest and order the responses. The policies of accountability were built on previously enacted provisions of fiscal controls and limitations.

With a political genesis driven by political forces during its formulation, the movement toward fiscal accountability was a political phenomenon that responded to specific problems and needs. Fiscal accountability did not appear as a generic or universally applicable technical device such as an explicit factor in a school foundation program formula.

Lastly, the movement toward fiscal accountability generates additional responsibilities not only for local school districts but also for state education agencies. School districts are required to respond to additional accountability mandates. State agencies are required to monitor the activities of school districts, develop and implement triggering devices which determine when state intervention is called for, and provide for that intervention which may include sanctions, revenue, advice and management services, and perhaps even a form of receivership.

Fiscal accountability as an emerging concept already suggests that it not only solves problems but also generates questions. What are the appropriate mechanisms to provide fiscal accountability? What factors determine the appropriate mechanism? What is the effect of fiscal accountability on school district authority and power? What is the effect of fiscal accountability on pupil equity? On taxpayer equity? On efficiency and effectiveness?

Clearly, professional and scholarly involvement is needed so that a carefully and rationally developed positive approach to fiscal accountability can be formulated to ensure that a piecemeal or patchwork policy does not prevail.

NOTES TO CHAPTER 9

1. Under a full disclosure procedure, a property tax rate is established that will provide a levy equal to the previous year's when applied to some percentage of the current year's tax base. In order to increase the levy above the amount derived by using the established rate, the local governing board must advertise its intent to set a higher rate, hold public hearings, and thereafter approve the higher rate by vote of the board.

2. Property tax rate limitation sets a maximum rate that may be applied against the assessed value of property.

3. Levy limitation places a maximum on the amount of revenue that can be raised by the property tax (for instance, 106 percent of the prior levy).
4. The information contained in this section was drawn from Castetter, Ferguson, and Heisler (1980).
5. See Florida Department of Education (1979) for the source of all information contained in this section.

REFERENCES

Advisory Commission on Intergovernmental Relations (ACIR). 1977. *State Limitations on Local Taxes and Expenditures.* Washington, D.C.: U.S. Government Printing Office.

Benson, Charles S. 1978. *The Economics of Public Education.* Boston: Houghton Mifflin.

Bidwell, Charles E. 1965. "The School as a Formal Organization." In *Handbook of Organizations,* edited by James G. March. Chicago: Rand McNally College Publishing Co.

Budgeting, Accounting, and Auditing Handbook. 1979. Salt Lake City: Utah State Board of Education.

Bureau of the Census. 1980. *Statistical Abstract of the United States.* Washington, D.C.: U.S. Government Printing Office.

Burke, Arvid J. 1956. "Finance in School Business Management." In *School Business Administration,* edited by Henry H. Linn. New York: Ronald Press.

Callahan, Raymond E. 1962. *Education and the Cult of Efficiency.* Chicago: University of Chicago Press.

Candoli, I. Carl; Walter G. Hack; John R. Ray; and Dewey H. Stollar. 1978. *School Business Administration: A Planning Approach.* Boston: Allyn and Bacon.

Castetter, William B.; Norma B. L. Ferguson; and Richard S. Heisler. 1980. *Guide to Pennsylvania School Finance.* Philadelphia: Center for Field Studies and Center for School Study Councils, Graduate School of Education, University of Pennsylvania.

Cincinnati v. *Walter,* 390 N.E.2d 813 (1979).

Cronin, Joseph M. 1980. *Big City School Bankruptcy.* Palo Alto, California: Stanford University, Institute for Research on Education Finance and Governance.

DeYoung, Chris A. 1956. "The School Budget." In *School Business Administration,* edited by Henry H. Linn. New York: Ronald Press.

Education Commission of the States (ECS). 1978. *School District Expenditures and Tax Controls.* Denver, Colorado.

Florida Department of Education. 1979. *1978–79 Florida Education Finance Program.* Tallahassee, Florida.

Fuhrman, Susan. 1978. "The Politics and Process of School Finance Reform." *Journal of Education Finance* 4, no. 2 (Fall): 158–178.

Fuhrman, Susan, with Joel Berke; Michael Kirst; and Michael Usdan. 1979. *State Education Politics: The Case of School Finance Reform.* Denver: Education Commission of the States.

League of Women Voters Education Fund (LWVEF). 1978. *Campaigning for Fair School Finance: Cases in Point.* Washington, D.C.: LWVEF.

Lessinger, Leon M. 1973. "Accountability and Humanism: A Productive Educational Complementarity." In *Accountability: Systems Planning in Education,* edited by Creta D. Sabine. Homewood, Ill.: E.T.C. Publications.

Levin, Richard A. 1977. "Property Tax Limits in Ohio." Paper presented to the 45th Annual Meeting of the National Association of Tax Administrators, June.

Menchik, Mark D., and Anthony Pascal. 1980. "Equity Effects of Restraints on Taxing and Spending." Rand Paper P–6469. Santa Monica, Calif.: The Rand Corporation.

Mikesell, John L. n.d. "The Season of Tax Revolt: Referenda on Tax Expenditures Control in 1978." Bloomington, Ind.: School of Public and Environmental Affairs, Indiana University. Mimeo.

Milstein, Mike M. 1976. *Impact and Responses: Federal Aid and State Education Agencies.* New York: Teachers College Press.

Odden, Allan, and John Augenblick. 1980. *School Finance Reform in the States: 1980.* Denver: Education Commission of the States.

Ohio Department of Education. 1980. "Factsheet." Columbus, Ohio, January.

Palaich, Robert; James Kloss; and Mary Frase Williams. 1980. *Tax and Expenditure Limitation Referenda: An Analysis of Public Opinion Voting Behavior and Campaigns in Four States.* Denver: Education Commission of the States.

Parham, David L. 1977. "A Financial Crisis in Review: The Cleveland Schools in 1977." Paper prepared for the Study Group on Racial Isolation in the Public Schools and Its Member Organizations from the Greater Cleveland Area, December.

Pascal, Anthony; Mark David Menchik; Jan M. Chaiken; Phyllis L. Ellickson; Warren E. Walker; Dennis E. De Tray; and Arthur E. Wise. 1979. *Fiscal Containment of Local and State Government.* Report R–2429–FF/RC. Santa Monica, Calif.: The Rand Corporation.

Senate Education Committee. 1978. "Cleveland City School District Fiscal Problems." Columbus, Ohio: Legislative Budget Office of the Ohio General Assembly.

Shannon, John, and Bruce Wallin. 1978. "The Tax Revolt—Implications for Education Policy Holders." Forum of Educational Organization Leaders. Washington, D.C.: Advisory Commission on Intergovernmental Relations, November.

Siegel, Peggy M. 1976. "The Politics of School Finance Reform." In *State Policy Making for the Public Schools*, edited by R.F. Campbell and T.L. Mazzoni. Berkeley: McCutchan Publishing Corp.

Tron, Esther O. 1976. "Fiscal Controls and Tax Requirements Imposed by States and Tax Options Available to School Districts." In *Selected Papers in School Finance 1976*, edited by E. Tron. Washington, D.C.: U.S. Government Printing Office.

_____. 1980. *Public School Finance Programs, 1978-79.* Washington, D.C.: U.S. Government Printing Office.

10 EDUCATIONAL NEEDS
Accounting for School Finance

Arthur E. Wise *
Linda Darling-Hammond **

OVERVIEW

Traditionally, school finance has been concerned with guaranteeing a minimum expenditure on the education of every student. In contrast, certain federal programs are intended to increase expenditures on students with certain characteristics. School finance *reform* began with a concern for disconnecting expenditure determination from the happenstance of local property wealth. Each of these policy emphases makes some assumptions about the educational needs of students.

By guaranteeing a minimum educational expenditure for every student, traditional school finance has assumed that the state's obligation is to meet a minimum set of a student's educational needs. To be sure, lengthy debates could be and were held on the question of whether a specific foundation amount was sufficient to pay for a

*Arthur E. Wise, Senior Social Scientist, Rand Corporation.

**Linda Darling-Hammond, Social Scientist, Rand Corporation.

An earlier version of this chapter was written under the auspices of the Rand Corporation's Policy Research Center in Educational Finance and Governance under contract with the Office of the Assistant Secretary for Education and the National Center for Education Statistics, Department of Health, Education, and Welfare.

The authors wish to thank Paul Hill and Aaron Gurwitz of the Rand Corporation and Leslie Silverman of the NCES for their assistance. The views presented are those of the authors.

281

minimally acceptable education program. The debates were settled politically; whether the foundation amounts were sufficient was subject to continuous reexamination. Title I assumed that students with certain characteristics merited an increment of resources. And one element of school finance reform assumed that all students were equally meritorious of the state's resources. The common characteristic of these policy emphases is that they are concerned with the distribution of resources, but they skirt the educational truism that students differ in their needs.

In recent years, decisions about the distribution of educational resources have often been accompanied by statewide school accountability plans. These plans institute methods for measuring school outcomes (often student achievement tests) and include procedures for addressing deficiencies revealed by the assessment measures. In some states like New Jersey, school finance reform and accountability mechanisms have gone hand in hand. In others, accountability plans have inherent resource implications, though often unmet. Where school districts, schools, or students fail to meet state-defined objectives, unmet needs presumably exist. Responses to these needs would require that they be defined and a method for addressing them be specified. Federal funding programs, too, have incorporated accountability mechanisms such as program evaluations and individualized education plans. Like state accountability plans, these include implicit or explicit standards and objectives for education which require consideration of student needs if they are to be met. Formal accountability systems have the effect of shifting policy concerns from the distribution of resources—a concern for inputs—to the effects of resources or programs—a concern for outcomes. Thus, they make it far more difficult for policymakers to ignore the fact that students differ in their needs. They also force policymakers to specify standards and objectives which, by their nature, define the quality of education for which the state is responsible (and to which the state's students are entitled).

Judgments about whether students are entitled to "minimum," "additional," or "equal" expenditures are discomforting to policymakers. They look arbitrary; they are arbitrary. Policymakers would prefer to have a rational or scientific basis for such decisions. In this way they would be relieved of the necessity of justifying differences on value or political grounds. They could then design school finance formulas "scientifically." This prospect is the policy-context of the present analysis.

Can a way be found to distribute funds rationally? The answer, as will be shown, is perplexing. *Apparently* rational systems can be found. Upon further scrutiny, these rational systems obscure judgments which must inevitably be made on nonrational grounds. The most critical judgment which must precede the measurement of student need involves both the definition of "need" and the source of that definition. In common usage, need refers to a lack of something requisite, desirable, useful, or essential. The concept has meaning only when a standard of reference is also defined, when it is known what the object is: requisite for what? Essential for the attainment of what goal? Further, the answers to these questions will depend upon who is doing the defining. Who decides what is essential or useful for whom? Is there a static, objective goal which is the same for all? Or is need a concept relative to the individual? There are, then, two intersecting dimensions of the needs concept which must be defined before measurement of student needs can be discussed. First, the goal(s) against which needs are to be measured must be articulated; these may be the same for all students or different for different groups or individuals. Second, the source of the criteria for needs assessment must be determined and legitimized; the source may be the state, the service deliverers, or the client. This determination goes to the root of questions about the purpose of education in a democratic society and about the role of the state, of professionals, and of consumers—parents and children—in shaping that education.

If the state's purpose in providing public education is to ensure that the populace will attain certain kinds of capabilities, such as reading and computational skills, then the state's responsibility may be seen as providing extra resources to those who have not attained the specified levels of capability. The goal for all students is uniform, and needs are measured according to a deficit model: the need is the difference between the state-defined goal and the student's level of attainment.

If, on the other hand, public education is meant to develop each student's potential to the maximum extent possible, then the state's responsibility to each student is far more complex. Goals vary for every student, and needs can be defined only in relation to someone's definition of each student's potential. Whose definition is acceptable? Does one rely upon the perceptions of service deliverers or clients, or perhaps the assessments made "objectively" by means of standardized tests? Does one seek to fulfill all potentials, or only some subset defined by the state? Does one hold the state accountable for provision of (and access to) services designed to offer opportunities for students' self-actualization, or for the outcomes exhibited by the students? Moreover, since resources are always limited, how does the state allocate scarce resources among students?

Obviously, the answers to these questions are politically and philosophically troublesome. They are most troublesome within the context of accountability. State systems of accountability, conceived according to rational management principles, require evidence that goals are being met, and necessitate adjustments in the system (or sanctions) when goals are not met. Since potentialist goals can never fully be met and since their definition is individual rather than collective in scope, they are not conducive to state accountability systems. Such systems, because they offer guarantees, tend to be collective and minimalist: they guarantee only that all students will receive at least X quantum of education. Though some groups of students may be declared entitled to different programs in order that they may reach X, no effective guarantee can be made that each student will be given a program that will allow him or her to reach maximum potential, for how would anyone know precisely what the state must be held accountable for, or when it has succeeded?

The critical issues which arise when one considers how to define and address educational needs within the context of system accountability revolve around the dialectic of two principles termed by Thomas F. Green the "best principle" and the "equal principle." The best principle is the proposition that each student is entitled to the education that is best for him or her; the equal principle is the proposition that each is entitled to receive an education at least as good as (equal to) that provided for others (Green 1980:114). The best principle typically operates through the political system where group interests generate client definitions of needs that will be accommodated if political accountability mechanisms operate effectively. The equal principle is seen at work in the legal system where individual rights to equal treatment are translated into state duties which must be performed collectively, but are enforced by individuals who seek recourse to legal accountability mechanisms.

The general goals of education incorporate both principles, and school policies seek to balance them in individual and collective cases. However, formal accountability mechanisms strive to translate general goals into specific goals or targets, the attainment of which can be objectively measured. Thus, the state must resolve the dialectic between best and equal through formal systems or processes rather than through personal or political interchanges. Because of the necessarily formal, legal, bureaucratic nature of state actions, state accountability systems which seek to take account of educational needs must rely upon certain rationalistic assumptions about schooling (Wise 1979).

1. Consensus on the objectives of education for all children can be readily reached, and they are the same for all children.

2. The objectives of education can be precisely stated.

3. The needs of students—the gap between their present state and the objectives—can be assessed. If the needs are assessed, they can be met.

4. Instructional interventions can be designed to meet those objectives.

5. The attainment of objectives can be accurately and fully assessed by objective means.

These assumptions—while questionable—form the basis for the systems of student needs assessment to be reviewed. While other methods can be imagined, these systems were selected because they are currently used for assessing students (though not all are used as a basis for distributing resources). The five systems are as follows:

- *Low test scores* reveal high educational need (relative to other students) and presumptively indicate that additional resources are required.

- *Minimum competency testing*—a variant of the low test score approach—is a macro-version of the model since it explicitly endorses the same objectives for all.

- *Poverty*, because of its association with low test scores and relatively fewer available educational resources, presumptively indicates that additional resources are required.

- The *individualized education plan*, by assessing a student's capability and needs, indicates what amounts and kinds of additional resources are required.

- *Learning time* is a new possibility explicitly based upon the idea that all students can attain mastery of subject matter if given enough time. Longer learning times presumably indicate a need for additional resources (for instance, longer school days or school years for some children).

INTRODUCTION

For most of this century, state governments have given aid to school districts to guarantee a minimum expenditure on the education of every student. In recent years, the federal government has given aid to school districts to provide an increase in educational expenditures for students of certain characteristics. State governments, too, have sometimes used student characteristics as the basis for additional allocations of school aid. In this chapter, the demand for funds created by differences in student characteristics is analyzed. This "demand," actual or potential, is reinforced by the existence and proliferation of educational accountability programs at both the state and federal levels. These programs are designed to provoke needs assessments through a process which leads from goal specification to student and program evaluation. When goals or objectives are not attained, unmet needs presumably exist. Student need, then, is an important component of any accountability model, even if funds are not allocated according to that criterion.

Student need as the basis for allocating educational resources is an attractive idea. It begins with the straightforward premise that students are different, that is, they have different needs. It continues with the premise that it is the obligation of the school to meet those different needs. It assumes that meeting those needs will require different quantities of resources.

Dissatisfaction with the distribution of resources to students based upon arbitrary judgments about what equality of educational opportunity demands has led to a search for measurable concepts of student need. The search for such concepts has been driven by the desire not merely to allocate resources but also to ensure educational results.

Student need, then, refers to characteristics of students which can be used as the basis for federal, state, or even local funding programs. In this view, measures of student need aggregate into measures of district need.

But the concept of student need is not nearly as straightforward as it first appears. First, it requires the selection of a desired educational result. Second, it requires ascertainment of the discrepancy between the desired result and the current state. Third, it requires the adoption of a policy that the discrepancy should be eliminated. The purpose of this chapter is to analyze alternative measures of student need, assess barriers to the use of the measures, and provide a preliminary assessment of the types of places likely to have concentrations of students with high measures.

In this chapter, existing and prospective measures of student need are identified, described, and critiqued. As measures of student need, the authors examine the traditional school finance approach, low test scores, minimum competency test scores, poverty, the individualized education plan, and learning time. *Technical*, *philosophical*, *cost*, and *political* barriers must be overcome before the concepts can be measured and used. The measures listed above range from those that are or can be technically implemented to those which must be developed. Some measures pose philosophical problems. Some would be expensive to administer. And some may be politically difficult to implement. An assessment of each measure along these four dimensions is made. Where possible, studies are reviewed to ascertain the kinds of places likely to receive disproportionate amounts of funds under a particular measure of student need.

MEASURES OF STUDENT NEED

The Traditional School Finance Approach

The central issue in school finance is the quantity of resources to be allocated to the education of each student. Traditionally, it was assumed that equality of educational opportunity in a state demanded a guaranteed minimum expenditure on the education of every student. This concept is embodied in the foundation program which stipulates a "satisfactory minimum offering," expressed in dollars per pupil, which shall be guaranteed to every student. When a locality cannot supply the minimum offering at the state-mandated local tax rate, the state makes up the deficiency. Conceptually, the foundation program has its roots in the writing of Ellwood P. Cubberley. He stated:

> Theoretically all the children of the state are equally important and are entitled to have the same advantages; practically this can never be quite true. The duty of the state is to secure for all as high a minimum of good instruction as

is possible, but not to reduce all to this minimum; to equalize the advantages to all as nearly as can be done with the resources at hand; to place a premium on those local efforts which will enable communities to rise above the legal minimum as far as possible; and to encourage communities to extend their educational energies to new and desirable undertakings (Cubberley 1905: 17).

The key elements of the foundation program are here—every child is to receive a *minimum* of resources, but individual school districts are to be free to provide more than a minimum of resources. Although Cubberley began his argument with an appeal to the equal principle, he quickly modified the concept to take account of what were considered to be practical realities, arriving at a formulation of "minimum equal" support.

In 1923, Strayer and Haig described their concept of the foundation program:

There exists today and has existed for many years a movement which has come to be known as the "equalization of educational opportunity" or the "equalization of school support." These phrases are interpreted in various ways. In its most extreme form the interpretation is somewhat as follows: The state should insure equal educational facilities to every child within its borders at a uniform effort throughout the state in terms of the burden of taxation; the tax burden of education should throughout the state be uniform in relation to tax-paying ability, and the provision for schools should be uniform in relation to the educable population desiring education. Most of the supporters of this proposition, however, would not preclude any particularly rich and costly educational program. They would insist that there be an adequate minimum offered everywhere, the expense of which should be considered a prior claim on the state's economic resources (1923: 173).

Again, the key elements of the foundation program are here—every child is to have access to "equal educational opportunity," but communities are to be free to offer particularly rich and costly educational programs. The foundation program fails to provide equality of educational opportunity because, in principle and in practice, it provides more educational resources to some students and less to others. The foundation program is predicated on the belief that the state is responsible for guaranteeing a minimum of educational resources to each student, irrespective of the needs of students.

The school finance lawsuits that began in the 1960s were brought to challenge the idea that the state is responsible for guaranteeing *merely* a minimum of educational resources (Wise 1968). The central premise was the idea that federal and state constitutions might be held to require an equal allocation of educational opportunity. The underlying constitutional principle was the equal protection of the laws. One possibility was that equal protection might be equated with equal opportunity which, in turn, might be equated with an equal allocation of resources. The final assumption generally made is that equal allocations of resources are purchased with equal expenditures per pupil. While each of these assumptions can be challenged, our purpose here is served by the general assumption that quantities of resources (whether minimum or equal) are used to meet student needs.

Barriers. The use of expenditures as a measure of student need is technically easy. If one holds the view that the guarantee of a minimum expenditure level approximates meeting a minimum set of needs, then traditional school finance formulas (including some modern variations) do the job. Or if one holds the view that all students are equally worthy of resources, then school finance formulas can be designed with relative ease. To be sure, there are technical problems associated with the issue of whether or not equal dollars lead to the purchase of equal resources in different regions or in schools of different size. These technical problems pale, however, when compared to problems associated with approaches to be considered later. There is a serious issue which the approach begs—the extent to which expenditures map onto student needs. This problem is more philosophical than technical and will be considered below.

A strong objection to the minimum expenditure approach is that it may be insufficient to meet the minimum needs of some students. The amount provided may be insufficient to provide some students with basic—or advanced—skills. Other needs of students—for example, special developmental programs of various kinds—are equally unrecognized by the minimum expenditures approach. A second strong objection is the equity argument. Why should the state support a financing system that provides smaller amounts of resources to some students than to others? The minimum expenditures approach cannot approximate satisfying either the best or the equal principle of educational system design.

The concept of equal expenditures faces philosophical objections from those who believe that equal education cannot provide the best education. As noted, it is opposed by those who believe that students of low demonstrated achievement have higher needs. (Of course, their opposition is relevant only in the circumstance in which low-achieving students are receiving the same amount of resources as average- and high-achieving students.) By reference to the principle that each student is entitled to that education which is best for him or her, those who recognize as critical the existence of student differences (along any educational dimension) reject the sufficiency of equal expenditures as satisfying the state's duty.

The obligation of the state is construed differently depending upon whether education is viewed as a right or as a requirement. If education is a requirement, that is, a duty owed by citizens to the state, as the compulsory character of elementary and secondary education suggests, then students are entitled only to that education deemed sufficient to fulfill the state's compelling interest. That interest is in the production of a functionally literate citizenry—a minimum standard. If education is a right of all students, then the principle of equality is paramount, for rights must be accorded to all on equal terms. However, recent constructions of student rights have inserted the principle of best into formulations of equality. Under the Education for All Handicapped Children Act, for example, handicapped students are entitled to an education "appropriate to their needs"; thus they should receive additional quantities of resources, not just collectively, but individually as well.

The traditional school finance approach is limited in satisfying this latter requirement both because it typically rests on a different concept of equality and because its reliance on formulas for distribution means that students must be treated as group members rather than as individuals. The existence of different concepts of entitlement poses a philosophical tension for school finance policymakers which is usually resolved by partially accommodating each point of view in finance plans subject to the constraints of costs and political pressures.

There are no *extraordinary* costs associated with the *administration* of the traditional school finance approach. The costs associated with the development of formulas, the assessment of property, and the equalization of assessed valuation are accepted administrative costs of supporting the schools. There are costs but they are already being met.

The costs of establishing higher foundation levels or of equalizing educational expenditures can be straightforwardly calculated. If equalization is to be at the current mean expenditure level, then no new financial costs are to be incurred. At any higher level, whether it be the 90th percentile or the 100th percentile, the cost can be readily calculated. Even the costs of allocating additional resources to classes of districts or students can be easily obtained if the number of recipients is known and stable.

The political barriers to the implementation of school finance reform are, by now, well known. Wealthy school districts and districts with low tax rates, their representatives in state legislatures, and those who oppose increased state expenditures tend to oppose school finance reform. Hence, those who favor reform have been forced to initiate lawsuits to achieve a result that majoritarian political decisionmaking cannot. Reform advocates are, of course, representatives of the "neediest" school districts and students.

Concentrations of student need as traditionally defined in school finance appear in school districts with low assessed valuation and low expenditure levels. However, the assumption that low school expenditure is associated with need may not coincide with need defined in other ways. More explicit measures of student need are discussed below.

Low Test Scores

Low educational achievement is often taken as the *prima facie* indicator of educational need. Yet what precisely does the concept assume? It assumes that there is an acceptable level of educational achievement that can be measured by objective testing. The acceptable level may be the level of achievement of the average student or of a superior student. The frame of reference is comparative and may be students in the school, the school district, the state, or the nation. It may be a group of students designated in some other way. In any of these cases, it assumes that the acceptable level should be the goal for all other students as well as the group which provides the norm. The concept—if it is to have meaning—must also come to terms with the nature or content of the educational achievement that is desired. What are the educational objectives being pursued?

The concept of low educational achievement is generally equated with low scores on achievement tests. Test results are the measure of the concept. Moreover, the comparative frame of references generally means that the tests to be considered are norm-referenced tests.

Thus, identifying low-achieving students requires a scoring procedure and a cut-off point. The grade-level equivalent computation may be made and students one year or more below grade level may be designated as low-achieving. Test scores may be converted to percentiles, deciles, or stanines, and a cut-off identified. A judgment is then made of the score of low-achieving students.

Alternatively, criterion-referenced tests may be employed.[1] These are tests that reveal the skills which students have mastered. A low-achieving student is one who fails to acquire all or some set of skills. Since few students master all skills, someone must judge the number or percentage of skills below which students will be considered low-achieving.

Judgments about low achievement require decisions about the content to be appraised. Is it the entire curriculum? Which learning objectives are to be appraised? Is it to be the basic skills?

Using low test scores to distribute state school funds has been discussed but never fully implemented in Michigan, New York, and California (Feldmesser 1975). Using test scores to distribute federal funds under Title I has received substantial attention at the instigation of former Congressman Albert Quie. That attention led to the creation of the Congressionally mandated study of Title I conducted by the National Institute of Education (NIE). That study and an earlier NIE-funded study by Robert A. Feldmesser are the major analyses of the effects of using test scores to distribute educational program funds.

Barriers. The use of tests for the distribution of funds faces technical questions associated with tests generally. Do tests measure aptitude, achievement, or test-taking ability? Are tests valid measures of learning? What skills can and cannot be measured by tests? Will testing for policy purposes lead to an overemphasis on testing? Will the curriculum be distorted? Still, in principle, it is not impossible to imagine using test results as a basis for distributing state or local funds.

Employing test scores as a basis for distributing funds creates countervailing incentives. On the one hand, the worse students perform, the more resources a district will receive. On the other hand, administrators, teachers, and students will want to perform as well as they can. These positive and negative incentives may neutralize each other. Moreover, testing could be performed by the state or a disinterested party, further neutralizing these incentives.

Test-based funding would appear to have the potential for targeting funds to students who do not perform well on tests. Several philosophical problems, however, remain unresolved.

First, those who advocate test-based funding have tended to assume that a single test score or two would be a sufficient basis for discriminating among students in the distribution of funds. Advocates have tended to think about such funding for compensatory education programs. In principle, test-based funding could be used for the full instructional program. In this case, serious questions would arise concerning the need for an array of tests in all subject-matter areas. Unless all subjects were tested, the curriculum would be distorted. Moreover, devising tests for all school objectives would prove difficult, controversial, and very expensive.

Second, questions are related to the cut-offs at which funding discrimination should be made. There is some difficulty choosing a score below which a student will be judged to require additional resources for compensatory services. If the bulk of funding were associated with test results, serious philosophical debates would arise over how steeply to scale the relationship of test results and funding. If the objective were to equalize educational results, low scores should yield high expenditures. However, the converse also is implied. High scores should yield low expenditures—a result which would not be universally applauded (as explained more fully below).

Finally, a profound philosophical problem is posed by the possibility that what students need may not be related to how they score on any single test or even a group of tests. That is, if students need different inputs or resources (rather than merely different amounts of the same thing) to maximize their individual potentials, then using static outcome measures as a standard for needs assessment is a philosophically unsatisfying solution. If students have varying relative abilities and interests across subject areas (ignoring for the moment noncognitive school functions) and schools are supposed to encourage individual student growth rather than producing standardized outcomes, then the achievement-deficiency model represented by the low test score approach is an inadequate policy tool. Conversely, use of the test score approach requires acceptance of a deficiency model of education, with its emphasis upon the appropriateness of standardized outcomes as a primary goal of schooling. Rarely is explicit acceptance of this model and its underlying assumptions made. Instead, the rhetoric of educational goal-setting leaves unresolved the question of whether goals should be the same for all children or somehow be plastic, depending upon individual abilities, interests, and desires.

The cost barriers to initiating a testing program, while high, are not insuperable. Many states are already moving in the direction of statewide testing. The NIE Compensatory Education Study estimated that a national testing program—suitable for the distribution of federal funds to the states—would cost $7.2 million. A national testing program suitable for distributing federal funds to school districts would cost $53 million (NIE 1977b). The costs associated with funding the program, of course, depend upon whether the program is supplementary or comprehensive—covering the distribution of some or all school funds.

As indicated by experience to date, political barriers to test-based funding are considerable. The radical change which test-based funding entails threatens all those who believe that they are relatively well served by the present arrangement. Advocates of Title I funding fear that the current appropriations would be allocated to students who are not poor. If the program were a general one, supporters of high-scoring students would likely oppose a policy which resulted in smaller amounts of resources for those who did well on tests.

Obviously, all school districts will have some students who score low on tests. This fact leads to some political support for the idea of test-based funding. There are even those who believe that the existence of test-based funding will generate an increase in the amount of funds appropriated for education.

The NIE Title I study provides some indication of the kinds of districts and populations which would benefit from a test-based allocation of compensatory education funds *relative* to an income-based allocation. *Assuming* that the total percentage of students served remained the same (15 percent), NIE compared the percentages of students served by both types of allocations:

Location

Nonmetropolitan areas would probably lose funds if achievement criteria were substituted for poverty criteria. By contrast, cities and suburbs would gain, but these gains are not statistically significant because the variation around the national trend is very high. Thus, urban and suburban districts in some areas are likely to gain funds, while those in other areas are likely to lose.

Demographic Composition

On average, school districts with high percentages of blacks would be likely to gain funds if an achievement-based allocation system were used. Districts with high proportions of whites would be likely to lose funds; there would generally not be major differences in funding for districts with high proportions of Spanish-surnamed children (NIE 1977b: 34–35).

NIE found, however, that the percentages served were highly sensitive to the definition of low achievement:

Parallel analyses were conducted using alternative definitions of low achievement ranging from the 7th to 30th percentiles. These analyses of alternative cutoffs indicate that the definition of low achievement used in an achievement-based funding system will have significant consequences for the distribution of funds. At cutoffs above the 15th percentile, the distribution of achievement eligibles resembles the distribution of the 5- to 17-year olds in the population. If the 28th percentile, for example, is used as the cutoff, 30% of the low achievers are in cities—a proportion very close to the proportion of all 5- to 17-year olds in these places. When achievement eligibility limits are set low, at the 7th percentile, approximately 42% of low-achieving children are in cities. Therefore, cities would receive proportionately more funds as the cutoff is lowered, and proportionately less as the cutoff is raised.

The reverse is likely to be true for suburban areas; they are likely to gain funds as the cutoff is raised. At lower cutoff levels, however, their share of funds is likely to approximate the share they currently receive. Nonmetropolitan areas are likely to lose about the same amount of funds in a shift from poverty to achievement for any cutoff between the 7th and 30th percentile.

The definition of low achievement would also affect the distributional consequences of a shift from poverty to achievement criteria for districts of varying racial/ethnic composition. As the cutoff point is increased, the proportion of achievement eligibles for districts with high concentrations of blacks declines, and the proportion of eligibles for districts with high proportions of whites increases (NIE 1977b: 35).

Finally, NIE warned that the pattern found for the nation as a whole would not hold in every state.

In short, concentrations of need identified by low test scores are highly sensitive to the cut-off score employed.

Minimal Competency Testing

Minimal competency testing is a variant of test-based funding that is associated with accountability. Current attention to it is so high that it deserves special treatment here.

The idea of mandating learning really began during the nation's bicentennial. In 1976, the concept of educational accountability appeared in strengthened form with the emergence of "minimal competency." In the words of the *National Assessment of Educational Progress Newsletter*, "One of the hottest issues in education today is minimal competency":

> Packed into those two words are images ranging from the simple implication that students need master only basic readin', writin' and 'rithmetic to a miscellany of complex, emotional and sometimes intertwined controversies (*NAEP* 1976:1).

The reader will by now anticipate the connotations of minimal competency:

> The latter cover teacher accountability, costs and logistics of extensive remedial classes, potential loss of school revenue, increased parental demand for schools to prepare their children to manage—at least with some minimum success—their lives after formal education ceases and the specter of a country-wide testing program that is defined and controlled by the federal government (*NAEP* 1976:1).

"Minimal competency," sometimes expanded to "minimal-competency-testing," joins together basic (minimum) skills, competency-based education, and assessment.

Perhaps the most comprehensive minimal competency testing legislation is Florida's Educational Accountability Act enacted in 1976. The law mandates learning while preserving many other elements of accountability. Its intent is in part to:

1. Guarantee to each student in the Florida system of public education that the system provides instructional programs which meet minimum performance standards compatible with the state's plan for education.

2. Provide a more thorough analysis of program costs and the degree to which the various districts are meeting the minimum performance standards established by the state board of education.

3. Provide information to the public about the performance of the
    Florida system of public education in meeting established goals
    and providing effective, meaningful, and relevant educational
    experiences designed to give students at least the minimum skills
    necessary to function and survive in today's society (Florida Stat-
    utes 1976).

While the minimum performance standards may appear to be characteristics of *programs*, it soon becomes clear that they are standards
for students to attain; in short, the system is to guarantee that each
student attain a specified standard.

Here the concern is with minimal competency testing as a basis for
measuring student need for a system of resource allocation. Florida
has already instituted a compensatory program policy. Funds appropriated for the program are allocated proportionately to each school
district on the basis of the number of students in grades three, five,
eight, and eleven whose scores on the Statewide Student Assessment
Test are at the 25th percentile or below. The districts make application to the state describing the remedial program to be offered. In
1978–79, Florida appropriated $26.5 million for the program.

Barriers.   The technical barriers presented in the earlier discussion of
low test scores as a basis for measuring student need are somewhat
pertinent here. Funds can be distributed on the basis of test scores.
With minimal competency testing, however, there are several offsetting pressures. On the one hand, the worse students perform, the
more resources flow to the district. On the other hand, students have
a positive incentive to do well since promotion and graduation are at
stake. Moreover, administrators are under substantial public pressure
to make their districts look as good as possible. How these pressures
will resolve themselves remains to be seen over time. One potential
problem at the local school district level might be the continual need
to alter staffing and programming levels to adjust to changes in the
failure rate. At the state level in Florida, that problem is accommodated by always serving the bottom quartile of test scores—a quartile that will always be with us. However, if the distribution of low
achievers shows marked instability, individual districts may have to
make substantial program adjustments from year to year.

The fact that minimal competency testing is operating or pending
in the majority of states would suggest that there are no insupera-

ble philosophical barriers. However, political acceptability does not assure legality or philosophical solvency, and some problems have already emerged.

In Florida and elsewhere, lawsuits have been and will be brought on civil rights grounds, threatening the future of the program. The use of tests for classifying students or assigning diplomas is troublesome when resource disparities are present, when remedial programs are not available, and when test bias is suspected (see McClung 1978; Tractenberg and Jacoby 1977). While allocating funds on the basis of minimal competency test scores may not bring legal challenges, assigning students to special programs on the basis of the scores may—particularly if a disproportionate number of the students are minority and if such programs are viewed as limiting, rather than expanding, the students' educational opportunities. Denying diplomas to students on the basis of minimal competency tests has already been the subject of legal controversy; the status of handicapped students is especially troublesome in this regard. The extent to which passing test scores really indicates preparation for adult life is another serious legal and philosophical issue. At the root of these controversies is the question, again, of whether education is a right or a requirement and whether the state's duty is to provide equal opportunities or to assure some standardized outcome of its certified graduates. At a minimum, the weight of legal opinion suggests that minimal competency testing must be accompanied by resource equalization. Allocating additional funds to aid low-scoring students might be seen as one means for advancing such equalization efforts.

Still unresolved are questions of how emphasis on minimal competency testing will affect the provision of resources (educational opportunities) to high-scoring students, and how it will affect the remainder of the (untested) curriculum. If competency testing drives resource allocations, will the breadth of educational offerings be diminished for all or some students? Will the goals of education be distorted or reduced? What will be the state's obligation to students who have passed the tests before their compulsory school years end? What is the state's duty to students who have not passed the tests before their final year?

These questions are related to the cost barriers of the competency testing approach. A supplementary funding program can be small or large. In most states *no* extra funds are provided for students who fail. In Florida, modest levels of funding have been provided in a way that school districts can count on them nearly as if they were another form of categorical aid. The true costs of successful remediation are not known and probably cannot be known. Students in a state with minimal competency testing are surely going to be intensively prepared to take the tests. Scores for all students may rise as a result. What will not be known is whether *educational achievement* (distinguished from test scores) is rising. Arbitrarily derived supplemental appropriations can be given to low-scoring students. Accurately determining costs for meeting student needs is very difficult — if not impossible.

Political barriers to the implementation of a funding based upon minimal competency testing are not high as long as the funds involved are marginal. If substantial portions of a state's resources were to be employed in this fashion, political opposition could be expected to emerge. Moreover, the philosophical and legal tensions underlying this approach could be expected to become more visible and subject to intensified debate.

Poverty

It has long been known that poverty is associated with low school achievement (Warner 1974). Moreover, poverty is itself often an indication that students do not have access to resources at home or in school. During the early and mid-1960s it became clear that the school finance system in the United States discriminated against children in poor schools and, in many instances, against poor children (Wise 1968). That realization was the beginning of two powerful social movements intended to remedy it. The first was Title I of the Elementary and Secondary Education Act of 1965. The second was the school finance reform movement.

Title I as part of the War on Poverty was designed to attack two aspects of the effects of poverty on education. First, low family income, associated with low parental educational levels, led to an inadequate educational environment in the home and often resulted in poor school achievement. Second, families with low income frequently lived in urban and rural areas where the expenditures on schools were relatively low. Title I has successfully channeled additional educational funds to the children of the poor (NIE 1978).[2]

The school finance reform movement had a similar objective — to increase investment in the education of the poor. However, because of the ways in which schools are financed and the ways in which data on school finance are assembled, school finance reform has tended to concentrate on poor school districts. *School finance reform was to render the expenditure on the education of a student independent of the resources of his local school district. However, the objective has gradually been transformed to the equalization of school district expenditures.* The question was raised of whether poor students lived in poor school districts, and it continues today to confuse the reform movement. Some poor students live in poor school districts; others do not.

The relation between poverty and low school achievement is well established. A background paper prepared by Alison Wolf for the NIE Compensatory Education Study reported on the strength of association between poverty and student achievement at three levels of analysis—the student, the school, and school district. She reported student-level correlations as high as .46; school-level correlations as high as .90; and district-level correlations as high as .60 (Wolf 1977:i–ii).

Clearly, poverty is a good indicator of the degree to which a student or group of students is likely to need special or additional educational resources.

Barriers.   Strictly speaking, there are no serious technical barriers to the use of low family income as an indicator of student need. There are, however, numerous problems associated with its use.

First, poverty measures are not integral to the current system of state and local financing of schools. Thus, special steps must be taken to incorporate them and keep them current.

Second, family income measures pertain to individuals rather than to districts. Thus, channeling resources to individuals based upon their poverty poses a challenge. The challenge is both bookkeeping and programmatic. The temptation to segregate students to ensure that they benefit from funds and programs is strong, a practice which may not be educationally desirable. Segregating students for bookkeeping convenience can lead to racial and social class isolation.

The major philosophical barrier to this approach is that some poor students are not low-achieving and that some nonpoor students are low-achieving. Some argue that, on the one hand, additional resources are given to students who do not require them. And, on the other hand, additional resources are not given to those who do require them. This argument, though, assumes once again that low achievement indicates need. One could argue, alternatively, that whatever the achievement level of poor students, if tangible resources (school and nonschool) make a difference, their achievement could be higher still given funds to equalize their environmental handicap. Thus, the notion of need as related to individual potential could provide a basis for allocating additional resources to poor students, regardless of their achievement levels, just as it is used to argue for special allocations to gifted and talented students who are said to be constrained from realizing their full potentials.

The special case of *additional* funds for the poor would be enormously exacerbated by the general case of distributing *all* funds on the basis of poverty—or wealth. The current system of school finance often has precisely the effect of distributing resources in proportion to wealth (or inversely proportional to poverty). Yet, a new system which explicitly made wealth or poverty the criterion for distributing funds would be explosive. If all funds were explicitly distributed on the basis of poverty (the poorer you were, the more you received), the rich would object. If all funds were distributed on the basis of wealth (the richer you were, the more you received), the poor would object, as they have and continue to do.

It may seem unlikely that poverty or wealth would become explicitly recognized in the distribution of general school funds. Yet, the newly reemerging debate over educational vouchers and tax credits is precisely on point. If parents are free to supplement vouchers or credits, the rich have the advantage. If parents are restricted from supplementing vouchers, then the rich will object. The distribution of equality of educational opportunity remains volatile—more so when personal wealth is explicitly recognized as a qualifying or disqualifying factor for additional funds.

There are no significant cost barriers to the implementation of poverty as a measure of student need. The administrative costs are already incorporated in federal legislation. Should states choose to recognize family income in the distribution of school funds (as, for example, in a family power-equalized voucher), some administrative costs would be associated with building family wealth measures into educational funding formulas.

The politics of poverty as an indicator of educational need are embedded in the philosophical considerations discussed above. The allocation of supplementary funding is well established politically. Indeed, some states now distribute categorical state aid on bases similar to Title I. The politics of general funding and poverty are another, more volatile matter.

It is perhaps worth noting here, parenthetically, that there is a view that all students are, in a sense, poor. It is their parents (or school districts) who differ in wealth. Current school finance legislation, in effect, classifies school districts on the basis of their property wealth—not family income. As a result of the way in which these laws operate, wealthy school districts enjoy the benefits of high expenditures for public education whereas poor districts must make do with low school expenditures. Under one definition, equality of educational opportunity will exist when a child's educational opportunity does not depend upon either his parents' economic circumstances or his geographical location. Thus, a school finance system which delivers equal quantities of resources to all students is one in which wealth is no longer a criterion for determining resource distribution. Concentrations of student need in this sense are equivalent to the number of students in the school district. While some will assert that children from poor families have greater educational need than children from wealthier families, the redress of current imbalances between the poorest and wealthiest school districts would even today increase the quantity of resources distributed to children from poor families.

Data compiled for the NIE Compensatory Education Study give some indication of how incremental increases based upon poverty would affect school districts of different characteristics (NIE 1977a: 117–118). One analysis compared the average per pupil allocation of Title I funds based upon fiscal characteristics of districts. Title I funds clearly reach children from poor families, but those children do not necessarily live in districts which are property-poor. Many, of course, live in cities which are close to or above average in property wealth. Obviously, school finance systems which allocate funds on the basis of family poverty will deliver funds to districts which serve the poor, but not necessarily to districts that are "poor" in property. However, to the extent that poverty is used, certain types of places will benefit disproportionately. Table 10–1 gives some indications of the effects on different types of places. In the Northeast, poor children tend to be located in cities; in the South, more numerous, they tend to be located in nonmetropolitan areas. A school finance system built on poverty measures would have different consequences in dif-

Table 10-1. Percent of Poor Children (Orshansky Formula) by Place, Type, and Region

	North East	North Central	South	West
Central city	8.7	7.8	13.1	4.6
Suburban	5.2	4.6	11.2	5.7
Nonmetropolitan	2.3	7.6	25.2	4.0
Total	16.2	20.0	49.5	14.3

Source: Adapted from NIE (1977a: 135).

ferent states; its distributional consequences would make it very different from existing school finance systems.

The "Individualized Education Plan"

P.L. 94–142, The Education for All Handicapped Children Act of 1975, calls for an individualized education program (IEP) for every handicapped child. The program is defined by law as:

> . . . a written statement for each handicapped child developed in any meeting by a representative of the local educational agency or an intermediate educational unit who shall be qualified to provide, or supervise the provision of, specially designed instruction to meet the unique needs of handicapped children, the teacher, the parents or guardian of such child, and, whenever appropriate, such child, which statement shall include (A) a statement of the present levels of educational performance of such child, (B) a statement of annual goals, including short-term instructional objectives, (C) a statement of the specific educational services to be provided to such child, and the extent to which such child will be able to participate in regular educational programs, (D) the projected date for initiation and anticipated duration of such services, and (E) appropriate objective criteria and evaluation procedures and schedules for determining, on at least an annual basis, whether instructional objectives are being achieved.

The purpose here is not to evaluate the IEP requirement of P.L. 94–142; rather, it is to assess the potential use of IEPs as the basis of a school finance system for all children.

The IEP is clearly intended to identify student need. If the IEP is to have practical effect, it must be used either to guide the teacher or the system of allocating resources or both. The concern here is with the latter.

The IEP as the basis for a school finance system would work as follows:

1. Measure the present level of performance of each child.

2. State annual instructional objectives for each child.

3. Calculate the differences between 2 and 1; these are the educational needs of the child.

4. Determine the specific educational resources necessary to meet those needs.

5. Determine the cost of those educational resources.

6. To determine the cost of meeting the needs of a class of students, sum individual costs.

7. To determine the cost of operating a school, sum classroom costs.

8. To determine the cost of operating a school district, sum school costs.

9. In steps 5–8, adjust for economies and diseconomies of scale and regional price level differences.

10. To determine the overall state budget, sum school district budgets and allocate costs between local school districts and the state.

11. If desired, to determine the federal budget, sum overall state budgets, and allocate costs between the state and the federal government.

Needless to say, a finance system based on IEP's is very different from systems now employed. It would, however, be consistent with an educational philosophy of meeting each child's needs.

Barriers. The steps enumerated are each logically derived from the idea of meeting each child's educational needs. Yet there are technical, philosophical, cost, and political problems associated with each step. Perhaps the easiest step is the measurement of the present level of performance of each child. However, decisions must be made concerning what is to be measured, a point related to the next step. The act of stating annual instructional objectives hides a multitude of difficulties concerning the overall curriculum and the curriculum for each child. The difficulties pertain to the breadth of the curriculum. How many objectives are there to be? Are they to be the same for all students? Step three lists the needs to be met; its problem is that it contains no principles for limiting the number of needs to be met. Will more able students have more of their needs met? Will less able students have only a basic curriculum? If objectives are static across the student population, will more able students be entitled to programs designed to enrich their progress past the minimal level? The next step—determining resources needed—may or may not pose a technical challenge. The decisions may be trivial—the child requires one-thirtieth of a teacher, for example. In this case, the new system would be the inverse of the current system in which one simply decides that one teacher can teach thirty children. Or the decisions may attempt to be sophisticated—a detailed specification of instructional treatments for each child. In this case, there will be questions as to whether the treatments will have their intended effects and what should be done if they do not. Managing a melange of ever-changing individual treatment packages for groups of children may prove nearly impossible.

Determining the needs of each child to be met requires the resolution of at least two philosophical questions. What are the goals of the school system? And, consistent with the norm of equality and given that resources are limited, which needs of which children are to be met?

Stating annual instructional objectives for each child requires a clear statement of the goals of education. The goals must be widely accepted, explicit, not inconsistent, and exhaustively stated. For some, the basics are sufficient—reading and arithmetic. For others, much more comprehensive goals are necessary. The goals cannot be left unstated or implicit or vague or given to the teacher for interpretation.

But students differ in their beginning level of performance; their rate of progress through the year will differ as well. The cost of meeting needs will differ for different students. How does one reconcile these differences with the demand of equal educational opportunity, particularly if equal educational opportunity bears some relation to equal resource allocation? No *principle* for reconciling the conflict-ing principles of "meeting student needs" and "equal resource allo-cation" is easily reachable.[3]

A variant of this problem is posed by the principle of limited resources. Since resources are limited, they must be allocated. Again, there is no clear principle for deciding the quantity of each student's needs to be met. And if one starts with individual student needs rather than budget constraints, is not one bound to go over budget?

The cost barriers posed by the IEP approach are substantial. The administrative costs would be high. Experience to date under P.L. 94-142 suggests that substantial time is required to develop IEPs. The testing required by this program also is demanding. The develop-ment of carefully specified instructional interventions would be diffi-cult as would the costing of these interventions. The experience of program budgeting is relevant here. Program budgeting is comparable to IEP construction in that program objectives and costs need to be related. The difference is the level at which objectives and costs are related: on the one hand, it is at the program level; on the other hand, it is at the student level. Experience with program budgeting proved to be very difficult and time-consuming. One can expect the same with IEPs (Marver and David 1978).

The programmatic costs—the school-budgeting process—are un-predictable. If the approach were taken seriously, student needs would drive the budget. In the real world of school budgeting, that cannot occur. The question then is whether there can be some ac-commodation between the IEP approach and a fixed budget. One answer is suggested by the IEPs constructed under P.L. 94-142 (see Kakalik 1978). IEPs can be constructed in isolation from budget decisions. They are nonetheless bounded by resource availability, since school personnel fit students to existing programs. In this case, they have some relation to resource allocation decisions, but the IEPs do not drive budget development. At the same time, these IEPs can-not be said to reflect student needs in an ideal sense. In short, pro-gram costs cannot be predicted until some of the difficulties posed can be resolved. Arbitrary decisions made about budget levels at any administrative level vitiate the novelty of the approach.

The major political barrier of the approach is probably its novelty. Its appeal derives from liberal educational philosophy which prom-ises to meet the needs of every student. The IEP is an administrative mechanism which is designed to deliver on that promise. Political acceptance will likely be determined largely by the resolution of the technical, philosophical, and cost questions described above.

Learning Time

A developing theoretical and empirical literature in educational research examines the relationship between time-on-task and learning. Under scrutiny is the apparent truism that more time spent on learning results in more learning. The literature recognizes another fact as well—that students differ in the speed with which they master new material. The time needed by a student to learn would be an intriguing measure of student need. The measures of student need examined in preceding sections of this report do not easily relate to costs. Time-needed-to-learn can be more easily costed and built into school finance formulas. The approach does not altogether avoid some of the problems associated with measures discussed earlier. It does, however, provide a novel way of relating need to cost.

In recent years, Benjamin Bloom (1976) has been espousing the theory of mastery learning. The central point of mastery learning is stated as follows:

> It made clear that if students are normally distributed with respect to *aptitude* for some subject and all students are given exactly the *same instruction* (the same in terms of amount and quality of instruction and learning time allowed), then achievement measured at the completion of the subject will be normally distributed. Under such conditions the relationship (correlation) between aptitude measured at the beginning of the instruction and achievement measured at the end of the instruction will be relatively high (typically about +.70). Conversely, if students are normally distributed with respect to aptitude, but the kind and quality of instruction and learning time allowed are made appropriate to the characteristics and needs of *each* learner, the correlation between aptitude measured at the beginning of instruction and achievement measured at the end of instruction should approach zero (Bloom 1976: 4).

For the present discussion, we will focus upon *learning time* and assume that the marginal cost of units of instruction neither increases nor decreases, and that every instructor can vary the kind and quality of instruction.

Bloom reviews a number of estimates of variation in learning time. Some estimates suggest that certain students require five times as much *elapsed* time as do other students. More carefully controlled studies provide a somewhat different picture. In particular, it has been found that under mastery teaching practices, the learning rates of students become more similar from the beginning of a course to the end of the course. At the beginning of three experimental courses, the fastest students learned from seven and one-half to three and one-third times faster than the slowest students. At the end of these courses, the fastest students learned four to two times faster than the slowest students. In a study which looked at time-on-task (time actually spent in learning activities), the slowest student began by requiring twice as much time as the faster, but by the end required only one and one-third as much time-on-task to learn. Substantial additional empirical support for the relationship between time and learning has been provided by the *Beginning Teacher Evaluation Study* conducted by the California State Commission for Teacher Preparation and Licensing (1978) under contract with the National Institute of Education. These differences in time can, in principle, be easily costed.

Learning time figures prominently in the ideal definition of the popular movement known as competency-based education (CBE). Perhaps the clearest definition of CBE is William Spady's:

> CBE [is] a data-based, adaptive, performance-oriented set of integrated processes that facilitate, measure, record, and certify within the context of flexible time parameters the demonstration of known, explicitly stated, and agreed upon learning outcomes that reflect successful functioning in life role (1976: 9-14).

It is important to note that CBE is already the subject of state legislation in a number of states. The importance of this observation is that it moves the idea of learning time as the basis of resource allocation closer to political reality. Unfortunately, while the idea of CBE has been implemented, the idea of flexible learning time has not. CBE obviously requires variable class hours, days, weeks, months, and possibly years. It would be as revolutionary as the idea of allocating resources on the basis of learning time. Indeed, the two have the same implications—more dollars for some students and less for others.

Barriers. As suggested already, learning time as a measure of student need has intuitive and practical appeal. No serious conceptual problems are associated with costing time, especially when compared to other measures. Conceptually sound measures can be crude or fine. The cost of additional instructional time can be calculated from minutes to years. Having said this, operating school systems in a manner consistent with the principles implied by mastery learning or CBE would require enormous changes from current practice. Here lie the technical barriers.

School districts would, for example, have to develop means for managing flexible schedules (varying in duration for different students and, presumably, teachers). In addition, learning speed ratios would have to be calculated for each student across many learning tasks and curricular areas, and these would have to be adjusted over time as the intended changes in learning rate took place.

On the philosophical front, learning time has an advantage over other measures that require broad consensus on the goals of education. Learning time can be assessed at the local level—even at the school level. The approach is compatible with the local determination of educational objectives. However, as noted at the outset, some conceptual problems associated with other measures cannot be avoided. Learning objectives must be established, and some means of determining the total size of the budget must be found.

Finally, both mastery learning and competency-based education are controversial. There is by no means universal agreement that they achieve what they purport to achieve—uniform learning achievement. More fundamentally, even if they can achieve the goal of uniform learning, there are serious philosophical questions as to the goal itself. While it may be quite true that all students can master a given set of learning objectives, if students vary in their individual potentials, some students will be able to learn more of some things (beyond the objectives) than others. Is this opportunity denied by sending them home when they have mastered the agreed-upon set? What is to be done for the faster students while the slower ones are catching up? Do some students attend school for four months each year while others attend year 'round? If, on the other hand, ultimate objectives vary for each student, the approach will aid some students to master "basic competencies" while others will receive another quality of educational experience.

The cost barriers to the learning time approach pale by comparison with the difficulties noted above. The variable learning rates cited by Bloom (1976) approximate the current variability in per pupil expenditures. In other words, the variability is not so large as to be beyond one's capacity to imagine the political system sustaining. The problem is that the current variability is due largely to the property wealth of school districts—not to objectively determined educational need.

The administrative costs of establishing a school finance system based on learning time would be very high. In fact, they would be so high that constructing a school finance system should not be the prime motivation for implementing such a system. Instead, the motivation should be the reform of the American educational system. Such reform would lead to dramatic changes in the delivery of instruction, age-grading, compulsory schooling, and so forth.

Operating costs of such a system are difficult to predict. They need to be no higher than current levels. Nonetheless, learning time does carry with it the same political liabilities as distribution of resources on the basis of low achievement scores. More able students will probably suffer reductions in resources made available to them. Bloom (1976) maintains that nearly all will learn at the level previously attained by only the most able. This prediction seems overly optimistic. Even CBE advocates worry that minimal competencies will become maximal expectations. Hence, the fear is that the standard of education will decline.

CONCLUSION

The preceding analysis suggests that variations from current practice with respect to the distribution of educational resources are possible. Educational resources can be distributed on the basis of student characteristics. However, the means to do so raise profound technical, philosophical, cost, and political problems. In certain instances, they require profound changes in the educational system, especially if they are actually implemented as opposed to being laid on the existing system. (Often, of course, such programs as competency-based education are mandated but their requirements for flexible time are not.)

Tying funds to student need involves the state in determinations of student capabilities and their relation to systemwide educational goals and objectives. A decision to use a particular method for measuring need requires making explicit the purposes of education and the state's responsibilities to its students. Resolving the ever-present tension between the goals of best and equal treatment—as must be done if resource allocations are driven by student characteristics—will be difficult because both are highly valued goals. Such resolution may require either a commitment to standardized outcomes for all students or acceptance of potentially unlimited client demands for services they feel are needed. The focus on educational inputs implicit in current school finance systems allows local systems to balance these objectives without reference to highly formalized, rationalistic procedures for statewide assessment of needs or outcomes.

The procedures required to implement the testing, IEP, and mastery learning approaches to measuring student need also raise the possibility of a new, more far-reaching kind of school accountability. Educational malpractice suits which have previously been brought before the courts have failed in large part because the duty of the state or school district has not been specified as precisely as it would be under a minimal competency testing law. Nor have the methods for achieving adequate outcomes been specified as precisely as they would be under legislation which requires the use of techniques such as individualized education plans, competency-based education, or mastery learning. In *Peter Doe v. San Francisco Unified School District*, one of the earliest educational malpractice lawsuits, the plaintiff's action was dismissed because the court could find no clearly definable duty of care owed to him by the state. The court commented that:

> Unlike the activity of the highway or the marketplace, classroom methodology affords no readily acceptable standards of care, or cause, or injury. The science of pedagogy itself is fraught with different and conflicting theories of how or what a child should be taught, and any layman might—and commonly does—have his own emphatic views on the subject (1976:860–861).

Formally mandating the above systems as a means for distributing resources will establish a standard of care based on some particular theory of "how or what a child should be taught." Prescribing educational practices in the absence of a highly developed science or technology of education may have unintended educational consequences while diverting attention from the equity concerns which have guided school finance in the past.

The analysis also raises questions about the current distribution of educational resources in the United States. Aggregating federal, state, and local funds, are more funds spent upon high-achieving or low-achieving students? Are more funds spent upon children from wealthy families or children from poor families? The need to answer these questions is extremely important. Until the answers are known, it may not be prudent to embark upon major new funding systems. One purpose of new systems is to redistribute funds in favor of poor and low-achieving students. That goal can be achieved by modifications of existing school finance practice. If the goal is to redirect funds, it can be reached in ways that do not require the imposition of highly rationalistic systems, the unintended consequences of which will be numerous. If the goal is to spend the same on poor or rich students, funds can be so directed. Similarly, if the goal is to spend more on poor or low-achieving students, funds can be so directed. How much more? Scientific answers to that question are unlikely. As in the past, the judgment must be political. If the goal is to raise achievement—as ultimately it must be—then the facile imposition of rationalistic systems is not certain to lead to that result (Wise 1978).

NOTES TO CHAPTER 10

1. Many experts believe the criterion-referenced testing is, in fact, similar to norm-referenced testing. For a discussion, see National Academy of Education (1978:13–16).
2. However, Title I allocates funds to schools on the basis of poverty, but students are selected to receive services on the basis of *achievement* (often loosely assessed, for instance, through teacher judgment). Low-achieving children from wealthy families in poor schools are *supposed* to get Title I services. A program truly based on poverty-as-need would give money directly to poor children, whatever their achievement levels. That, in fact, is the only system consistent with the Title I rhetoric, which talks about serving "disadvantaged" or "deprived" children. The clearest meaning of disadvantaged or deprivation is that children do not have access to resources; that would apply to poor children whether they were high-achieving or not.
3. Economic marginal decisionmaking is not appropriate because its objective is efficiency, not equality.

REFERENCES

Bloom, Benjamin S. 1976. *Human Characteristics and School Learning.* New York: McGraw-Hill.

California State Commission for Teacher Preparation and Licensing. 1978. *Beginning Teacher Evaluation Study.* Report to National Institute for Education.

Cubberley, Ellwood P. 1905. *School Funds and Their Apportionment.* New York: Teachers College, Columbia University.

Feldmesser, Robert A. 1975. "The Use of Test Scores as a Basis for Allocating Educational Resources: A Synthesis and Interpretation of Knowledge and Experience." Princeton: Educational Testing Service. Mimeo.

Florida Statutes, Chapter 72–223, §1 (1976).

Green, Thomas F. 1980. *Predicting the Behavior of the Educational System.* Syracuse, N.Y.: Syracuse University Press.

Kakalik, James S. 1978. *Cost of Special Education.* Progress Reports. Santa Monica, Calif.: The Rand Corporation.

McClung, Merle Steven. 1978. "Are Competency Testing Programs Fair? Legal?" *Phi Delta Kappan* 59 (February): 397–400.

Marver, James D., and Jane L. David. 1978. *Three States' Experiences with I.E.P. Requirements Similar to 94–192.* Stanford, Calif.: Stanford Research Institute.

National Academy of Education. 1978. "Improving Educational Achievement." Report submitted to ASE.

National Assessment of Educational Progress (NAEP) Newsletter 9, no. 3 (June 1976): 1.

National Institute of Education (NIE). 1977a. *Title I Funds Allocation: The Current Formula.* Washington, D.C.

_____. 1977b. *Using Achievement Test Scores to Allocate Title I Funds.* Washington, D.C.

_____. 1978. *Compensatory Education Study: A Final Report.* Washington, D.C.

Peter Doe v. San Francisco Unified School District, 131 Cal. Rptr. 854, 860–861 (1976).

Spady, William. 1976. "Competency Based Education: A Bandwagon in Search of a Definition." *Educational Research* 6, no. 1 (January): 9–14.

Strayer, George D., and Robert M. Haig. 1923. *The Financing of Education in the State of New York.* New York: Macmillan Co.

Tractenberg, Paul L., and Elaine Jacoby. 1977. "Pupil Testing: A Legal View." *Phi Delta Kappan* 59 (December): 249–254.

Warner, W. Lloyd. 1944. *Who Shall Be Educated?* New York: Harper and Brothers.

Wise, Arthur E. 1968. *Rich Schools, Poor Schools: The Promise of Equal Educational Opportunity.* Chicago: University of Chicago Press.

_____ . 1978. "Minimum Competency Testing: Another Case of Hyperrationalization." *Phi Delta Kappan* 59 (May): 596–598.

_____ . 1979. *Legislated Learning: The Bureaucratization of the American Classroom.* Berkeley: University of California Press.

Wolf, Alison. 1977. "The Relationship Between Poverty and Achievement." Unpublished paper, Washington, D.C.: National Institute of Education.

11 ADEQUACY IN EDUCATIONAL PROGRAMS
A Legal Perspective

*Martha M. McCarthy**

The emphasis in public school finance reform efforts gradually has shifted from equity to adequacy issues. Resource equalization among school districts within states is viewed as a necessary, but not a sufficient, condition to improve public education. Legislative and judical bodies are exhibiting increasing interest in the adequacy of educational offerings. Citizen demands for greater accountability from schools are resulting in a proliferation of program requirements as well as standards for pupil performance. Many legal mandates are placing an obligation on school districts to provide an "adequate basic education" or "appropriate services" to prepare students for future adult roles. Yet, the precise meaning of these terms and their translation into funding schemes remain somewhat illusive.

In this chapter, the topic of educational adequacy is addressed from a legal perspective. No attempt is made to offer conclusions as to how educational adequacy *should* be defined and attained in public schools. Rather, the intent is to present an overview of legislative, judicial, and administrative responses to educational adequacy concerns and to explore the implications of these mandates. Instead of providing answers, this chapter is designed to raise questions, the answers to which may have a significant impact on the future direction of educational reform efforts.

*Martha M. McCarthy, Associate Professor, Educational Administration, Indiana University.

This investigation focuses primarily on the following dimensions of the legal mandates: (1) the sources of the mandates (i.e., constitutional, statutory, administrative, or judicial at both state and federal levels); (2) the procedures used to establish standards of educational adequacy; (3) the measures used to assess program adequacy (i.e., input and output measures); and (4) the targets of the mandates (i.e., the general school population and special need students). For organizational purposes the chapter is divided into five sections. Initially, the concepts of equity and adequacy are distinguished in the context of school finance litigation. In the next two sections, state mandates establishing standards of adequacy for the general public school program are explored, first in terms of resource input standards and then in terms of school output standards. The fourth section focuses on federal mandates pertaining to educational adequacy for students with identified special needs, that is, the handicapped, English-deficient, and culturally or racially disadvantaged. The final section entails a discussion of several unresolved issues and their implications for future school reform efforts.

FROM EQUITY TO ADEQUACY

The concepts of equity and adequacy have distinctly different educational applications. Equity connotes fair, unbiased treatment. The notion of equity does not imply that individuals must be treated equally in all circumstances; indeed, unequal treatment of persons not similarly situated may be necessary to ensure equity. Adequacy, in contrast to equity, connotes the state of being sufficient for a particular purpose.[1] Once the threshold standard of sufficiency is established, a single entity, such as a school or program, can be judged as to whether it satisfies the standard.

Both equity and adequacy can be evaluated from many perspectives, such as resource inputs, educational opportunities, or student outcomes (see Berne and Stiefel 1979; ECS 1980; and Wise 1976). But determinations of equity and adequacy are not necessarily related. Two schools may provide equitable opportunities for students, regardless of whether they satisfy the established threshold of adequacy. Likewise, equity is not a prerequisite for adequacy, unless the threshold criteria include this specification. Thus, fiscal resources for all schools within a state might be deemed adequate despite significant disparities among districts.

In the remainder of this section, the equity–adequacy distinction is illuminated through a review of selected school finance cases. Legal developments in two states, New Jersey and Washington, are examined in some detail as they are illustrative of the evolution from equity to adequacy concerns.

The Quest for Equity

Conceptually, minimum foundation programs are grounded in the notion that a guaranteed level of fiscal support for all school districts within a state will assure educational adequacy. While the adequacy of foundation levels has been questioned, most legal challenges to such programs have focused on equity issues. It has been alleged that disparities in fiscal capacity or per pupil expenditures among school districts in a state deprive some children of their right to equal access to educational resources. The concern in these suits has not been to guarantee "enough" education, a minimally adequate education, or an education appropriate to the unique needs of students, but rather to reduce interdistrict inequities in state school finance schemes.

The widely publicized California school finance litigation exemplifies this genre of cases. In *Serrano* v. *Priest* (1971, 1976; see also *Van Dusartz* 1971) the California Supreme Court twice reviewed the state's scheme for funding schools with its heavy reliance on local property taxes. The court held that the scheme violated the state constitution by conditioning the level of school revenues on school district wealth. While not assessing whether all school districts had *sufficient* resources to attain the state's educational purposes, the California Supreme Court concluded that the gross *disparities* in revenues among districts violated protected rights. The state legislature was ordered to design a finance scheme that would be fiscally neutral, in that the amount spent for education could not be a function of wealth other than the wealth of the state as a whole. Clearly, the court's focus in this litigation was on the equalization of fiscal resources.

In other states, such as Connecticut (*Horton* 1974) and Wyoming (*Washakie County* 1980) courts have invalidated public school funding schemes due to resource inequities among districts.[2] The Connecticut Supreme Court acknowledged that evidence is inconclusive as to whether or not increased expenditure per pupil produces better educated students. It reasoned, however, that evidence is "highly persuasive" that "disparities in expenditure per pupil tend to result in disparities in educational opportunity" (*Horton* 1974: 118). While suggesting that educational programs and services in low wealth districts might be deficient, the court based its decision on an assessment of equity – not adequacy – among school districts.

Minimum Adequacy Standard

In contrast to the preceding cases, some challenges to state school finance schemes, although initiated on equal protection grounds, actually have been resolved on the basis of whether or not fiscal resources have been considered *adequate* to ensure all children a minimum education. The Supreme Court followed this reasoning in the landmark decision, *San Antonio Independent School District* v. *Rodriguez* (1973). Despite Justice Marshall's contention that the issue raised in *Rodriguez* involved equity rather than adequacy (1973: 72–82),[3] the majority concluded that the constitutional test was whether Texas provided "a minimum statewide educational program" to assure "a basic education" for every child (1973: 48–49). The constitutionality of the school finance scheme was judged by whether each child would have an opportunity to acquire the minimal skills necessary to exercise the fundamental rights of citizenship. The Court noted that the Texas Educational Code mandated a minimum school expenditure level, ensured free textbooks and transportation, and prescribed pupil–teacher ratios, teacher qualification criteria, and certification standards. Such assurances of educational adequacy satisfied the *Rodriguez* majority.

Following the rationale espoused in *Rodriguez*, several challenges to inequities in state school finance schemes have been resolved on the basis of whether courts have concluded that adequate fiscal resources have been available for all students to receive a minimum education. Applying this logic, the Supreme Court of Oregon (*Olsen* 1976) held that the state constitution was satisfied if the state provided for "minimum educational opportunities" in all school districts and permitted "the districts to exercise local control over what they desire and can furnish, over the minimum (1976: 148). Courts in other states, such as Idaho (*Thompson*), Montana (*Woodahl* 1974), Michigan (*Milliken* 1973), Ohio (*Cincinnati* 1979), and Arizona (*Shofstall* 1973), similarly have upheld school finance schemes challenged as inequitable, reasoning that the schemes have guaranteed an adequate level of support to satisfy minimum state standards. These courts have not offered guidance as to what constitutes an adequate education; instead, they have accepted existing state input requirements as appropriate measures of educational adequacy.

Other courts, however, have found educational funding schemes inadequate to fulfill state constitutional and statutory obligations. Litigation in New Jersey and Washington is examined below as it has provided the impetus for legislative activity to define the components of an adequate basic education program.

New Jersey

The lengthy litigation involving the New Jersey school finance scheme provides an example of a shift in judicial focus from equity in tax capacity and fiscal resources to adequacy in educational opportunities. In the original *Robinson* v. *Cahill* (1973) decision, the trial court and subsequently state Supreme Court interpreted New Jersey's constitutionally mandated "thorough and efficient system of free public schools" as the provision of educational opportunities necessary in contemporary society to equip children for roles as citizens and competitors in the labor market. The New Jersey Supreme Court also elaborated on the state's responsibility to delineate the content of the required program and to ensure its adequate funding.

In subsequent litigation, the state high court has been called upon several times to assess legislative efforts to comply with its 1973 decision (see *Robinson* 1973, 1975a, 1975b, 1976a, 1976b). Increasingly the judicial mandates have focused on ensuring *adequacy* in educational opportunities rather than *equity* among districts in resource distribution. In 1975, upon reviewing the legislative scheme for the fourth time, the court praised the state department of education's efforts to "establish the components of a thorough and efficient system of education by the formulation of standards, goals, and guidelines by which the school districts and the Department may in collaboration improve the quality of the educational opportunity offered all children (1975b: 719). The court cautioned, however, that educational guidelines alone, without a redistribution of funds, would not satisfy the constitutional mandate. Thus, the court ordered a redistribution of state aid if the legislature did not develop its own plan within five months. In a separate opinion, one justice asserted that the court should have gone farther in imposing a duty on the state to assure educational adequacy by prescribing statewide standards for the operation of public schools (1975b: 726).

In response to *Robinson IV* (1975b) the New Jersey legislature enacted the Public School Education Act which specified the following major elements of a thorough and efficient system of free public schools:

1. Establishment of educational goals at both the state and local levels;

2. Encouragement of public involvement in the establishment of educational goals;

3. Instruction intended to produce the attainment of reasonable levels of proficiency in the basic communications and computational skills;

4. A breadth of program offerings designed to develop the individual talents and abilities of pupils;

5. Programs and supportive services for all pupils, especially those who are educationally disadvantaged or who have special educational needs;

6. Adequately equipped, sanitary and secure physical facilities and adequate materials and supplies;

7. Qualified instructional and other personnel;

8. Efficient administrative procedures;

9. An adequate State program of research and development; and

10. Evaluation and monitoring programs at both the state and local levels (N.J.S.A., 1980).

The act's explicit goal was not to ensure equity among school districts but to provide all children within the state "the educational opportunity which will prepare them to function politically, economically and socially in a democratic society."

The state supreme court assessed the constitutionality of this legislation in 1976. Assuming that full funding was forthcoming, the court concluded that the act was constitutional (*Robinson* 1976a). Within a year, however, the court was called upon to render its sixth *Robinson* (1976b) decision, in which it enjoined public officials in

New Jersey from expending any funds for the support of public schools (excluding certain fixed costs) due to the legislature's failure to provide funds for the 1975 act. After being closed for one week, schools were reopened because of the adoption of a state income tax to support the act.

From 1973 until 1976 the New Jersey Supreme Court appeared to shift its major concern from equity in fiscal resources to adequacy in educational programs measured by statewide standards with a focus on basic skills. The court has indicated that as long as the state fully funds an *adequate* education for all students, local districts can be authorized to go beyond that level. Thus, equalization of educational expenditures within the state, although the focus of the original *Robinson* suit, has not been judicially required.

The questions that remain unanswered are (1) whether the guaranteed program (regardless of inequities among districts in expenditures) is adequate to ensure that the prescribed skills are mastered, and (2) whether these skills are adequate to prepare students for their future roles as citizens and competitors in the labor market. Currently, evidence is not available documenting that New Jersey's required program will ensure acquisition of the specified skills or that mastery of minimum academic skills (primarily in reading and mathematics) is sufficient to equip individuals to compete in a complex technological society (see Levin 1979; Wise 1979).

Washington

Litigation and legislation in the state of Washington are also illustrative of a change in focus from equity to adequacy concerns. In 1974 the state's system for funding public schools was challenged as failing to make ample provision for a basic education for all children in the state as prescribed by the Washington Constitution (*Northshore* 1974). Further, it was alleged that children and taxpayers were denied equal protection because of differences in assessed property valuation per pupil among school districts. The Washington Supreme Court rejected these allegations and held that there was no evidence of a violation of equal protection guarantees. The Court relied on *Rodriguez* in concluding that the Washington system of funding schools was a "proper" and "pragmatic" method of discharging its duty to educate the children within its borders. The court concluded that there was no evidence presented that any children were denied access to "certain minimum and reasonable standardized" educational opportunities.

Four years later, however, the same court interpreted differently the constitutionally mandated "paramount duty" placed on the legislature to make ample provision for a basic education for all children within the state (*Seattle* 1978). Specifically, the court declared that students in every school district have a constitutional right to an *adequately funded* basic education program which must be supported from "definite and certain sources" (1978: 96–97). The court noted that the state's educational obligation extends beyond mere reading, writing, and arithmetic. It must prepare children to participate effectively and intelligently in the political system and compete in a free enterprise economic system. Although asked to give judicial guidelines as to the specific elements of the minimum program that must be provided, the court deferred to the state legislature to determine the program's substantive content.

In direct response to the judicial mandate, the state legislature replaced its minimum foundation program with a funding scheme based on staff units to fully support the basic education program (SSB 1979; see also ECS 1980). A designated number of full-time equivalent students, excluding certain categories of special need students, generates one staff unit (with modifications for unique school district characteristics). Additional staff units are provided for support services, and state categorical programs continue to fund special education, compensatory education, and other special programs. Local districts may supplement the basic education program up to 10 percent of the previous year's level of funding. Since the state funding formula is part of the Basic Education Act, it is not subject to legislative budget revisions unless the act itself is amended.

The Washington legislation has had an equalizing effect in that all school districts are assured full funding of the basic education program. The adequacy of the guaranteed program, however remains the source of debate. Components of this program have been determined by existing practices rather than by data relating program features to the attainment of specific educational goals. Essentially, the content of the required curriculum (which includes basic skill and work skill instruction) reflects the norm already in operation as to the type and duration of programs offered in schools within the state. Conceivably, the legislature could decide to eliminate any feature—even reading instruction—from the required program. Since full state funding of educational expenditures other than the basic program is not guaranteed, determination of this program's content is of paramount importance.

Judicial Limitations

Developments in both New Jersey and Washington highlight the limits of judicial influence in assuring educational adequacy. Courts can declare that all students have a right to a minimally adequate education, but this may be an empty right. Where components of the minimum program are based on past practices or possibly determined by the strength of lobbying efforts, it may be that the state-supported program is not *actually adequate.*

Currently, there is little agreement as to what a minimally adequate education should entail. There is general support for the idea that education should be sufficient to prepare children to participate in a democratic form of government and to compete in a free enterprise economy, but specific features of the minimum education necessary to attain these goals remain ill-defined. The translation of instructional adequacy into resource specifications is even more problematic. If educational funds are directly tied to the state-guaranteed program, there must be assurances that the program is indeed sufficient for the state's educational goals to be attained.

Courts have been reluctant to define educational adequacy and to prescribe specific standards against which to assess program adequacy. Such determinations require more technical knowledge than do assessments of equity. For example, a court can determine if all children within a state are provided an equal opportunity to take foreign languages, but the decision as to whether or not such an opportunity *should* be a part of the basic education program requires substantial professional knowledge as well as public endorsement (see Levin 1979). Courts have declined to enter the thicket of determining how much education is "enough" to be considered minimally adequate. Instead, they have deferred to legislative bodies to make such decisions in settings that are presumably less adversarial than courtrooms.

The judiciary plays a crucial role in interpreting legislative and administrative enactments, but the components of an adequate education and measures of adequacy seem likely to be established in other forums. The next three sections focus on various state and federal attempts to define educational adequacy through input and output standards for the general school population and special need students.

STATE-MANDATED INPUT STANDARDS OF ADEQUACY

States that partcipated in the recent federally funded project (under P.L. 93–380, Section 842) to study and recommend changes in school finance systems were requested to describe the process by which educational adequacy was defined and to assess the effects of recommended funding programs on the attainment of educational adequacy (see Furno 1980). Of the thirty-five states submitting state plans, over half reported that there was no identifiable process for defining educational adequacy. Only one state, Alabama, produced a document recommending standards for judging educational adequacy. Two states indicated that measures of student performance were used to assess adequacy; and in the remaining states, adequacy primarily was gauged in terms of minimum program specifications. These reports revealed that where educational adequacy was defined at all, such definitions usually were limited to school input requirements devised by state education departments. In this section, selected state accreditation and school approval schemes are reviewed to illustrate the types of input standards currently being imposed.

Models for state school approval systems have been provided by private accrediting agencies. Several of the regional accreditation associations have pioneered in establishing input standards to evaluate the adequacy of schools in areas such as institutional purpose; organization, administration, and control; instructional program; professional staff; pupil personnel services; extraclassroom activities; instructional media program; financial support; and school facilities, materials, and equipment (NCACS 1980). To receive accreditation from a regional association, schools are required to conduct a comprehensive self-study that includes the development of a plan to correct deficiencies to satisfy the criteria. Furthermore, a school's funding level must be sufficient to meet or exceed the association's standards in providing the staff, facilities, services, and materials needed to accomplish the school's purpose. While private accreditation standards are flexible to provide for variations among schools in purposes and programs, such variations are expected to exist within a "common framework of preconditions" for quality education.

Relying on many of the procedures and criteria used by the private associations, most states have implemented some type of school accreditation or approval scheme. As with the regional associations, standards for state approval are based primarily on an assessment of school inputs (for instance, facilities, length of school term, course offerings, staff qualifications and utilization, class size, instructional materials). There is wide divergence among the states as to the specificity of minimum state requirements. The most comprehensive standards are found in states with a history of a high level of state support, particularly those in the Southeast. In some states, schools or school districts are classified in various categories according to accreditation standards,[4] but such classification schemes usually do not include penalties or incentives for school districts as long as minimum criteria are satisfied.

In approximately half of the states, procedures have been adopted in which school districts engage in a process of evaluating their own educational programs with technical assistance provided by state education department personnel (ERC 1980:11). In these self-assessments, school districts are required to identify their needs, design goals and objectives, develop strategies to meet the objectives, and devise evaluation systems. Thus, standards by which adequacy is judged may vary among school districts according to locally identified needs and goals. In some states, school district participation in these self-evaluation programs is voluntary, whereas in others, participation is required as a condition of receiving state financial support.

Several states use a combination of voluntary and mandatory accreditation procedures. In Colorado, all school districts must receive "Standard Accreditation" which signifies that the district satisfies minimum criteria adopted by the state board of education. In addition, school districts can participate in the optional "Accreditation by Contract" program in which the district makes a commitment to implement a comprehensive and continuous school improvement plan. Participating districts make a contract with the state board of education to identify goals and objectives and strategies to attain them (ERC 1980:12).

In a few states, school districts must participate in a self-evaluation process as well as satisfy minimum state standards in order to receive state education funds. In Texas, for example, all districts must comply with detailed state requirements ("Principles and Standards") and develop a five-year plan for improvement to qualify for state financial support (ERC 1980: 11). The required planning process includes establishing district goals for student achievement, conducting a self-study to identify student learning needs, and identifying strategies and resources to attain the goals.

As discussed in the preceding section, a few state legislatures have statutorily prescribed the components of the minimum or basic education program that must be provided by all school districts within the state. Washington's legislation is perhaps the most explicit, but other states, such as South Carolina, have legislated standards that school districts must satisfy in providing the required minimum program. Such statutory standards are usually comparable to school approval or accreditation requirements promulgated by administrative agencies in other states.

Virginia is somewhat unique in that its school approval procedures emanate from a state constitutional mandate to devise educational "standards of quality" (VSDE 1980). Virginia's revised state constitution provides that standards of quality for schools must be prescribed by the state board of education, subject to revision only by the Virginia General Assembly. The state formula for funding schools is based on a guaranteed level of support per pupil to implement these standards. Requirements are quite specific as to program offerings, staff qualifications, testing procedures, pupil–teacher ratios, and special education programs. Each school district must develop an annual plan to meet state accreditation standards, and a state-appointed evaluation team assesses the plan's implementation. In addition to the annual plan, each district is required biannually to revise a six-year school improvement plan.

Currently, school accreditation or approval schemes supply the primary criteria by which educational adequacy is assessed in most states. These standards focus on educational inputs, and the relationship between these input requirements and the attainment of desired outcomes has not been systematically documented. Also, there is wide divergence among states in how such program specifications are translated into school funding schemes. Often personnel requirements are directly reflected in funding formulas, and a few states guarantee full support of the required minimum instructional program. However, in some instances, standards imposed on schools by departments of education have become more detailed without significant changes in educational funding schemes. The percentage of school funds supplied by several states has actually declined in recent years, although state-imposed requirements pertaining to program components have become more extensive.[5]

STATE-MANDATED OUTPUT STANDARDS OF ADEQUACY

The notion that adequacy in educational outcomes should be a goal of schooling is not a novel idea. Indeed, efforts to attain equity in the distribution of fiscal resources or adequacy in educational inputs have been based on the premise that such reforms ultimately will effect positive educational results. Many state constitutions explicitly or implicitly address the importance of education in relation to desired societal or individual outcomes. Compulsory attendance laws are grounded in the belief that a certain number of years of schooling is necessary to prepare individuals for citizenship and for competition in a free enterprise economy.[6]

Recently, the assumption that time spent in school per se will produce the expected societal and individual benefits has been seriously questioned. Assurances have been sought that the envisioned outcomes of schooling are indeed being attained. However, conversion of the global statements of desired outcomes into specific measurable skills (school outputs) which can then be linked with instructional programs and resources has not yet been accomplished. What should students learn to ensure adequate preparation for adult roles? How should this be measured? Who should be held accountable for pupil achievement? What level of achievement is enough? Should performance standards be the same for all children or should they differ according to individual student characteristics?

Educational Malpractice Litigation

Questions pertaining to the school's responsibility to assure adequacy in outputs have been raised, although not answered, in suits seeking damages from school districts for instructional negligence. In the now famous *Peter W.* (1976) case, plaintiffs asserted that the San Francisco school district was liable for damages because a student was successfully passed from grade to grade and was graduated from high school with the ability to read only at the fifth grade level (see also *Donohue* 1978). Thus, he was allegedly unprepared for employment because of the school district's negligence. The court, however, dismissed the suit. Noting the complexities of the learning process, the court concluded that the plantiffs did not prove that the school district's negligence *caused* the student's illiteracy.

In a more recent New York instructional negligence case, the plaintiff alleged that he was misclassified and instructed in classes for the mentally retarded for twelve years despite the school psychologist's recommendation that he be retested within two years of his original evaluation (*Hoffman* 1978). The two lower courts awarded damages because of the affirmative acts of negligence on the part of school personnel which placed crippling burdens on the student in terms of future employment opportunities. However, the New York Court of Appeals reversed the lower court rulings and held that public policy considerations precluded the judiciary from substituting its judgment for that of professional educators and government officials charged with administering public schools.

To date, claims that school districts are legally responsible to ensure a specified level of student achievement have not prevailed. But such allegations seem destined to continue. As legislative bodies become more specific in delineating the outcomes that can be expected from public education and the components of guaranteed educational programs, future plaintiffs may be more successful in substantiating negligence charges. Conceivably, courts may award damages if state-mandated skills are not acquired or if the skills taught do not adequately prepare students for adult roles (see Wise 1979:182).

Accountability Mandates

Partly in response to threats of malpractice suits, there has been a proliferation of state laws to ensure accountability for school outputs. Borrowing strategies from business management, legislatures have mandated the implementation of various educational accountability schemes such as Planning, Programming, Budgeting Systems (PPBS), Management Information Systems (MIS), and Performance-Based Education (PBE) (see generally CAP 1974). Although many of the strategies are intended to enhance the effectiveness of the total educational enterprise, there is a clear emphasis on improving the school's product in terms of pupil performance. Colorado's Educational Accountability Act, for example, calls for an assessment of "whether decisions affecting the educational process are advancing or impeding student achievement" (Col. Rev. Stat. Ann. 1980). In many states, accountability mandates require the development of performance objectives, the identification of programs and services to meet these objectives, and the implementation of a plan to evaluate pupil progress. In several states, such as Florida, Maryland, and Mississippi, performance objectives are described at the state level. However, most of the educational accountability mandates do not include penalties for schools or students who fail to meet the objectives.

Some accountability laws provide for the establishment of elaborate statewide student assessment programs. Among the purposes ascribed to such testing programs are to provide data for: (1) measuring the adequacy and efficiency of educational programs; (2) evaluating the effectiveness of public schools; and (3) analyzing costs and benefits of various educational programs (see Webster 1973:74). Over two-thirds of the states currently operate some type of standardized achievement testing program. The tests are usually norm-referenced and primarily measure basic academic skills in reading, mathematics, and language arts (see Clasby 1975). Many states use testing materials and procedures developed by the National Assessment of Educational Progress (NAEP) which was established in 1969 through a contractual arrangement between the federal government and the Education Commission of the States.[7]

Michigan's student assessment program exemplifies a testing program that is a part of a comprehensive educational planning model (see Murphey and Cohen 1974). Criterion-referenced tests which relate to multiple state goals and objectives are used. The assessment program, adopted in 1970, constitutes one phase of the state educational evaluation process. Unlike many state accountability provisions, the Michigan legislation provides for the reallocation of educational funds to provide remedial assistance for students identified as having the greatest educational needs in basic skills.

Minimum Competency Testing Programs

One particular type of student assessment strategy, minimum competency testing (MCT), warrants some elaboration. No topic has received more attention than MCT as a means to assure that students master certain skills in public schools. In a 1978 survey of the fifty states, *Today's Education* defined MCT as "any program of assessment, evaluation, certification, or testing (not necessarily paper and pencil) that is designed to determine whether individual students have reached a minimum level of performance predetermined as satisfactory" (1978: 33). While the focus of MCT programs is on the assessed competency of each *individual learner*, an underlying assumption is that such programs will make school districts more accountable for teaching the required skills.

Minimum competency testing has at least been discussed in every state during the past decade, and thirty-six states have laws or administrative regulations pertaining to MCT. Without question, competency testing has become a pervasive and controversial national movement. Notable state programs include Florida's Functional Literacy Skills Program, New York's Pupil Evaluation Program, and Maryland's Alternative Accountability Pilot Project (see generally *Viewpoints* 1980). There even has been a movement to establish national standards such as the Mottl Bill, introduced in Congress in 1978, which would have established a national commission on basic education to develop reading, writing, and arithmetic skills tests for specified grades (see Harty 1980).

In some states, competency standards are mandated at the state level, while in others, standards are devised locally. There is also diversity in how competency tests are used. In seventeen states, students must pass competency examinations as a prerequisite to graduation from high school. In other states, local school boards have the option of determining how to use the tests, or MCT is used solely to identify remediation needs among students.

The Education Commission of the States reported in 1978 that all but one of the states using MCT as part of minimum requirements for high school graduation included measures of competence in reading, writing, and arithmetic, and over half focused solely on this triad (Pipho 1978a). Only a few states reported that MCT programs addressed consumerism, problem-solving ability, and other areas that might be classified as life skills. Thus, it appears that MCT programs primarily have been restricted to an assessment of student performance in the basic skills area. It is unclear if this focus exists because of consensus that these skills are the most important in assuring future success in life or because they are more easily assessed using current psychometric knowledge (Thomas 1980; see also AASA 1978; McClung 1979; Pipho 1978b).

Florida's minimum competency testing program has perhaps received the greatest national attention among MCT efforts. Florida's commitment to educational accountability started in the late 1960s and culminated in the Educational Accountability Act (1976) which mandated minimum graduation standards for students graduating from high school in 1979 (Fla. Stat. 1980). Requirements included mastery of basic skills in reading, writing, and mathematics; completion of a minimum number of courses; and satisfactory performance on functional literacy tests. Florida's state education department defined functional literacy as the ability to apply basic skills in reading, writing, and mathematics to practical problems and tasks encountered in everyday life. In 1981, the Fifth Circuit Court of Appeals upheld the use of functional literacy tests to classify students for remediation purposes, but ruled that such tests could not be used as a prerequisite to graduation without proof of their curricular validity (Debra P. 1981).[8] While recognizing the state's authority to establish performance standards, the court emphasized that tests used as a graduation requirement must cover what has been taught.

The implementation of MCT programs remains plagued by unanswered questions. How should minimum competencies be identified? How should competence be assessed? What level of mastery should be considered minimum? What should be done with students who do not demonstrate competence? How should competency requirements be reflected in the allocation of educational resources? Currently, student assessment programs primarily focus on selected academic skills, and the validity and reliability of the testing procedures have not been sufficiently documented. Moreover, there is inconclusive research linking success in future adult roles to a minimum level of achievement in the skill areas presently being assessed.

STUDENTS WITH SPECIAL NEEDS

In the latter 1960s, courts rejected allegations that the federal Constitution requires educational resources to be expended according to pupils' needs. In finding such an assertion to be nonjusticiable, an Illinois federal district court concluded that the Constitution offered "no discoverable and manageable standards" by which a court could assess whether or not students' needs were being adequately addressed (*McInnis* 1969; see also *Burruss* 1970). Recently, however, a new wave of educational needs cases, based primarily on federal statutory protections, have been more successful. In these cases, courts have assessed the adequacy of particular instructional services and programs in light of the characteristics of the students being served.

This change in judicial posture over the past decade appears to have occurred primarily because legislative bodies have prescribed standards for courts to use in evaluating program adequacy for certain types of pupils. Special interest groups have become better organized and more aggressive in securing legislation outlining the educational rights of children with disabilities. Thus, the judiciary no longer is forced to evaluate educational needs cases on federal constitutional grounds which offer no "manageable standards" for determining whether or not rights have been violated.

The most definitive pronouncements pertaining to educational standards of adequacy for special need students have emanated from the federal level and have focused primarily on the handicapped, English-deficient, and culturally or racially disadvantaged. Courts in conjunction with Congress have moved along the continuum from ensuring equal access to educational opportunities for all children to ensuring *instructional adequacy* for certain students. Indeed, these mandates have gone beyond minimum adequacy in requiring that *appropriate* programs be provided to address identified needs.

Handicapped Students

While courts initially relied on constitutional guarantees to enforce handicapped children's rights to attend school (see *Mills* 1972), it soon became clear that mere access to school was a hollow victory if handicapped children, once enrolled, were not provided special services. Thus, Congress became active in defining the rights of handicapped students to appropriate educational programs at public expense.

Two pieces of federal legislation in particular, Section 504 of the Rehabilitation Act of 1973 and the Education for All Handicapped

Children Act of 1975 (P.L. 94–142), seem destined to have a significant impact on future activity to devise standards of adequacy for public schools. Section 504, a civil rights law, prohibits discrimination against otherwise qualified individuals in programs or activities receiving federal financial assistance (29 U.S.C. 794 1976). This law deals with employment practices and higher education as well as the rights of handicapped elementary and secondary students to appropriate educational programs. This last provision is closely coordinated with Public Law 94–142 which provides a source of federal financial assistance to defray some of the excess costs associated with providing a free appropriate education for handicapped children (20 U.S.C. 1401 1976).

Public Law 94–142 is unprecedented in that it requires state and local education agencies to assure program adequacy for handicapped students and specifies the form that such assurances must take. For example, the mandated individualized educational program (IEP) is one strategy to guarantee that appropriate instruction is provided for handicapped children in the least restrictive environment. The IEP, designed by a planning team, must contain goals for each handicapped child, short-term and long-range objectives to attain the goals, specification of the services that will be provided, and an evaluation schedule.

The due process requirements contained in Public Law 94–142 represent another mechanism to ensure educational adequacy. Handicapped children and their parents are guaranteed elaborate procedural safeguards prior to any change in a child's instructional assignment. Thus, "procedural adequacy" must be provided in connection with all placement decisions. Some courts have even held that the suspension of a handicapped child for disciplinary reasons constitutes a program change which must be accompanied by procedures to determine a more appropriate alternative placement for the child (see *Southeast Warren* 1979; *Stuart* 1978). The rationale for these extensive due process requirements is that they will deter improper placements and permanent assignments to special classes or schools.

In contrast to Public Law 94–142's specificity in regard to the development of IEPs for handicapped children and procedural safeguards that must be followed in making placement changes, the act does not specify the particular components of the programs that must be provided. Such components are expected to vary depending on each child's deficiencies. While the act stipulates that handicapped children are entitled to special education and related services, questions persist as to exactly what programs and services must be provided in order to satisfy the federal mandates. Courts play an important role in resolving conflicts over what constitutes an appropriate program for specific handicapped children. It seems clear that "appropriate" means more than merely providing access to "some" educational opportunity. However, it seems unlikely that appropriate means that each handicapped child is entitled to the *best* possible program available. What remains controversial is where on the continuum between these extremes lies the acceptable interpretation. Some courts have taken the position that Public Law 94-142 places an obligation on schools to "maximize the self-sufficiency" of handicapped children (see *Armstrong* 1980; *Kruelle* 1980)[9] or to provide programs to enable such children to reach their "full potential" commensurate with the opportunity provided for nonhandicapped pupils (see *Rowley* 1980). Several courts have required school districts to address noneducational needs of disabled students by providing psychotherapy (see *Matter of "A" Family* 1979) and catheterization services (see *Tatro* 1979) if necessary for the children to benefit from educational offerings. The judiciary also has held school districts responsible for private placements for handicapped children (even in a different state) if programs available within the public school system have not been considered appropriate for certain students (see *Matter of Suzanne* 1976).[10]

It appears that a higher threshold of adequacy is being applied to programs for the handicapped in contrast to programs for the general school population. Whereas the basic education program usually is considered sufficient if it satisfies minimum input requirements, programs for the handicapped must be *appropriate* to address the students' educational (and perhaps noneducational) needs. Courts increasingly are being asked to assess whether particular offerings for handicapped pupils are appropriate to satisfy statutory mandates, and the trend in recent decisions is toward placing additional responsibilities on school districts to meet the total needs of disabled students.

It seems likely that the fiscal and educational implications of this legal activity will reach far beyond the handicapped. With special interest groups vying for limited resources, educational offerings for the "normal" child undoubtedly will be affected. A New York federal district court has noted that the federal and state mandates on behalf of handicapped children "may necessitate a sacrifice in services now afforded children in the rest of the school system (*Lora* 1978). Although there are federal funds available to defray some of the excess costs associated with meeting the needs of disabled pupils, the major fiscal burden still remains with state and local education agencies. Courts have been unsympathetic when school districts have used "lack of funds" as the rationale for denying the educational rights of the handicapped (see *Elliot* 1978; *Lora* 1978; *Mills* 1972). Thus, school priorities may have to be rearranged in order to comply with the legal requirements.

Possibly, nonhandicapped students will begin capitalizing on the mandates for the handicapped in making similar demands for year round programs and special services to maximize their learning potential. Allegations that *all* children have a right to individualized educational programs may be in the not-too-distant future. Already, a small school system in Nebraska has reported positive results from its use of IEPs for all pupils within the district (*Education USA* 1980a). Nebraska has made state funds available for other school systems that wish to implement such a program. Also, a Wisconsin statute suggests, but does not require, that the equivalent of an IEP be developed for truant students (Kreunen 1980). If state legislatures ultimately should adopt a standard of educational adequacy that places a responsibility on schools to provide *appropriate programs* to meet the unique needs of *all pupils* (as currently required only for the handicapped), a substantial increase in educational funds would be required. Also, more complex pupil weighting schemes would be necessary so that funding formulas could accurately reflect the costs associated with addressing the complete range of students' needs.

English-deficient Students

Similar to cases pertaining to handicapped children, suits on behalf of English-deficient students have gone beyond demands for equity in treatment and have asserted that children with English language deficiencies are entitled to special programs in public schools because of their unique needs. Plaintiffs have alleged that non-English-speaking children have been functionally excluded from school when special instruction has not been provided to assist them in learning English.

In a case of first impression, *Lau* v. *Nichols* (1974), the United States Supreme Court ruled that Title VI of the Civil Rights Act of 1964 entitles non-English-speaking students to special instructional assistance in mastering the English language. This 1974 decision is extremely significant because for the first time, the Supreme Court concluded that there were judicially manageable standards to use in assessing the adequacy of educational programs in meeting the needs of students. The Court reviewed the substance of the instructional offerings and placed an obligation on school officials to augment programs for particular pupils. In response to the Supreme Court ruling, the Department of Health, Education, and Welfare issued informal guidelines, known as the *Lau* Remedies, to aid local schools in designing programs for children with limited ability to speak English.

Controversy has continued, however, as to precisely what obligations are placed on school districts to meet the needs of English-deficient children. Some courts have concluded that compensatory English instruction rather than bilingual instruction satisfies the legal requirements (see *Guadalupe* 1978; *Keyes* 1975). However, other courts have reasoned that instruction in a student's native language is necessary to meet the needs of non-English-speaking children (see *Morales* 1975; *United States* 1971).[11] In 1980, the Department of Education proposed regulations pursuant to Title VI in an attempt to clarify the responsibilities placed on school districts to provide appropriate programs for these pupils (see *Federal Register* 1980). The proposed *Lau* rules required transitional bilingual instruction to be provided for children with severe English deficiencies.

The *Lau* rules created substantial controversy in educational and legislative forums as to the Department of Education's authority to place specific program requirements on public schools. National education interest groups charged that the proposed regulations would subvert the authority of local school districts to design the curriculum and possibly set a dangerous precedent as to future federal regulation of *what* constitutes adequate instruction and *how* such instruction should be provided (*Education Daily* 1980a). Moreover, it was estimated that implementation of the regulations would cost school districts between 200 and 400 million dollars a year in addition to federal and state funds already being spent on bilingual education. Congress also voiced concern over the *Lau* rules by attaching riders to bills stipulating that the Department of Education could not issue final bilingual regulations until June 1981 to provide lawmakers sufficient time to study the issue (*Education Daily* 1980b). Reacting to the massive negative sentiment, in January 1981, Education Secretary Terrel Bell withdrew the controversial proposed rules which he called "inflexible, unworkable, and incredibly costly" (*Education Daily* 1981).

The withdrawal of the *Lau* rules has elicited mixed responses. It has been assailed by civil rights activists as a sign that the Department of Education under the Reagan administration intends to be less assertive in promulgating regulations to protect the civil rights of students. However, education groups have applauded the move as a victory for advocates of local control. While Secretary Bell has affirmed the department's commitment to ensure equal educational opportunities for all children, he also has indicated that the department will move cautiously in designing regulations to ensure that local flexibility is maintained. Possibly, the department's action in connection with the *Lau* rules is an indication that federal regulatory agencies will play a less active role in determining public school policies and practices than has been true during the past decade.

Culturally or Racially Disadvantaged Students

The most massive federal attempt to assure educational adequacy for culturally disadvantaged children is represented by Title I of the Elementary and Secondary Education Act of 1965. With this law, the federal government began a series of efforts to improve educational opportunities for disadvantaged students. Title I has provided substantial federal financial assistance to school districts with "concentrations of children from low-income families" to address "the special educational needs of educationally deprived children" (20 U.S.C. 241 1976). In order to receive Title I funds, school districts must comply with detailed program specifications. The federal government not only has provided financial support for special services under Title I but also has required participating school districts to engage in a systematic evaluation of the effects of Title I projects in terms of pupil achievement.

While states can exercise discretion in accepting or rejecting Title I categorical aid, they do not have such leeway in connection with federal directives clarifying the constitutional or statutory rights of pupils. Courts have interpreted the U.S. Constitution and civil rights laws as placing an *obligation* on school districts to provide special services for students who have been educationally deprived. Illustrative are the various types of compensatory education programs that have been mandated in desegregation orders (see *Morgan* 1975; *United States* 1971).

In 1977, the Supreme Court specifically recognized the authority of the federal judiciary to place such instructional requirements on school districts to fulfill constitutional obligations to minority students. It approved lower court rulings that required new programs in remedial reading and communication skills, counseling and career guidance, in-service teacher training, and nondiscriminatory testing as part of the desegregation plan for the Detroit school system (*Milliken* 1977). Following this decision, remedial or compensatory programs have frequently been ordered to overcome the consequences of past racial discrimination. For example, federal courts have mandated the provision of educational programs and other ancillary relief in desegregation schemes for school districts such as Wilmington, Delaware, and Cleveland, Ohio (*Evans* 1978; *Reed* 1978). Recently, the judiciary has reflected the sentiment that student reassignment alone cannot counteract the effects of discriminatory practices; there must be assurances that instructional programs and services adequately address the educational deficiencies of minority pupils.

The recognition that children who have been traditionally deprived are entitled to compensatory programs is indicative of the recent judicial and legislative sensitivity to the special needs of students. Legislation and litigation on behalf of the culturally and racially disadvantaged, the handicapped, and the English-deficient, in concert, may have a significant impact on standards of educational adequacy ultimately adopted for *all* students. As other groups of pupils begin capitalizing on these mandates to demand special services and programs, a decision will have to be made as to whether public schools have an obligation to meet the unique needs of all pupils and maximize the learning potential of every child.[12] Perhaps this legal activity will force some consensus regarding the *types* of student needs that should be addressed by public schools and the *criteria* that should be used to assess whether programs are adequate to meet those needs.

UNRESOLVED ISSUES

Legal activity to ensure educational adequacy is in its embryonic stage, and thus far has generated more questions than answers. Many unresolved issues have been noted in the preceding overview of the legal mandates. A few of these issues warrant additional comment.

Adequacy for What?

By definition, "adequacy" means sufficiency *for a given purpose.* The adequacy of educational programs or school funding plans cannot be assessed accurately until there is some agreement regarding *for what* the programs and funding schemes must be sufficient. Currently, the purposes ascribed to public education are often ambiguous or all-encompassing. Global goal statements that schools should prepare students for adult roles or maximize their potential provide little guidance as to the specific components that should be included in educational programs.

It appears that federal, state, and local policymakers are determining the school's goals through the imposition of input and output standards. Some of these requirements seem to be grounded in conflicting notions as to the purposes of public education. Additional responsibilities are being placed on schools by different levels of government without consensus that public schools *can* (or should) assume these responsibilities. Public education cannot solve all of society's problems. Possibly, schools are attempting to perform some functions that could be handled more effectively by other public agencies. Realistic purposes for public education need to be delineated so that resources can be concentrated on finding the most appropriate means to attain them. Until such purposes are identified and translated into specific objectives for schools, it seems likely that definitions of educational adequacy will remain ambiguous.

Adequacy for Whom?

Closely related to the issue of deciding for what public education must be adequate is the issue of determining *for whom* it must be adequate. Presently, standards to assess program adequacy vary according to the students being served. In most states, the regular education program for the general school population is considered adequate if it satisfies minimum input requirements, whereas programs for certain special need students must satisfy more stringent criteria, that is, they must be *appropriate* to meet the unique characteristics of the pupils.

Mandates on behalf of the handicapped and English-deficient have provided the impetus for efforts to secure similar protections for other special need students (for instance, gifted, culturally disadvantaged). As legislative directives continue to place additional obligations on public schools to appropriately serve certain pupils, the regular school program is bound to feel the impact. There already is a noticeable backlash directed toward recent federal mandates pertaining to special need pupils. For example, the required individualized educational programs for handicapped children have been criticized as placing unrealistic demands on schools and siphoning resources from the regular instructional program (*Education U.S.A.* 1980a). Also, the U.S. Department of Education's proposed bilingual education regulations have been denounced as usurping the discretion of local school districts to design curricular programs (*Education Daily* 1980a).

Without clear priorities for public education, the components of the instructional program (and measures of educational adequacy) may be determined by the strength of lobbying efforts. Difficult questions must be answered regarding the scope of the school's responsibility to meet the needs of pupils. Should a substantial portion of the limited educational resources be expended to toilet-train students or to provide catheterization and psychotherapy services? Do gifted and talented students have the right to demand a publicly supported private education if the public school is not meeting their needs? Should public schools be responsible for preschool and adult education programs? Are some students entitled to appropriate programs, designed to meet their special needs, while other pupils are entitled only to minimally adequate programs? Without answers to these and similar questions, it seems likely that child advocacy groups will continue to compete for assurances of educational adequacy for their respective constituencies.

How To Assess Adequacy

Precise definitions of educational adequacy have not emerged; therefore, minimum input standards for the basic education program generally serve as "proxies" for a definition of adequacy. It is assumed that schools are providing adequate educational programs if such minimum criteria are satisfied. However, a program conceivably could be considered adequate using input standards even though the skills that the program is designed to impart are not actually mastered by students. Mandated pupil–teacher ratios provide an example of input requirements that are based on inconclusive research as to the effects of class size on pupil achievement (see Glass and Smith 1979; Shapson et al. 1980). Only with more sophisticated data relating desired outcomes to specific program components and resources can input standards of educational adequacy be defended.

It is ironic that there is substantial legal activity to create educational program specifications that presuppose a firm knowledge base as to the merits of certain programs in attaining desired outcomes, but there is little support for actual research in this area. Less than 1 percent of education funds are earmarked for research activities. In some instances, input standards have been based on what schools already *are* doing rather than on a systematic assessment of what schools *should* be doing. Also, child advocacy groups and teacher organizations often have determined the components of state-required basic programs.

While it might appear that the use of output instead of input standards of adequacy is more defensible, this approach as currently used does not offer a panacea. Most attempts to assess adequacy in terms of pupil performance are limited to measures of academic achievement in a few skill areas that lend themselves to group-administered testing procedures. However, there are no assurances that these are the only (or most important) skills necessary to attain the desired outcomes (for instance, success in various life roles) or that the assessment strategies are valid and reliable.

Some states have addressed educational adequacy concerns by establishing process standards (requiring school districts to engage in self-evaluation studies) in addition to statewide minimum input or output criteria. Such mandated self-evaluations usually entail a procedure whereby school districts assess their own needs, develop goals, and design strategies to attain the goals. Since adequacy is judged in part by whether the school district's program is considered sufficient to meet locally identified goals, criteria might vary considerably within a single state.

Input, output, and process requirements are being imposed simultaneously on school districts within some states. Yet, little coordination of these efforts is apparent (see ERC 1980). Statewide student assessment programs often are operated independently of activity to monitor local district self-evaluations and to devise state minimum criteria for school inputs. In some situations, student performance standards seem to bear little relationship to adopted program requirements. While a few states are attempting to address these inconsistencies through accountability mandates that include input, output, and process standards as part of a unified educational planning and evaluation model, the incongruities between means and ends have not been resolved.

Also, the translation of program requirements or student performance standards into criteria to assess resource adequacy has not received sufficient attention. For example, if all students are expected to master certain competencies before leaving public schools, provisions must be made for the students who will be more costly to educate than others. Similarly, if statewide input standards are used, allowances must be made for the fact that the required programs and services will be more costly to provide in some school districts than in others. Furthermore, if adequacy is to be assessed on the basis of whether schools are meeting the needs of each individual learner, more sophisticated systems of reflecting the costs associated with addressing various types of students' needs will have to be devised. Also, if educational goals and measures of program adequacy are locally developed, new configurations in school finance schemes may be necessary to respond to differences among districts. Unless input and output requirements are directly reflected in funding schemes, school districts may be faced with continually increasing demands and decreasing resources to meet the demands.

Federal and State Roles

Although the federal Constitution delegates *no* responsibility for education to the federal government and state constitutions place *total* responsibility for education on state governments, these absolutes are not reflected in reality. Through its authority to tax and expend funds for the general welfare and to enact laws to protect individual civil rights, the federal government has had a significant influence on public schools. This influence is readily apparent in areas such as vocational education, career education, special education, and programs for the disadvantaged. Indeed, federal education regulations have increased over ten-fold since 1965, and federal involvement in public education seems likely to continue.

While it appears inevitable that the educational adequacy movement will result in more centralized determination of educational policies,[13] the respective roles of state and federal governments remain unclear. One might assume that the roles will be determined to a large extent by the amount of financial assistance supplied by each level of government. However, the increased centralization of policies has not been directly reflected in more centralized fiscal support. That is, federal requirements (for example, Section 504 of the Rehabilitation Act) often have not been accompanied by federal funds to implement the mandates. Also, in several states where mandated program requirements have become more extensive, the percentage of school funds provided by the state actually has declined.

Currently, federal and state roles in establishing standards of adequacy for public schools seem to be distinguished primarily on the basis of the *targets* of the mandates. State legislatures and administrative agencies are the central actors in specifying program requirements and output standards for the general school population. On the other hand, Congress and federal agencies are taking the lead in establishing standards of adequacy for special need students. In some instances, overlapping and even contradictory requirements are being imposed on schools by different levels of government.[14] As additional special interest groups secure federal and state statutory protections, the tension between levels of government in prescribing requirements for public schools is likely to become more pronounced. The judiciary ultimately may be called upon to determine whether the federal government has acted beyond its constitutional authority by imposing certain program specifications on state and local education agencies.

The Judicial Role

While courts do not enact laws, they often shape the law through interpretations of state and federal constitutional and statutory mandates. The judiciary has the potential to influence significantly the educational adequacy movement through its use of these interpretive powers. However, the extent that courts are willing to intervene in this technical-political domain is still unclear.

A few state courts have relied on state constitutional provisions in concluding that students have a right to a fully supported basic education. Also, the Supreme Court has indicated that the federal Constitution entitles all citizens at least to "some" education, even though equity in school resources and offerings is not required (*San Antonio* 1973). Possibly, federal courts will rely more heavily on the fourteenth amendment due process clause in declaring that students have a constitutional right to a minimum education. The due process clause has been used to assert that citizens are entitled to a minimum level of certain essential goods or welfare services (see *Bell* 1971; *Goldberg* 1970; *Slochover* 1956). Support for the argument that education is one of these protected goods is provided by the Supreme Court's recognition that students have a state-created property right to an education which cannot be impaired without due process of law (*Goss* 1975).

However, judicial endorsement of a state or federal constitutional right to a minimally adequate education may be a vacuous right if the components of the guaranteed program are left to political determination. Courts have refrained from defining how much education is "enough" and have deferred to legislative bodies to make such decisions. The judiciary can decree that students are entitled to an adequate education, but this right will not become substantive until there is a workable definition of what educational adequacy entails.

Will courts become assertive in delineating the *specific features* of an adequate education? Does the judiciary provide the appropriate forum for such technical decisions to be made, or should issues involving large-scale social change be left to legislatures? Is judicial intervention necessary due to the inaction of other branches of government? Justices themselves are not in aggreement as to whether courts should play an activist role or adopt a position of restraint in this arena.

Although it remains uncertain if courts will begin prescribing the components of a state's basic education program, the judiciary has been willing to assess whether or not schools are in compliance with legislative and administrative mandates. With the proliferation of school input requirements emanating from both federal and state levels, perhaps the major judicial contribution to the adequacy movement will be in clarifying vague statutory language and evaluating whether specific school offerings satisfy legislative and administrative directives. Illustrative is the litigation pertaining to the educational rights of handicapped children in which courts have ruled that particular programs and services must be provided in order to satisfy federal mandates. As legislative bodies become more active in prescribing the school's responsibilities, courts may become inclined to award damages to students if legislated services are not provided, specified skills are not taught, or the skills taught do not produce the promised results.

CONCLUSION

The school finance reform movement has evolved into an educational reform movement, and it seems clear that equalization of resources alone cannot remedy deficiencies in state educational systems. Distributional equity is not the only or even the primary topic of current concern. In a 1980 national survey of educational policymakers considered knowledgeable in the area of school finance, respondents considered adequacy issues to be the most pressing problems in financing public schools (Ward 1981). The critical question is no longer whether educational adequacy will be addressed, but rather, how it will be defined, measured, and translated into funding schemes.

The quest for educational adequacy is generating substantial legislative, administrative, and judicial activity. Yet, thus far, there is little agreement as to what this term actually means. The apparent paradox must be resolved: courts, legislatures, and administrative agencies are reluctant to define educational adequacy; but at the same time, input and output standards of adequacy are being established at an escalating rate. In essence, adequacy *is being defined* by the standards imposed, even though such standards may be based on faulty assumptions regarding for what and for whom educational programs should be adequate. Solutions are being implemented without thorough exploration of the problems they are designed to solve or the outcomes they are intended to achieve. Unless the incongruities between means and ends are addressed, the proliferation of legal mandates establishing educational input and output standards will not assure that educational programs are in fact adequate.

NOTES TO CHAPTER 11

1. Adequacy is defined as "the state of being sufficient for a specific requirement; lawfully and reasonable sufficient" (*Webster's* 1973).

2. A New York court has used a different rationale to invalidate the state scheme for funding schools under equal protection guarantees. In addition to holding that students in property-poor districts were denied the educational resources available to students in wealthier districts, the court ruled that the state aid formula did not make allowances for the variations in educational costs among school districts or the reduced purchasing power of the urban educational dollar. Accordingly, the legislature was instructed to redesign its financing scheme to give adequate attention to certain municipal and educational overburdening conditions that affect the large cities and the schools located within their boundaries (*Levittown* 1978).

3. He also questioned the majority's conclusion that the Texas minimum foundation program guaranteed an adequate education for every child (*Rodriguez* 1973: 86-87), and drew attention to the problem of assessing what is "enough" education to satisfy constitutional guarantees (1973: 89-90).

4. In Missouri, for example, the state education department classifies all public school districts into one of three categories based on input standards (see Furno 1980).

5. For example, in Virginia state-mandated program requirements have become more detailed, but the portion of school funds supplied by the state has decreased (see Salmon and Shotwell 1978).

6. Even the *San Antonio* (1973: 36-37) majority indicated that a minimum education is necessary for meaningful participation in the political system. In 1972 the Supreme Court suggested that an education through the eighth grade would satisfy governmental interests by ensuring an educated citizenry (*Wisconsin* 1972).

7. The NAEP was instituted to examine changes in pupil achievement over time in ten areas in order to provide data for national educational policy (see Tyler 1975).

8. Students also alleged that the tests were racially and culturally biased in that a disproportionate number of minority students did not pass.

The court concluded that the immediate use of the tests as a graduation requirement would punish minority students for deficiencies caused by past racial discrimination in the state.

9. It should be noted that in the Pennsylvania case (*Armstrong* 1980), the federal district court held that P.L. 94–142 mandates a uniform goal to maximize the self-sufficiency of all handicapped children, but the Third Circuit Court of Appeals reasoned that the act instead places a responsibility on state and local education agencies to devise appropriate goals and programs for individual handicapped children.

10. Also, school districts must incur the full cost of transporting handicapped children to attend special classes or schools (see *In the Matter of James A. Stevenson* 1976).

11. Courts also have addressed the rights of students who speak "black English" to receive special assistance in learning to use standard English (see *Martin Luther King* 1979).

12. The Supreme Court of West Virginia has interpreted a thorough and efficient system of schools as one that develops every child to "his or her capacity" in basic skill areas, knowledge of government, self-knowledge, work-training and advanced academic training, recreational pursuits, interests in all creative arts, and social ethics. Thus, the West Virginia high court has indicated that the state constitution requires public schools to maximize the potential of each learner (*Pauley* 1979).

13. There is some sentiment that the promulgation of educational policies by higher levels of government—while appropriate to address equity issues— will not solve educational inadequacies (see Wise 1979).

14. To illustrate, P.L. 94–142 has been interpreted as requiring year-round programs for severely handicapped children, but some states have laws or regulations that restrict the length of the public school term to 180 days (see *Armstrong* 1980).

REFERENCES

American Association of School Administrators (AASA). 1978. *The Competency Movement*. Arlington, Virginia.

Armstrong v. Kline , 476 F. Supp. 583 (E.D. Pa. 1979), *modified and remanded*, 629 F.2d 269 (3d Cir. 1980).

Bell v. Burson, 402 U.S. 535 (1971).

Berne, Robert, and Leanna Stiefel. 1979. "Concepts of Equity and Their Relationship to State School Finance Plans." *Journal of Education Finance* 5 (Fall): 109–32.

Burruss v. Wilkerson, 310 F. Supp. 572 (W.D. Va. 1969), *aff'd mem.*, 397 U.S. 44 (1970).

Cincinnati v. Walter, 390 N.E. 812 (Ohio 1979), *cert. denied*, 444 U.S. 1015 (1980).

Clasby, Mariam. 1975. *A Survey of Statewide Testing Programs.* Syracuse, N.Y.: Syracuse University Research Corp.

Colo. Rev. Stat. Ann. § 22-7-102(a)(1980).

Cooperative Accountability Project (CAP). 1974. *Legislation by the States: Accountability and Assessment in Education.* Denver, Colorado.

Debra P. v. Turlington, 474 F. Supp. 244 (M.C. Fla. 1979), *aff'd. in part, vacated and remanded in part*, 644 F.2d 397 (5th Cir. 1981).

Donohue v. Copiague Union Free Schools, 407 N.Y.S.2d 874 (App. Div. 1978), *aff'd* 391 N.E. 2d 1352 (N.Y. 1979).

Education Commission of the States (ECS). 1980. *School Finance Reform in the States: 1979.* Denver, Colorado.

Education Daily. 1980a. 13, no. 172 (September 3): 3.

Education Daily. 1980b. 13, no. 218 (November 7): 5.

Education Daily. 1981. 14, no. 22 (February 3): 1-2.

Education Review Committee (ERC). 1980. "Methods Other States Use to Assure Quality in the Public Schools." Columbus, Ohio: General Assembly.

Education U.S.A. 1980a. 22, no. 50 (August 11):369.

Education U.S.A. 1980b. 23, no. 3 (September 15): 17-24.

Elliot v. Board of Educ. of City of Chicago, 380 N.E.2d 1137 (Ill. App. 1978).

Evans v. Buchanan, 447 F. Supp. 982 (D. Del. 1978).

Federal Register. 45, no. 152 (August 5, 1980).

Fla. Stat. §§ 232.245(3), 232.246(1)-(3). 1980.

Furno, Orlando. 1980. *State Equalization Plans.* Washington, D.C.: Department of Education.

Glass, Gene, and Mary Smith. 1979. "Meta-analysis of Research on Class Size and Achievement." *Educational Evaluation and Policy Analysis* 1: 2-16.

Goldberg v. Kelly, 397 U.S. 254 (1970).

Goss v. Lopez, 419 U.S. 565 (1975).

Guadalupe Organization, Inc. v. Tempe Elementary School Dist. No. 3, 587 F.2d 1022 (9th Cir. 1978).

Harty, Harold. 1980. "Implementation of Minimum Competency Testing Programs." *Viewpoints in Teaching and Learning* 56 (Summer): 3.

Hoffman v. Board of Educ. of the City of New York, 410 N.Y.S.2d 99 (App. Div. 1978), *rev'd* 424 N.Y.S.2d 376 (Ct. App. 1979).

Horton v. Meskill, 332 A.2d 113 (Conn. 1974).

"Impact of Minimum Competency Testing in Florida." *Today's Education* 67 (1978): 33.

Keyes v. School Dist. No. 1, 521 F.2d 465 (10th Cir. 1975).

Kreunen, Warren L. 1980. "The Law and the Handicapped Student." Paper presented at the National Organization on Legal Problems of Education Annual Convention, Boston, Massachusetts, November 14.

Kruelle v. Briggs, 489 F. Supp. 169 (D. Del. 1980).

Lau v. Nichols, 414 U.S. 563 (1974).

Levin, Betsy. 1979. "The Courts, Congress, and Educational Adequacy: The Equal Protection Predicament." *Maryland Law Review* 39 no. 2: 256.

Levittown Union Free School Dist. v. Nyquist, 408 N.Y.S.2d 606 (Sup. Ct., Nassau County, 1978).

Lora v. Board of Educ., 456 F. Supp. 1211 (E.D.N.Y. 1978).

McClung, Merle. 1979. "Competency Testing Programs: Legal and Educational Issues." *Fordham Law Review* 47 (April): 651–712.

McInnis v. Shapiro, 293 F. Supp. 327 (N.D. Ill. 1968), *aff'd mem. sub. nom.*, McInnis v. Ogilvie, 394 U.S. 322 (1969).

Martin Luther King Junior Elementary School Children v. Ann Arbor School Dist. Bd., 473 F. Supp. 1371 (E.D. Mich. 1979).

In the Matter of "A" Family, 602 P.2d 157 (Mont. 1979).

In the Matter of James A. Stevenson, 385 N.Y.S.2d 477 (Family Ct., St. Lawrence County, 1976).

In the Matter of Suzanne, 381 N.Y.S.2d 628 (Family Ct., Westchester County, 1976).

Milliken v. Bradley (Milliken II), 433 U.S. 267 (1977).

Milliken v. Green, 212 N.W.2d 711 (Mich. 1973).

Mills v. Board of Education, 348 F. Supp. 866 (D.D.C. 1972).

Morales v. Shannon, 516 F.2d 411 (5th Cir. 1975).

Morgan v. Kerrigan, 401 F. Supp. 216 (D. Mass. 1975), *aff'd* 530 F.2d 401 (1st Cir. 1976).

Murphey, Jerome T., and David Cohen. 1974. "Accountability in Education— The Michigan Experience." *Public Interest* 36 (Summer): 53–81.

N.J.S.A. 18A: 7A–5. 1980.

North Central Association of Colleges and Schools (NCACS). 1980. *Policies and Standards for the Approval of Secondary Schools 1980–1981.* Boulder, Colorado.

Northshore School Dist. No. 417 v. Kinnear, 530 P.2d 178 (Wash. 1974).

Olsen v. State of Oregon, 554 P.2d 139 (1976).

Pauley v. Kelly, 255 S.E.2d 859 (W. Va. 1979).

Pennsylvania Ass'n for Retarded Children v. Commonwealth, 343 F. Supp. 279 (E.D. Pa. 1972).

Peter W. v. San Francisco Unified School Dist., 131 Cal. Rptr. 854 (Cal. App. 1976).

Pipho, Chris. 1978a. *State Activity—Minimal Competency Testing.* Denver, Colo.: Education Commission of the States.

———. 1978b. *Update VIII: Minimum Competency Testing.* Denver, Colo.: Education Commission of the States.

Reed v. Rhodes, 455 F. Supp. 546 (N.D. Ohio 1978).

Robinson v. Cahill, 287 A.2d 187 (N.J. Super. 1972), *aff'd as modified*, 303 A.2d 273 (N.J. 1973) (Robinson I).

Robinson II, 306 A.2d 65 (1973).

Robinson III, 339 A.2d 193 (1975a).

Robinson IV, 351 A.2d 713 (1975b).

Robinson V, 355 A.2d 129 (1976a).

Robinson VI, 358 A.2d 457 (1976b).

Rowley v. Board of Educ. of the Hendrick Hudson Central School Dist., 483 F. Supp. 528 (S.D.N.Y. 1980), *aff'd.* 632 F.2d 945 (2d Cir., July 17, 1980).

Salmon, Richard, and Ralph Shotwell. 1978. "Virginia School Finance Reform: Status Quo Maintained." *Journal of Education Finance* 3 (Spring): 527.

San Antonio Independent School Dist. v. Rodriguez, 411 U.S. 1 (1973).

Seattle School Dist. No. 1 of King County v. State of Washington, 585 P.2d 71 (Wash. 1978).

Serrano v. Priest, 96 Cal. Rptr. 601 (1971).

Serrano v. Priest, 135 Cal. Rptr. 345 (1976).

Shofstall v. Hollins, 515 P.2d 590 (Ariz. 1973).

Shapson, Stan; Edgar N. Wright; Gary Eason; and John Fitzgerald. 1980. "An Experimental Study of the Effects of Class Size." *American Educational Research Journal* 17 (Spring): 141–152.

Slochover v. Board of Higher Education, 350 U.S. 551 (1956).

Southeast Warren Community School Dist. v. Department of Public Instruction, 285 N.W.2d 173 (Iowa 1979).

Stuart v. Nappi, 443 F. Supp. 1235 (D. Conn. 1978).

Engrossed Substitute Senate Bill (SSB) No. 2709, State of Washington.

Tatro v. State of Texas, 481 F. Supp. 1224 (N.D. Tex. 1979), *vacated and remanded*, 625 F.2d 557 (5th Cir. 1980).

Thomas, Charles. 1980. "The Minimum Competencies of Minimum Competency Testing." *Viewpoints in Teaching and Learning* 56 (Summer): 30.

Thompson v. Engelking, 537 P.2d 635 (Idaho 1975).

Tyler, Ralph. 1975. *Update on Education*. Denver, Colo.: Education Commission of the States.

United States v. Texas, 342 F. Supp. 24 (E.D. Tex. 1971), *aff'd* 466 F.2d 518 (5th Cir. 1972).

20 U.S.C. 241a *et seq.* (1976a).

20 U.S.C. § 1401 *et seq.* (1976b).

29 U.S.C. § 794 (1976).

Van Dusartz v. Hatfield, 334 F. Supp. 870 (D. Minn. 1971).

Viewpoints in Teaching and Learning 56 (Summer 1980).

Virginia State Department of Education (VSDE). 1980. *Standards of Quality for Public Schools of Virginia 1980–82*. Richmond, Virginia.

Ward, Cynthia. 1981. "Opinion Survey of School Finance Project." *Journal of Education Finance* 6, no. 4 (Spring): 505–511.

Washakie County School Dist. No. 1 v. Herschler, 606 P.2d 310 (Wyo. 1980).